CRITICAL SURVEY

OF

LONG FICTION

Gothic Novelists

Editor

Carl Rollyson
Baruch College, City University of New York

SALEM PRESS
Ipswich, Massachusetts • Hackensack, New Jersey

Cover photo:
Charlotte Brontë (© Bettmann/Corbis)

978-1-4298-3678-4

CONTENTS

CONTRIBUTORS

Tel Asiado
Chatswood, New South Wales

Kirk H. Beetz
Original Contributor

Bernadette Lynn Bosky
Yonkers, New York

Faith Hickman Brynie
Bigfork, Montana

Karen Carmean
Original Contributor

Diane D'Amico
Original Contributor

J. Madison Davis
Original Contributor

Paul J. deGategno
Original Contributor

Bill Delaney
Original Contributor

Kenneth Friedenreich
Original Contributor

William J. Heim
Original Contributor

Terry Heller
Original Contributor

Earl G. Ingersoll
SUNY-College at Brockport

Rebecca Kuzins
Pasadena, California

Lawrence F. Laban
Original Contributor

Mary E. Mahony
Wayne County Community College

Patricia Marks
Original Contributor

Charles E. May
California State University, Long Beach

Laurence W. Mazzeno
Alvernia College

Sally Mitchell
Original Contributor

Earl Paulus Murphy
Original Contributor

Martha Nochimson
Original Contributor

Holly L. Norton
University of Northwestern Ohio

Lisa Paddock
Cape May Court House, New Jersey

Makarand Paranjape
Original Contributor

Robert C. Petersen
Original Contributor

Jan St. Martin
Original Contributor

Joachim Scholz
Original Contributor

Traci S. Smrcka
Hardin-Simmons University

Karen F. Stein
University of Rhode Island

Judith L. Steininger
Milwaukee School of Engineering

Jennifer L. Wyatt
Original Contributor

THE GOTHIC NOVEL

The gothic novel is a living tradition, a form that enjoys great popular appeal while pro-
voking harsh critical judgments. It began with Horace Walpole's *The Castle of Otranto*
(1765), then traveled through Ann Radcliffe, Matthew Gregory Lewis, Charles Robert
Maturin, Mary Wollstonecraft Shelley,Edgar Allan Poe, Charlotte Brontë and Emily
Brontë, Nathaniel Hawthorne, Charles Brockden Brown, Bram Stoker, Charles Dickens,
Thomas Hardy, Henry James, and many others into the twentieth century, where it surfaced,
much altered and yet spiritually continuous, in the work of writers such as William Faulkner,
D. H. Lawrence, Iris Murdoch, John Gardner (1933-1982), Joyce Carol Oates, and Doris
Lessing and in the popular genres of horror fiction and some women's romances.

The externals of the gothic, especially early in its history, are characterized by sublime
but terrifying mountain scenery; bandits and outlaws; ruined, ancient seats of power; morbid death imagery; and virgins and charismatic villains, as well as hyperbolic physical
states of agitation and lurid images of physical degradation. Its spirit is characterized by a
tone of high agitation and unresolved or almost-impossible to resolve anxiety, fear,
unnatural elation, and desperation.

The first gothic novel is identifiable with a precision unusual in genre study. Walpole
(1717-1797), the earl of Orford, began writing *The Castle of Otranto* in June, 1764,; he
finished it in August and published it in an edition of five hundred copies in early 1765.
Walpole was a historian and essayist whose vivid and massive personal correspondence
remains essential reading for the eighteenth century background. Before writing *The Castle of Otranto*, his only connection with the gothic was his estate in Twickenham, which he
called Strawberry Hill. It was built in the gothic style and set an architectural trend, as his
novel would later set a literary trend.

Walpole did not dream of what he was about to initiate with *The Castle of Otranto*; he
published his first edition anonymously, revealing his identity, only after the novel's great
success, in his second edition of April, 1765. At that point, he no longer feared mockery of
his tale of a statue with a bleeding nose and mammoth, peregrinating armor, and an ancient castle complete with ancient family curse. With his second edition, he was obliged to
add a preface explaining why he had hidden behind the guise of a preface proclaiming the
book to be a "found manuscript," printed originally "in Naples in the black letter in 1529."
The reader of the first edition was told that *The Castle of Otranto* was the long-lost history
of an ancient Catholic family in the north of England. The greater reading public loved it,
and it was reprinted in many editions. By 1796, it had been translated into French and
Spanish and had been repeatedly rendered into dramatic form. In 1848, the novel was still
active as the basis for successful theatrical presentations, although the original gothic
vogue had passed.

Close upon Walpole's heels followed Radcliffe, Lewis, and Maturin. These three authors, of course, were not the only imitators ready to take advantage of the contemporary

trend (there were literally hundreds of those), but they are among the few who are still read, for they made their own distinctive contributions to the genre's evolution. Radcliffe (1764-1823) was born just as Walpole's *The Castle of Otranto* was being published. She was reared in a middle-class milieu, acquainted with merchants and professionals; her husband was the editor of *The English Chronicle* and a fellow of the Society of Antiquaries. She lived a quiet life, was likely asthmatic, and seems to have stayed close to her hearth. Although she never became a habitué of literary circles and in her lifetime only published a handful of works, she is considered the grande dame of the gothic novelists and enjoyed a stunning commercial success in her day; she is the only female novelist of the period whose work is still read.

Radcliffe's works include *The Castles of Athlin and Dunbayne* (1789), *A Sicilian Romance* (1790), *The Romance of the Forest* (1791), *The Mysteries of Udolpho* (1794), *The Italian: Or, The Confessional of the Black Penitents* (1797), and *Gaston de Blondeville* (1826). She also wrote an account of a trip through parts of northern Europe, *A Journey Made in the Summer of 1794 Through Holland and the Western Frontier of Germany* (1795). Her remarkably sedate life contrasts strikingly with the melodramatic flamboyance of her works. Her experiences also fail to account for her dazzling, fictional accounts of the scenery of Southern Europe, which she had never seen.

Lewis, called Monk Lewis in honor of his major work, conformed in his life more closely to the stereotype of the gothic masters. Lewis (1775-1818) was a child of the upper classes, the spoiled son of a frivolous beauty, whom he adored. His parents' unhappy marriage ended when he was at Westminster Preparatory School. There was a continual struggle between his parents to manage his life—his father stern and aloof, his mother extravagant and possessive.

Lewis spent his childhood treading the halls of large, old manses belonging both to family and to friends. He paced long, gloomy corridors—a staple of the gothic—and peered up at ancient portraits in dark galleries, another permanent fixture in gothic convention. Deeply involved with the literati of his day, Lewis (also homosexual) found an equivocal public reception, but his novel *The Monk: A Romance* (1796; also known as *Ambrosio: Or, The Monk*), an international sensation, had an enormous effect on the gothic productions of his day. Lewis died on board ship, a casualty of a yellow-fever epidemic, in the arms of his valet, Baptista, and was buried at sea.

Lewis's bibliography is as frenetic as his biography. Although his only gothic novel is the infamous *The Monk*, he spent most of his career writing plays heavily influenced by gothic conventions; he also translated many gothic works into English and wrote scandalous poetry. Among his plays are *Village Virtues* (pb. 1796), *The Castle Spectre* (pr. 1797), *The East Indian* (pr. 1799), *Adelmorn the Outlaw* (pr., pb. 1801), and *The Captive* (pr. 1803). He translated Friedrich Schiller's *The Minister* (1797) and August von Kotzebue's *Rolla: Or, The Peruvian Hero* (1799). He became notorious for his poetic work *The Love of Gain: A Poem Initiated from Juvenal* (1799), an imitation of Juvenal's thirteenth satire.

Maturin (1780-1824) is the final major gothic artist of the period. He was a Protestant clergyman from Dublin and a spiritual brother of the Marquis de Sade. He also was a protégé of Sir Walter Scott and an admirer of Lord Byron. His major gothic novel is *Melmoth the Wanderer* (1820), as shocking to its public as was Lewis's *The Monk*. An earlier Maturin gothic was *Fatal Revenge: Or, The Family of Montorio* (1807). His other works include the novel *The Milesian Chief* (1812); a theological novel, *Women: Or, Pour et Contre* (1818); a tragedy, *Bertram: Or, The Castle of St. Aldobrand* (pr., pb. 1816), produced by Edmund Kean; and the novel *The Albigenses* (1824).

Among the legions of other gothic novelists, a few writers (especially the following women, who are no longer generally read) have made a place for themselves in literary history. These writers include Harriet Lee, known for *The Canterbury Tales* (1797-1805), written with her sister, Sophia Lee, author also of *The Recess: Or, A Tale of Other Times* (1783); Clara Reeve (*The Champion of Virtue: A Gothic Story*, 1777; also known as *The Old English Baron: A Gothic Story*); Regina Maria Roche (*The Children of the Abbey*, 1796); Charlotte Smith (*Emmeline; Or, The Orphan of the Castle—A Novel*, 1788); Charlotte Dacre (*Zofloya: Or, The Moor—A Romance of the Fifteenth Century*, 1806); and Mary Anne Radcliffe (*Manfroné: Or, The One Handed Monk—A Romance*, 1809).

Critics generally agree that the period gothics, while having much in common, divide into relatively clear subclassifications: the historical gothic, the school of terror, and the *Schauer-Romantik* school of horror. All gothics of the period return to the past, are flushed with suggestions of the supernatural, and tend to be set amid ruined architecture, particularly a great estate house gone to ruin or a decaying abbey. All make use of stock characters. These will generally include one or more young and innocent virgins of both sexes; monks and nuns, particularly of sinister aspect; and towering male and female characters of overpowering will whose charismatic egotism knows no bounds.

Frequently the novels are set in the rugged mountains of Italy and contain an evil Italian character. Tumultuous weather often accompanies tumultuous passions. The gothic genre specializes in making external conditions metaphors of human emotions, a convention thought to have been derived in part from the works of William Shakespeare. Brigands are frequently employed in the plot, and most gothics of the period employ morbid, lurid imagery, such as a body riddled with worms behind a moldy black veil.

The various subdivisions of the gothic may feature any or all of these conventions, being distinguished by relative emphasis. The historical gothic, for example, reveals the supernatural against a genuinely historical background, best exemplified by the works of the Lee sisters, who, although their own novels are infrequently read today, played a part in the evolution of the historical novel through their influence on Sir Walter Scott. The school of terror provided safe emotional titillation—safe, because the morbidity such novels portray takes place not in a genuine, historical setting, but in some fantasy of the past, and because the fearful effects tend to be explained away rationally at the end of the respective work. Radcliffe is the major paradigm of this subgroup. The *Schauer-Romantik* school of horror, best represented by Lewis and Maturin, did not offer the reassurance of a moral, rational order. These works tend to evoke history but stir anxiety without resolving or relieving it. They are perverse and sadistic, marked by the amoral use of thrill.

There are very few traditional gothic plots and conventions; a discrete set of such paradigms was recycled and refurbished many times. Walpole's *The Castle of Otranto*, Radcliffe's *The Mysteries of Udolpho*, Lewis's *The Monk*, and Maturin's *Melmoth the Wanderer* represent the basic models of the genre.

THE CASTLE OF OTRANTO

The Castle of Otranto, emphatically not historical gothic, takes place in a fantasy past. It is not of the school of terror either; although it resolves its dilemmas in a human fashion, it does not rationally explain the supernatural events it recounts. This earliest of the gothics trembles between horror and terror.

The story opens with Manfred, Prince of Otranto, ready to marry his sickly son, Conrad, to the beautiful Isabella. Manfred, the pattern for future gothic villains of towering egotism and pride, is startled when his son is killed in a bizarre fashion. The gigantic statuary helmet of a marble figure of Alphonse the Good has been mysteriously transported to Manfred's castle, where it has fallen on and crushed Conrad.

Manfred precipitously reveals that he is tired of his virtuous wife, Hippolita, and, disdaining both her and their virtuous daughter, Mathilda, attempts to force himself on the exquisite, virginal Isabella, his erstwhile daughter-in-law elect. At the same time, he attempts to blame his son's death on an individual named Theodore, who appears to be a virtuous peasant lad and bears an uncanny resemblance to the now helmetless statue of Alfonso the Good. Theodore is incarcerated in the palace but manages to escape. Theodore and Isabella, both traversing the mazelike halls of Otranto to escape Manfred, find each other, and Theodore manages to set Isabella free. She finds asylum in the Church of St. Nicholas, site of the statue of Alfonso the Good, under the protection of Father Jerome, a virtuous friar. In the process of persuading Jerome to bring Isabella to him, Manfred discovers that Theodore is actually Jerome's long-lost son. Manfred threatens Theodore in order to maneuver Jerome into delivering Isabella. The long-lost relative later became a popular feature of the gothic.

Both Isabella and Theodore are temporarily saved by the appearance of a mysterious Black Knight, who turns out to be Isabella's father and joins the forces against Manfred. A round of comings and goings through tunnels, hallways, and churches ensues. This flight through dark corridors also became almost mandatory in gothic fiction. In the course of his flight, Theodore falls in love with Mathilda. As the two lovers meet in a church, Manfred, "flushed with love and wine," mistakes Mathilda for Isabella. Wishing to prevent Theodore from possessing the woman he thinks is his own beloved, Manfred mistakenly stabs his daughter. Her dying words prevent Theodore from revenging her: "Stop thy impious hand . . . it is my father!"

Manfred must now forfeit his kingdom for his bloody deed. The final revelation is that Theodore is actually the true Prince of Otranto, the direct descendant of Alfonso the Good. The statuary helmet flies back to the statue; Isabella is given to Theodore in marriage, but only after he completes a period of mourning for Mathilda; and order is restored. The flight of the helmet remains beyond the pale of reason, as does the extraordinary, rigid virtue of the sympathetic characters, but Manfred's threat to the kingdom is ended. Here is the master plot for the gothic of the Kingdom.

THE MYSTERIES OF UDOLPHO

Radcliffe's *The Mysteries of Udolpho* presents apparently unnatural behavior and events but ultimately explains them all. Not only will the sins of the past be nullified, but also human understanding will penetrate all the mysteries. In *The Mysteries of Udolpho*, the obligatory gothic virgin is Emily St. Aubert; she is complemented by a virginal male named Valancourt, whom Emily meets while still in the bosom of her family. When her parents die, she is left at the mercy of her uncle, the villainous Montoni, dark, compelling, and savage in pursuit of his own interests. Montoni whisks Emily away to Udolpho, his great house in the Apennines, where, desperate for money, he exerts himself on Emily in hopes of taking her patrimony while his more lustful, equally brutal friends scheme against her virtue. Emily resists, fainting and palpitating frequently. Emily's propensity to swoon is very much entrenched in the character of the gothic heroine.

Emily soon escapes and, sequestered in a convent, makes the acquaintance of a dying nun, whose past is revealed to contain a murder inspired by lust and greed. Her past also contains Montoni, who acquired Udolpho through her evil deeds. Now repenting, the nun (née Laurentini de Udolpho) reveals all. The innocent victim of Laurentini's stratagems was Emily's long-lost, virtuous aunt, and Udolpho should have been hers. Ultimately, it will belong to Emily and Valancourt.

This novel contains the obligatory gothic flights up and down dimly lit staircases and halls and into dark turrets; there are also fabulous vistas of soul-elevating charm in the Apennines, which became a hallmark of gothic, and blood-chilling vistas of banditti by torch and moonlight. There is also mysterious music that seems to issue from some supernatural source and a mysterious disappearance of Emily's bracelet, both later revealed to be the work of Valancourt. A picture of the first marchioness of Udolpho, who looks unaccountably like Emily, threatens to reveal some irregularity about Emily's birth but in the end reveals only that the poor, victimized marchioness was Emily's aunt. In Udolpho, in a distant turret, Emily finds a body being devoured by worms. Emily is thrown into a frenzy, fearing that this is the corpse of her deluded aunt, Montoni's wife, but it is revealed to be a wax effigy placed there long ago for the contemplation of some sinning cleric, as a penance. The dark night of the soul lifts, and terror yields to the paradise that Emily and Valancourt will engender. This is the master plot for personal gothic: the gothic of the family.

Radcliffe was known to distinguish between horror and terror and would have none of the former. Terror was a blood-tingling experience of which she approved because it would ultimately yield to better things. Horror she identified with decadence, a distemper in the blood that could not be discharged but rendered men and women inactive with fright. Lewis's *The Monk* demonstrates Radcliffe's distinction.

THE MONK

Lewis's *The Monk* concerns a Capuchin friar named Ambrosio, famed throughout Madrid for his beauty and virtue. He is fervent in his devotion to his calling and is wholly enchanted by a picture of the Virgin, to which he prays. A young novice of the order named Rosario becomes Ambrosio's favorite. Rosario is a beautiful, virtuous youth, as Ambrosio thinks, but one night Ambrosio perceives that Rosario has a female breast, and that "he" is in fact "she": Mathilda, a daughter of a noble house, so enthralled by Ambrosio that she has disguised herself to be near him.

Mathilda is the very image of the picture of the Virgin to which Ambrosio is so devoted, and, through her virginal beauty, seduces Ambrosio into a degrading sexual entanglement that is fully described. As Mathilda grows more obsessed with Ambrosio, his ardor cools. To secure him to her, she offers help in seducing Antonia, another virginal beauty, Ambrosio's newest passion. Mathilda, the madonna-faced enchantress, now reveals that she is actually a female demon. She puts her supernatural powers at Ambrosio's disposal, and together they successfully abduct Antonia, although only after killing Antonia's mother. Ambrosio then rapes Antonia in the foul, suffocating stench of a charnel house in the cathedral catacombs. In this scene of heavy breathing and sadism, the monk is incited to his deed by the virginal Antonia's softness and her pleas for her virtue. Each tear excites him further into a frenzy, which he climaxes by strangling the girl.

Ambrosio's deeds are discovered, and he is tried by an inquisitorial panel. Mathilda reveals his union with Satan through her. The novel ends with Satan's liberation of Ambrosio from the dungeon into which the inquisitors have thrown him. Satan mangles Ambrosio's body by throwing him into an abyss but does not let him die for seven days (the de-creation of the world?). During this time, Ambrosio must suffer the physical and psychological torments of his situation, and the reader along with him. The devil triumphs at the end of this novel. All means of redressing virtue are abandoned, and the reader is left in the abyss with Ambrosio.

MELMOTH THE WANDERER

The same may be said of Maturin's *Melmoth the Wanderer*, a tale of agony and the failure of redemption. The book may be called a novel only if one employs the concept of the picaresque in its broadest sense. It is a collection of short stories, each centering on Melmoth, a damned, Faust-like character. Each tale concerns Melmoth's attempt to find someone to change places with him, a trade he would gladly make, as he has sold his soul to the devil and now wishes to be released.

The book rubs the reader's nerves raw with obsessive suffering, detailing scenes from the Spanish Inquisition that include the popping of bones and the melting of eyeballs. The book also minutely details the degradation of a beautiful, virginal island maiden named Immalee, who is utterly destroyed by the idolatrous love of Melmoth. The last scene of the book ticks the seconds of the clock as Melmoth, unable to find a surrogate, awaits his fall into Satan's clutches. The denouement is an almost unbearable agony that the reader is forced to endure with the protagonist. Again the horror is eternal. There will never be any quietus for either Ambrosio or Melmoth, or for the reader haunted by them. These are the molds for the gothic of damnation.

THE MODERNIZATION OF THE GOTHIC

The reading public of the late eighteenth and early nineteenth centuries was avid for both horror and terror, as well as for supernatural history. Such works were gobbled greedily as they rolled off the presses. Indeed, the readers of the gothic may have begun the mass marketing of literature by ensuring the fortunes of the private lending libraries that opened in response to the gothic binge. Although the libraries continued after the gothic wave had crested, it was this craze that gave the libraries their impetus. Such private lending libraries purchased numerous copies of long lists of gothic works and furnished subscribers with a list from which they might choose. Like contemporary book clubs, the libraries vied for the most appetizing authors. Unlike the modern clubs, books circulated back and forth, not to be kept by subscribers.

William Lane's Minerva Public Library was the most famous and most successful of all these libraries. Lane went after the works of independent gothic authors but formed the basis of his list by maintaining his own stable of hacks. The names of most of the "stable authors" are gone, and so are their books, but the titles linger on in the library records, echoing one another and the titles of the more prominent authors: *The Romance Castle* (1791), *The Black Forest: Or, The Cavern of Horrors* (1802), *The Mysterious Omen: Or, Awful Retribution* (1812).

By the time *Melmoth the Wanderer* had appeared, this trend had run its course. Only hacks continued to mine the old pits for monks, nuns, fainting innocents, Apennine banditti, and Satanic quests, but critics agree that if the conventions of the gothic period from Walpole to Maturin have dried out and fossilized, the spirit is very much alive. Many modern novels set miles from an abbey and containing not one shrieking, orphaned virgin or worm-ridden corpse may be considered gothic. If the sophisticated cannot repress a snicker at the obvious and well-worn gothic conventions, they cannot dismiss the power and attraction of its spirit, which lives today in serious literature.

Modern thinking about gothic literature has gravitated toward the psychological aspects of the gothic. The castle or ruined abbey has become the interior of the mind, racked with anxiety and unbridled surges of emotion, melodramatically governed by polarities. The traditional gothic is now identified as the beginning of neurotic literature. In a perceptive study of the genre, *Love, Misery, and Mystery: Feeling in Gothic Fiction* (1978), Coral Ann Howells points out that the gothic literature of the eighteenth century was willing to deal with the syntax of hysteria, which the more prestigious literature, controlled by classical influences, simply denied or avoided. Hysteria is no stranger to all kinds of literature, but thinking today seeks to discriminate between the literary presentation of hysteria or neuroticism as an aberration from a rational norm and the gothic presentation of neuroticism as equally normative with rational control, or even as the dominant mode.

The evolution of the modern gothic began close to the original seedbed, in the works of Edgar Allan Poe. In "The Fall of the House of Usher," for example, the traditional sins of the gothic past cavort in a mansion of ancient and noble lineage. A young virgin is subjected to the tortures of the charnel house; the tomb and the catacombs descend directly from Lewis. So, too, do the hyperbolic physical states of pallor and sensory excitement. This tale is also marked, however, by the new relationship it seeks to demonstrate between reason and hysterical anxiety.

Roderick Usher's boyhood friend, the story's narrator, is a representative of the normative rational world. He is forced to encounter a reality in which anxiety and dread are the norm and in which the passions know no rational bounds. Reason is forced to confront the reality of hysteria, its horror, terror, and power. This new psychological development of the gothic is stripped of the traditional gothic appurtenances in Poe's "The Tell-Tale Heart," where there are neither swooning virgins nor charnel houses, nor ruined, once-great edifices, save the ruin of the narrator's mind. The narrator's uncontrollable obsessions both to murder and to confess are presented to stun the reader with the overwhelming force of anxiety unconditioned by rational analysis.

Thus, a more modern gothic focuses on the overturning of rational limits as the source of horror and dread, without necessarily using the conventional apparatus. More examples of what may be considered modern gothic can be found in the works of Nathaniel Hawthorne (1804-1864). Although Hawthorne was perfectly capable of using the conventional machinery of the gothic, as in *The House of the Seven Gables* (1851), he was one of the architects of the modern gothic. In Hawthorne's forward-looking tales, certain combinations of personalities bond, as if they were chemical compounds, to form anxiety systems that cannot be resolved except by the destruction of all or part of the human configuration. In *The Scarlet Letter* (1850), for example, the configuration of Hester, Chillingsworth, and Dimmesdale forms an interlocking system of emotional destruction that is its own Otranto. The needs and social positions of each character in this trio impinge on one another in ways that disintegrate "normal" considerations of loyalty, courage, sympathy, consideration, and judgment. Hester's vivacity is answered in Dimmesdale, whose violently clashing aloofness and responsiveness create for her a vicious cycle of fulfillment and rejection. Chillingsworth introduces further complications through another vicious cycle of confidence and betrayal. These are the catacombs of the modern gothic.

Another strand of the modern gothic can be traced to *Frankenstein* (1818), by Mary

Wollstonecraft Shelley (1979-1851). The novel was published just as the gothic genre was on the wane. Shelley's story represents an important alternative for the gothic imagination. The setting in this work shifts from the castle to the laboratory, forming the gothic tributary of science fiction. Frankenstein reverses the anxiety system of the gothic from the past to the future. Instead of the sins of the fathers—old actions, old human instincts rising to blight the present—human creativity is called into question as the blight of the future. Frankenstein's mind and laboratory are the gothic locus of "future fear," a horror of the dark side of originality and birth, which may, as the story shows, be locked into a vicious cycle with death and sterility. A dread of the whole future of human endeavor pursues the reader in and out of the dark corridors of *Frankenstein*.

Bram Stoker's *Dracula* (1897) may be considered an example of a further evolution of the gothic. Here one finds a strong resurgence of the traditional gothic: the ruined castle, bandits ranging over craggy hills, the sins of the past attacking the life of the present, and swooning, morbidly detailed accounts of deaths. The attendant supernatural horror and the bloodletting of the vampires, their repulsive stench, and the unearthly attractiveness of Dracula's vampire brides come right out of the original school of *Schauer-Romantik* horror. The utterly debilitating effect of the vampire on human will is, however, strong evidence for those critics who see the gothic tradition as an exploration of neurosis.

Stoker synthesizes two major gothic subclassifications in his work, thereby producing an interesting affirmation. Unlike the works of Radcliffe and her terror school, *Dracula* does not ultimately affirm the power of human reason, for it never explains away the supernatural. On the other hand, Stoker does not invoke his vampires as totally overwhelming forces, as in the horror school. *Dracula* does not present a fatalistic course of events through which the truth will not win out. Humankind is the agency of its salvation, but only through its affirmation of the power of faith. Reason is indeed powerless before Dracula, but Dr. Van Helsing's enormous faith and the faith he inspires in others are ultimately sufficient to resolve gothic anxiety, without denying its terrifying power and reality.

THE GOTHIC IN THE TWENTIETH CENTURY AND LATER

Significantly, in the contemporary gothic, reason never achieves the triumph it briefly found through the terror school. Twentieth and twenty-first century gothic tends toward the *Schauer-Romantik* school of horror. Either it pessimistically portrays an inescapable, mind-forged squirrel cage, or it optimistically envisions an apocalyptic release through faith, instinct, or imagination, the nonrational human faculties. For examples of both twentieth century gothic trends, it may be instructive to consider briefly William Faulkner (1897-1962), whose works are frequently listed at the head of what is called the southern gothic tradition, and Doris Lessing (born 1919), whose later works took a turn that brought them into the fold of the science-fiction branch of gothic. If there remains any doubt about the respectability of the genre and its writers, it may be noted here that both Faulkner and Lessing are winners of the Nobel Prize in Literature.

Faulkner's fictions have all the characteristic elements of the southern gothic: the traditional iconography; decaying mansions and graveyards; morbid, death-oriented actions and images; sins of the past; and virgins. *The Sound and the Fury* (1929) is concerned with the decaying Compson house and family, the implications of past actions, and Quentin's morbid preoccupation with death and virginity; it features Benjy's graveyard and important scenes in a cemetery. *As I Lay Dying* (1930) is structured around a long march to the cemetery with a stinking corpse. *Absalom, Absalom!* (1936) is full of decaying houses and lurid death scenes and features prominently three strange virgins—Rosa Coldfield, Judith Sutpen, and Clytie—or five if Quentin and Shreve are to be counted. In this work, the past eats the present up alive and the central figure, Thomas Sutpen, is much in the tradition of the charismatic, but boundlessly appropriating, gothic villain.

These cold gothic externals are only superficial images that betray the presence of the steaming psychological modern gothic centers of these works. Like Hawthorne, Faulkner creates interfacing human systems of neurosis whose inextricable coils lock each character into endless anxiety, producing hysteria, obsession, and utter loss of will and freedom. The violence and physical hyperbole in Faulkner reveal the truly gothic dilemmas of the characters, inaccessible to the mediations of active reason. As in Hawthorne, the combinations of characters form the catacombs of an inescapable though invisible castle or charnel house. Through these catacombs Faulkner's characters run, but they cannot extricate themselves and thus simply revolve in a maze of involuted thought. The Compsons bind one another to tragedy, as do the Sutpens and their spiritual and psychological descendants.

There is, however, an alternative in the modern gothic impulse. In her insightful, imaginative study of the modern evolution of the gothic, *Ghosts of the Gothic: Austen, Eliot, and Lawrence* (1980), Judith Wilt assigns Lessing a place as the ultimate inheritor of the tradition. Lessing does portray exotic states of anxiety, variously descending into the netherworld (*Briefing for a Descent into Hell*, 1971) and plunging into outer space (the Canopus in Argos series), but Wilt focuses on *The Four-Gated City* (1969). This novel has both the trappings and the spirit of the gothic. The book centers on a doomed old house and an old, traditional family succumbing to the sins of the past. These Lessing portrays as no less than the debilitating sins of Western culture, racist, sexist, and exploitive in character. Lessing does indeed bring down this house. Several of the major characters are released from doom, however, by an apocalyptic World War III that wipes away the old sins, freeing some characters for a new, fruitful, life without anxiety. Significantly, this new world will be structured not on the principles of reason and logic, which Lessing excoriates as the heart of the old sins, but on the basis of something innately nonrational and hard to identify. It is not instinct and not faith, but seems closest to imagination. Lessing's ultimately hopeful vision, it must be conceded, is not shared by most contemporary practitioners of the genre.

The gothic enjoyed a resurgence in the 1980's that critics identified as a significant literary trend. Typical of the diversity of writers mentioned under this rubric are those represented in a collection edited by Patrick McGrath (born 1950): *The New Gothic: A Collection of Contemporary Gothic Fiction* (1991; with Bradford Morrow). McGrath, himself a writer of much-praised gothic fictions, assembled work by veteran novelists such as Robert Coover and John Hawkes as well as younger (now established) writers such as Jamaica Kincaid and William T. Vollmann; the group includes both the best-selling novelist Peter Straub and the assaultive experimental novelist Kathy Acker. These works were first collected by McGrath in the journal *Conjunctions* (1989), in which he contributed an essay outlining some of the characteristics of the new gothic. While resisting any attempt at rigid definition (the gothic, he says, is "an air, a tone, a tendency"; it is "not a monolith"), he acknowledges that all the writers whom he places in this group "concern themselves variously with extremes of sexual experience, with disease and social power, with murder and terror and death." That much might be said about most gothic novelists from the beginnings of the genre.

What perhaps differentiates many of the writers whom McGrath discusses from their predecessors—what makes the new gothic new—is a more self-consciously transgressive stance, evident in McGrath's summation of the vision that he and his fellow writers share.

> Common to all is an idea of evil, transgression of natural and social law, and the gothic, in all its suppleness, is the literature that permits that mad dream to be dreamt in a thousand forms.

Among popular-fiction writers, the gothic split into two main genres, one based on supernatural or psychological horror and the other based on women's fiction, featuring romance and, often, historical settings. Moreover, combinations of the two traditions most approach the hyperreal intensity and blend of fear and passion seen in the original gothic: for example, the saga of the Dollanganger family by V. C. Andrews (1923-1986) or the Blood Opera series—*Dark Dance* (1992), *Personal Darkness* (1993), and *Darkness, I* (1994)—by Tanith Lee (born 1947).

While horror writers often substitute the suburbs or small town for the isolated castle—and sometimes psychic abilities, deranged computers, or psychotic killers for ghostly nuns and predatory villain-heroes—they continue to explore the intense feeling, perilous world, tense social situations, and alluring but corrupt sexuality of the original gothic. Unlike the romantic gothic, which has seen periods of quiescence and revival, an unbroken line of the horror gothic persisted from *The Castle of Otranto* through *Dracula* and into the twentieth century with books such as *Ghost Stories of an Antiquary* (1904), by M. R. James (1862-1936), and the works of Walter de la Mare (1873-1956) and H. P. Lovecraft (1890-1937).

These stories continue the trend—seen in Poe, Hawthorne, Faulkner, and others—of maintaining morbid and sensational gothic elements while rooting the terror in psychology and even epistemology. Often, hauntings reveal, or are even replaced by, obsession and paranoia. Before the burgeoning of the modern commercial horror novel, Shirley

Jackson (1916-1965), in two eerie and lyrical novels, *The Haunting of Hill House* (1959) and *We Have Always Lived in the Castle* (1962), uses the traditional gothic form and many of its motifs, with both psychological sophistication and true terror. Robert Bloch (1917-1994), with his novel *Psycho* (1959), also updates and psychologizes gothic conventions, substituting an out-of-the-way motel for a castle and explicitly invoking Sigmund Freud.

The horror genre grew with the (arguably) gothic novel *The Exorcist* (1971), by William Peter Blatty (born 1928), and with *Rosemary's Baby* (1967), by Ira Levin (1929-2007). The novel transplants to a New York City apartment building the hidden secret, supernatural menace, and conspiracies against the heroine of early gothics. Although the horror market withered in the 1990's, four best-selling authors continued in the gothic-horror vein: Dean R. Koontz (born 1945), Straub, Stephen King (born 1947), and Anne Rice (born 1941).

While much of Koontz's horror is better classified as horror-adventure, lacking the brooding neuroses and doubts about rationality prevalent in gothic fiction, gothic aspects do dominate his novels *Whispers* (1980), *Shadowfires* (1987), *Dean Koontz's Frankenstein: Prodigal Son* (2005; with Kevin J. Anderson), *Dean Koontz's Frankenstein: City of Night* (2005; with Edward Gorman), and *Dean Koontz's Frankenstein: Dead or Alive* (2007; with Gorman). Koontz's *Demon Seed* (1973) exemplifies the techno-gothic: A threatening setting and pursuing lover combine in a robot intelligence, which runs the house and wants to impregnate the heroine. Rice explores the gothic's lush, dangerous sexuality and burden of the past in the novels of the Vampire Chronicles, including *Interview with the Vampire* (1976), *The Vampire Lestat* (1985), *The Tale of the Body Thief* (1992), *Memnoch the Devil* (1995), *Blood and Gold: Or, The Story of Marius* (2001), and *Blood Canticle* (2003).

Straub's *Julia* (1975; also known as *Full Circle*), is a drawing-room gothic novel, focusing on the haunting—supernatural, mentally pathological, or both—of a woman dominated by her husband and his disturbing, enmeshed family. In *Ghost Story* (1979), *Shadowland* (1980), and others, Straub widens the focus, exploring and critiquing the small town, boys' school, or suburban setting while developing gothic themes, including dangerous secrets, guilt, ambivalent eroticism, and a threat from the past. In *Lost Boy, Lost Girl* (2003), the threats include a pedophile serial killer, a haunted house, and a missing man's obsession with his dead mother. Straub explores other genres as well, especially the mystery, but maintains a gothic tone and intensity.

Similarly, King's early work is more strictly gothic, such as *'Salem's Lot* (1975), in which vampires spread through a small town in Maine, and *The Shining* (1977), a story of madness and terror in an isolated, empty hotel. However, many later works, even mimetic ones such as *Gerald's Game* (1992), *Dolores Claiborne* (1993), *Bag of Bones* (1998), *From a Buick Eight* (2002), and *Cell* (2006), continue gothic themes and often a gothic tone. King is the undisputed best-selling author of the genre, having sold more than 330 million copies of his novels. Straub and King, admirers of one another's work, have collaborated on two fantasy novels, *The Talisman* (1984), and a sequel, *Black House* (2001).

The prolific Joyce Carol Oates (born 1938), author of more than fifty novels, has created several memorable gothic works, including a Gothic Saga series comprising *Bellefleur* (1980) and its sequels. Another memorable work is *Zombie* (1995), an exploration of the mind of a serial killer, based on the life of Jeffrey Dahmer. New voices on the gothic-novel scene include Donna Tartt (born c. 1964), author of *The Secret History* (1992) and *The Little Friend* (2002), and Elizabeth Kostova (born 1964), whose first novel, *The Historian* (2005), became a best seller and was translated into close to thirty languages.

Along with terror and horror, sentimental and romantic elements were established in the original gothic in the works of Ann Radcliffe, Clara Reeve, Susanna Rowson (1762-1824), and the Brontë sisters. In 1938, *Rebecca*, by Daphne du Maurier (1907-1989), the story of a young woman's marriage to a wealthy English widower with a secret, conveyed many gothic conventions to a new audience, paving the way for the genre of gothic romance. Combining mystery, danger, and romantic fantasy, such books tend to feature innocent but admirable heroines, a powerful male love interest and his isolated estate, ominous secrets (often linked to a woman from the love interest's past, as in *Rebecca*), and exotic settings that are remote in place and time.

In the early 1960's, editor Gerald Gross of Ace Books used the term "gothic" for a line of paperbacks aimed at women, featuring primarily British authors such as Victoria Holt (pseudonym for Eleanor Alice Burford Hibbert, 1906-1993), Phyllis A. Whitney (1903-2008), and Dorothy Eden (1912-1982). The mystery and love plots are inextricable, and the novels feature many gothic elements, including besieged heroines; strong, enigmatic men; settings that evoke an atmosphere of tension and justified paranoia; heightened emotional states; doubled characters (including impersonation); and lurid, sometimes cruel, sexuality. In the 1970's and later, erotic elements flourished and became more explicit, resulting in the new category of the erotic gothic.

Martha Nochimson
Updated by Bernadette Lynn Bosky

BIBLIOGRAPHY

Brown, Marshall. *The Gothic Text*. Stanford, Calif.: Stanford University Press, 2005. Scholarly examination of what it means to designate a literary work as "gothic." Brown explicates the antecedents of and ideologies that were contemporary to the birth of gothic literature. Brown also examines definitive gothic authors and works.

Ellis, Markman. *The History of Gothic Fiction*. New York: Columbia University Press, 2000. Historical survey of the gothic novel, with analyses of the female gothic, revolution and libertinism, science and conspiracy, vampires and credulity, and zombies and the occultation of slavery.

Frank, Frederick S. *Guide to the Gothic*. Lanham, Md.: Scarecrow Press, 1984.

_____. *Guide to the Gothic II*. Lanham, Md.: Scarecrow Press, 1995. Annotated bibliographies on gothic fiction and literary analyses of gothic works. With Frank's updated 1995 guide, impressively complete and helpful.

Geary, Robert F. *The Supernatural in Gothic Fiction: Horror, Belief, and Literary Change.* Lewiston, N.Y.: Edwin Mellen Press, 1992. Gothic fiction often contains elements of the supernatural. Geary discusses the most common works using use the supernatural as a theme.

Haggerty, George E. *Queer Gothic.* Urbana: University of Illinois Press, 2006. Considers the subtext of homoeroticism in gothic fiction. Examines topics such as gothic fiction and the history of sexuality, the gothic and the "erotics of loss," and the influence of gothic novelist Anne Rice on the "queering of culture."

Jackson, Anna, Karen Coats, and Roderick McGillis, eds. *The Gothic in Children's Literature: Haunting the Borders.* New York: Routledge, 2007. Argues that the gothic has always been a part of children's literature, contrary to assumptions about the gothic as a forbidden realm for adults only. Examines "the early intersection of the gothic and children's literature and the contemporary manifestations of the gothic impulse."

Kilgour, Maggie. *The Rise of the Gothic Novel.* Reprint. New York: Routledge, 1997. Explores the gothic novel's beginnings and its growth in popularity among writers, readers, and publishers. Includes bibliographical references and an index.

Mussell, Kay. *Women's Gothic and Romantic Fiction: A Reference Guide.* Westport, Conn.: Greenwood Press, 1981. Concise and insightful overviews and lengthy bibliographies concerning the female gothic, from Ann Radcliffe to commercial gothic romances of the late twentieth century.

Norton, Rictor, ed. *Gothic Readings: The First Wave, 1764-1840.* Reprint. New York: Leicester University Press, 2006. Study of the first novels of gothic literature. Edited collection of intelligent, readable essays.

Punter, David, and Glennis Byron. *The Gothic.* Malden, Mass.: Blackwell, 2004. Discusses backgrounds, contexts, themes, and motifs, and provides detailed introductions to dozens of individual authors. Includes a chronology and a bibliography.

Punter, David, ed. *A Companion to the Gothic.* Malden, Mass.: Blackwell, 2000. Twenty-four critical essays by leading scholars in the field, exploring the gothic's progression in Western literary history.

Varma, Devendra P. *The Gothic Flame: Being a History of the Gothic Novel in England—Its Origins, Efflorescence, Disintegration, and Residuary Influences.* Metuchen, N.J.: Scarecrow Press, 1987. Originally published in 1957, this groundbreaking study of the early gothic (1764-1826) provides descriptions, analyses, classifications, and a detailed history.

Wright, Angela. *Gothic Fiction.* New York: Palgrave Macmillan, 2007. From the perspective of aesthetic, political, psychoanalytic, and gender criticism, Wright explores "the moral and political panic" that accompanied the earliest rise of gothic fiction. Follows with a study of how the gothic survived the panic and then thrived as a serious form of literature.

WILLIAM HARRISON AINSWORTH

Born: Manchester, Lancashire, England; February 4, 1805
Died: Reigate, Surrey, England; January 3, 1882
Also known as: T. Hall

PRINCIPAL LONG FICTION

Sir John Chiverton, 1826 (with John Partington Aston)
Rookwood, 1834
Crichton, 1837
Jack Sheppard, 1839
The Tower of London, 1840
Guy Fawkes, 1841
Old Saint Paul's, 1841
The Miser's Daughter, 1842
Windsor Castle, 1843
Saint James's: Or, The Court of Queen Anne, 1844
James the Second, 1848
The Lancashire Witches, 1849
The Flitch of Bacon, 1854
The Star-Chamber, 1854
The Spendthrift, 1856
Mervyn Clitheroe, 1858
Ovingdean Grange, 1860
The Constable of the Tower, 1861
The Lord Mayor of London, 1862
Cardinal Pole, 1863
John Law, 1864
Auriol, 1865
The Spanish Match, 1865
The Constable de Bourbon, 1866
Old Court, 1867
Myddleton Pomfret, 1868
The South-Sea Bubble, 1868
Hilary St. Ives, 1869
Talbot Harland, 1871
Tower Hill, 1871
Boscobel, 1872
The Manchester Rebels of the Fatal '45, 1872 (originally published as *The Good Old Times*)

Merry England, 1874
The Goldsmith's Wife, 1875
Preston Fight, 1875
Chetwynd Calverley, 1876
The Leaguer of Latham, 1876
The Fall of Somerset, 1877
Beatrice Tyldesley, 1878
Beau Nash, 1879
Stanley Brereton, 1881

OTHER LITERARY FORMS

Most of the work that William Harrison Ainsworth (AYNZ-wurth) produced in forms other than the novel was limited to juvenilia. Before he had reached the age of nineteen, he had published dramas, poems, essays, tales, and translations in local Manchester periodicals. He also wrote several short books of verse and a brief political pamphlet before he became known as a novelist. Later, he contributed some reviews and verse to annuals and magazines. The songs and ballads scattered throughout his novels were collected for separate publication in 1855 and reprinted in 1872. Ainsworth's association with periodicals was long and significant, and most of his novels were first published as magazine serials. He served as editor with the periodicals *Bentley's Miscellany* (1839-1841 and 1854-1868), *Ainsworth's Magazine* (1842-1854), and the *New Monthly Magazine* (1846-1870).

ACHIEVEMENTS

William Harrison Ainsworth has often been considered the heir of Sir Walter Scott. After writing two books that were criticized for glamorizing criminals, he produced dozens of solid historical novels that were entertaining, moral, and educational. Some of these works feature real historical figures; others use invented characters who take part in significant historical events. Ainsworth's books have vivid scenes and exciting conflicts. They are filled with accurate details about costume, food, ceremony, and architecture. Although *Windsor Castle* and *The Tower of London* are novels, generations of tourists used them for guidebooks. Ainsworth covered the significant monarchs that were too recent to be in William Shakespeare's plays. Most ordinary people in the nineteenth century gleaned their sense of English history largely from the works of Scott, Shakespeare, and Ainsworth.

Ainsworth, however, contributed virtually nothing to the development of the novel as a literary form; he merely did what Scott had done before him—and not nearly so well. The literary novel was turning to realistic social and psychological examinations of contemporary life. Ainsworth is significant for the roles he played as an author and as an editor of popular literature. His books refined and preserved elements of popular theater and gothic fiction, adapting them to mid-nineteenth century modes of publication. His novels are characterized by heightened confrontations and recurring climaxes; the techniques of suspended narration and the resources of serial construction; supernatural excitements, vivid tableaux, and memorable spectacles; a preference for romantic underdogs; and moral simplicity. Ainsworth made these touchstones of popular writing briefly respectable and then handed them down to the authors who catered to the much broader mass reading public of the late nineteenth century.

BIOGRAPHY

William Harrison Ainsworth was born February 4, 1805, to a prosperous family in Manchester, England. His father was a solicitor who had a substantial house on a good street, a suburban summer residence, and a fondness for collecting information about crime and criminals. Even before he could read, Ainsworth adored his father's stories of highwaymen and ghosts. Although he was brought up in a strict atmosphere of Whiggism and Nonconformity, Ainsworth also grew to love lost causes. From early youth he adopted Jacobite and Tory ideals.

When he was twelve years old, Ainsworth was sent to the Manchester Free Grammar School. He became passionately fond of the stage, and from the age of fifteen wrote and acted in plays with schoolboy friends. One of them, *Giotto: Or, The Fatal Revenge*, included a dreadful storm, terrible and mysterious events, signs of the supernatural, and minute descriptions of scenery, buildings, and costumes.

In the next few years, Ainsworth published anonymous or pseudonymous pieces in a number of magazines, briefly edited a periodical of his own, and wrote to Charles Lamb for advice about two metrical tales and three short songs that he published in 1822 as *Poems* by Cheviot Ticheburn. Leaving school at seventeen, Ainsworth became an articled clerk; in 1824, when his father died, he went to London for further legal education. At the age of twenty-one he qualified as a solicitor. In 1826, however—almost as soon as he had finished preparing to practice law—he published the historical romance he had written with a fellow clerk in Manchester, married Anne Frances "Fanny" Ebers, and took over the publishing and bookselling branches of his father-in-law's business.

Ainsworth hoped to conduct a gentlemanly trade that would publish good books that were not popular enough for other publishing houses, but he soon found the prospects were not what he had imagined; although he met many authors and produced some good works, his firm's biggest success was a cookbook. In 1829, after returning briefly to law, he became part of the circle formed by William Maginn to contribute to *Fraser's Magazine for Town and Country*—a circle that included Theodore Hook, Samuel Taylor Coleridge, Thomas Carlyle, and William Makepeace Thackeray and was therefore intimately linked to literary fashion. Ainsworth started begging friends for plots. Finally, inspired by Ann Radcliffe's gothic fiction, he published *Rookwood* in April, 1834, a work that was an immediate success with both critics and public.

The next ten or twelve years were Ainsworth's best. His novels sold phenomenally. For much of the time he was producing two at once: *Guy Fawkes* ran in *Bentley's Miscellany* between January, 1840, and November, 1841, while at the same time *The Tower of London* came out in monthly parts in 1840, and *Old Saint Paul's* was serialized in the *Sunday Times* during 1841. Even while writing two novels at once, Ainsworth was a successful and conscientious editor. He succeeded Charles Dickens at the helm of *Bentley's Miscellany* in 1839 and then, in 1842, began *Ainsworth's Magazine*. He was also a social celebrity who gave elaborate dinners for friends, including virtually everyone active in literature in England during the 1840's.

By the decade's end, Ainsworth was rerunning his early novels in *Ainsworth's Magazine* and repeating scenes and characters in the new books he wrote. In 1853 he moved to Brighton. Although he continued to write constantly for almost thirty more years and although, as an editor, he still influenced the course of popular fiction, he was no longer—physically, creatively, or socially—at the heart of nineteenth century literature.

Almost nothing is known of Ainsworth as a private person. Neither of his wives shared his public life. Fanny, who bore him three daughters, separated from him three years before she died in 1838. Sarah Wells, who gave him another daughter in 1867, was married to Ainsworth secretly sometime before they moved to Reigate in 1878. There he continued to write for whatever he could earn. His last novel was being serialized in a provincial newspaper when he died on January 3, 1882.

ANALYSIS

Popular fiction requires, above all else, a work that holds the reader's interest. The best popular authors, furthermore, are generally those who believe and delight in the books they write. William Harrison Ainsworth began to publish just after Sir Walter Scott's death. At that time there was as yet no clearly discernible indication of the direction fiction would take, but there was a vogue for stories about history and crime. These topics suited Ainsworth's personal taste—his early interest in his father's tales, his love of acting exciting roles, his fondness for Scott, Lord Byron, Christopher Marlowe, and for gothic novelists such as Matthew Gregory Lewis and Ann Radcliffe. Before long, the vogue for such stories had passed. Its other practitioners, including Charles Dickens, moved on to different styles and themes, but Ainsworth remained in the groove he had carved. His method of composition bred a narrative technique that secured the reader's involvement but did not encourage analytical thought.

Ainsworth's mind was attracted by snatches of legend, by the mood surrounding a place, by the intensely realized scenes without antecedents or consequences that often feature in daydreams. His books have very complicated stories but often lack plot in the sense of shape, point, or consequence. His most successful works gain apparent unity because they are linked to a single place or use a well-known historical event as a frame. Ainsworth was not creative in the broad sense; he depended on research because it supplied a mass of details that helped disguise the fact that he lacked Scott's ability to create the texture and spirit of the past. The accurate details also gave Ainsworth's books respectability for a mass public that was becoming increasingly self-conscious; historical distance permitted both Ainsworth and his readers to be emotionally involved in scenes of horror, conflict, and danger.

Ainsworth's stories are far too complicated to summarize. In each novel, at least three or four series of events move simultaneously; typically, one is historical, one uses fictional characters acting in historical events, and a third involves comic figures. Each individual story line is itself intricate. In any plot, at any moment, present action may be suspended by the entrance of a stranger who proceeds to recount the course of his life to date, and the stranger's narrative may itself be suspended for its own internal interruptions. The method is not, strictly speaking, dramatic, because the reader is likely to forget just what question is driving the story onward. The individual scenes, however, are vividly realized. Inevitably, at the end of an installment, one set of characters is left dangling, and a new set is taken up in the next. Ainsworth's creative use of the breaks imposed by the medium (in this case serialization) and his control of lighting effects and angles of vision anticipate the techniques of popular film and television.

Especially useful for creating effects, the topics of history and the supernatural were used by Ainsworth because they supplied cruelty, torture, flight, combat, and chills down the spine, tools for the manipulation of emotions. The supernatural elements that appear in almost all of Ainsworth's novels are used primarily for effect; Ainsworth neither explains the uncanny events nor (as serious gothic novelists would) explores the mystery of evil. Elements of reality, such as murders, storms, and riots, arouse emotional responses, and the unreality of the supernatural may, like the distance of history, help rationalist readers from an industrialized world to release emotions that are no longer acceptable in daily life.

Ainsworth virtually always includes at least one character who is disguised, who is using a false name, or who has mysterious, confused, obscure parentage. Readers of Ainsworth's books soon learn that they can never be certain who the characters really are. The stories of concealed parentage and shifting identity allow readers in the most humdrum circumstances to step imaginatively into the shoes of a countess, a knight, or even royal offspring, secure in the expectation that anyone might turn out to be royalty in disguise. The device is a psychological strategy for Ainsworth, the bourgeois son of a Nonconformist family from a bleak industrial town who chose to become a Royalist, a Tory, and a Jacobite. It is also a paradigm for the escapism beloved by readers who found themselves increasingly interchangeable cogs in the nineteenth century's bureaucratic and commercial machines.

ROOKWOOD

An immediate best seller, *Rookwood* not only is typical Ainsworth but also might serve as a model to teach generations of adventure writers about constructing narrative books.

The opening sentence reveals two people seated in a burial vault at midnight. The rest of the long first paragraph holds the reader's curiosity about these people in abeyance while it describes the architecture and effigies of the mausoleum in order to create an air of foreboding. The first chapter alternates passages of partial exposition with scenes of strong emotion, and the second chapter is a chase built from a series of captures, struggles, and escapes. At the second chapter's climax, Luke Rookwood—the protagonist—dives into a pool and does not emerge; the chapter ends, leaving him underwater. The next several chapters introduce other characters, new lines of action, and a great deal more historical exposition before telling the reader what happened to Luke.

Rookwood virtually catalogs the devices made popular by gothic novelists thirty years earlier. In the opening chapter, Ainsworth introduces the inheritance theme and Luke's confused parentage, a death omen, croaking ravens, a Gypsy queen, a preserved corpse with a significant ring on its finger, an evil Jesuit, a moving statue, a dead hand, and writing on a wall. The rest of the book supplies duels between relatives, a deathbed curse, a runaway bride, a portrait that changes expression, underground caverns, a supernatural summons, a miniature with an inscription that gives a clue to the past, a rediscovered marriage certificate, secret passageways, stormy nights, an interrupted burial, a purely incidental death by thunderbolt, corpses swaying from a gibbet, talismans, a deserted priory where Gypsies dwell, a character who masquerades as a ghost, infallible prophecies in verse, love potions, a marriage in a subterranean shrine (formerly an anchorite's cell) with a corpse on the altar, disguises, a bride substituted for another in the dark, a heroine drugged into passivity, a battle between Gypsies and highwaymen, and a faithless lover who dies from kissing a poisoned lock of hair. In the final scene, the villainess is shoved by a statue into a sarcophagus, where she perishes.

Like the typical gothic romance, *Rookwood* has a Byronic hero of mixed good and evil (Luke), a persecuted maiden (Eleanor), and a romantic hero who gets the girl (Ranulph). Ranulph and Eleanor are uninteresting, and even Luke is not very successful; he arouses some sympathy at the outset because he is an underdog, but his transformation to villain is not explored fully enough to be convincing. To berate Ainsworth for lack of originality, however, is to miss the point. He used the traditional gothic devices for the very reason that they were conventional; they had become a code, an emotional shorthand that triggered known responses. Ainsworth was thus able to control the reader's mood, orchestrate the emotional response, and build to repeated transports of excitement.

The most interesting character in *Rookwood* is Dick Turpin, the highwayman. He appears in an outstanding sequence that has little to do with the book's plot: After accidentally killing one of his friends, Turpin rides on horseback with a pistol in each hand and the reins between his teeth, barely ahead of pursuers, the entire distance from London to York. The action peaks every twenty miles or so when Turpin encounters characters from the main plot or exerts a superhuman effort to outfight or outrun the law.

Rookwood was almost totally unplanned; Ainsworth's visit to a gloomy mansion inspired him to attempt a deliberate imitation of the work of Ann Radcliffe. He researched thieves' cant so he could include English highwaymen in place of Italian bandits; he interspersed dramatic songs, comic ballads, and Gypsy dances as if he were writing a melodrama for the stage; and he decided how to solve the mysteries as he went along. The most telling indication of Ainsworth's relationship to his work is that he wrote the twenty-five thousand words of Turpin's ride to York in a day and a night of work. He was so fully absorbed by the scene and its emotion that he wrote continuously until it was finished.

THE TOWER OF LONDON

Setting remained an essential stimulus to Ainsworth's imagination. The architectural-historical books, of which *The Tower of London* is a good example, were largely responsible for his reputation as a novelist who supplied education along with excitement. The single setting and the historical events should have helped Ainsworth focus the novel. The story that he chose, however, illuminates the artistic difficulties that grew from his ability to become wholly absorbed in his characters' emotions

The Tower of London covers the struggle for the throne between the Protestant Lady Jane Grey and the Catholic Queen Mary. The book opens with a magnificent processional, described in exhaustive detail from contemporary sources. Within the frame of this processional, Ainsworth dangles passages of historical exposition, scenes from an assassination conspiracy, confrontations between as-yet-unidentified characters, a thunderstorm, a warning from an old crone, a moment of love at first sight, and other elements that establish emotional tone and provide the narrative hook. The handling of the historical plot line, however, shows how little the story element mattered to Ainsworth; he frequently reminds readers of the outcome already determined by history, so that curiosity about the ending is not a prime motive for reading on.

The book is a good example of Ainsworth's visual imagination and the reciprocal influence of novel and stage. Ainsworth worked closely with his illustrator, George Cruikshank. After their previous collaboration on *Jack Sheppard*, they had seen that Cruikshank's illustrations were almost immediately turned into living tableaux for stage versions of the book. Before beginning each monthly part of *The Tower of London*, Ainsworth and Cruikshank visited the Tower together and decided on the exact setting. They examined the architectural detail, explored the possibilities for light and shadow and composing human forms, and decided what events would take place. Ainsworth apparently learned from the stage how to control the source of light. He conceals the identities of characters by showing them in profile against backlight, he blinds onlookers with sudden brightness, and, inevitably, he extinguishes candles or torches at crucial moments.

Ainsworth continued to manipulate feelings by using dungeons, secret passageways, and torture chambers; he describes—with full detail—a martyr burned at the stake and a prisoner gnawed by rats. The humor supplied in *The Tower of London* in a running subplot about three giants and a dwarf is also largely visual.

Ainsworth has trouble linking the characters from history with the fictional people acting out his typical story of concealed birth, attempted seduction, and true love. The historical scenes are sometimes well realized, in particular the scenes between Lady Jane and Lord Dudley that dramatize the conflict of patriotism and faith. Nevertheless, Ainsworth's emotional connection to the characters—which makes the scenes so powerful—virtually prevents him from shaping any opinion on the moral conflict. Although the book depicts a struggle in which Queen Mary is generally seen as the villain, he cannot despise her. At any given moment, his sympathy is entirely engaged by the character at the center of the scene he is writing. Thus, even with the Tower imposing unity, the book remains a collection of vivid fragments.

OLD SAINT PAUL'S

By the time of *Old Saint Paul's*, serious literary critics were beginning to dismiss Ainsworth and his novels. The best they could say was that his books were educational, but critic Richard Henry Hengist Horne, in *A New Spirit of the Age* (1844), objected that even the history was nothing but "old dates, old names, old houses, and old clothes" and called *Old Saint Paul's* "generally dull, except when it is revolting." Part of the problem, for critics, was the simple fact that Ainsworth had become so popular. *Old Saint Paul's* was apparently the first novel serialized in an English newspaper. The *Sunday Times* paid Ainsworth one thousand pounds for first rights alone; after the book had run in weekly installments through 1841, he was able to sell it again in monthly parts, in three volumes, and in a steady stream of cheap, illustrated, and popular editions.

Artistically, the book is one of Ainsworth's most competent; a coherent invention integrates the history, the melodrama, and even the comedy. The story follows London grocer Stephen Bloundel and his family through the plague of 1665 and the fire of 1666. Most of the characters are fictional, although one historical person, the libertine earl of Rochester, provides a unifying strand by pursuing the grocer's blue-eyed daughter Amabel from one end of the tale to the other. The story lines are adroitly interwoven (perhaps because Ainsworth was not tied to actual historical confrontations), and the comic subplot involving a hypochondriac servant advances and comments on the main action while it supplies laughs. Memorable minor characters include the plundering nurse Judith Malmayns and the religious fanatic Solomon Eagle.

As always, Ainsworth is best at painting scenes. The novel features unforgettable pictures of London with green grass in the streets, of live burials and mass graves, of Saint Paul's filled with victims of plague, of King Charles II in a mad masque of death. In *Rookwood* (as in gothic novels in general) the past simply provides distance and strangeness; it gives readers an excuse to enjoy vicariously passion, cruelty, and sheer excitement. *Old Saint Paul's* allows the same indulgence of feelings, but the novel's scenes of death and sexual passion have a legitimate relationship to the heightened sense of life and death implicit in the historical events.

The moral outlook of *Old Saint Paul's* suggests one reason Ainsworth remained popular with middle-class and lower-middle-class readers long after the literary mainstream had left him behind. The grocer Stephen Bloundel is a rock of individualism and self-sufficiency; as a husband and a father he knows what is best for his family, rules with an iron hand, and preserves not only their lives but also (even in the face of fire) most of their goods. The protagonist—Bloundel's apprentice Leonard Holt—is intelligent, industrious, ambitious, loyal, and as successful as any Horatio Alger hero. His master makes him a partner; his suggestions about fighting the fire are so practical that King Charles gives him a title. Furthermore, his girlfriend turns out to be an heiress in disguise and somehow, during a week of unrelieved firefighting, he manages to acquire new clothes suited to his improved station in life. Although Rochester and his crowd are seen as evil libertines through most of the book, Leonard has no ill feeling toward them at the end. This paradoxical moral attitude—which despises the upper classes for idleness and sexuality yet rewards the industrious hero by giving him wealth and a title—is virtually universal in the cheap literature of the mid-nineteenth century.

LATER CAREER

The historical vein supplied boundaries and permissible exaggerations that gave free play to what Ainsworth could do well. He was much less successful when he attempted a partly autobiographical book in the manner of Dickens's *David Copperfield* (1849-1850, serial; 1850, book)—Ainsworth's was titled *Mervyn Clitheroe*—or when he wrote sensation novels (including *Old Court*, *Myddleton Pomfret*, and *Hilary St. Ives*). The most popular form of the 1860's (and the direct ancestor of thrillers and detective stories), the sensation novel required tight plotting and a convincing contemporary milieu; Ainsworth's modern tales used his typical devices of misplaced inheritance, concealed identity, and inexplicable supernatural events, but the gaps tended to show when the actors wore modern dress.

If he was not particularly adept at writing sensation novels, however, Ainsworth was good at finding people who could. His middlebrow popular magazines effectively encouraged tight serial construction, the accumulation of incidents, and the interweaving of plots so that each installment could end in suspense. He discovered and encouraged two of the best-selling authors of the 1860's and 1870's, Ouida (Marie Louise de la Ramée) and Mrs. Henry Wood, whose famous *East Lynne* was written for *New Monthly Magazine* between 1859 and 1861, when Ainsworth was its editor. He reputedly read all submissions and wrote letters of advice to young authors. He also knew how to promote himself and was not above giving dinners to cultivate the influential librarian Charles Edward Mudie.

After the success of *Rookwood* in 1834, Ainsworth was a novelist everyone read. His first books were reviewed by leading journals; Ainsworth's *Jack Sheppard* sold more copies on first appearance than did Dickens's *Oliver Twist*, which came out at the same time. By the late 1860's, however, some of Ainsworth's novels were published only in penny magazines and sixpenny paperback editions. By the end of the century, his works were generally considered boys' reading; he became known as a novelist to be classed with such writers as Frederick Marryat and G. A. Henty.

Ainsworth had not changed; the novel and the reading public had. The division between mass literature and serious literature grew wider as the number of literate consumers for popular fiction burgeoned. Eight of Ainsworth's novels ran as serials in *Bow Bells*, a penny-weekly magazine that featured household advice and needlework patterns; the romantic-historical-gothic mode continued popular in *Bow Bells* and persisted as a women's escapist form into the twentieth century. At a Manchester testimonial in 1881, it was said that the Free Library had 250 volumes of Ainsworth's works in order to meet the demand by readers from the artisan class. The influence of his technique can be traced, finally, through the Jack Harkaway serials at the end of the century and on into the Hardy Boys books, which share with Ainsworth's best novels the spooky buildings, caves and underground passages, effective use of lighting, suspended narration, and exclamation marks at the ends of chapters.

Sally Mitchell

OTHER MAJOR WORK

POETRY: *Ballads*, 1855.

BIBLIOGRAPHY

Abbey, Cherie D., ed. *Nineteenth-Century Literature Criticism*. Detroit, Mich.: Gale Research, 1986. Presents information on Ainsworth's writing in its two forms, the Newgate novels and the historical romances, and includes some biographical details. Also includes extracts from reviews and essays from the 1830's through 1979, which are helpful in assessing critical responses to Ainsworth.

Carver, Stephen James. *The Life and Works of the Lancashire Novelist William Harrison Ainsworth, 1805-1882*. Lewiston, N.Y.: Edward Mellen Press, 2003. Provides extensive analysis of Ainsworth's writings and outlines the contributions Ainsworth made to periodical literature. Includes bibliographies of both Ainsworth's work and secondary literature.

Collins, Stephen. "Guy Fawkes in Manchester: The World of William Harrison Ainsworth." *Historian* 188 (Winter, 2005): 34-37. Explores Harrison's life and works. Maintains that Harrison was one of the nineteenth century authors "responsible for placing some of the most memorable historical legends in the public psyche," as illustrated by his novels about Dick Turpin and Jack Sheppard. Focuses on Ainsworth's novel *Guy Fawkes*, in which the author sets the Gunpowder Plot in his native Manchester.

Hollingsworth, Keith. *The Newgate Novel, 1830-1847: Bulwer, Ainsworth, Dickens, and Thackeray*. Detroit, Mich.: Wayne State University Press, 1963. Discusses the Newgate theme in nineteenth century literature, including critical commentary on Ainsworth's Newgate fiction and his association with Charles Dickens. Valuable for placing Ainsworth within this genre. Also covers his later writings and his work as editor of *New Monthly Magazine.*

Kelly, Patrick. "William Ainsworth." In *Victorian Novelists After 1885.* Vol. 1 in *Dictionary of Literary Biography*, edited by Ira B. Nadel and William E. Fredeman. Detroit, Mich.: Gale Research, 1983. Provides some helpful background information on Ainsworth's early years, the influences on his writing, and his later years as an editor. Cites *Rookwood* and *Jack Sheppard* as novels worthy of attention, and also discusses the novel *Crichton.* Notes the influence of Sir Walter Scott on Ainsworth's historical novels.

Mitchell, Rosemary. "Experiments with History: The Later Novels of W. H. Ainsworth and Their Illustrations and the Decline of the Picturesque Historical Novel." In *Picturing the Past: English History in Text and Image, 1830-1870.* New York: Oxford University Press, 2000. Chapter on Ainsworth's later historical novels is part of a study of nineteenth century history books, history textbooks, and historical novels that focuses on Victorians' attitudes toward British history. Demonstrates how the text and images in popular and scholarly publications contributed to Victorian cultural identities.

Sharpe, James. *Dick Turpin: The Myth of the English Highwayman.* London: Profile, 2004. Biography explores how the criminal's legend was recounted in eighteenth and nineteenth century literature, including a discussion of Ainsworth's treatment of Turpin in his historical novel *Rookwood.*

Worth, George J. *William Harrison Ainsworth.* New York: Twayne, 1972. Discusses the major aspects of Ainsworth's writing and provides background information on his long life. Describes the author as an "intriguing novelist" who "deserves to be read."

MARGARET ATWOOD

Born: Ottawa, Ontario, Canada; November 18, 1939
Also known as: Margaret Eleanor Atwood

PRINCIPAL LONG FICTION
The Edible Woman, 1969
Surfacing, 1972
Lady Oracle, 1976
Life Before Man, 1979
Bodily Harm, 1981
The Handmaid's Tale, 1985
Cat's Eye, 1988
The Robber Bride, 1993
Alias Grace, 1996
The Blind Assassin, 2000
Oryx and Crake, 2003
The Penelopiad: The Myth of Penelope and Odysseus, 2005

OTHER LITERARY FORMS

A skillful and prolific writer, Margaret Atwood has published many volumes of poetry. Collections such as *Double Persephone* (1961), *The Animals in That Country* (1968), *The Journals of Susanna Moodie* (1970), *Procedures for Underground* (1970), *Power Politics* (1971), *You Are Happy* (1974), *Two-Headed Poems* (1978), *True Stories* (1981), *Interlunar* (1984), and *Morning in the Burned House* (1995) have enjoyed a wide and enthusiastic readership, especially in Canada. During the 1960's, Atwood published in limited editions poems and broadsides illustrated by Charles Pachter: *The Circle Game* (1964), *Kaleidoscopes Baroque: A Poem* (1965), *Speeches for Dr. Frankenstein* (1966), *Expeditions* (1966), and *What Was in the Garden* (1969).

Atwood has also written books for children, including *Up in the Tree* (1978), which she also illustrated, and *Rude Ramsay and the Roaring Radishes* (2004). Her volumes of short stories, a collection of short fiction and prose poems (*Murder in the Dark*, 1983), a volume of criticism (*Survival: A Thematic Guide to Canadian Literature*, 1972), and a collection of literary essays (*Second Words*, 1982) further demonstrate Atwood's wide-ranging talent. In 1982, Atwood coedited *The New Oxford Book of Canadian Verse in English*. She has also written articles and critical reviews too numerous to list. She has contributed prose and poetry to literary journals such as *Acta Victoriana* and *Canadian Forum*, and her teleplays have been aired by the Canadian Broadcasting Corporation.

ACHIEVEMENTS

Early in her career, Margaret Atwood received critical recognition for her work. This is particularly true of her poetry, which has earned her numerous awards, including the E. J. Pratt Medal in 1961, the President's Medal from the University of Western Ontario in 1965, and the Governor-General's Award, Canada's highest literary honor, for *The Circle Game* in 1966. Twenty years later, Atwood again won this prize for *The Handmaid's Tale*. Atwood won first prize in the Canadian Centennial Commission Poetry Competition in 1967 and won a prize for poetry from the Union League Civic and Arts Foundation in 1969. She has received honorary doctorates from Trent University and Queen's University. Additional honors and awards she has received include the Bess Hoskins Prize for poetry (1974), the City of Toronto Award (1977), the Canadian Booksellers Association Award (1977), the St. Lawrence Award for Fiction (1978), the Canada Council Molson Prize (1980), and the Radcliffe Medal (1980). *The Blind Assassin* won the 2000 Booker Prize, and Atwood received Spain's Prince of Asturias literary prize for 2008.

BIOGRAPHY

Margaret Eleanor Atwood was born in Ottawa, Ontario, Canada, on November 18, 1939, the second of Carl Edmund Atwood and Margaret Killam Atwood's three children. At the age of six months, she was backpacked into the Quebec wilderness, where her father, an entomologist, pursued his special interests in bees, spruce budworms, and forest tent caterpillars. Throughout her childhood, Atwood's family spent several months of the year in the bush of Quebec and northern Ontario. She did not attend school full time until she was twelve.

Though often interrupted, Atwood's education seems to have been more than adequate. She was encouraged by her parents to read and write at an early age, and her creative efforts started at five, when she wrote stories, poems, and plays. Her serious composition, however, did not begin until she was sixteen.

In 1961, Atwood earned her B.A. in the English honors program from the University of Toronto, where she studied with poets Jay Macpherson and Margaret Avison. Her M.A. from Radcliffe followed in 1962. Continuing graduate work at Harvard in 1963, Atwood interrupted her studies before reentering the program for two more years in 1965. While she found graduate studies interesting, Atwood directed her energies largely toward her creative efforts. For her, the Ph.D. program was chiefly a means of support while she wrote. Atwood left Harvard without writing her doctoral thesis.

Returning to Canada in 1967, Atwood accepted a position at Sir George Williams University in Montreal. By this time, her poetry was gaining recognition. With the publication of *The Edible Woman* and the sale of its film rights, Atwood was able to concentrate more fully on writing, though she taught at York University and was writer-in-residence at the University of Toronto. In 1973, Atwood divorced her American husband of five years, James Polk. After the publication of *Surfacing*, she was able to support herself through her creative efforts. She moved to a farm near Alliston, Ontario, with Canadian novelist Graeme Gibson; the couple's daughter, Eleanor Jess Atwood Gibson, was born in 1979. In 1980, Atwood and her family returned to Toronto, where Atwood and Gibson became active in the Writers' Union of Canada, Amnesty International, and the International Association of Poets, Playwrights, Editors, Essayists, and Novelists (PEN).

ANALYSIS

For Margaret Atwood, an unabashed Canadian, literature became a means to cultural and personal self-awareness. "To know ourselves," she writes in *Survival*, "we must know our own literature; to know ourselves accurately, we need to know it as part of literature as a whole." Thus, when she defines Canadian literary concerns she relates her own as well, for Atwood's fiction grows out of this tradition. In her opinion, Canada's central reality is the act of survival: Canadian life and culture are decisively shaped by the demands of a harsh environment. Closely related to this defining act of survival, in Atwood's view, is the Canadian search for territorial identity—or, as literary theorist Northrop Frye put it, "Where is here?"

Atwood's heroines invariably discover themselves to be emotional refugees, strangers in a territory they can accurately label but one in which they are unable to feel at home. They are alienated not only from their environment but also from language itself; for them, communication becomes a decoding process. To a great degree, their feelings of estrangement extend from a culture that, having reduced everything to products, threatens to consume them. Women are particularly singled out as products, items to be decorated and sold as commodities, though men are threatened as well. Indeed, Canadian identity as a whole is in danger of being engulfed by an acquisitive American culture, though Atwood's "Americans" symbolize exploitation and often turn out to be Canadian nationals.

Reflective of their time and place, Atwood's characters are appropriately ambivalent. Dead or dying traditions prevent their return to the past, a past most have rejected. Their present is ephemeral at best, and their future inconceivable. Emotionally maimed, her heroines plumb their conscious and unconscious impressions, searching for a return to feeling, a means of identification with the present.

Atwood often couches their struggle in terms of a journey, which serves as a controlling metaphor for inner explorations: The unnamed heroine of *Surfacing* returns to the wilderness of Quebec, Lesje Green of *Life Before Man* wanders through imagined Mesozoic jungles, Rennie Wilford of *Bodily Harm* flies to the insurgent islands of Ste. Agathe and St. Antoine. By setting contemporary culture in relief, these primitive sites define the difference between nature and culture and allow Atwood's heroines to gain new perspectives on their own realities. They can see people and places in relation to each other, not as isolated entities. Ultimately, however, this resolves little, for Atwood's novels end on a tenuous note. Although her heroines come to terms with themselves, they remain estranged.

Supporting her characters' ambivalence is Atwood's versatile narrative technique. Her astringent prose reflects their emotional numbness; its ironic restraint reveals their wariness. Frequent contradictions suggest not only the complexity of her characters but also the antagonistic times they must survive. By skillful juxtaposition of past and present through the use of flashbacks, Atwood evokes compelling fictional landscapes that ironically comment on the untenable state of modern men and women. Still, there remains some hope, for her characters survive with increased understanding of their world. Despite everything, life does go on.

SURFACING

The first of Atwood's novels to arouse critical praise and commentary, *Surfacing* explores new facets of the bildungsroman. What might have been a conventional novel of self-discovery develops into a resonant search for self-recovery imbued with mythic overtones and made accessible through Atwood's skillful use of symbol and ritual. At the same time, Atwood undercuts the romantic literary conventions of ultimate self-realization as a plausible conclusion. To accept the heroine's final emergence as an end in itself is to misread this suggestively ironic novel.

The unnamed heroine of *Surfacing*, accompanied by her lover, Joe, and a married couple named David and Anna, returns to the Canadian wilderness where she was reared in hopes of locating her missing father. His sudden disappearance has recalled her from a city life marked by personal and professional failures that have left her emotionally anesthetized. While her external search goes forward, the heroine conducts a more important internal investigation to locate missing "gifts" from both parents. Through these, she hopes to rediscover her lost ability to feel. In order to succeed, however, she will need to expose the fiction of her life.

At the outset of her narrative, the heroine warns her readers that she has led a double life when she recalls Anna's question, "Do you have a twin?" She denies having one, for she apparently believes the elaborate fiction she has created, a story involving a spurious marriage, divorce, and abandonment of her child. As additional protection, the heroine has distanced herself from everyone. She refers to her family as "they," "as if they were somebody else's family." Her relationship with Joe is notable for its coolness, and she has known Anna, described as her best friend, for only two months.

By surrounding herself with friends whose occupation of making a film significantly titled *Random Samples* reveals their rootlessness, the heroine seeks to escape the consequences of her actions. Indeed, she describes herself both as a commercial artist, indicating her sense of having sold out, and as an escape artist. Reluctantly approaching the past she sought to escape, the heroine feels as if she is in foreign territory.

That she feels alienated by the location of her past is not surprising, for she is an outsider in a number of telling ways: of English descent in French territory; a non-Catholic, indeed nonreligious, person among the devout; a woman in a man's world. Her French is so halting that she could be mistaken for an American, representing yet another form of alienation, displacement by foreigners. Most of all, she is a stranger to herself. Rather than focusing on her self-alienation, she is consumed by the American usurpation of Canada, its wanton rape of virgin wilderness; this allows her to avoid a more personal loss of innocence.

Canada's victimization by Americans reflects the heroine's victimization by men. Having been subjected to the concept that "with a paper bag over their head they're all the same," the protagonist is perceived as either contemptible or threatening. Her artistic skills are denigrated by a culture in which no "important" artists have been women. Even her modest commercial success is treated as a personal assault by Joe, who has an "unvoiced claim to superior artistic skills." By telling herself that the wilderness can never recover from abuse, the protagonist denies her own recovery. Although she feels helpless at the beginning of the novel, she soon rediscovers her own capabilities, and as these are increasingly tested, she proves to be a powerful survivor. Thus, the wilderness, a self-reflection, provides the key to self-discovery.

Perhaps the most important lesson the heroine learns is that the wilderness is not innocent. Her encounter with and response to a senselessly slaughtered heron evoke a sense of complicity, leading her to reflect on similar collusion in her brother's animal experiments when they were children. Finding her refuge in childhood innocence blocked, the heroine goes forward with her search. Once again, nature provides information, for in discovering her father's body trapped under water, she finally recognizes her aborted child, her complicity in its death by yielding to her lover's demands. On a broader scale, she acknowledges death as a part of life and reclaims her participation in the life process by conceiving a child by Joe.

In a ceremony evocative of primitive fertility rites, she seduces her lover. Then, assured of her pregnancy, she undergoes a systematic purgation in order to penetrate to the very core of reality. During this process, the protagonist discovers her parents' gifts—her father's sense of sight and her mother's gift of life. With body and mind reunited, she takes an oath in which she refuses to be a victim. Whole, she feels free to reenter her own time, no longer either victim or stranger.

Atwood's procedure for bringing her heroine to this state of consciousness is remarkable for its intricacy. Though she distrusts language, the protagonist proceeds to tell her story by describing what she sees. Since she has lost her ability to feel, much of this description seems to be objective—until the reader realizes just how unreliable her impressions can be. Contradictions abound, creating enormous uncertainty as intentional and unintentional irony collide, lies converge, and opinion stated as fact proves to be false. Given this burden of complexity, any simple conclusion to *Surfacing* is out of the question. Clearly, Atwood hints at a temporary union with Joe, but this is far from resolving the heroine's dilemma. Outer reality, after all, has not altered. Atwood's open-ended conclusion is thus both appropriate and plausible, for to resolve all difficulties would be to give in to the very romantic conventions that her fiction subverts.

LIFE BEFORE MAN

Coming after the gothic comedy of *Lady Oracle*, *Life Before Man* seems especially stark. Nevertheless, its similarity with all of Atwood's novels is apparent. A penetrating examination of contemporary relationships, it peels away protective layers of deceptions, stripping the main characters until their fallible selves are presented with relentless accuracy. Lesje Green and Elizabeth and Nate Schoenhof are adrift in a collapsing culture in which they struggle to survive. As she focuses on each character, Atwood reveals unrecognized facets of the others.

In this novel, wilderness and culture converge in the Royal Ontario Museum, where Lesje works as a paleontologist and Elizabeth works in public relations. There is little need for the bush country of Quebec, since culture is something of a jungle itself. Unlike the Mesozoic, however, the present anticipates its own extinction because of abundant evidence: pollution, separatist movements, political upheaval, lost traditions, disintegrating families. Humanity is in danger of drowning in its own waste. Whatever predictability life held in the past seems completely absent; even holidays are meaningless. Still, the novel is fascinated with the past, with the behavior of animals, both human and prehistoric, and with the perpetuation of memory, particularly as it records the history of families.

As in *Surfacing*, a violent death precipitates emotional withdrawal. Most affected is Elizabeth Schoenhof, whose lover Chris has blown off his head as a final gesture of defiance, the ultimate form of escape. His act destroys Elizabeth's sense of security, which resides both in her home and in her ability to manipulate or predict the actions of others. A supreme manipulator, Elizabeth attempts to make everyone act as reasonably as she. Not surprisingly, Elizabeth has at least two selves speaking different languages, genteel chic and street argot, and what passes for "civilized" behavior is merely an escape from honest confrontation with such basic human emotions as love, grief, rejection, and anger. In fact, all of the novel's characters prefer escape to self-realization, and while they pay lip service to social decorum, they quietly rebel.

Their rebellious emotions are reflected in the larger world, a political world aflame with separatist zeal. René Lévesque, with whom Nate identifies, is gaining momentum for the separation of Quebec and the reestablishment of French as the major language, threatening to displace the English. Indeed, the world seems to be coming apart as international, national, and personal moves toward separation define this novel's movement. As a solution, however, separation fails to satisfy the characters' need to escape, for no matter how far they run, all carry the baggage of their past.

Elizabeth in particular has survived a loveless past, including abandonment by both parents, the painful death of her alcoholic mother, her sister's mental breakdown and drowning, and her Auntie Muriel's puritanical upbringing. All of this has turned Elizabeth into a determined survivor. Beneath her polished exterior is a street fighter from the slums, a primitive. Indeed, Elizabeth recognizes an important part of herself in Chris. Nate and Lesje share a different kind of past, where love created as much tension as affection.

Lesje's Jewish and Ukrainian grandmothers treated her as disputed territory, speaking to her in languages she could not understand and driving her to seek refuge in her fantasy world of Lesjeland.

Feeling like a refugee in treacherous territory, each character attempts to build a new, stable world, notwithstanding the continual impingement of the old, messy one. Nate, having forsaken his mother's futile idealistic causes to save the world, falls in love with Lesje, whom he envisions as an exotic subtropical island free from rules. For a time, Elizabeth inhabits a clean expanse of space somewhere between her bed and the ceiling, and Lesje explores prehistoric terrain, wishing for a return to innocence. When these fantasies diminish in power, the characters find substitutes, challenging the reader to reexamine the novel's possibilities.

Despite its bleak tone, its grimy picture of a deteriorating culture, its feeling of estrangement and futility, and its rejection of simplistic resolutions, *Life Before Man* is not without hope. Each character emerges at the end of this novel with something he or she has desired. Nate has Lesje, now pregnant with his child—a child who, in turn, confirms Lesje's commitment to life by displacing her preoccupation with death. Having exorcised the evil spirits of her past, Elizabeth experiences a return of direct emotion.

There is, however, a distinct possibility that the apparent resolution is as ambivalent as that of *Surfacing*. What appears to be a completely objective third-person point of view, presiding over chapters neatly cataloged by name and date, sometimes shifts to the first person, an unreliable first person at that. Through her revolving characters, their identification with one another, and their multiple role reversals, Atwood creates contradictory, problematic, and deceptive human characters who defy neat categorization. Taken separately, Nate, Elizabeth, and Lesje can easily be misinterpreted; taken as a whole, they assume an even more complex meaning, reflecting not only their own biased viewpoints but also the reader's. Atwood's ability to capture such shifting realities of character and place is one of her chief artistic distinctions.

BODILY HARM

Rather like the narrator of *Surfacing*, Rennie Wilford in *Bodily Harm* has abandoned her past, the stifling world of Griswold, Ontario, to achieve modest success as a freelance journalist. To Rennie, Griswold represents values of duty, self-sacrifice, and decency found comic by modern-day standards. It is a place where women are narrowly confined to assigned roles that make them little better than servants. Rennie much prefers city life, with its emphasis on mobility and trends such as slave-girl bracelets and pornographic art. In fact, Rennie has become an expert on just such trends, so adept that she can either describe or fabricate one with equal facility. Having learned to look only at surfaces, Rennie has difficulty accepting the reality of her cancerous breast, which *looks* so healthy.

Her cancer serves as the controlling metaphor in the novel, spreading from diseased personal relationships to a political eruption on St. Antoine. Indeed, the world seems shot through with moral cancer. The symptoms are manifest: Honesty is a liability, friends are "contacts," lovers are rapists, pharmacists are drug pushers, and no one wants to hear about issues. What should be healthy forms of human commerce have gone out of control, mirroring the rioting cells in Rennie's breast. When confronted by yet another manifestation of this malaise, a would-be murderer who leaves a coil of rope on her bed, Rennie finds a fast escape route by landing a magazine assignment on St. Antoine.

Her hopes of being a tourist, exempt from participation and responsibility, are short-lived as she is drawn into a political intrigue more life-threatening than her cancer. Before reaching St. Antoine, she learns of its coming election, ignoring Dr. Minnow's allusions to political corruption and makeshift operations. What puzzles her most about their conversation is his reference to the "sweet Canadians." Is he being ironic or not, she wonders. Her superficial observations of island life reveal little, though plenty of evidence points to a violent eruption. Rennie seems more concerned about avoiding sunburn and arrest for drug possession than she is about the abundant poverty and casual violence. Her blindness allows her to become a gunrunner, duped by Lora Lucas, a resilient survivor of many injurious experiences, and Paul, the local connection for drugs and guns, who initiates Rennie into genuine, albeit unwilling, massive involvement.

As a physical link to life, Paul's sexual attention is important to Rennie, who appreciates the value of his touch. His hands call forth the "missing" hands of her grandmother, her doctor's hands, and Lora's bitten hands, hands that deny or offer help. Paul's "aid" to the warring political factions, like Canada's donation of canned hams and Rennie's assistance, is highly questionable, and the results are the reverse of what was planned. Trying to escape from his botched plan, Rennie is brought to confront her own guilt.

Again, Atwood uses flight as a route to self-discovery and deprivation as a source of spiritual nourishment. In Rennie's case, however, these are externally imposed. In her underground cell, with only Lora as company, Rennie ultimately sees and understands the violent disease consuming the world, a disease growing out of a human need to express superiority in a variety of ways and at great spiritual expense. Rennie becomes "afraid of men because men are frightening." Equally important, she understands that there is no difference between *here* and *there*. Finally, she knows that she is not exempt: "Nobody is exempt from anything."

If she survives this ordeal, Rennie plans to change her life, becoming a reporter who will tell what truly happened. Once again, however, Atwood leaves this resolution open to questions. Rennie is often mistaken about what she sees and frequently misinterprets events. Her entire story may well be a prison journal, an account of how she arrived there. When projecting her emergence from prison, she uses the future tense. For Atwood's purposes, this is of relative unimportance, since Rennie has been restored in a way she never anticipated. In the end, stroking Lora's battered hand, Rennie finally embodies the best of Griswold with a clear vision of what lies beneath the surface of human reality.

THE HANDMAID'S TALE

In *The Handmaid's Tale*, Atwood's fiction turns from the realistic to the speculative, though she merely takes the political bent of the 1980's to its logical—and chilling—conclusion. Awash in a swill of pollution, promiscuity, pornography, and venereal disease, late twentieth century America erupts into political and religious battles. Rising from the ashes is the Republic of Gilead, a theocracy so conservative in its reactionary bent that women are channeled into roles as Daughters, Wives, Marthas (maids), Econowives, or Handmaids (mistresses). The narrator, Offred (referring to her status as a possession *of* her master), is among the first group of Handmaids, fertile women assigned to high-ranking government officials. Weaving between her past and present in flat, almost emotionless prose, Offred draws a terrifying picture of a culture retreating to religious fundamentalist values in the name of stability. At first her prose seems to be accurate, a report from an observer. Deeper in the story, readers come to understand that Offred is numb from all that has changed in her life. Besides, she does not trust anyone, least of all herself. Still, as a survivor, she determines to stay alive, even if that means taking risks.

Her loss of freedom and identity create new hungers in Offred: curiosity about the world, a subversive desire for power, a longing for feeling, a need to take risks. In many ways, *The Handmaid's Tale* is a novel about what loss creates. Gilead, in fact, is created partially in response to men's loss of feeling, according to Fred, Offred's Commander. Offred, however, takes little comfort in his assurance that feeling has returned.

As she knows, feeling is ephemeral, often unstable, impossible to gauge. Perhaps this is why her characterization of others in the novel seems remote. While Offred observes gestures, facial movements, and voice tone, she can only guess at intent. Implicit in the simplest statement may be an important message. Offred thus decodes all kinds of communication, beginning with the Latin inscription she finds scratched in her wardrobe: "Nolite te bastardes carborundorum." Even this injunction, however, which becomes her motto, is a corruption. Though desperate for communication, Offred cautiously obscures her own message. Her struggle to understand reflects Atwood's familiar theme of the inability for an individual truly to understand another person, another situation.

By having Offred acknowledge the impossibility of accurately decoding messages, Atwood calls attention to the narrative itself. Another interesting fictional element is the narrative's remove in time. Offred tells her story in the present, except when she refers to her life before becoming a Handmaid. Ironically, readers learn that not only is she telling her story after events, but her narrative has been reconstructed and presented to an audience at a still greater temporal remove. All of this increases the equivocal quality of the novel and its rich ambiguity.

While Atwood demands attention, she provides direction in prefatory quotations. Most revealing is her quotation from Jonathan Swift's "A Modest Proposal." Like Swift's satire, Atwood's skates on the surface of reality, often snagging on familiar actions and only slightly exaggerating some attitudes, especially those commonly held about women.

Perennial issues of a woman's place, the value of her work, and her true role in society are at the center of this novel.

CAT'S EYE

These concerns appear again in *Cat's Eye*, but in a more subdued form. In subject and theme, *Cat's Eye* is an artistic retrospective. Elaine Risley, a middle-aged painter, is called to Toronto to prepare for her first artistic retrospective. Risley takes the occasion to come to terms with the dimensions of self in time, which she perceives as a "series of transparencies, one laid on top of another." Her return to Toronto, where she grew up, gives her an opportunity to look through the layers of people and events from her present position on the curve of time. This perspective, often ironic and tenuous, allows Risley to accept herself, including her foibles.

Cat's Eye takes full advantage of Atwood's visual style as it reiterates the importance of perspective in relation to change. The novel's art theme emphasizes interpretation while simultaneously satirizing the kind of inflated yet highly subjective criticism published for public consumption. Atwood's most personal novel to date, *Cat's Eye* tackles the physics of life and art and arrives at Atwood's least ambiguous conclusion. Returning to her family in Vancouver, Risley notes that the starlight she sees is only a reflection. Still, she concludes, "it's enough to see by."

THE ROBBER BRIDE

In *The Robber Bride* communication as a decoding process occurs both figuratively and literally, as one of the four protagonists, the historian Antonia "Tony" Fremont, seeks to discover the underlying meaning of the past. In her own storytelling she sometimes uses a reverse code, transforming herself into her imagined heroine Ynot Tnomerf. In fact, each of the women in the novel has renamed herself to gain distance from past traumas: Karen becomes Charis to cast out the memory of sexual abuse; Tony hopes to escape the "raw sexes war" that characterized her family; Roz Grunwald becomes Rosalind Greenwood as her family climbs the social ladder.

Although cast in comic form, the novel explores issues of identity, reality versus fiction, and women's friendship. The three friends meet for lunch and reminisce about their betrayal at the hands of Zenia, a mysterious femme fatale who seduced Tony's and Roz's husbands and Charis's lover. Zenia has multiple stories about her origins, all dramatic but plausible. She ensnares her victims by preying on their fears and hopes. Speaking about the novel, Atwood has remarked that Zenia is the equivalent of the fiction writer, a liar, a trickster who creates stories to captivate her audience.

ALIAS GRACE

Alias Grace is a historical novel based on the real case of Grace Marks, a nineteenth century Irish immigrant to Canada who was accused of being an accomplice in the murder of her employer and his housekeeper-mistress. The novel combines gothic elements, social commentary, and conventions of nineteenth century fiction to tell its story. Spinning out several parallel courtship plots, the novel elucidates the implications of class and gender: Servant women were often the victims of wealthy employers or their employers' bachelor sons. Grace's friend Mary Whitney dies of a botched abortion when she becomes pregnant.

The story is told through letters and narration by Grace and Dr. Simon Jordan, a young physician who has been employed by Grace's supporters to discover the truth of the murder. Dr. Jordan is a foil to Grace: As her fortunes rise, his fall. Hoping to win a pardon from her prison sentence, the shrewd Grace narrates her life story in great detail but claims she cannot clearly remember the events surrounding the murder. Dr. Jordan hopes to restore her faulty memory and to learn the facts of the case. However, in an ironic twist of plot, he becomes embroiled in a shabby romantic liaison and, to avoid the consequences, flees Canada in haste. He is injured while serving as a physician in the American Civil War and loses his recent memory. Grace is released from prison, given a job as a housekeeper, and marries her employer. Dr. Jordan remains in the care of his mother and the woman she has chosen to be her son's wife. At the end of the novel all the plot threads are conveniently tied together as in the conventional nineteenth century novel, but at the heart of the story Grace herself remains a mystery.

THE BLIND ASSASSIN

Some of Atwood's loyal readers may have looked to *The Blind Assassin* as an opportunity for the Nobel Committee to grace the author with its literature prize. It is a "big novel," not merely because it runs well over five hundred pages but also because it offers a large slice of Canadian history in the twentieth century—or, perhaps more accurately, modern history, in its sweep through the two world wars and the Great Depression. It is a family chronicle of at least three generations of the Chase family, a wealthy, socially prominent family whose progenitor enriched his heirs from the manufacture of buttons and underwear. Stylistically, *The Blind Assassin* is an especially complex text, a series of nested narratives, for the most part under the control of the novel's octogenarian narrator, Iris Chase Griffen, telling the story as a memoir of essentially how she has survived the rest of her family. Because she has a heart condition, Iris is racing against time to finish her story, the most important prospective reader of which is her lost granddaughter Sabrina.

Iris begins with the blunt statement, "Ten days after the war [World War II] ended, my sister Laura drove a car off a bridge," which this memoir promises to explain. Many readers of *Alias Grace* were disappointed because they expected to know eventually whether or not Grace was guilty of murder, but the opening pages of *The Blind Assassin* give a strong sense that Iris not only knows "whodunit" but will eventually divulge that information.

Before Iris can do so, she must explain everything that led up to that fatal day in 1945.

She tells how her father survived World War I—unlike his brothers—and struggled with his business through the Depression to save his workers' jobs, only to accept a merger that cost them those jobs and doomed Iris to a loveless marriage with his business rival, who delighted in leaving bruises on her body where only he could enjoy them as the stigmata of his domination. In rapid fashion Iris loses the only man she ever loved, then her sister and her husband to suicide, and finally her daughter is taken from her as well—a tragic sequence of events reminiscent of Greek tragedy.

ORYX AND CRAKE

Atwood has encouraged readers to approach *Oryx and Crake* as a "bookend" to *The Handmaid's Tale*. *Oryx and Crake* is also set in a future United States. It involves speculation concerning humankind's uses of science, but Atwood rejects the term "science fiction" for this novel as well as for *The Handmaid's Tale*, preferring instead to call them "speculative fiction." She has been adamant in arguing that all the scientific elements she needed for *Oryx and Crake*'s future world, in which global warming and genetic engineering are the dominant forces, are either already in play or merely extensions of the present.

Oryx and Crake represents a new departure for the author as her first novel with a male viewpoint character. Snowman, short for "The Abominable Snowman," struggles to survive in a postapocalyptic world. Snowman was once "Jimmy," the childhood chum of Crake, a boy wonder of bioengineering. In its earlier stages, bioengineering was a boy's game of dreaming up hybrids such as the "rakunk," a mixture of raccoon and skunk. Now the field has developed into procedures such as NooSkins, which gradually replace human skin for a youthful appearance.

As a young man, Crake moves into a powerful position in which he seduces Oryx, whom Jimmy and Crake "met" as boys surfing child pornography online, as well as Jimmy, as his instruments in a master plan to eradicate humanity and replace it with the Children of Crake, creatures he has genetically engineered to survive, as *Homo sapiens* no longer can, in the global swamp generated by contamination of the atmosphere and the melting of the polar icecaps. These Frankenstein's "monsters" will inherit a brave new world from which Snowman and a few remaining humans will soon depart.

THE PENELOPIAD

Commissioned by Canongate Books for its series The Myths, *The Penelopiad* offers the long-suffering wife of Odysseus an opportunity to tell her side of the story from the Underworld more than three millennia after her death. Half of the novel is her memoir, a genre to which Atwood has become attracted in her later years.

Penelope begins with her unhappy childhood as the daughter of an indifferent water spirit and a royal father who foolishly sought immortality by attempting to drown her when the Oracle prophesied that Penelope would weave his shroud—actually it was her father-in-law whose shroud she would famously weave—but she was saved by a flotilla of ducks, thus earning the nickname "Duckie." From childhood she was tormented with the name by her beautiful cousin Helen, whose abduction by or elopement with Prince Paris would start the Trojan War.

Accordingly, if Penelope would cast herself as a figure in Greek tragedy—Atwood's theater adaptation has been successfully staged—Helen is the nemesis who brought about a fall from the good fortune of her early married life with Odysseus, whom she grew to love, even if she could never trust him because he was a "storyteller" and because he had his eye on Helen. Like Iris with her writer-lover, Penelope learned to tell stories after making love. Almost obsessed with her cousin as rival for Odysseus's love, Penelope devotes her energies to managing Ithaca so well that Odysseus upon his return will tell his wife she is worth a thousand Helens.

Atwood has stated that she took the Canongate assignment because she had been haunted as an early teenager by the summary execution of Penelope's twelve maids by Odysseus and Telemachus. The maids function as a Greek chorus of cynical commentary on the royals. They are Penelope's confidants, spies, and helpers with the unweaving of the shroud their mistress must finish before choosing a new husband. At least one disclosed the shroud ruse, and Penelope may have feared they would accuse her of adultery. The big question is whether Penelope colluded in their murder. Like Grace, Penelope never reveals any guilt.

Atwood's vision is as informed and humane as that of any contemporary novelist. Challenging her readers to form their own judgments, she combines the complexity of the best modern fiction with the moral rigor found in the works of the great nineteenth century novelists. Atwood's resonant symbols, her ironic reversals, and her example challenge readers and writers alike to confront the most difficult and important issues of today's world.

Karen Carmean; Karen F. Stein
Updated by Earl G. Ingersoll

OTHER MAJOR WORKS

SHORT FICTION: *Dancing Girls, and Other Stories*, 1977; *Bluebeard's Egg*, 1983; *Murder in the Dark: Short Fictions and Prose Poems*, 1983; *Wilderness Tips*, 1991; *Good Bones*, 1992 (also known as *Good Bones and Simple Murders*, 1994); *Moral Disorder*, 2006.

POETRY: *Double Persephone*, 1961; *The Circle Game*, 1964 (single poem), 1966 (collection); *Kaleidoscopes Baroque: A Poem*, 1965; *Talismans for Children*, 1965; *Expeditions*, 1966; *Speeches for Dr. Frankenstein*, 1966; *The Animals in That Country*, 1968; *What Was in the Garden*, 1969; *The Journals of Susanna Moodie*, 1970; *Procedures for Underground*, 1970; *Power Politics*, 1971; *You Are Happy*, 1974; *Selected Poems*, 1976; *Two-Headed Poems*, 1978; *True Stories*, 1981; *Snake Poems*, 1983; *Interlunar*, 1984; *Selected Poems II: Poems Selected and New, 1976-1986*, 1987; *Selected Poems, 1966-1984*,

1990; *Poems, 1965-1975*, 1991; *Poems, 1976-1989*, 1992; *Morning in the Burned House*, 1995; *Eating Fire: Selected Poems, 1965-1995*, 1998; *The Door*, 2007.

NONFICTION: *Survival: A Thematic Guide to Canadian Literature*, 1972; *Days of the Rebels, 1815-1840*, 1977; *Second Words: Selected Critical Prose*, 1982; *Margaret Atwood: Conversations*, 1990; *Deux sollicitudes: Entretiens*, 1996 (with Victor-Lévy Beaulieu; *Two Solicitudes: Conversations*, 1998); *Negotiating with the Dead: A Writer on Writing*, 2002; *Moving Targets: Writing with Intent, 1982-2004*, 2004 (also known as *Writing with Intent: Essays, Reviews, Personal Prose, 1983-2005*, 2005); *Waltzing Again: New and Selected Conversations with Margaret Atwood*, 2006 (with others; Earl G. Ingersoll, editor); *Payback: Debt and the Shadow Side of Wealth*, 2008.

CHILDREN'S LITERATURE: *Up in the Tree*, 1978; *Anna's Pet*, 1980 (with Joyce Barkhouse); *For the Birds*, 1990; *Princess Prunella and the Purple Peanut*, 1995 (illustrated by Maryann Kowalski); *Bashful Bob and Doleful Dorinda*, 2004 (illustrated by Dušan Petricic); *Rude Ramsay and the Roaring Radishes*, 2004 (illustrated by Dušan Petricic).

EDITED TEXTS: *The New Oxford Book of Canadian Verse in English*, 1982; *The Oxford Book of Canadian Short Stories in English*, 1986 (with Robert Weaver); *The CanLit Foodbook: From Pen to Palate, a Collection of Tasty Literary Fare*, 1987; *The Best American Short Stories 1989*, 1989 (with Shannon Ravenel); *The New Oxford Book of Canadian Short Stories in English*, 1995 (with Robert Weaver).

MISCELLANEOUS: *The Tent*, 2006.

BIBLIOGRAPHY

Bloom, Harold, ed. *Margaret Atwood*. Philadelphia: Chelsea House, 2000. Collection of essays by literary critics provides analyses of Atwood's major novels. Includes brief biography, chronology of Atwood's life, and an informative editor's introduction.

Brown, Jane W. "Constructing the Narrative of Women's Friendship: Margaret Atwood's Reflexive Fiction." *Literature, Interpretation, Theory* 6 (1995): 197-212. Argues that Atwood's narrative reflects the struggle of women to attain friendship and asserts that Atwood achieves this with such reflexive devices as embedded discourse, narrative fragmentation, and doubling.

Cooke, Nathalie. *Margaret Atwood: A Biography*. Toronto, Ont.: ECW Press, 1998. Although this is not an authorized biography, Atwood answered Cooke's questions and allowed her access, albeit limited, to materials for her research. A more substantive work than Sullivan's biography *The Red Shoes* (cited below).

Howells, Coral Ann. *Margaret Atwood*. New York: St. Martin's Press, 1996. Lively critical and biographical study elucidates issues that have energized all of Atwood's fiction: feminist issues, literary genres, and her own identity as a Canadian, a woman, and a writer.

_____, ed. *The Cambridge Companion to Margaret Atwood*. New York: Cambridge

University Press, 2006. Collection of twelve excellent essays provides critical examination of Atwood's novels as well as a concise biography of the author.

McCombs, Judith, ed. *Critical Essays on Margaret Atwood*. Boston: G. K. Hall, 1988. Indispensable volume comprises thirty-two essays, including assessments of patterns and themes in Atwood's poetry and prose. Discusses her primary works in chronological order, beginning with *The Circle Game* and ending with *The Handmaid's Tale*. An editor's introduction provides an illuminating overview of Atwood's writing career. Includes a primary bibliography to 1986 and a thorough index.

Stein, Karen F. *Margaret Atwood Revisited*. New York: Twayne, 1999. Presents a thorough overview of Atwood's writings in all genres. Includes references and a selected bibliography.

Sullivan, Rosemary. *The Red Shoes: Margaret Atwood, Starting Out*. Toronto, Ont.: HarperFlamingo Canada, 1998. Biography focuses on Atwood's early life, until the end of the 1970's. Attempts to answer the question of how Atwood became a writer and to describe the unfolding of her career.

Wilson, Sharon Rose. *Margaret Atwood's Fairy-Tale Sexual Politics*. Jackson: University Press of Mississippi, 1993. One of the most extensive and thorough investigations available of Atwood's use of fairy-tale elements in her graphic art as well as her writing. Covers her novels up to *Cat's Eye*.

_____, ed. *Margaret Atwood's Textual Assassinations: Recent Poetry and Fiction*. Columbus: Ohio State University Press, 2003. Collection of scholarly essays examines Atwood's work, with a focus on her writings published since the late 1980's. Includes discussion of the novels *Cat's Eye*, *The Robber Bride*, *Alias Grace*, and *The Blind Assassin*.

CHARLOTTE BRONTË

Born: Thornton, Yorkshire, England; April 21, 1816
Died: Haworth, Yorkshire, England; March 31, 1855
Also known as: Currer Bell

PRINCIPAL LONG FICTION
Jane Eyre: An Autobiography, 1847
Shirley, 1849
Villette, 1853
The Professor, 1857

OTHER LITERARY FORMS

The nineteen poems selected by Charlotte Brontë (BRAHNT-ee) to print with her sister Anne's work in *Poems by Currer, Ellis, and Acton Bell* (1846) were her only other works published during her lifetime. The juvenilia produced by the four Brontë children—Charlotte, Emily, Anne, and Branwell—between 1824 and 1839 are scattered in libraries and private collections. Some of Charlotte's contributions have been published in *The Twelve Adventurers, and Other Stories* (1925), *Legends of Angria* (1933), *The Search After Happiness* (1969), *Five Novelettes* (1971), and *The Secret and Lily Hart* (1979). A fragment of a novel written during the last year of Brontë's life was published as *Emma* in the *Cornhill Magazine* in 1860 and is often reprinted in editions of *The Professor*. The *Complete Poems of Charlotte Brontë* appeared in 1923. Other brief selections, fragments, and ephemera have been printed in *Transactions and Other Publications of the Brontë Society*. The nineteen-volume *Shakespeare Head Brontë* (1931-1938), edited by T. J. Wise and J. A. Symington, contains all of the novels, four volumes of life and letters, two volumes of miscellaneous writings, and two volumes of poems.

ACHIEVEMENTS

Charlotte Brontë brought to English fiction an intensely personal voice. Her books show the moral and emotional growth of her protagonists almost entirely by self-revelation. Her novels focus on individual self-fulfillment; they express the subjective interior world not only in thoughts, dreams, visions, and symbols but also by projecting inner states through external objects, secondary characters, places, events, and weather. Brontë's own experiences and emotions inform the narrative presence. "Perhaps no other writer of her time," wrote Margaret Oliphant in 1855, "has impressed her mark so clearly on contemporary literature, or drawn so many followers into her own peculiar path."

The personal voice, which blurs the distances separating novelist, protagonist, and reader, accounts for much of the critical ambivalence toward Brontë's work. Generations of unsophisticated readers have identified with Jane Eyre; thousands of romances and

Charlotte Brontë
(Library of Congress)

modern gothics have used Brontë's situations and invited readers to step into the fantasy. Brontë's novels, however, are much more than simply the common reader's daydreams. They are rich enough to allow a variety of critical approaches. They have been studied in relation to traditions (gothic, provincial, realistic, Romantic); read for psychological, linguistic, Christian, social, economic, and personal interpretations; and analyzed in terms of symbolism, imagery, metaphor, viewpoint, narrative distance, and prose style. Because the novels are so clearly wrought from the materials of their author's life, psychoanalytic and feminist criticism has proved rewarding. In Brontë's work, a woman author makes significant statements about issues central to women's lives. Most of her heroines are working women; each feels the pull of individual self-development against the wish for emotional fulfillment, the tension between sexual energies and social realities, the almost unresolvable conflict between love and independence.

BIOGRAPHY

Charlotte Brontë was the third of six children born within seven years to the Reverend Patrick Brontë and his wife Maria Branwell Brontë. Patrick Brontë was perpetual curate of Haworth, a bleak manufacturing town in Yorkshire, England. In 1821, when Charlotte was five years old, her mother died of cancer. Three years later, the four elder girls were sent to the Clergy Daughters' School at Cowan Bridge—the school that appears as Lowood in *Jane Eyre*. In the summer of 1825, the eldest two daughters, Maria and Elizabeth, died of tuberculosis. Charlotte and Emily were removed from the school and brought home. There were no educated middle-class families in Haworth to supply friends and companions for the Brontë children; they lived with a noncommunicative aunt, an elderly servant, and a father much preoccupied by his intellectual interests and his own griefs.

In their home and with only one another for company, the children had material for both educational and imaginative development. Patrick Brontë expected his children to read and to carry on adult conversations about politics. He subscribed to *Blackwood's Edinburgh Magazine*, where his children had access to political and economic essays, art criticism, and literary reviews. They had annuals with engravings of fine art; they taught themselves to draw by copying the pictures in minute detail. They were free to do reading that would not have been permitted by any school of the time—by the age of thirteen, Charlotte Brontë was fully acquainted not only with John Milton and Sir Walter Scott but also with Robert Southey, William Cowper, and (most important) Lord Byron.

In 1826, Branwell was given a set of wooden toy soldiers, and the four children used these as characters in creative play. The individual soldiers gradually took on personal characteristics and acquired countries to rule. The countries needed cities, governments, ruling families, political intrigues, legends, and citizens with private lives, all of which the children happily invented. In 1829, when Charlotte Brontë was thirteen, she and the others began to write down materials from these fantasies, producing a collection of juvenilia that extended ultimately to hundreds of items: magazines, histories, maps, essays, tales, dramas, poems, newspapers, wills, speeches, scrapbooks. This enormous creative production in adolescence gave concrete form to motifs that were later transformed into situations, characters, and concerns of Charlotte Brontë's mature work. It was also a workshop for literary technique; the young author explored prose style, experimented with viewpoint, and discovered how to control narrative voice. A single event, she learned, could be the basis for both a newspaper story and a romance, and the romance could be told by one of the protagonists or by a detached observer.

Because Patrick Brontë had no income beyond his salary, his daughters had to prepare to support themselves. In 1831, when she was almost fifteen, Charlotte Brontë went to Miss Wooler's School at Roe Head. After returning home for a time to tutor her sisters, she went back to Miss Wooler's as a teacher. Over the next several years, all three sisters held positions as governesses in private families. None, however, was happy as a governess; aside from the predictable difficulties caused by burdensome work and undisciplined children, they all suffered when separated from their shared emotional and creative life. A possible solution would have been to open their own school, but they needed some special qualification to attract pupils. Charlotte conceived a plan for going abroad to study languages. In 1842, she and Emily went to Brussels to the Pensionnat Héger. They returned in November because of their aunt's death, but in the following year Charlotte went back to Brussels alone to work as a pupil-teacher. An additional reason for her return to Brussels was that she desired to be near Professor Constantine Héger, but at the end of the year she left in misery after Héger's wife had realized (perhaps more clearly than did Charlotte herself) the romantic nature of the attraction.

In 1844, at the age of twenty-eight, Charlotte Brontë established herself permanently at Haworth. The prospectus for "The Misses Brontë's Establishment" was published, but no pupils applied. Branwell, dismissed in disgrace from his post as tutor, came home to drink, take opium, and disintegrate. Charlotte spent nearly two years in deep depression: Her yearning for love was unsatisfied, and she had repressed her creative impulse because she was afraid her fantasies were self-indulgent. Then, with the discovery that all three had written poetry, the sisters found a new aim in life. A joint volume of poems was published in May, 1846, though it sold only two copies. Each wrote a short novel; they offered the three together to publishers. Emily Brontë's *Wuthering Heights* (1847) and Anne Brontë's *Agnes Grey* (1847) were accepted. Charlotte Brontë's *The Professor* was refused, but one editor, George Smith, said he would like to see a three-volume novel written by its author. *Jane Eyre* was by that time almost finished; it was sent to Smith on August 24, 1847, and impressed him so much that he had it in print by the middle of October.

Jane Eyre was immediately successful, but there was barely any time for its author to enjoy her fame and accomplishment. Within a single year, her three companions in creation died: Branwell on September 24, 1848; Emily on December 19, 1848; and Anne on May 28, 1849. When Charlotte Brontë began work on *Shirley*, she met with her sisters in the evenings to exchange ideas, read aloud, and offer criticism. By the time she finished the manuscript, she was alone.

Brontë's sense that she was plain, "undeveloped," and unlikely to be loved seems to have been partly the product of her own psychological condition. She had refused more than one proposal in her early twenties. In 1852 there was another, from Arthur Bell Nicholls, curate at Haworth. Patrick Brontë objected violently and dismissed his curate. Gradually, however, the objections were worn away. On June 29, 1854, Charlotte Brontë and the Reverend Nicholls were married and, after a brief honeymoon tour, took up residence in Haworth parsonage. After a few months of apparent content—which did not prevent her from beginning work on another novel—Charlotte Brontë died on March 31, 1855, at the age of thirty-eight; a severe cold made her too weak to survive the complications of her early pregnancy.

ANALYSIS

The individualism and richness of Charlotte Brontë's work arise from the multiple ways in which Brontë's writing is personal: observation and introspection, rational analysis and spontaneous emotion, accurate mimesis and private symbolism. Tension and ambiguity grow from the intersections and conflicts among these levels of writing and, indeed, among the layers of the self.

Few writers of English prose have so successfully communicated the emotional texture of inner life while still constructing fictions with enough verisimilitude to appear realistic. Brontë startled the Victorians because her work was so little influenced by the books of her own era. Its literary forebears were the written corporate daydreams of her childhood and the Romantic poets she read during the period when the fantasies took shape. Certain characters and situations that crystallized the emotional conflicts of early adolescence became necessary components of emotional satisfaction. The source of these fantasies was, to a degree, beyond control, occurring in the region the twentieth century has termed "the unconscious"; by writing them down from childhood on, Brontë learned to preserve and draw on relatively undisguised desires and ego conflicts in a way lost to most adults.

The power and reality of the inner life disturbed Brontë after she had passed through adolescence; she compared her creative urge to the action of opium and was afraid that she might become lost in her "infernal world." When she began to think of publication, she deliberately used material from her own experience and reported scenes and characters in verifiable detail. In this way, she hoped to subdue the exaggerated romanticism—and the overwrought writing—of the fantasy fictions. "Details, situations which I do not understand and cannot personally inspect," she wrote to her publisher, "I would not for the world meddle with." Her drawing from life was so accurate that the curates and the Yorkes in *Shirley* were recognized at once by people who knew them, and Brontë lost the protection that her pseudonym had provided.

The years of practice in writing fiction that satisfied her own emotional needs gave Brontë the means to produce powerful psychological effects. She uses a variety of resources to make readers share the protagonist's subjective state. The truth of the outside world is only that truth which reflects the narrator's feelings and perceptions. All characters are aspects of the consciousness that creates them: Brontë uses splitting, doubling, and other fairy-tale devices; she replicates key situations; she carefully controls the narrative distance and the amount of information readers have at their disposal.

The unquietness that Brontë's readers often feel grows from the tension between direct emotional satisfactions (often apparently immature) on one hand and, on the other, mature and realistic conflicts in motive, reason, and sense of self. Read as a sequence, the four completed novels demonstrate both Brontë's development and the story of a woman's relationship to the world. Brontë's heroines find identity outside the enclosed family popularly supposed to circumscribe nineteenth century women. Isolation allows the heroines' self-development, but it impedes their romantic yearning to be lost in love.

THE PROFESSOR

At the beginning of *The Professor*, William Crimsworth is working as a clerk in a mill owned by his proud elder brother. He breaks away, goes to Brussels to teach English, survives a brief attraction to a seductive older woman, and then comes to love Frances Henri, an orphaned Anglo-Swiss lace mender who had been his pupil.

Brontë's narrative devices supply shifting masks that both expose and evade the self. The epistolary opening keeps readers from identifying directly with Crimsworth but draws them into the novel as recipients of his revelations. The masculine persona, which Brontë used frequently in the juvenilia, gives her access to the literary mainstream and creates possibilities for action, attitude, and initiative that did not exist in models for female stories. The juvenile fantasies supply the feud between two brothers; the Belgian scenes and characters come from Brontë's own experiences. Although nominally male, Crimsworth is in an essentially female situation: disinherited, passive, timid. He has, furthermore, an exaggerated awareness and fear of the sexual overtones in human behavior.

Biographical details also go into the making of Frances Henri, the friendless older student working to pay for her lessons in the Belgian school. The poem that Frances writes is one Brontë had created out of her own yearning for Professor Héger. In *The Professor*, the dream can come true; the poem awakens the teacher's response.

Like the central figures in all Brontë novels, both Crimsworth and Frances enact a Cinderella plot. Each begins as an oppressed outcast and ends successful, confident, and satisfactorily placed in society. The details of Crimsworth's story work both symbolically and functionally. The imprisoning situations in the factory and the school reflect his perception of the world. At the same time, these situations are created by his own inner barriers. His bondage as a despised clerk is self-induced; he is an educated adult male who could move on at any time. In Belgium, he plods a treadmill of guilt because of Zoraïde Reuter's sexual manipulativeness—for which he is not responsible. His self-suppression is also seen through Yorke Hunsden, who appears whenever Crimsworth must express strong emotion. Hunsden voices anger and rebellion not permitted to the male/female narrator and becomes a voyeuristic alter ego to appreciate Frances and love.

The novel is weakest when it fails to integrate the biography, the emotion, and the ideas. True moral dilemmas are not developed. The heroine, seen through sympathetic male eyes, wins love for her writing, her pride, and her self-possession, and she continues to work even after she has a child. Brontë solves her chronic romantic dilemma (How can a strong woman love if woman's love is defined as willing subordination?) by letting Frances vibrate between two roles: She is the stately directress of the school by day, the little lace mender by night.

JANE EYRE

In *Jane Eyre*, Brontë created a story that has the authority of myth. Everything that had deeply affected her is present in the book's emotional content. The traumatic experiences of maternal deprivation, the Clergy Daughters' School, and Maria's death create the events of Jane's early life. The book also taps universal feelings of rejection, victimization, and loneliness, making them permissible by displacement: The hateful children are cousins, not siblings; the bad adult an aunt, not a mother. Rochester's compelling power as a lover derives from neither literal nor literary sources—Rochester is the man Brontë had loved for twenty years, the duke of Zamorna who dominates the adolescent fantasies, exerting a power on both Jane and the reader that can hardly be explained by reason. Jane defied literary convention because she was poor, plain, and a heroine; she defied social convention by refusing to accept any external authority. Placed repeatedly in situations that exemplify male power, Jane resists and survives. At the end of the narrative, she is transformed from Cinderella to Prince Charming, becoming the heroine who cuts through the brambles to rescue the imprisoned sleeper. Identification is so immediate and so close that readers often fail to notice Brontë's control of distance, in particular the points of detachment when an older Jane comments on her younger self and the direct addresses from Jane to the reader that break the spell when emotions become too strong.

Place controls the book's structure. Events at Gateshead, Lowood, Thornfield, and Moor House determine Jane's development; a brief coda at Ferndean provides the resolution. Each of the four major sections contains a figure representing the sources of male power over women: John Reed (physical force and the patriarchal family), Reverend Brocklehurst (the social structures of class, education, and religion), Rochester (sexual attraction), and St. John Rivers (moral and spiritual authority). Jane protects herself at first by devious and indirect means—fainting, illness, flight—and then ultimately, in rejecting St. John Rivers, by direct confrontation. Compelled by circumstances to fend for herself, she comes—at first instinctively, later rationally—to rely on herself.

The book's emotional power grows from its total absorption in Jane's view of the world and from the images, symbols, and structures that convey multiple interwoven reverberations. The red room—which suggests violence, irrationality, enclosure, rebellion, rebirth, the bloody chamber of emerging womanhood—echoes throughout the book. The Bridewell charade, Jane's paintings, the buildings and terrain, and a multitude of other details have both meaning and function. Characters double and split: Helen Burns (mind) and Bertha Mason (body) are aspects of Jane as well as actors in the plot. Recurring images of ice and fire suggest fatal coldness without and consuming fire within. Rochester's sexuality is the most threatening and ambiguous aspect of masculine power because of Jane's own complicity and her need for love. Her terrors and dreams accumulate as the marriage approaches; there are drowning images, abyss images, loss of consciousness. She refuses to become Rochester's mistress, finally, not because of the practical and moral dangers (which she does recognize) but because she fears her own willingness to make a god of him. She will not become dependent; she escapes to preserve her self.

As Jane takes her life into her own hands, she becomes less needy. After she has achieved independence by discovering a family and inheriting money, she is free to seek out Rochester. At the same time, he has become less omnipotent, perhaps a code for the destruction of patriarchal power. Thus, the marriage not only ends the romance and resolves the moral, emotional, and sexual conflicts but also supplies a satisfactory woman's fantasy of independence coupled with love.

SHIRLEY

For the book that would follow *Jane Eyre*, Brontë deliberately sought a new style and subject matter. *Shirley*, set in 1812, concerns two public issues still relevant in 1848—working-class riots and the condition of women. Brontë did historical research in newspaper files. She used a panoramic scene, included a variety of characters observed from life, and added touches of comedy. *Shirley* is told in the third person; the interest is divided between two heroines, neither of whom is a persona. Nevertheless, Brontë is strongly present in the narrative voice, which remains objective only in scenes of action. The authorial commentary, more strongly even than the events themselves, creates a tone of anger, rebellion, suffering, and doubt.

The novel is clearly plotted, although the mechanics are at times apparent. Brontë shifts focus among characters and uses reported conversations to violate the time sequence so that she can arrange events in the most effective dramatic order. Robert Moore, owner of a cloth mill, arouses the workers' wrath by introducing machinery. Caroline Helstone loves Robert, but her affection is not reciprocated. Although Caroline has a comfortable home with her uncle the rector, she is almost fatally depressed by lack of love and occupation. Property owner Shirley Keeldar discovers that having a man's name, position, and forthrightness gives her some power but fails to make her man's equal; she is simply more valuable as a matrimonial prize. Louis Moore, Shirley's former tutor, loves her silently because he lacks wealth and social position. Eventually Robert, humbled by Shirley's contempt and weakened by a workman's bullet, declares his love for Caroline, who has in the meantime discovered her mother and grown much stronger. Shirley's union with Louis is more ambivalent; she loves him because he is a master she can look up to, but she is seen on her wedding day as a pantheress pining for virginal freedom.

The primary source of women's tribulation is dependency. Caroline Helstone craves occupation to fill her time, make her financially independent, and give her life purpose. Women become psychologically dependent on men because they have so little else to think about. Brontë examines the lives of several old maids; they are individuals, not stereotypes, but they are all lonely. Shirley and Caroline dissect John Milton, search for female roots, and talk cozily about men's inadequacies. They cannot, however, speak honestly to each other about their romantic feelings. Caroline must hold to herself the deep pain of unrequited love.

Although *Shirley* deliberately moves beyond the isolated mythic world of *Jane Eyre* to put women's oppression in the context of a society rent by other power struggles (workers against employers, England against France, Church against Nonconformity), the individualistic ending only partially resolves the divisions. Brontë's narrative tone in the final passage is bleak and bitter. She reminds readers that *Shirley*'s events are history. Fieldhead Hollow is covered by mills and mill housing; magic is gone from the world.

VILLETTE

Villette is Brontë's most disciplined novel. Because *The Professor* had not been published, Brontë was able to rework the Brussels experience without masks, as a story of loneliness and female deprivation, deliberately subduing the wish fulfillment and making her uncompromising self-examination control form as well as feeling. Lucy Snowe is a woman without money, family, friends, or health. She is not, however, a sympathetic, friendly narrator like Jane Eyre. Her personality has the unattractiveness that realistically grows from deprivation; she has no social ease, no warmth, no mental quickness. Furthermore, her personality creates her pain, loneliness, and disengagement.

In the book's early sections, Lucy is not even the center of her narrative. She watches and judges instead of taking part; she tells other people's stories instead of her own. She is so self-disciplined that she appears to have neither feelings nor imagination, so restrained that she never reveals the facts about her family or the incidents of her youth that might explain to readers how and why she learned to suppress emotion, hope, and the desire for human contact. Despite—or perhaps because of—her anesthetized feeling and desperate shyness, Lucy Snowe drives herself to actions that might have been inconceivable for a woman more thoroughly socialized. Thrust into the world by the death of the elderly woman whose companion she had been, she goes alone to London, takes a ship for the Continent, gets a job as nursemaid, rises through her own efforts to teach in Madame Beck's school, and begins laying plans to open a school of her own.

The coincidental and melodramatic elements of the story gain authenticity because they grow from Lucy's inner life. When she is left alone in the school during vacation, her repressed need to be heard by someone drives her to enter the confessional of a Catholic church. Once the internal barrier is breached, she immediately meets the Bretton family. Realistically, she must have known they were in Villette; she knew that "Dr. John" was Graham Bretton, but she withheld that information from the reader both because of her habitual secretiveness and also because she did not really "know" the Brettons were accessible to her until she was able to admit her need to reach out for human sympathy. The characterization of Paul Emanuel gains richness and detail in such a manner that readers realize—before Lucy herself dares admit it—that she is interested in him. The phantom nun, at first a night terror of pure emotion, is revealed as a prankish disguise when Lucy is free to express feelings directly.

The novel's ending, however, is deliberately ambiguous, though not in event. (Only the most naïve readers dare accept Brontë's invitation to imagine that Paul Emanuel escapes drowning and to "picture union and a happy succeeding life.") The ambiguity grows from Lucy's earlier statement: "M. Emanuel was away for three years. Reader, they were the three happiest years of my life." In those years, Lucy Snowe prospered, became respected, expanded her school. Her happiness depends not on the presence of her beloved but rather on the knowledge that she is loved. With that knowledge, she becomes whole and independent. No longer telling others' stories, she speaks directly to the reader about her most private concerns. Only when her lover is absent, perhaps, can a woman treasure love and emotional satisfaction while yet retaining the freedom to be her own person.

Sally Mitchell

OTHER MAJOR WORKS

POETRY: *Poems by Currer, Ellis, and Acton Bell*, 1846 (with Emily Brontë and Anne Brontë); *The Complete Poems of Charlotte Brontë*, 1923.

CHILDREN'S LITERATURE: *The Twelve Adventurers, and Other Stories*, 1925 (C. K. Shorter and C. W. Hatfield, editors); *Legends of Angria*, 1933 (Fannie E. Ratchford, compiler); *The Search After Happiness*, 1969; *Five Novelettes*, 1971 (Winifred Gérin, editor); *The Secret and Lily Hart*, 1979 (William Holtz, editor).

MISCELLANEOUS: *The Shakespeare Head Brontë*, 1931-1938 (19 volumes; T. J. Wise and J. A. Symington, editors).

BIBLIOGRAPHY

Barker, Juliet. *The Brontës*. New York: St. Martin's Press, 1995. This massive study of the entire Brontë family sometimes overwhelms with detail, but it presents a complete picture of one of English literature's most intriguing and productive families. Barker's analysis of the juvenilia, in particular, constitutes a major contribution to Brontë scholarship. Not surprisingly, the author has more to say about Charlotte than about other members of the family.

Edwards, Mike. *Charlotte Brontë: The Novels*. New York: St. Martin's Press, 1999. Extracts sections from *Jane Eyre*, *Shirley*, and *Villette* to analyze the layers of meaning and the combination of realism and fantasy in these texts.

Fraser, Rebecca. *The Brontës: Charlotte Brontë and Her Family*. New York: Crown, 1988. Thorough and engrossing biography of Charlotte Brontë and the rest of the Brontë family is carefully researched and annotated and offers a vividly written portrait of the Brontës and their world. Makes use of letters, published and unpublished manuscripts, and contemporary news sources to examine this complex literary family.

Gaskell, Elizabeth C. *The Life of Charlotte Brontë*. 1857. Reprint. London: Penguin Books, 1975. Still an indispensable source for any student of Charlotte Brontë's life, this biography offers the insights that Gaskell gained through her long friendship with Brontë. Herself a popular novelist of the time, Gaskell creates a memorable picture of Brontë both as a writer and as a woman.

Glen, Heather. *Charlotte Brontë: The Imagination in History*. New York: Oxford University Press, 2002. Presents analysis of all of Brontë's novels and contradicts previous biographical works with evidence that Brontë was more artistically sophisticated and more engaged in contemporary social issues than many scholars have asserted.

_____, ed. *The Cambridge Companion to the Brontës*. New York: Cambridge University Press, 2002. Collection of essays examines the lives and work of the three sisters. Includes analysis of all of Charlotte's novels, a feminist perspective on the sisters' work, and a discussion of the Brontës and religion.

Gordon, Lyndall. *Charlotte Brontë: A Passionate Life*. New York: W. W. Norton, 1994. Written with the blessing of the Brontë Society, which granted access to and permission to reproduce from its copious archives. Readable account of Brontë's life and literary output makes good use of the materials provided by the society.

Ingham, Patricia. *The Brontës*. New York: Oxford University Press, 2006. Chronological examination of the three sisters' lives and works includes chapters detailing the literary context in which they wrote and their treatment of social class issues, with particular focus on *Shirley*, and of gender in *Jane Eyre*. Includes bibliography, index, list of relevant Web sites, and list of film and television adaptations of the sisters' books.

Menon, Patricia. *Austen, Eliot, Charlotte Brontë, and the Mentor-Lover*. New York: Palgrave Macmillan, 2003. Examines how Brontë, Jane Austen, and George Eliot handled matters of gender, sexuality, family, behavior, and freedom in their work.

Plasa, Carl. *Charlotte Brontë*. New York: Palgrave Macmillan, 2004. Assesses Brontë's writings by viewing them from a postcolonial perspective. Examines her novels and other works in terms of their treatment of miscegenation, colonization, slavery, and the Irish famine.

Rollyson, Carl, and Lisa Paddock. *The Brontës A to Z: The Essential Reference to Their Lives and Work*. New York: Facts On File, 2003. Takes an encyclopedic approach to the family, including ill-starred brother Branwell. Offers synopses of the novels and discussions of poems as well as details of the lives of the authors. Includes reproductions of illustrations from early editions of the works.

EMILY BRONTË

Born: Thornton, Yorkshire, England; July 30, 1818
Died: Haworth, Yorkshire, England; December 19, 1848
Also known as: Emily Jane Brontë; Ellis Bell

PRINCIPAL LONG FICTION
Wuthering Heights, 1847

OTHER LITERARY FORMS

Poems by Emily Brontë and her sisters Charlotte and Anne are collected in the volume *Poems by Currer, Ellis, and Acton Bell* (1846). Juvenilia and early prose works by Brontë on the imaginary world of Gondal have all been lost.

ACHIEVEMENTS

Emily Brontë occupies a unique place in the annals of literature. Her reputation as a major novelist stands on the merits of one relatively short novel that was misunderstood and intensely disliked upon publication, yet no study of British fiction is complete without a discussion of *Wuthering Heights*. The names of the novel's settings and characters, particularly Heathcliff, have become part of the heritage of Western culture, familiar even to those who have neither read the novel nor know anything about its author's life and career. Several film and television versions, two of the most popular of which were released in 1939 and 1970, have helped perpetuate this familiarity.

The literary achievement of *Wuthering Heights* lies in its realistic portrayal of a specific place and time and in its examination of universal patterns of human behavior. Set in Yorkshire in the closing years of the eighteenth century, the novel delineates the quality of life in the remote moors of northern England and also reminds the reader of the growing pains of industrialization throughout the nation. In addition, more than any other novel of the period, *Wuthering Heights* presents in clear dialectic form the conflict between two opposing psychic forces, embodied in the settings of the Grange and the Heights and the people who inhabit them. Although modern readers often apply the theories of Sigmund Freud and Carl Jung to give names to these forces, Brontë illustrated their conflict long before psychologists pigeonholed them. *Wuthering Heights* is so true in its portrayal of human nature that it fits easily into many theoretical and critical molds, from the historical to the psychological. The novel may be most fully appreciated, however, as a study of the nature of human perception and its ultimate failure in understanding human behavior. This underlying theme, presented through the dialectic structure of human perception, unites many of the elements that are sometimes singled out or overemphasized in particular critical approaches to the novel.

Brontë's skill is not confined to representing the world and the human forces at work

Emily Brontë
(Library of Congress)

within her characters, great as that skill is. She has also created a complex narrative structure built on a series of interlocking memories and perceptions, spanning three generations and moving across several social classes. Told primarily from two often unreliable and sometimes ambiguous first-person points of view, the novel illustrates through its structure the limitations of human intelligence and imagination. Faced with choosing between Lockwood's and Nelly Dean's interpretations of Heathcliff's life, the reader can only ponder that human perception never allows a full understanding of another soul.

BIOGRAPHY

Emily Jane Brontë was born at Thornton, in Bradford Parish, Yorkshire, on July 30, 1818, the fifth child of the Reverend Patrick and Maria Brontë. Patrick Brontë had been born in county Down, Ireland, one of ten children, on March 17, 1777. He was a schoolteacher and tutor before he obtained his bachelor of arts degree from Cambridge in 1806, from where he was ordained to curacies, first in Essex and then in Hartshead, Yorkshire. He married Maria Branwell, of Penzance, in Hartshead on December 19, 1812, and in

1817, they moved to Thornton. The other children in the family at the time of Emily's birth were Maria, Elizabeth, Charlotte, and Patrick Branwell; another daughter, Anne, was born two years later. Charlotte and Anne Brontë also became writers.

In early 1820, the family moved to Haworth, four miles from the village of Keighley, where the Reverend Brontë was perpetual curate until his death in 1861. Maria Brontë died on September 15, 1821, and about a year later, her elder sister, Elizabeth Branwell, moved in to take care of the children and household. She remained with them until her own death in 1842.

Life at Haworth was spartan but not unpleasant. There was a close and devoted relationship among the children, especially between Charlotte and Emily. Reading was a favorite pastime, and a wide range of books, including the novels of Sir Walter Scott and the poetry of William Wordsworth and Robert Southey, as well as the more predictable classics, was available to the children. Outdoor activities included many hours of wandering through the moors and woods. Their father wanted the children to be hardy and independent, intellectually and physically, indifferent to the passing fashions of the world.

Maria, Elizabeth, and Charlotte had already been sent away to a school for clergymen's daughters, at Cowan Bridge, when Emily joined them in November, 1824. Emily was not happy in this confined and rigid environment and longed for home. Two of the sisters, Elizabeth and Maria, became ill and were taken home to die during 1825; in June, Charlotte and Emily returned home as well.

From 1825 to 1830, the remaining Brontë children lived at Haworth with their father and their aunt, Miss Branwell. In June, 1826, their father gave them a set of wooden toy soldiers, a seemingly insignificant gift that stimulated their imaginative and literary talents. The children devoted endless energy to creating an imaginary world for the soldiers. During these years, Charlotte and her brother Branwell created in their minds and on paper the land of "Angria," while Emily and Anne were at work on "Gondal." Although all of these early prose works have been lost, some of Emily's poetry contains references to aspects of the Gondal-Angria creations.

In July, 1835, Emily again joined Charlotte, already a teacher, at the Roe Head school. She remained only three months, returning home in October. Three years later, she accepted a position as governess in a school in Halifax for about six months but returned to Haworth in December; Charlotte joined her there early in the following year. During 1839 and 1840, the sisters were planning to establish their own school at Haworth, but the plan was never carried through.

Charlotte left home again to serve as a governess in 1841, and in February, 1842, she and Emily went to Mme Héger's school in Brussels to study languages. They returned to Haworth in November because of Miss Branwell's death. Charlotte went back to Brussels to teach in 1843, but Emily never left Yorkshire again.

From August, 1845, the Brontë children were again united at Haworth. They did not have much contact with neighbors, whose educational level and intellectual interests were much inferior to theirs. They kept busy reading and writing, both fiction and poetry. *Wuthering Heights* was probably begun in October, 1845, and completed sometime in 1846, although it was not published until December, 1847, after the success of Charlotte's *Jane Eyre* (1847).

Meanwhile, the sisters published *Poems by Currer, Ellis, and Acton Bell* in May, 1846. Finding a press was very difficult, and the sisters chose the pseudonyms to avoid personal publicity and to create the fiction of male authorship, more readily acceptable to the general public. The reaction was predictable, as Charlotte noted: "Neither we nor our poems were at all wanted." The sisters were not discouraged, however, and they continued to seek publishers for their novels.

The first edition of *Wuthering Heights* was published in 1847 by T. C. Newby, with Anne's *Agnes Grey* as the third volume. It was a sloppy edition and contained many errors. The second edition, published in 1850, after the author's death, was "corrected" by Charlotte. The public reaction to *Wuthering Heights* was decidedly negative; readers were disturbed by the "wickedness" of the characters and the "implausibility" of the action. Until Charlotte herself corrected the misconception, readers assumed that *Wuthering Heights* was an inferior production by the author of *Jane Eyre*.

In October, 1848, Emily became seriously ill with a cough and cold. She suffered quietly and patiently, even refusing to see the doctor who had been called. She died of tuberculosis at Haworth on December 19, 1848. She was buried in the church alongside her mother, her sisters Maria and Elizabeth, and her brother Branwell.

These facts about Emily Brontë's life and death are known, but her character will always remain a mystery. Her early prose works have been lost, only three personal letters survive, and her poems give little insight into her own life. Most information about the Brontë family life and background comes from Mrs. Elizabeth Gaskell's biography of Charlotte and the autobiographical comments on which she based her work. Charlotte comments that Emily was "not a person of demonstrative character" and that she was "stronger than a man, simpler than a child." She had a nature that "stood alone." The person behind this mystery is revealed only in a reading of *Wuthering Heights*.

ANALYSIS: WUTHERING HEIGHTS

Wuthering Heights is constructed around a series of dialectic motifs that interconnect and unify the elements of setting, character, and plot. An examination of these motifs will give the reader the clearest insight into the central meaning of the novel. Although *Wuthering Heights* is a "classic," as Frank Kermode has noted, precisely because it is open to many different critical methods and conducive to many levels of interpretation, the novel grows from a coherent imaginative vision that underlies all the motifs. That vision demonstrates that all human perception is limited and failed. The fullest approach to Emily Brontë's novel is through the basic patterns that support this vision.

Wuthering Heights concerns the interactions of two families, the Earnshaws and

Lintons, over three generations. The novel is set in the desolate moors of Yorkshire and covers the years from 1771 to 1803. The Earnshaws and Lintons are in harmony with their environment, but their lives are disrupted by an outsider and catalyst of change, the orphan Heathcliff. Heathcliff is, first of all, an emblem of the social problems of a nation entering the age of industrial expansion and urban growth. Although Brontë sets the action of the novel entirely within the locale familiar to her, she reminds the reader continually of the contrast between that world and the larger world outside.

Aside from Heathcliff's background as a child of the streets and the description of urban Liverpool, from which he is brought, the novel contains other reminders that Yorkshire, long insulated from change and susceptible only to the forces of nature, is no longer as remote as it once was. The servant Joseph's religious cant, the class distinctions obvious in the treatment of Nelly Dean as well as of Heathcliff, and Lockwood's pseudosophisticated urban values are all reminders that Wuthering Heights cannot remain as it has been, that religious, social, and economic change is rampant. Brontë clearly signifies in the courtship and marriage of young Cathy and Hareton that progress and enlightenment *will* come and the wilderness *will* be tamed. Heathcliff is both an embodiment of the force of this change and its victim. He brings about a change but cannot change himself. What he leaves behind, as Lockwood attests and the relationship of Cathy and Hareton verifies, is a new society, at peace with itself and its environment.

It is not necessary, however, to examine in depth the Victorian context of *Wuthering Heights* to sense the dialectic contrast of environments. Within the limited setting that the novel itself describes, society is divided between two opposing worlds: Wuthering Heights, ancestral home of the Earnshaws, and Thrushcross Grange, the Linton estate. Wuthering Heights is rustic and wild; it is open to the elements of nature and takes its name from "atmospheric tumult." The house is strong, built with narrow windows and jutting cornerstones, fortified to withstand the battering of external forces. It is identified with the outdoors and nature and with strong, "masculine" values. Its appearance, both inside and out, is wild, untamed, disordered, and hard. The Grange expresses a more civilized, controlled atmosphere. The house is neat and orderly, and there is always an abundance of light—to Brontë's mind, "feminine" values. It is not surprising that Lockwood is more comfortable at the Grange, since he takes pleasure in "feminine" behavior (gossip, vanity of appearance, adherence to social decorum, romantic self-delusion), while Heathcliff, entirely "masculine," is always out of place there.

Indeed, all of the characters reflect, to greater or lesser degrees, the masculine and feminine values of the places they inhabit. Hindley and Catherine Earnshaw are as wild and uncontrollable as the Heights: Catherine claims even to prefer her home to the pleasures of heaven. Edgar and Isabella Linton are as refined and civilized as the Grange. The marriage of Edgar and Catherine (as well as the marriage of Isabella and Heathcliff) is ill-fated from the start, not only because she does not love him, as her answers to Nelly Dean's catechism reveal, but also because both are so strongly associated with the values of their homes that they lack the opposing and necessary personality components. Catherine is too willful, wild, and strong; she expresses too much of the "masculine" side of her personality (the animus of Jungian psychology), while Edgar is weak and effeminate (the anima). They are unable to interact fully with each other because they are not complete individuals themselves. This lack leads to their failures to perceive each other's true needs.

Even Cathy's passionate cry for Heathcliff, "Nelly, I *am* Heathcliff," is less love for him as an individual than the deepest form of self-love. Cathy cannot exist without him, but a meaningful relationship is not possible because Cathy sees Heathcliff only as a reflection of herself. Heathcliff, too, has denied an important aspect of his personality. Archetypally masculine, Heathcliff acts out only the aggressive, violent parts of himself.

The settings and the characters are patterned against each other, and explosions are the only possible results. Only Hareton and young Cathy, each of whom embodies the psychological characteristics of both Heights and Grange, can successfully sustain a mutual relationship.

This dialectic structure extends into the roles of the narrators as well. The story is reflected through the words of Nelly Dean—an inmate of both houses, a participant in the events of the narrative, and a confidant of the major characters—and Lockwood, an outsider who witnesses only the results of the characters' interactions. Nelly is a companion and servant in the Earnshaw and Linton households, and she shares many of the values and perceptions of the families. Lockwood, an urban sophisticate on retreat, misunderstands his own character as well as the characters of others. His brief romantic "adventure" in Bath and his awkwardness when he arrives at the Heights (he thinks Cathy will fall in love with him; he mistakes the dead rabbits for puppies) exemplify his obtuseness. His perceptions are always to be questioned. Occasionally, however, even a denizen of the conventional world may gain a glimpse of the forces at work beneath the surface of reality. Lockwood's dream of the dead Cathy, which sets off his curiosity and Heathcliff's final plans, is a reminder that even the placid, normal world may be disrupted by the psychic violence of a willful personality.

The presentation of two family units and parallel brother-sister, husband-wife relationships in each also emphasizes the dialectic. That two such opposing modes of behavior could arise in the same environment prevents the reader from easy condemnation of either pair. The use of flashback for the major part of the narration—it begins in medias res—reminds the reader that he or she is seeing events out of their natural order, recounted by two individuals whose reliability must be questioned. The working out of the plot over three generations further suggests that no one group, much less one individual, can perceive the complexity of the human personality.

Taken together, the setting, plot, characters, and structure combine into a whole when they are seen as parts of the dialectic nature of existence. In a world where opposing forces are continually arrayed against each other in the environment, in society, in families, and in relationships, as well as within the individual, there can be no easy route to perception of another human soul. *Wuthering Heights* convincingly demonstrates the complexity of this dialectic and portrays the limitations of human perception.

Lawrence F. Laban

OTHER MAJOR WORKS

POETRY: *Poems by Currer, Ellis, and Acton Bell*, 1846 (with Charlotte Brontë and Anne Brontë); *The Complete Poems of Emily Jane Brontë*, 1941 (C. W. Hatfield, editor); *Gondal's Queen: A Novel in Verse by Emily Jane Brontë*, 1955 (Fannie E. Ratchford, editor).

NONFICTION: *Five Essays Written in French*, 1948 (Lorine White Nagel, translator); *The Brontë Letters*, 1954 (Muriel Spark, editor).

BIBLIOGRAPHY

Barnard, Robert. *Emily Brontë*. New York: Oxford University Press, 2000. Barnard, chairman of the Brontë Society, provides an incisive overview of Brontë's life and work. Includes bibliography, maps, illustrations (some in color), index, and chronology.

Benvenuto, Richard. *Emily Brontë*. Boston: Twayne, 1982. Brief biography of the Brontë sister whose life remains relatively obscure. Although only three of her letters survive, Benvenuto stays within the documentary record to provide a convincing portrait of her life and personality.

Berg, Maggie. *"Wuthering Heights": The Writing in the Margin*. New York: Twayne, 1996. Provides a good introduction to Emily Brontë's masterpiece. A chronology of her life and works is followed by a section devoted to the literary and social context of the novel and a reading emphasizing the importance of the novel's "marginal spaces," such as the diary that Catherine keeps in the blank spaces of books.

Davies, Stevie. *Emily Brontë: Heretic*. London: Women's Press, 1994. Feminist interpretation of Brontë's life and work contradicts the legends of Brontë's sexual innocence and unworldliness, showing how *Wuthering Heights* and the author's poetry offer evidence of her sophistication and sexuality.

Frank, Katherine. *A Chainless Soul: A Life of Emily Brontë*. Boston: Houghton Mifflin, 1990. Biographical study demonstrates the complex relationships between Emily Brontë and her family members.

Glen, Heather, ed. *The Cambridge Companion to the Brontës*. New York: Cambridge University Press, 2002. Essays examining the lives and work of the three sisters include analysis of *Wuthering Heights* and Emily's poetry, a feminist perspective on the sisters' work, and a discussion of the Brontës and religion.

Liddell, Robert. *Twin Spirits: The Novels of Emily and Anne Brontë*. London: Peter Owen, 1990. Presents analysis of *Wuthering Heights* and includes a companion essay on Anne Brontë's 1848 novel *The Tenant of Wildfell Hall*, showing that the latter is Anne's answer to Emily's novel.

Miller, Lucasta. *The Brontë Myth*. London: Jonathan Cape, 2001. Biography of the Brontës emphasizes how previous biographers have shaped readers' understanding of the three sisters' lives and work. Corrects misinformation contained in nineteenth century biographies, which exaggerated the authors' miserable childhoods, as well as in later books that interpreted their work from Freudian, feminist, and poststructural perspectives.

Pykett, Lyn. *Emily Brontë*. Savage, Md.: Barnes & Noble, 1989. Feminist assessment of Brontë's work suggests that *Wuthering Heights* is a distinctive novel because of the particular way it combines the female gothic genre and the realistic domestic novel that was becoming popular in Brontë's lifetime.

Rollyson, Carl, and Lisa Paddock. *The Brontës A to Z: The Essential Reference to Their Lives and Work*. New York: Facts On File, 2003. Covers every aspect of the three sisters' lives and work in more than five hundred alphabetically arranged essays. Includes seventeen pages of plot summary and analysis for *Wuthering Heights*.

Vine, Steve. *Emily Brontë*. New York: Twayne, 1998. Presents biographical information as well as critical analysis of *Wuthering Heights* and Brontë's poetry. Intended as an introduction for general readers.

Winnifrith, Tom, ed. *Critical Essays on Emily Brontë*. New York: G. K. Hall, 1997. Collection of two dozen essays by distinguished critics focuses on a range of topics, including Brontë's religion, her reading and education, *Wuthering Heights*, and her poetry. In one essay, Virginia Woolf compares *Wuthering Heights* to Charlotte Brontë's *Jane Eyre*.

CHARLES BROCKDEN BROWN

Born: Philadelphia, Pennsylvania; January 17, 1771
Died: Philadelphia, Pennsylvania; February 22, 1810

OTHER LITERARY FORMS

Charles Brockden Brown published two parts of a dialogue on the rights of women, *Alcuin: A Dialogue*, in 1798; the last two sections appeared in William Dunlap's 1815 biography of Brown. Many of Brown's essays on literature have been collected in *Literary Essays and Reviews* (1992), edited by Alfred Weber and Wolfgang Schäfer. His later political and historical essays, originally published in magazines and as pamphlets, have not been collected. Several of Brown's fictional fragments appear in *Carwin, the Biloquist, and Other American Tales and Pieces* (1822) and in the Dunlap biography, notably the Carwin story and "Memoirs of Stephen Calvert." Several collected editions of Brown's novels were published in the nineteenth century. Harry Warfel's edition of *The Rhapsodist, and Other Uncollected Writings* (1943) completes the publication of most of Brown's literary works. Some of Brown's letters have appeared in scattered books and essays, but no collection of letters has yet been published.

ACHIEVEMENTS

The significant portion of Charles Brockden Brown's literary career lasted little more than one year, in the period 1798-1800, during which he published the four novels for which he is best known: *Wieland, Ormond, Arthur Mervyn*, and *Edgar Huntly*. Although Brown's career began with the essays comprising "The Rhapsodist" in 1789 and continued until his death, most of his other fiction, poetry, and prose is thought to be of minor importance.

Brown's literary reputation rests heavily on his historical position as one of the first significant American novelists. An English reviewer wrote in 1824 that Brown "was the first writer of prose fiction of which America could boast." Brown's contemporaries recognized his abilities, and he received praise from William Godwin, John Keats, and Percy Bysshe Shelley. Although his American reputation remained unsteady, he was read by nineteenth century novelists such as James Fenimore Cooper, Edgar Allan Poe, and

Charles Brockden Brown
(Library of Congress)

Herman Melville. In the twentieth and twenty-first centuries, scholars and advanced students of American culture have been Brown's most frequent readers; they have rediscovered him in part because his concerns with identity and choice in a disordered world prefigured or initiated some of the major themes of American fiction.

Brown's four best-known novels begin the peculiarly American mutation of the gothic romance. Some similarities can be seen between Brown's novels and the political gothic of Godwin and the sentimental gothic of Ann Radcliffe, but Brown's adaptations of gothic conventions for the exploration of human psychology, the analysis of the mind choosing under stress, and the representation of a truly incomprehensible world suggest that he may be an important bridge between the popular gothic tradition of eighteenth century England and the American gothic strain that is traceable through Poe, Melville, and Nathaniel Hawthorne to Henry James, William Faulkner, and such late twentieth century novelists as Joyce Carol Oates.

BIOGRAPHY

Born on January 17, 1771, Charles Brockden Brown was the fifth son of Elijah Brown and Mary Armitt Brown. Named for a relative who was a well-known Philadelphia official, Brown grew up in an intellectual Quaker family where the works of contemporary radicals such as Godwin and Mary Wollstonecraft were read, even though they were unacceptable by society's norms. Brown's health was never good; his parents tended to protect him from an active boy's life and to encourage his reading. When he was eleven, he began his formal education at the Friends' Latin School in Philadelphia under Robert Proud, a renowned teacher and scholar who later wrote *The History of Pennsylvania* (1797). Proud encouraged Brown to strengthen his constitution by taking walks in the country, similar to those Edgar Huntly takes with Sarsefield in *Edgar Huntly*. After five or six years in Latin School, Brown began the study of law under Alexander Willcocks (variously spelled), a prominent Philadelphia lawyer. Although he studied law for five or six years, until 1792 or 1793, he never practiced.

During Brown's years studying law, he taught himself French and increasingly leaned toward literary work. He became a member of the Belles Lettres Club, which met to discuss current literary and intellectual topics. In 1789, he published his first work, "The Rhapsodist," in the *Columbian Magazine*. In 1790, he met and became friends with Elihu Hubbard Smith of Litchfield, Connecticut, a medical student with literary interests. Smith encouraged Brown's literary aspirations, helping to draw him away from law. Brown's acquaintance with Smith brought him to New York City in 1794, where he came to know the members of the Friendly Club, a group of young New York intellectuals, one of whom was to be his first biographer, William Dunlap.

During this period, Brown wrote poetry, and by 1795 he had begun a novel. He began active publishing in 1798 in the Philadelphia *Weekly Magazine*. In the summer of 1798, when he was visiting Smith in New York, he published *Wieland*. Smith died during the yellow fever outbreak of that summer; Brown also became ill, but he recovered. In 1799, Brown suddenly became an extremely busy writer. He published two novels and part of a third and also founded *The Monthly Magazine and American Review*. In 1800, he published the second half of *Arthur Mervyn*, abandoned his magazine, and joined his brothers in business. After publishing his last two novels in 1801, he turned to political and historical writing. His 1803 pamphlet on the Louisiana Territory was widely read and provoked debate in Congress. In 1803, he began another magazine, *The Literary Magazine and American Register*, which lasted until 1806. His final magazine venture was *The American Register: Or, General Repository of History, Politics, and Science* (1807-1810). He was working on a geography publication when he died on February 22, 1810, of tuberculosis, a disease that had pursued him most of his life.

The details of Brown's personal and intellectual life are known primarily through his writings. He married Elizabeth Linn on November 19, 1804, and his family eventually included three sons and a daughter. There is evidence that Brown entertained the liberal Quaker ideas of his parents, the Deism of Smith, and the ideas of the English radicals at various times. His dialogue on the rights of women, *Alcuin*, advocates sound education and political equality for women and, in the two parts published after his death, even suggests a utopian state of absolute social equality between the sexes in which there would be no marriage. Although he entertained such radical ideas in his youth, Brown seems to have become more conservative with maturity, affirming in his later works the importance of both reason and religion in living a good life.

ANALYSIS

Charles Brockden Brown's aims in writing, aside from attempting to earn a living, are a matter of debate among critics. In his preface to *Edgar Huntly*, he makes the conventional claim of novelists of the time, that writing is "amusement to the fancy and instruction to the heart," but he also argues the importance as well as the richness of American materials:

> One merit the writer may at least claim:—that of calling forth the passions and engaging the sympathy of the reader by means hitherto unemployed by preceding authors. Puerile superstition and exploded manners, Gothic castles and chimeras, are the material usually employed for this end. The incidents of Indian hostility, the perils of the Western wilderness, are far more suitable; and for a native of America to overlook these would admit of no apology.

This statement suggests several elements of Brown's primary achievement, the development of gothic conventions for the purposes of exploring the human mind in moments of ethically significant decision. Such an achievement was important for its example to later American novelists.

AMERICAN GOTHIC

Brown's novels are like William Godwin's in their use of radical contemporary thought; they are like Ann Radcliffe's in that they continue the tradition of the rationalized gothic. Brown, however, proves in some ways to be less radical than Godwin, and his fictional worlds differ greatly from Radcliffe's. Brown brings into his novels current intellectual debates about education, psychology and reason, epistemology, ethics, and religion. Characters who hold typical attitudes find themselves in situations that thoroughly test their beliefs. The novels do not seem especially didactic; they are rather more like Radcliffe's romances in form. A central character or group undergoes a crisis that tests education and belief. Brown's novels tend to be developmental, but the world he presents is so ambiguous and disorderly that the reader is rarely certain that a character's growth really fits the character better for living.

This ambiguity is only one of the differences that make Brown appear, in retrospect at least, to be an Americanizer of the gothic. In one sense, his American settings are of little significance, since they are rather simple equivalents of the castle grounds and wildernesses of an Otranto or Udolpho; on the other hand, these settings are recognizable and much more familiar to American readers. Rather than emphasizing the exoticism of the gothic, Brown increases the immediacy of his tales by using American settings.

Brown also increases the immediacy and the intensity of his stories by setting them close to his readers in time. Even though his novels are usually told in retrospect by the kinds of first-person narrators who would come to dominate great American fiction, the narratives frequently lapse into the present tense at crises, the narrators becoming transfixed by the renewed contemplation of past terrors. Brown avoids the supernatural; even though his novels are filled with the inexplicable, they do not feature the physical acts of supernatural beings. For example, Clara Wieland dreams prophetic dreams that prove accurate, but the apparently supernatural voices that waking people hear are hallucinatory or are merely the work of Carwin, the ventriloquist. All of these devices for reducing the distance between reader and text contribute to the success of Brown's fast-paced if sometimes overly complicated plots, but they also reveal the author's movement away from Radcliffe's rationalized gothic toward the kind of realism that would come to dominate American fiction in the next century.

Perhaps Brown's most significant contribution to the Americanization of the gothic romance is his representation of the human mind as inadequate to its world. Even the best minds in his works fall victim to internal and external assaults, and people avoid or fall into disaster seemingly by chance. In Radcliffe's fictional world, Providence actively promotes poetic justice; if the hero or heroine persists in rational Christian virtue and holds to his or her faith that the world is ultimately orderly, then weaknesses and error, villains and accidents will be overcome, and justice will prevail. In Brown's novels, there are no such guarantees. At the end of *Wieland*, Clara, the narrator, reflects, "If Wieland had framed juster notions of moral duty, and of the divine attributes; or if I had been gifted with ordinary equanimity or foresight, the double-tongued deceiver would have been baffled and repelled." Clara's moralizing is, in fact, useless, even to herself. She was not so "gifted"; therefore, she could never have escaped the catastrophes that befell her. Furthermore, she persists in seeing Carwin, the "double-tongued deceiver," as a devil who ruined her brother, even though Carwin is no more than a peculiarly gifted and not very moral human being. Clara is able to moralize in this way only because, for the time being, disasters do not threaten her. Placed once again in the situation in which she completed the first portion of her narrative, she would again reject all human comfort and wish for death. Brown's fictional worlds defy human comprehension and make ethical actions excessively problematic.

This apparent irony in *Wieland* illustrates a final significant development in Brown's adaptation of the gothic romance. Although it is difficult, given his sometimes clumsy work, to be certain of what he intends, Brown seems to have experimented with point of view in ways that foreshadow later works. *Arthur Mervyn*, written in two parts, seems a deliberate experiment in multiple points of view. As Donald Ringe has noted, while the first part, told primarily from Mervyn's point of view, emphasizes Mervyn's naïve victimization by a sophisticated villain, the second part, told from a more objective point of view, suggests that Mervyn may unconsciously be a moral chameleon and confidence man. This shifting of point of view to capture complexity or create irony reappears in the works of many major American novelists, notably Herman Melville (for example, in "Benito Cereno") and William Faulkner.

By focusing on the mind dealing with crises in an ambiguous world, making his stories more immediate, and manipulating point of view for ironic effect, Brown helped to transform popular gothic conventions into tools for the more deeply psychological American gothic fiction that would follow.

WIELAND

Clara Wieland, the heroine of *Wieland*, is a bridge between the gothic heroine of Radcliffe and a line of American gothic victims stretching from Edgar Allan Poe's narrators in his tales of terror through Henry James's governess in *The Turn of the Screw* (1898) to Faulkner's Temple Drake and beyond. Her life is idyllic until she reaches her early twenties, when she encounters a series of catastrophes that, it appears, will greatly alter her benign view of life. When her disasters are three years behind her and she has married the man she loves, Clara returns to her view that the world is reasonably orderly and that careful virtue will pull one through all difficulties.

The novel opens with an account of the Wieland family curse on the father's side. Clara's father, an orphaned child of a German nobleman cast off by his family because of a rebellious marriage, grows up apprenticed to an English merchant. Deprived of family love and feeling an emptiness in his spiritual isolation, he finds meaning when he chances upon a book of a radical Protestant sect. In consequence, he develops an asocial and paranoid personal faith that converts his emptiness into an obligation. He takes upon himself certain duties that will make him worthy of the god he has created. These attitudes dominate his life and lead eventually to his "spontaneous combustion" in his private temple on the estate he has developed in America. The spiritual and psychological causes of this disaster arise in part from his guilt at failing to carry out some command of his personal deity, perhaps the successful conversion of American Indians to Christianity, the project that brought him to America. Clara's uncle presents this "scientific" explanation of her father's death and, much later in the novel, tells a story indicating that such religious madness has also occurred on her mother's side of the family. Religious madness is the familial curse that falls upon Clara's immediate family: Theodore Wieland, her brother; his wife, Catharine; their children and a ward; and Catharine's brother, Pleyel, whom Clara comes to love.

The madness strikes Theodore Wieland; he believes he hears the voice of God commanding him to sacrifice his family if he is to be granted a vision of God. He succeeds in killing all except Pleyel and Clara. The first half of the novel leads up to his crimes, and the second half deals primarily with Clara's discoveries about herself and the world as she learns more details about the murders. Clara's ability to deal with this catastrophe is greatly complicated by events that prove to be essentially unrelated to it but coincide with it. In these events, the central agent is Carwin.

Carwin is a ventriloquist whose background is explained in a separate short fragment, "Memoirs of Carwin the Biloquist." Because ventriloquism is an art virtually unknown in Clara's world, Carwin seems monstrous to her. As he explains to Clara near the end of the novel, he has been lurking about the Wieland estate, and his life has touched on theirs in several ways. He has used his art to avoid being detected in his solitary night explorations of the grounds. The apparently supernatural voices he has created may have contributed to the unsettling of Theodore Wieland, but Wieland's own account during his trial indicates other more powerful causes of his madness. Much more dangerous to Clara has been Carwin's affair with her housekeeper, Judith, for by this means he has come to see Clara as a flower of human virtue and intellect. He is tempted to test her by creating the illusion that murderers are killing Judith in Clara's bedroom closet. This experiment miscarries, leading Clara to think she is the proposed victim. He later uses a "supernatural" voice that accidentally coincides with one of her prophetic dreams; though his purpose is to frighten her away from the place of his meetings with Judith, Carwin confirms Clara's fears and superstitions. He pries into her private diary and concocts an elaborate lie about his intention to rape her when he is caught. Out of envy and spite and because he is able, Carwin deceives Pleyel into thinking that Clara has surrendered her honor to him.

Throughout these deceptions, Carwin also fosters in Clara the superstition that a supernatural being is watching over and protecting her by warning her of dangers. Carwin's acts are essentially pranks; he never intends as much harm as actually occurs when his actions become threads in a complex net of causality. The worst consequence of his pranks is that Pleyel is convinced that Clara has become depraved just at the moment when she hopes that he will propose marriage, and this consequence occurs because Carwin overestimates Pleyel's intelligence. Pleyel's accusation of Clara is quite serious for her because it culminates the series of dark events that Clara perceives as engulfing her happy life. Carwin's scattered acts have convinced her that rapists and murderers lurk in every dark corner and that she is the center of some impersonal struggle between forces of good and evil. Pleyel's accusation also immediately precedes her brother's murders. These two crises nearly destroy Clara's reason and deprive her of the will to live.

The attack on Clara's mind is, in fact, the central action of the novel. All the gothic shocks come to focus on her perception of herself. They strip her of layers of identity until she is reduced to a mere consciousness of her own integrity, a consciousness that is then challenged when she comes to understand the nature of her brother's insanity. When all the props of her identity have been shaken, she wishes for death. Tracing her progress toward the wish for death reveals the central thematic elements of the novel.

The attack on Clara's mind is generated from poles represented by her brother and Pleyel. Wieland crumbles from within, and Pleyel is deceived by external appearances. Each falls prey to the weakness to which he is most susceptible. Clara's more stable mind is caught in the midst of these extremes. Theodore Wieland has the family temperament, the tendency to brood in isolation over his spiritual state and over "last things." Pleyel is the lighthearted and optimistic rationalist, skeptical of all religious ideas, especially any belief in modern supernatural agencies. While Wieland trusts his inner voice above all, Pleyel places absolute faith in his senses. Both are certain of their powers to interpret their experience accurately, and both are wrong on all counts. Wieland sees what he wants to see, and Pleyel's senses are easily deceived, especially by the skillful Carwin. Wieland interprets his visions as divine revelations even though they command murder, and Pleyel believes Clara is polluted even though such a belief is inconsistent with his lifelong knowledge of her.

Clara's sense of identity first suffers when her idyllic world begins to slip away. Her world becomes a place of unseen and unaccountable danger. As her anxiety increases, she finds herself unable to reason about her situation. Brown shows this disintegration in one of his more famous scenes, when Clara comes to believe there is someone in her closet, yet persists in trying to enter it even though she has heard the murderers there and even after her protecting voice has warned her away. Critics take various attitudes toward this scene, which prolongs the reader's wait to learn who is in the closet in order to follow minutely Clara's thoughts and reactions. Brown creates suspense that some critics have judged overwrought, but his main purpose is clearly the close analysis of a strong mind coming apart under great pressure. Even though Pleyel's mistakes emphasize the inadequacy of individual rationality to the complexity of the world, that faculty remains the isolated person's only means of active defense. As Clara's rationality disintegrates, her helplessness increases.

Seeing her world divide into a war between good and evil in which her reason fails to help her, Clara's anxiety develops into paranoia. After Carwin tells how he intended to rape her, she begins to see him as a supernatural agent of Satan. When Pleyel accuses her of self-transforming wickedness with Carwin, Clara loses her social identity. Unable to change Pleyel's mind, she can see recent events only as a devilish plot against her happiness. Just when she thinks she is about to complete her identity in marriage, she is denied the opportunity. When she loses the rest of her family as a result of Wieland's insanity, she loses the last supporting prop of her identity, leaving only her faith in herself, her consciousness of her own innocence, and her belief that the satanic Carwin has caused all of her catastrophes.

Two more events deprive Clara of these remaining certainties. She learns that Wieland, rather than Carwin, whom she has suspected, is the murderer, and when she understands Wieland's motives, she loses confidence in her perceptions of herself, for should she be similarly transformed, she would be unable to resist. In fact, she sees herself, prostrate and wishing for death, as already transformed: "Was I not likewise transformed from rational and human into a creature of nameless and fearful attributes?" In this state, she understands her brother's certainty of his own rectitude. She cannot know herself. When she finally meets Carwin and hears how trivial and without malice his acts have been, she is unable to believe him, unable to give up her belief that she is the victim of a supernatural agency. Like Wieland, whom she meets for the last time on the same evening she talks with Carwin, she insists that divinity stands behind her disasters; the paranoid Wielands stand at the head of the line of American monomaniacs of whom Melville's Ahab is the greatest example. Deprived of her ordered world, Clara asserts against it an order that gives her reason, at least, to die. Wieland himself commits suicide when Carwin convinces him he has listened to the wrong voice.

Criticism has been rightly skeptical of the apparent clumsiness of the last chapter, Clara's continuation of the narration three years after Wieland's suicide. That chapter tidies up what had appeared earlier to be a subplot involving the Wielands' ward, Louisa Conway, and it also puts together a conventional happy ending. The recovered Clara marries Pleyel after he resolves several complications, including learning the truth about Clara and losing his first wife. Although it remains difficult to determine what Brown intended, it is unlikely that a writer of Brown's intelligence, deeply interested in the twistings of human thought, could be unaware that Clara's final statement is a manifest tissue of illusion. No attainable human virtue could have saved her or Wieland from the web of events in which they became enmeshed. That she persists in magnifying Carwin's responsibility shows that she fails to appreciate the complexity of human events even as Carwin himself has failed. That the Conway/Stuart family disasters of the last chapter recapitulate her own emphasizes Clara's failure to appreciate fully the incomprehensibility of her world.

Brown apparently intended in the final chapter to underline the illusory quality of social normality. When life moves as it usually does, it appears to be orderly, and one's ideas of order, because they are not seriously challenged, seem to prevail and become a source of comfort and security. That these ideas of order all break down when seriously challenged leads Clara to the wisdom of despair: "The most perfect being must owe his exemption from vice to the absence of temptation. No human virtue is secure from degeneracy." Such wisdom is not, however, of much use under normal conditions and is of no use at all in a crisis. Perhaps more useful is Clara's reflection as she looks back from the perspective of three years, her idea that one's perceptions and interpretations, because of their imperfection, must be tested over time and compared with those of other observers. The Wieland family curse and Pleyel's errors might be moderated if each character relied less on his or her unaided perceptions and interpretations. In the midst of chaos, however, this maxim may be no more helpful than any other; Clara, for example, violently resists the sympathy of friends who might help to restore the order of her mind.

Although not a great novel, *Wieland* is both intrinsically interesting and worthy of study for the degree to which it foreshadows developments of considerable importance in the American novel. By subjecting Clara to a completely disordered world and by taking her through a loss of identity, Brown prepares the way for greater American gothic protagonists from Captain Ahab to Thomas Sutpen.

EDGAR HUNTLY

Edgar Huntly appears at first to be a clumsily episodic adventure novel, but the more closely one looks at it, the more interesting and troubling it becomes. The protagonist-narrator, Edgar Huntly, writes a long letter to his betrothed, Mary Waldegrave, recounting a series of adventures in which he has participated. This letter is followed by two short ones from Huntly to his benefactor, Sarsefield, and one final short letter from Sarsefield to Huntly. The last letter suggests some of the ways in which the apparent clumsiness becomes troubling. Midway through the novel, Edgar learns that he will probably be unable to marry his fiancé, for her inheritance from her recently murdered brother seems not really to belong to her. Later, it appears that the return of Edgar's recently well-married friend, Sarsefield, once again puts him in a position to marry, but Sarsefield's last letter raises doubts about this event that remain unresolved. The reader never learns whether Edgar and Mary are united. The purpose of Sarsefield's letter is to chastise Edgar.

Edgar's main project in the novel becomes to cure the mad Clithero, who mistakenly believes he has been responsible for the death of Sarsefield's wife, formerly Mrs. Lorimer. By the end of his adventures, Edgar understands the degree to which Clithero is mistaken about events and believes that when Clithero learns the truth, he will be cured. To Edgar's surprise, when Clithero learns the truth, he apparently sets out to really kill his benefactor, Mrs. Sarsefield. Edgar writes his two letters to Sarsefield to warn of Clithero's impending appearance and sends them directly to Sarsefield, knowing that his wife may well see them first. She does see the second letter, and collapses and miscarries as a result. Sarsefield chastises Edgar for misdirecting the letters, even though Sarsefield knew full well from the first letter that the second was on its way to the same address. While, on one hand, Edgar's error seems comically trivial, especially in comparison with the misguided benevolence that drives him to meddle with Clithero, on the other hand, the consequences are quite serious, serious enough to make one question why Edgar *and* Sarsefield are so stupid about their handling of the letters. The reader is left wondering what to make of Edgar and Sarsefield; does either of them know what he is doing?

The novel seems intended in part as a demonstration that one is rarely if ever aware of what one is doing. Paul Witherington has noted that the novel takes the form of a quest that never quite succeeds, a story of initiation in which repeated initiations fail to take place. Edgar returns to his home shortly after the murder of his closest friend, Waldegrave, in order to solve the crime and bring the murderer to justice. When he sees Clithero, the mysterious servant of a neighbor, sleepwalking at the murder scene, he suspects Clithero of the murder. When he confronts Clithero, Edgar learns the story of his past. In Ireland, Clithero rose out of obscurity to become the favorite servant of Mrs. Lorimer. His virtue eventually led to Mrs. Lorimer's allowing an engagement between Clithero and her beloved niece. This story of virtue rewarded turned sour when, in self-defense, Clithero killed Mrs. Lorimer's blackguard twin brother. Mrs. Lorimer believed her life to be mysteriously entwined with her brother's and was convinced that she would die when he did. Clithero believed her and was convinced that by killing the father of his bride-to-be he had also killed his benefactor. In a mad refinement of benevolence, he determined to stab her in order to spare her the pain of dying from the news of her brother's death. Failing with the sword, he resorted to the word, telling her what had happened. Upon her collapse, he took flight, ignorant of the actual consequences of his act. Mrs. Lorimer did not die; she married Sarsefield and they went to America. Although Clithero's guilt seems unconnected with the murder of Waldegrave, except that the event has renewed Clithero's anguish over what he believes to be his crime, Edgar still suspects him. Furthermore, Clithero's story has stimulated Edgar's benevolence.

Edgar becomes determined to help Clithero, for even if he is Waldegrave's murderer, he has suffered enough. Clithero retires to the wilderness of Norwalk to die after telling his story to Edgar, but Edgar pursues him there to save him. After three trips filled with wilderness adventures, Edgar receives a series of shocks. He meets the man who is probably the real owner of Mary's inheritance and loses his hope for a speedy marriage. Fatigued from his adventures in the wilderness and frustrated in his efforts to benefit Clithero, perhaps guilty about prying into Clithero's life and certainly guilty about his handling of Waldegrave's letters, he begins to sleepwalk. His sleepwalking mirrors Clithero's in several ways, most notably in that he also hides a treasure, Waldegrave's letters, without being aware of what he is doing. After a second episode of sleepwalking, he finds himself at the bottom of a pit in a cave with no memory of how he arrived there; this is the second apparent diversion from his quest for Waldegrave's murderer.

Edgar takes three days to return to civilization, moving through a fairly clear pattern of death and rebirth that parallels the movement from savagery to civilization. His adventures—drinking panther blood, rescuing a maiden, fighting Native Americans, losing and finding himself in rough terrain, nearly killing his friends, and successfully evading his own rescue while narrowly escaping death several times—are filled with weird mistakes and rather abstract humor. For example, he is amazed at his physical endurance. When he finds himself within a half-day's walk of home, he determines, despite his three days of privation, to make the walk in six hours. Six hours later, he has not yet even gained the necessary road, and, though he knows where he is, he is effectively no closer to home than when he started out. Although he has endured the physical trials, he has not progressed.

Of his earlier explorations of the wilderness, Edgar says, "My rambles were productive of incessant novelty, though they always terminated in the prospects of limits that could not be overleaped." This physical nature of the wilderness is indicative of the moral nature of human life, which proves so complex that while people believe they can see to the next step of their actions, they find continually that they have seen incorrectly. Edgar repeatedly finds himself doing what he never thought he could do and failing at what he believes he can easily accomplish. The complexities of his wilderness experience are beyond the reach of this brief essay, but they seem to lead toward the deeper consideration of questions Edgar raises after hearing Clithero's story:

If consequences arise that cannot be foreseen, shall we find no refuge in the persuasion of our rectitude and of human frailty? Shall we deem ourselves criminal because we do not enjoy the attributes of Deity? Because our power and our knowledge are confined by impassable boundaries?

In order for Edgar to be initiated and to achieve his quest, he needs to come to a just appreciation of his own limits. Although he can see Clithero's limitations quite clearly, Edgar fails to see his own, even after he learns that he has been sleepwalking, that he has been largely mistaken about the events surrounding the Indian raid, that he has mistaken his friends for enemies, and that he has made many other errors that might have caused his own death. Even after he learns that an American Indian killed Waldegrave and that his efforts with Clithero have been largely irrelevant, he persists in his ignorant attempt to cure the madman, only to precipitate new disasters. Edgar does not know himself and cannot measure the consequences of his simplest actions, yet he persists in meddling with another equally complex soul that he understands even less. Before Clithero tells Edgar his story, he says: "You boast of the beneficence of your intentions. You set yourself to do me benefit. What are the effects of your misguided zeal and random efforts? They have brought my life to a miserable close." This statement proves prophetic, for prior to each confrontation with Edgar, Clithero has determined to try to live out his life as best he can; each of Edgar's attempts to help drives Clithero toward the suicide that he finally commits.

Insofar as Edgar's quest is to avenge his friend's murder, he succeeds quite by accident. Insofar as his quest is for ethical maturity, he fails miserably, but no one else in the novel succeeds either. If a measure of moral maturity is the ability to moderate one's passions for the benefit of others, no one is mature. The virtuous Mrs. Lorimer cannot behave rationally toward her villainous brother, and her suffering derives ultimately from that failure. Clithero will murder out of misguided benevolence. Sarsefield, a physician, will let Clithero die of wounds received from American Indians because he believes that to Clithero, "consciousness itself is the malady, the pest, of which he only is cured who ceases to think." Even though Edgar must assent to this statement—concluding, "Disastrous and humiliating is the state of man! By his own hands is constructed the mass of misery and error in which his steps are forever involved"—he still wishes to correct some of Clithero's mistakes. In doing so, he provokes Clithero's suicide. No character understands him- or herself, his or her limitations, or his or her actions thoroughly; in the case of each of these characters, benevolence issues in murder, direct or indirect. One of the novel's many ironies is that among Edgar, Sarsefield, and Clithero, only Clithero is never morally responsible for a death other than his own.

In *Edgar Huntly*, as in *Wieland*, the stage of human action is beyond human comprehension. In *Wieland*, although there is no sanctuary for the virtuous, virtue remains valuable at least as a source of illusions of order, but in *Edgar Huntly* positive virtue becomes criminal because of inevitable human error. The phenomenon of sleepwalking and the motif of ignorance of self encourage the reader to consider those darker motives that may be hidden from the consciousness of the characters. Edgar must indeed affirm that people are criminal because they do not have "the attributes of Deity."

Wieland and *Edgar Huntly* are good examples of Brown's interests and the complexity of his fiction. The wedding of serious philosophical issues with forms of the popular gothic novel accounts for Brown's distinctive role in the development of the American novel and his continuing interest for students of American culture.

Terry Heller

OTHER MAJOR WORKS

SHORT FICTION: *Carwin, the Biloquist, and Other American Tales and Pieces*, 1822; *The Rhapsodist, and Other Uncollected Writings*, 1943.

NONFICTION: *Alcuin: A Dialogue*, 1798; *Literary Essays and Reviews*, 1992 (Alfred Weber and Wolfgang Schäfer, editors).

BIBLIOGRAPHY

Allen, Paul. *The Late Charles Brockden Brown*. Edited by Robert E. Hemenway and Joseph Katz. Columbia, S.C.: J. Faust, 1976. Begun in the early nineteenth century, this biography was later expanded upon by William Dunlap. Despite some inaccuracies, this work became the basis for subsequent studies.

Axelrod, Alan. *Charles Brockden Brown: An American Tale*. Austin: University of Texas Press, 1983. Study of Brown's work focuses primarily on four novels: *Wieland, Ormond, Arthur Mervyn*, and *Edgar Huntly*. Includes bibliographical references and an index.

Barnard, Philip, Stephen Shapiro, and Mark L. Kamrath, eds. *Revising Charles Brockden Brown: Culture, Politics, and Sexuality in the Early Republic*. Knoxville: University of Tennessee Press, 2004. Collection of thirteen essays addresses various aspects of Brown's works, placing them within the context of the political and ideological issues of his time. Among the topics discussed are the culture of the Enlightenment and questions of gender and sexuality.

Christopherson, Bill. *The Apparition in the Glass: Charles Brockden Brown's American Gothic*. Athens: University of Georgia Press, 1993. Chapter 2 provides a good discussion of the American romance, and separate chapters are devoted to Brown's novels *Wieland, Ormond, Arthur Mervyn*, and *Edgar Huntly*.

Clark, David L. *Charles Brockden Brown: Pioneer Voice of America*. 1952. Reprint. New York: AMS Press, 1966. Still one of the most complete books on Brown available. Combines biography, criticism, and liberal quotations from Brown's papers. Some of Brown's letters were published for the first time in the original edition of this work.

Clemit, Pamela. *The Godwinian Novel: The Rational Fictions of Godwin, Brockden Brown, Mary Shelley*. New York: Oxford University Press, 1993. Discusses the influence of British novelist William Godwin on Brown, examining elements of the Godwinian novel in *Wieland*. Includes bibliographical references and index.

Grabo, Norman S. *The Coincidental Art of Charles Brockden Brown*. Chapel Hill: University of North Carolina Press, 1981. Scholarly yet easy-to-read analysis of Brown's major fiction focuses on the psychology of the characters and what they reveal about Brown's own mind.

Hinds, Elizabeth Jane Wall. *Private Property: Charles Brockden Brown's Gendered Economics of Virtue*. Newark: University of Delaware Press, 1997. Contains chapters on economics and gender issues in the 1790's and separate chapters on each of Brown's major novels. Includes detailed notes and a bibliography.

Kafer, Peter. *Charles Brockden Brown's Revolution and the Birth of American Gothic*. Philadelphia: University of Pennsylvania Press, 2004. Focuses on *Wieland* in explaining how Brown adapted the European gothic novel into a purely American genre. Describes the social and political influences on Brown's work.

Ringe, Donald A. *Charles Brockden Brown*. Rev. ed. Boston: Twayne, 1991. Contains some of the most helpful criticism of Brown's works to be found. Discusses each of the novels and provides a chronology of Brown's life and writings. Includes an annotated bibliography.

Watts, Steven. *The Romance of Real Life: Charles Brockden Brown and the Origins of American Culture*. Baltimore: Johns Hopkins University Press, 1994. Discusses Brown's work from the perspective of the emergence of a capitalistic culture at the beginning of the nineteenth century. Addresses the author's major novels as well as his essays, private correspondence, and other materials.

WILKIE COLLINS

Born: London, England; January 8, 1824
Died: London, England; September 23, 1889

<small>PRINCIPAL LONG FICTION</small>
Antonina: Or, The Fall of Rome, 1850
Basil: A Story of Modern Life, 1852
Hide and Seek, 1854
The Dead Secret, 1857
The Woman in White, 1860
No Name, 1862
Armadale, 1866
The Moonstone, 1868
Man and Wife, 1870
Poor Miss Finch: A Novel, 1872
The New Magdalen, 1873
The Law and the Lady, 1875
The Two Destinies: A Romance, 1876
My Lady's Money, 1878
The Fallen Leaves, 1879
The Haunted Hotel: A Mystery of Modern Venice, 1879
A Rogue's Life, 1879
Jezebel's Daughter, 1880
The Black Robe, 1881
Heart and Science, 1883
I Say No, 1884
The Evil Genius: A Dramatic Story, 1886
The Guilty River, 1886
The Legacy of Cain, 1889
Blind Love, 1890 (completed by Walter Besant)

<small>OTHER LITERARY FORMS</small>

In addition to his novels, Wilkie Collins produced a biography of his father in 1848 as well as travel books, essays and reviews, and a number of short stories. He also wrote and adapted plays, often in collaboration with Charles Dickens.

<small>ACHIEVEMENTS</small>

Wilkie Collins's reputation more than a century after his death rests almost entirely on two works: *The Woman in White*, first published serially in *All the Year Round* from November 26, 1859, to August 25, 1860; and *The Moonstone*, published in 1868. Mystery author Dorothy L. Sayers called the latter work "probably the finest detective story ever written." No chronicler of crime and detective fiction can fail to include Collins's important contributions to the genre; simply for the ingenuity of his plots, Collins earned the admiration of T. S. Eliot. *The Woman in White* and *The Moonstone* have also been adapted numerous times for the stage, film, radio, and television. For an author so conscientious and industrious, however—Collins averaged one "big" novel every two years in his maturity—to be known as the author of two books would hardly be satisfactory. The relative obscurity into which most of Collins's work has fallen cannot be attributed completely to the shadow cast by his friend and sometime collaborator Charles Dickens, to his physical infirmities and his addiction to laudanum, or to the social vision that led him to write a succession of thesis novels. Indeed, the greatest mystery Collins left behind concerns the course of his literary career and subsequent reputation.

BIOGRAPHY

A pencil drawing of the author titled "Wilkie Collins by his father William Collins, R. A." survives; it shows a pretty, if serious, round face. The features beneath the end of the boy's nose are shaded, giving particular prominence to the upper face and forehead. The viewer is at once drawn to the boy's eyes; they are large, probing, mysterious—hardly the eyes of a child. Perhaps the artist-father sought to impart to his elder son some of his own austere, pious nature. William Collins (1788-1847), whose life began on the verge of one great European revolution and ended on the verge of another, was no revolutionary himself, nor was he the bohemian others of his calling imagined themselves. Instead, he was a strict Sabbatarian, an individual who overcame by talent and perseverance the disadvantages of poverty. The novelist's paternal grandfather was an art dealer, a restorer, and a storyteller who lovingly trained and cajoled his son in painting and drawing. William Collins did not begin to taste success until several years after the death of his father in 1812, but gradually commissions and patrons did come, including Sir Robert Peel. Befriended by noted artists such as Sir David Wilkie and Washington Allston, William Collins was at last elected to the Royal Academy in 1820. Two years later, he married Harriet Geddes. The names of both of their sons, born in 1824 and 1828, respectively, honored fellow artists: William Wilkie Collins and Charles Allston Collins.

Little is known of Wilkie Collins's early years, save that they appear to have been relatively tranquil. By 1833, Collins was already enrolled at Maida Hill Academy. In 1836, William Collins elected to take his family to Italy, where they remained until the late summer of 1838. The return to London required taking new lodgings at Regent's Park, and the fourteen-year-old Wilkie Collins was sent to boarding school at Highbury. By the close of 1840, he was presumably finished with school. His father's health began to fail, and the senior Collins made known his wish that Wilkie take holy orders, though the son apparently had no such inclination. The choice became university or commerce. Wilkie Collins chose business, and he became an apprentice to the tea merchants Antrobus and Company in 1841. He performed well there and was able to take a leave in order to accompany his father to Scotland the following summer. While still an apprentice, Collins began to write occasional pieces, and in August, 1843, the *Illuminated Magazine* published his first signed story, "The Last Stage Coachman." A novel about Polynesia was also written but discarded. In 1844, Collins traveled to Paris with his friend Charles Ward, and he made a second visit in 1845. While William Collins's health began to deteriorate more rapidly, his son was released from his apprenticeship and decided on the study of law. In February, 1847, William Collins died.

Wilkie Collins emulated his father's self-discipline, industry, and especially his love of art and beauty, yet if one judges by the series of self-serving religious zealots who populate Collins's fiction, one must assume that, while he respected his father's artistic sensibilities, he did not admire his pious ardor. Instead, Wilkie Collins seems in most things to have taken the example of his mother, a woman of loving good nature and humor with whom both he and his brother Charles remained close until her death. Nevertheless, William Collins near the end of his life had asked Wilkie to write his biography, providing the opportunity for the young man's first published book, *Memoirs of the Life of William Collins, R. A.*, published in 1848 in two volumes. While the narrator tends toward self-effacement and burdens his readers with minute detail, the work is nevertheless a formidable accomplishment. His research in preparing the book led Collins into correspondence with the American writer Richard Henry Dana, Jr., and with a circle of established and rising artists, including E. M. Ward (brother of his friend Charles), Augustus Egg, John Everett Millais, Holman Hunt, and the Rossettis. At this time, Collins completed his historical novel *Antonina*, which is filled with gothic violence and adventure, a work that attracted the serious attention of John Ruskin. It was published in 1850, the same year that saw the production of Collins's first publicly staged dramatic work, *A Court Duel*, which he had adapted from the French. With the success of his play and the surprisingly positive reception of *Antonina*, Collins began to enjoy a rising reputation.

In January, 1851, Richard Bentley published Collins's account of a Cornwall hiking trip taken during the summer of 1850 as *Rambles Beyond Railways*. Two months later, Egg introduced the twenty-seven-year-old Collins to Dickens, and the initial contact resulted in Collins's taking part in Dickens's theatrical *Not So Bad as We Seem: Or, Many Sides to a Character* (pb. 1851), written by Edward Bulwer-Lytton. Until Dickens's death in 1870 he and Collins remained staunch friends, though there is some indication that there was friction between the two authors following Collins's success with *The Moonstone* and Dickens's supposed attempt to outdo his junior with his novel *The Mystery of Edwin Drood* (1870), which remained unfinished at Dickens's death.

In 1852, after having tried to sell the version of a story that would become "Mad Monkton" to Dickens, Collins published the story "A Terribly Strange Bed" (anthologized often since) in *Household Words*, a magazine edited by Dickens from 1850 to 1859.

The following years saw considerable collaboration between the two authors, not the least of which were Collins's stories for the Christmas annuals such as *Mr. Wray's Cash-Box: Or, The Mask and the Mystery* (1852), the collaboration *The Seven Poor Travellers* (1854), *The Wreck of the Golden Mary* (1856), a work often attributed to Dickens until the late twentieth century, the novel *The Dead Secret*, and numerous other stories and articles. In 1853, Collins, Dickens, and Egg traveled together in Italy and Switzerland. Four years later, Dickens produced Collins's play *The Frozen Deep*, later noting that the self-sacrifice of the central character, Richard Wardour (played by Dickens), provided the germ for *A Tale of Two Cities* (1859). Although never published as a play, *The Frozen Deep* was published in 1866 as part of a collection of short stories.

The impact each had on the writing of the other has long been a topic of controversy and speculation for critics and biographers; generally unchallenged is the influence of Collins's meticulous plotting on the work of his senior. In turn, Dickens often corrected and refined by suggestion Collins's fiction, although he never agreed with Collins's practice of including prefaces that upbraided critics and the public alike. When Collins published *Basil* (having included for Bentley's publication in book form the first of those vexing prefaces), he forwarded the volume to Dickens. After a two-week silence, there came a thoughtful, admiring reply: "I have made Basil's acquaintance," wrote Dickens at the end of 1852, "with great gratification, and entertain high respect for him. I hope that I shall become intimate with many worthy descendants of his, who are yet in the limbo of creatures waiting to be born." Collins did not disappoint Dickens on that count over their years of friendship and collaboration; indeed, they became "family" when Charles Allston Collins married Dickens's daughter Kate.

Household Words faded in 1859 along with Dickens's association with the publishers Bradbury and Evans. Dickens's new periodical, *All the Year Round* (1859-1870), began auspiciously with the publication of *A Tale of Two Cities*. After the run of that novel, he needed something to keep public interest in the new magazine from abating, and Collins provided it with *The Woman in White*. This work's monumental success put Collins into that rarest literary circle: that of well-to-do authors. Its success also coincided with important personal events in Collins's life.

Collins had lived the life of a bachelor, residing with his brother and mother at least into his early thirties. Their house was often open to guests. On one such evening, the author and his brother escorted home the artist John Everett Millais through then-rural North London. Suddenly, a woman appeared to them in the moonlight, attired in flowing robes, all in white. Though distraught, she regained her composure and vanished as quickly as she had appeared. The author was most astounded and insisted he would discover the identity of the lovely creature. J. G. Millais, the painter's son, who later narrated this anecdote in a life of his father, did not reveal the lady's ultimate identity, saying, "Her subsequent history, interesting as it is, is not for these pages." The woman was Caroline Elizabeth Graves, born 1834, mother of a little girl, Harriet. Her husband, G. R. Graves, may or may not have been dead. Of him, only his name is known. Clearly, however, the liaison between Caroline Graves and Wilkie Collins was fully under way when he began to write *The Woman in White.*

From at least 1859, the couple lived together in a secret relationship known only to their closest friends, until the autumn of 1868, when for obscure reasons Caroline married the son of a distiller, John C. Clow. Collins, not one to waste time, started a new liaison with Martha Rudd. This union produced three children: Marian (1869), Harriet Constance (1871), and William Charles (1874). The children took the surname Dawson, but Collins freely admitted his paternity. By this time, too, Caroline and her daughter returned, and Harriet Graves for a time served as her mother's lover's amanuensis; Collins adopted her as his daughter. A lover of hearty food, fine champagne, and good cigars, Collins appears to have lived in private a life that would have shocked many of his readers. Still, Collins treated his "morganatic family" quite well: He provided handsomely for his natural and adopted children and for their mothers. When she died in 1895 at age sixty-one, Caroline Elizabeth Graves was interred beside the author of *The Woman in White.*

As Collins's private life began taking on its unconventional proportions in the 1860's, his public career grew more distinguished. His output for *All the Year Round* in shorter forms declined; he simply did not need the money. In March, 1861, his novel *No Name*, a didactic work about inheritance, began its run in the magazine; it was published in volume form in December, 1862. A year later, Collins resigned his editorial assignment for Dickens's periodical and also published, with Sampson Low, Son, and Company, *My Miscellanies*, bringing together, in two volumes, work that had first appeared in the two Dickens periodicals. After about seven years of almost obsessive productivity, Collins relented, but only for a time; he began his novel *Armadale* in the spring of 1864, for serial publication in the *Cornhill Magazine* in Britain and *Harper's Monthly* in the United States. This exploration of inherited and personal guilt remains one of Collins's most adept and popular novels; it is also his longest. He wrote a dramatic version of the novel in 1866, but the play was not produced until it appeared in 1876 as *Miss Gwilt.*

In 1867, Collins and Dickens began their last collaboration, the play *No Thoroughfare* (pr., pb. 1867), an adventure set in the Alps and perhaps not unaffected by the two men's shared Swiss journey many years before. By this time, too, Collins began to suffer tremendously from the good living he had long enjoyed—gout of the areas around the eyes caused him excruciating pain, requiring the application of bandages for weeks at a time. To allay the ache, Collins developed a habit for laudanum, that tincture of opium that fills the darker recesses of middle-Victorian culture. It was in this period of alternating pain and bliss that Collins penned *The Moonstone*, for *All the Year Round*, beginning in January, 1868. The novel was an uncontestable triumph; Collins himself thought it wonderfully wrought.

The Moonstone had hardly begun its run, however, when Collins's mother died, and later that same year, Caroline married Clow. When the novel was finished, Collins again turned to the stage, writing *Black and White* with his friend Charles Fechter, an actor; the play successfully opened in March, 1869. At the end of the year, the serialization of *Man and Wife* began in *Harper's Weekly* and in January, 1870, in *Cassell's Magazine*. Posterity has judged *Man and Wife* more harshly than did its first readers. It was a different kind of novel from *The Moonstone*: It attacked society's growing obsession with athleticism and castigated marital laws that Collins believed to be cruel, unfair, and unrealistic. According to Collins's modern biographer Kenneth Robinson, *Man and Wife* was the turning point in Collins's career, the start of the "downhill" phase of the writer's life. The novel sold well after its serialization; Collins also wrote a four-act dramatic version that was not produced on the stage until 1873.

At the same time, Collins adapted *No Name* for the theater and, in 1871, *The Woman in White*. The stage version of *The Woman in White* opened at the Olympic Theatre in October and ran for five months before going on tour. The same year saw the beginning of a new novel in serial form, *Poor Miss Finch*, about a blind woman who falls in love with an epileptic whose cure turns him blue. When she is temporarily cured of her affliction, she finds herself in a dilemma about her blue lover, whose healthy twin also desires her love. A year later, the indefatigable Collins published *The New Magdalen* in a magazine called *Temple Bar*; the novel's heroine, a virtuous prostitute, outraged contemporary critics, but the work's dramatization in 1873 was greeted with enthusiasm.

As his work increasingly turned to exposing social hypocrisies, Collins sought, as a writer of established repute, to regulate the body of his published work. Since *Basil*, wholesale piracy of his writings had angered him and hurt his finances. By the early 1870's, he had reached agreements with the German publisher Tauchnitz and with Harper & Brothers in the United States, and, by 1875, with Chatto & Windus in Britain. Chatto & Windus not only bought all extant copyrights to Collins's work but also became his publisher for the rest of his life. This arrangement was finalized in the year after Collins, like his friend Dickens before him, had undertaken a reading tour of the United States and Canada.

The years 1875 and 1876 saw the publication of two popular but lesser novels, *The Law and the Lady* and *The Two Destinies*. The next year was marked, however, by the successful dramatization of *The Moonstone* and the beginning of Collins's friendship with Charles Reade. In 1879, Collins wrote *The Haunted Hotel* for the *Belgravia Magazine*, a ghost story fresh in invention that extends one's notions about the genre. Meanwhile, however, Collins's health became less certain and his laudanum doses became more frequent and increasingly potent. The decade took away many close friends, beginning with Dickens and, later, his brother Charles, then Augustus Egg.

In the last decade of his life, Collins became more reclusive, although not much less productive. He adapted his 1858 play *The Red Vial* into the novel *Jezebel's Daughter*. He also began, for serialization in the *Canadian Monthly*, the novel *The Black Robe*, the central figure of which is a priest plotting to encumber the wealth of a large estate. This work has been regarded as the most successful of his longer, late novels. It was followed by a more controversial novel, *Heart and Science*, a polemic against vivisection that appeared in 1883. The same year saw Collins's last theatrical work, *Rank and Riches*, an unqualified disaster that brought the leading lady to tears before the first-act curtain and that led her leading man, G. W. Anson, to berate the audience. Collins thereafter gave up writing for the stage, save a one-performance version of *The Evil Genius* in 1885; the work was quickly recast as a novel that proved his single most lucrative publication.

Although 1884 saw the passing of Reade, his closest friend of the time, Collins continued to write steadily. *The Guilty River* made its appearance in the *Arrowsmith Christmas Annual* for 1886; in 1887, Chatto & Windus published *Little Novels*, collecting earlier stories. Two works also appeared that ended the battle Collins had long waged with critics. A young man, Harry Quilter, published an encomiastic article for the *Contemporary Review*, "A Living Story-Teller." Collins himself wrote "How I Write My Books" for the newspaper *The Globe*, an account of his work on *The Woman in White*. As his health at last began to fail precipitously in 1888, Collins completed his final serial novel, *The Legacy of Cain*. It appeared in three volumes the following year, at a time when he was finishing the writing of *Blind Love* for the *Illustrated London News*. On the evening of June 30, 1889, Collins suffered a stroke. He requested that Walter Besant, then traveling in the north, return and complete the tale.

Collins had long before befriended Dickens's physician and neighbor, Frank Beard, who did what little could be done to comfort Collins in his final days. Just past midmorning on September 23, 1889, Wilkie Collins died, Beard at his bedside. Four days following his death, Collins was buried at Kensal Green; his procession was headed by Caroline Graves, Harriet Graves, and his surviving literary, theatrical, and household friends. Despite infirmities, Collins had lived a life long and full, remaining productive, industrious, and successful throughout his career.

ANALYSIS

At its best, Wilkie Collins's fiction is characterized by a transparent style that occasionally pleases and surprises the reader with an apt turn of word or phrase, by a genius for intricate plots, by a talent for characterization that in at least one instance must earn the epithet "Miltonic," and by an eye for detail that seems to make the story worth telling. These are the talents of an individual who learned early to look at things like a painter, to see the meaning, the emotion behind the gesture or pose—a habit of observation that constituted William Collins's finest bequest to his elder son.

NARRATIVE STYLE AND PLOTTING

The transparency of Collins's style rests on his adherence to the conventions of the popular fiction of his day. More so than contemporaries, he talks to readers, cajoles them, often protesting that the author will recede into the shadows in order that readers may judge the action for themselves. The "games"—as one critic has observed—that Collins plays with readers revolve about his mazelike plots, his "ingenuous" interruptions of the narrative, and his iterative language, symbolic names, and metaphors. Thus, at the beginning of "Mrs. Zant and the Ghost," published in *Little Novels*, the narrator begins by insisting that this tale of "supernatural influence" occurs in the daylight hours, adding, "The writer declines to follow modern examples by thrusting himself and his opinions on the public view. He returns to the shadow from which he has emerged, and leaves the opposing forces of incredulity and belief to fight the old battle over again, on the old ground." The apt word is "shadow," for certainly, this story depicts a shadow world. At its close, when the preternatural events have occurred, the reader is left to assume a happy resolution between the near victim Mrs. Zant and her earthly rescuer, Mr. Rayburn, through the mood of the man's daughter:

> Arrived at the end of the journey, Lucy held fast by Mrs. Zant's hand. Tears were rising in the child's eyes. "Are we to bid her good-bye?" she said sadly to her father.
>
> He seemed to be unwilling to trust himself to speak; he only said, "My dear, ask her yourself."
>
> But the result justified him. Lucy was happy again.

Here, Collins's narrator has receded like Mrs. Zant's supernatural protector, leaving the reader to hope and to expect that Mrs. Zant can again find love in this world.

This kind of exchange—direct and inferred—between author and reader can go in other directions. For example, when, near the middle of *The Woman in White*, one realizes that Count Fosco has read—as it were—over one's shoulder the diary of Miss Halcolmbe, the author surely intends that one should feel violated while at the same time forced into collusion with the already attractive, formidable villain.

Because Collins's style as narrator is so frequently self-effacing, it sustains the ingenuity of his plots. These are surely most elaborate in *The Woman in White* and *The Moonstone*. In both cases, Collins elects to have one figure, party to the main actions, assemble the materials of different narratives into cohesive form. It is a method far less tedious than that of epistolary novels and provides for both mystery and suspense. Although not the ostensible theme in either work, matters of self-identity and control over one's behavior operate in the contest between virtue and vice, good and evil. Thus, Laura Fairlie's identity is obliterated in an attempt to wrest from her her large fortune; thus, Franklin Blake, heavily drugged, unconsciously removes a gem that makes him the center of elaborate investigation. In each novel, the discovery of the actual circumstances restores identity to the character. The capacity to plot allows Collins to surprise his readers profoundly: In *The Woman in White*, one is astounded to be confronted by Laura Fairlie standing in the churchyard, above her own grave. In *The Moonstone*, one is baffled when the detective, Sergeant Cuff, provides a plausible solution to the theft of the diamond that turns out to be completely incorrect.

Collins's novels of the 1860's find the author having firmly established his transparent detachment from the subjects at hand, in turn giving full scope to his meticulous sense of plot. *No Name* and *Armadale* are no less complex in their respective actions than their more widely read counterparts. It is interesting to note, however, that all of these novels explore matters of identity and motive for action; they attest to Collins's ability to relate popular tales that encompass more serious issues.

CHARACTERIZATION

Because he had a painter's eye for detail, Collins was a master of characterization, even when it appears that a character is flat. Consider, for example, this passage from "Miss Dulane and My Lord," published in *Little Novels*:

> Mrs. Newsham, tall and elegant, painted and dyed, acted on the opposite principle in dressing, which confesses nothing. On exhibition before the world, this lady's disguise asserted she had reached her thirtieth year on her last birthday. Her husband was discreetly silent, and Father Time was discreetly silent; they both knew that her last birthday had happened thirty years since.

Here an incidental figure in a minor tale remains fixed, the picture of one comically out of synchronization with her own manner; before she has uttered a syllable, one dislikes her. Consider, on the other hand, the initial appearance of a woman one will grow to like and admire, Marian Halcolmbe, as she makes her way to meet Walter Hartright in *The Woman in White*:

> She turned towards me immediately. The easy elegance of every movement of her limbs and body as soon as she began to advance from the far end of the room, set me in a flutter of expectation to see her face clearly. She left the window—and I said to myself, The lady is dark. She moved forward a few steps—and I said to myself, The lady is young. She approached nearer—and I said to myself (with a sense of surprise which words fail me to express), The lady is ugly!

This passage reveals not only Collins's superb sense of pace, his ability to set a trap of astonished laughter, but also some of Hartright's incorrect assumptions about the position he has taken at Limmeridge House; for example, that the two young women he will instruct are pampered, spoiled, and not worth his serious consideration. Preeminently, it shows the grace of Marian Halcombe, a grace that overcomes her lack of physical beauty in conventional senses and points to her indefatigable intelligence and loyalty, so crucial to future events in the novel. Marian is, too, a foil for her half sister, Laura Fairlie, the victim of the main crimes in the book. While one might easily dismiss Laura Fairlie with her name—she is fair and petite and very vulnerable—she also displays a quiet resilience and determination in the face of overwhelming adversaries.

The most memorable of Collins's characters is Count Fosco in the same novel, whose name immediately suggests a bludgeon. Collins gives the job of describing Fosco to Marian Halcombe: "He looks like a man who could tame anything." In his characterization of Fosco, Collins spawned an entire race of fat villains and, occasionally, fat detectives, such as Nero Wolfe and Gideon Fell. One is not surprised that Sydney Greenstreet played both Fosco and his descendant, Caspar Gutman, in the 1948 film version of *The Woman in White* and the 1941 film version of Dashiell Hammett's *The Maltese Falcon* (1930). In one of his best speeches, Fosco reveals the nature of his hubris, his evil genius:

> Crimes cause their own detection, do they? . . . there are foolish criminals who are discovered, and wise criminals who escape. The hiding of a crime, or the detection of a crime, what is it? A trial of skill between the police on one side, and the individual on the other. When the criminal is a brutal, ignorant fool, the police in nine cases out of ten win. When the criminal is a resolute, educated, highly-intelligent man, the police in nine cases out of ten lose.

In pitting decent people against others who manipulate the law and social conventions to impose their wills, Collins frequently creates characters more interesting for their deficiencies than for their virtues. His novels pit, sensationally at times, the unsuspecting, the infirm, or the unprepossessing against darker figures who are usually operating under the scope of social acceptance. Beneath the veneer of his fiction, one finds in Collins a continuing struggle to legitimate the illegitimate, to neutralize hypocrisy, and to subvert the public certainties of his era.

Kenneth Friedenreich

OTHER MAJOR WORKS

SHORT FICTION: *Mr. Wray's Cash-Box: Or, The Mask and the Mystery*, 1852; *The Seven Poor Travellers*, 1854; *After Dark*, 1856; *The Wreck of the Golden Mary*, 1856; *The Lazy Tour of Two Idle Apprentices*, 1857 (with Charles Dickens); *The Queen of Hearts*, 1859; *The Frozen Deep*, 1866; *Miss or Mrs.?, and Other Stories*, 1873; *The Frozen Deep, and Other Stories*, 1874; *Alicia Warlock: A Mystery, and Other Stories*, 1875; *The Guilty River*, 1886; *Little Novels*, 1887; *The Yellow Tiger, and Other Tales*, 1924.

PLAYS: *The Lighthouse*, pr. 1855; *The Red Vial*, pr. 1858; *No Thoroughfare*, pr., pb. 1867 (with Charles Dickens); *The Woman in White*, pr., pb. 1871 (adaptation of his novel); *Man and Wife*, pr. 1873 (adaptation of his novel); *The New Magdalen*, pr., pb. 1873 (adaptation of his novel); *The Moonstone*, pr., pb. 1877 (adaptation of his novel).

NONFICTION: *Memoirs of the Life of William Collins, R. A.*, 1848 (2 volumes); *Rambles Beyond Railways*, 1851; *The Letters of Wilkie Collins*, 1999 (William Baker and William M. Clarke, editors); *The Public Face of Wilkie Collins: The Collected Letters*, 2005 (4 volumes; William Baker, editor).

MISCELLANEOUS: *My Miscellanies*, 1863; *The Works of Wilkie Collins*, 1900, 1970 (30 volumes).

BIBLIOGRAPHY

Bachman, Maria K., and Don Richard Cox, eds. *Reality's Dark Light: The Sensational Wilkie Collins*. Knoxville: University of Tennessee Press, 2003. Collection of fourteen essays analyzes Collins's novels, focusing on the themes and techniques that he introduced to the genre. Includes analysis of *The Moonstone* and *The Woman in White* as well as some of his lesser-known novels.

Gasson, Andrew. *Wilkie Collins: An Illustrated Guide*. New York: Oxford University Press, 1998. Well-illustrated volume provides an alphabetical guide to the characters, titles, and terms in Collins's works. Also includes a chronology, the Collins family tree, maps, and a bibliography.

Nayder, Lillian. *Wilkie Collins*. New York: Twayne, 1997. Good introductory study of the author features analysis of his novels and other works, placing them within the context of the political and cultural issues of Collins's time.

O'Neill, Philip. *Wilkie Collins: Women, Property, and Propriety*. New York: Macmillan, 1988. Seeks to move the discussion of Collins away from popularist categories by using modern feminist criticism deconstructively to open up a more considered version of his thematic material. Contains a full bibliography.

Page, Norman, ed. *Wilkie Collins: The Critical Heritage*. London: Routledge & Kegan Paul, 1974. Collection reprints critical responses to Collins's works from 1850 through 1891. Includes a short bibliography.

Peters, Catherine. *The King of Inventors: A Life of Wilkie Collins*. Princeton, N.J.: Princeton University Press, 1991. Comprehensive biography draws on a newly discovered autobiography by Collins's mother and on thousands of Collins's unpublished letters. Supplemented by detailed notes and bibliography.

Pykett, Lyn. *Wilkie Collins*. New York: Oxford University Press, 2005. Traces the various debates that have arisen since 1980, when literary critics began seriously reevaluating Collins's work. The essays focus on Collins's preoccupation with the themes of social and psychological identity, class, gender, and power.

_____, ed. *Wilkie Collins*. New York: St. Martin's Press, 1998. Provides an excellent introduction to Collins for the beginning student. Includes bibliographical references and an index.

Taylor, Jenny Bourne, ed. *The Cambridge Companion to Wilkie Collins*. New York: Cambridge University Press, 2006. All aspects of Collins's writing are discussed in this collection of thirteen essays. His common themes of sexuality, marriage, and religion are examined, as well as his experiences with publishing companies and the process of adapting his works for film. Includes a thorough bibliography and index.

Thoms, Peter. *The Windings of the Labyrinth: Quest and Structure in the Major Novels of Wilkie Collins*. Athens: Ohio University Press, 1992. Focuses on seven major novels, analyzing the theme of the quest in *Basil, Hide and Seek, The Dead Secret, The Woman in White, No Name, Armadale*, and *The Moonstone*.

WALTER DE LA MARE

Born: Charlton, Kent, England; April 25, 1873
Died: Twickenham, Middlesex, England; June 22, 1956
Also known as: Walter John de la Mare; Walter Ramal

<small>PRINCIPAL LONG FICTION</small>
Henry Brocken, 1904
The Return, 1910
The Three Mulla-Mulgars, 1910 (reprinted as *The Three Royal Monkeys: Or,
   The Three Mulla-Mulgars*, 1935)
Memoirs of a Midget, 1921
At First Sight: A Novel, 1928

<small>OTHER LITERARY FORMS</small>

Walter de la Mare (deh-luh-MAYR) was a prolific author of poetry, short stories, and nonfiction. Like his novels, de la Mare's poetry and short fiction range from works written explicitly for children (for which he is best remembered) to works intended for adults. Poetry collections such as *Songs of Childhood* (1902) and *A Child's Day: A Book of Rhymes* (1912) reveal his understanding of the pleasures and frustrations of childhood, an understanding that made *The Three Mulla-Mulgars* a favorite with children. De la Mare's poetry for adults embodies his belief that human beings live in two coexistent worlds: the world of everyday experience and the world of the spirit, which is akin to dreaming.

Dreams and the nature of the imagination are frequent themes in both de la Mare's fiction and his poetry. These and other interests are more explicitly revealed in his essays and in his work as an editor. Not much given to analysis, de la Mare was primarily an appreciative critic. Of the anthologies he edited, *Behold, This Dreamer!* (1939) is perhaps the most revealing of the influences that shaped his work.

<small>ACHIEVEMENTS</small>

Walter de la Mare published only five novels, one of which, *At First Sight*, is more a long short story than a true novel. His fiction is metaphorical and resembles his poetry in its concerns. Much of what he wanted to communicate in his writing is best suited to short works, and therefore his novels are haphazardly successful. In spite of the difficulties of his novels, his contemporary critics in general had a high regard for him as a novelist. Edward Wagenknecht, an important historian of the novel, ranked *Memoirs of a Midget* as one of the best twentieth century English novels. Indeed, in his essay on de la Mare in *Cyclopedia of World Authors* (1958), Wagenknecht emphasizes *Memoirs of a Midget* at the expense of de la Mare's other writings.

De la Mare's novels, however, were not as widely read in their time as his poetry and

Walter de la Mare
(Library of Congress)

short fiction, and today they are seldom read at all. The lack of modern attention to de la Mare's novels is caused less by any absence of merit than by the predictable drop in reputation that many authors undergo in the literary generation after their deaths. Although his novels are unlikely to regain their popularity with a general readership, serious students of twentieth century English literature will almost certainly return to de la Mare's novels as his generation's writings are rehabilitated among scholars.

BIOGRAPHY

Judging from the few published accounts of those who knew him, Walter de la Mare was a quiet and unpretentious man. One can reasonably infer from the absence of autobiographical material from an otherwise prolific writer that he was a private man. He seems to have lived his adventures through his writing, and his primary interests seem to have been of the intellect and spirit.

Walter John de la Mare was born in Charlton, Kent, on April 25, 1873, to James Edward de la Mare and Lucy Sophia Browning de la Mare, a Scot. While attending St. Paul's Cathedral Choir School, Walter de la Mare founded and edited *The Choiristers' Journal*, a school magazine. In 1890, he entered the employ of the Anglo-American Oil Company, for which he served as a bookkeeper until 1908. During these years, he wrote essays, stories, and poetry that appeared in various magazines, including *Black and White* and *The Sketch*. In 1902, his first book—and one of his most lastingly popular—was published, the collection of poetry *Songs of Childhood*. He used the pseudonym "Walter Ramal," which he also used for the publication of the novel *Henry Brocken* in 1904, then dropped. He married Constance Elfrida Igpen in 1899, with whom he had two sons and two daughters. His wife died in 1943.

De la Mare's employment at the Anglo-American Oil Company ended in 1908, when he was granted a Civil List pension of a yearly one hundred pounds by the British government. Thus encouraged, he embarked on a life of letters during which he produced novels, poetry, short stories, essays, one play, and edited volumes of poetry and essays. These many works display something of de la Mare's intellect, if not of his character. They reveal a preoccupation with inspiration and dreams, an irritation with Freudians and psychologists in general (too simplistic in their analyses, he believed), a love of romance, and a love for the child in people. The works indicate a complex mind that preferred appreciation to analysis and observation to explanation.

ANALYSIS

Walter de la Mare's novels are diverse in structure, although unified by his recurring themes. *Henry Brocken* is episodic, with its protagonist moving from one encounter to another. *The Return* has all the trappings of the gothic, with mysterious strangers, supernatural events, and unexplained happenings. *The Three Mulla-Mulgars* is a children's story, with a direct narrative and a clear objective toward which the novel's actions are directed. *Memoirs of a Midget* is Victorian in structure and is filled with incidents and coincidences; it emphasizes character over the other aspects of novel writing. *At First Sight* is really a long short story, what some might call a novella; its plot is simple, the problem its protagonist faces is straightforward, and it has only the barest attempt at a subplot.

HENRY BROCKEN

Early in his literary career, de la Mare concluded that there were two ways of observing the world: inductive and deductive. Induction was a child's way of understanding his environment, through direct experience, whereas deduction was associated with adolescents and adults—the environment was kept at an emotional and intellectual distance. De la Mare believed that reality is best understood in relation to the self and best interpreted through imagination; childlike—as opposed to *childish*—observation is subjective, and childlike imagination can make and remake reality according to the imaginer's desires. Henry Brocken, the eponymous protagonist of de la Mare's first novel, is such a childlike observer. Critics are often confused by his adult behavior; they fail to understand that Brocken is intended to be childlike rather than childish.

Dreams are a part of the human experience that can be made and remade according to the subjective dictates of the self; de la Mare believed that dreams revealed a truer reality than that found in the waking experience. Given de la Mare's beliefs, Brocken's use of dreams to meet with famous literary characters seems almost natural. Brocken is able to converse with characters from the works of such authors as Geoffrey Chaucer, Jonathan Swift, and Charlotte Brontë. The characters are often living lives that are barely implied in their original author's works. Jane Eyre, for instance, is with Rochester long after the conclusion of Brontë's *Jane Eyre* (1847). *Henry Brocken* is about imagination and what it can do to reality. Great literary characters can seem more real than many living people. De la Mare represents this aspect of the imaginative response to literature by showing characters maturing and changing in ways not necessarily envisioned by their creators. Criseyde, for example, is not only older but also wiser than in Chaucer's *Troilus and Criseyde* (1382). What is imagined can have a life of its own, just as dreams can be more alive than waking experience.

THE THREE MULLA-MULGARS

The Three Mulla-Mulgars seems to be an interruption in the development of de la Mare's themes of imagination, dreams, and reality. In it, three monkeys—called "Mulgars"—search for the Valley of Tishnar and the kingdom of their uncle Assasimmon. During their travels, the three—Nod, Thimble, and Thumb—have adventures among the various monkey species of the world and encounter danger in the form of Immanala, the source of darkness and cruelty. Although a children's story, and although humorous and generally lighthearted, *The Three Mulla-Mulgars* contains the spiritual themes typical of de la Mare's best work. Nod, although physically the weakest of the three monkeys, is spiritually gifted; he can contact the supernatural world in his dreams and is able to use the Moonstone, a talisman; Immanala is essentially a spiritual force; it can strike anywhere and can take any form; it can make dreams—which in the ethos of de la Mare are always akin to death—into the "Third Sleep," death. The quest for the Valley of Tishnar is a search for meaning in the Mulla-Mulgars' lives; their use of dreams, a talisman, and their conflict with Immanala make the quest spiritual as well as adventurous.

THE RETURN

The Return represents a major shift in de la Mare's approach to fiction, both long and short. Before *The Return*, he presented his iconoclastic views in the guise of children's stories and allegories—as if his ideas would be more palatable in inoffensive fantasies than in the form of the adult novel. In *The Return*, de la Mare took an important step toward his masterpiece, *Memoirs of a Midget*, by creating a novel featuring adult characters with adult problems.

The Return seems gothic on its surface. Arthur Lawford, weak from a previous illness, tires while walking in a graveyard. He naps beside the grave of Nicholas Sabathier, a man who committed suicide in 1739. Lawford awakens refreshed and vigorous, but to his dismay he discovers that his face and physique have changed. Later, a mysterious stranger, Herbert Herbert, reveals that Lawford resembles a portrait of Sabathier, and Herbert's sister Grisel becomes a powerful attraction for Lawford—she seems to be an incarnation of the lover who may have driven Sabathier to kill himself. The plot, when examined by itself, seems trite and melodramatic, yet de la Mare makes the events frightening, in part because he imbues the novel with genuine metaphysical questions and in part because he believes in his story.

Belief is always a problem in fiction, particularly fantastic fiction. Part of what makes hackwork poor literature is insincerity in the author—that is, the author does not believe that the work is valid, important, or worthy of belief. De la Mare clearly believes that the love story in *The Return* is important, that the novel's themes are valid, and that its events can be believed. His sincerity endows the novel's events with poetic power. The question of Lawford's identity thus becomes disturbing for the reader: De la Mare is saying that no one's identity is certain. Soon after Lawford's physical metamorphosis, his speech takes on a dual sound, as if he and Sabathier are speaking simultaneously. His conversations with Grisel are discussions between the corporeal Lawford and Grisel and between Sabathier and his past love.

In *The Return*, de la Mare's notions about the human spirit being part of two coexistent worlds are made graphic. Lawford becomes a citizen of everyday reality and of the greater reality of the spirit. He can see the world out of time, past and present; he battles both corporeal and supernatural foes; he is at once Sabathier and an ordinary, middle-aged Englishman. Although a part of two realities, he is accepted by neither. His friends and neighbors want him jailed or locked up in a madhouse; Grisel tells him that he cannot have her, although she shares his love, because he is not free of the burdens of his old world. The dilemma of Lawford, trapped as he is between the two worlds, is representative of the human condition: everyone is trapped between two realities because everyone, whether he chooses to recognize it or not, is spiritual as well as physical. So thick with double meanings and disturbing confusions is *The Return* that its almost too convenient resolution—on All Angels Eve, the night on which Sabathier had committed suicide, Lawford is freed of Sabathier's spiritual tug—is a relief. Lawford is free to pretend that what he sees is all that exists, and so is the novel's reader.

MEMOIRS OF A MIDGET

Greeted from its publication with praise for its characterization and graceful prose, *Memoirs of a Midget* is generally regarded by critics as de la Mare's masterpiece. The novel allows multiple readings; most critics readily recognize de la Mare's unusually successful development of a character's point of view, and they note the subtlety of his social commentary, but they often fail to recognize the novel's informing purpose. The story is simple on its surface. Miss M., also known as Midgetina, is a perfectly formed midget. The novel describes her childhood and emergence as an adult. Her point of view as a small adult is carefully created. The bulk of the novel is devoted to her twentieth year, during which she confronts her selfhood and comes to understand that there is a world of the spirit that is greater than the physical one in which she is a social amusement.

The novel has a Victorian flavor, and many of the characters have a Dickensian vitality. One of the most memorable characters is Mr. Anon, a misshapen hunchback who is only a little taller than Miss M. Mr. Anon transforms Miss M. from a social manipulator into a thoughtful person. He loves her—probably, he says, because she is one of the few people close to his size. His ugliness is repulsive, and Miss M. wants to keep him as a friend, but not as a lover. She joins a circus in order to become independent and quickly becomes a main attraction. In order to save Miss M. from possible recognition when Mrs. Monnerie, Miss M.'s former patroness, attends the circus, Mr. Anon takes her place in a pony-riding act. He is thrown from the pony and is injured; he later dies in Miss M.'s arms. Some critics contend that at Mr. Anon's death Miss M. finally loves him. What is probable is that she believes that his inner self—his spirit—is beautiful and more real than his ugly physical form. Later, Miss M. disappears from a locked room. Her housekeeper, Mrs. Bowater, who commands the only entrance and exit to the room, hears a male voice from within even though no one had entered through the door. Upon investigation, Mrs. Bowater finds a note that reads, "I have been called away."

The character of Miss M. is well suited to de la Mare's purposes. She is small and treated like a child by other characters, and thus her perspective is like that of a child. Reared in seclusion by indulgent parents, she emerges into society with much of her childlike ability to experience the world inductively still intact. She is an adult with an adult's thinking capacity, enabling her to understand as well as know the world. She is an excellent vehicle for de la Mare's ideas about the nature of the human spirit. She observes the best and worst in people, and she sees that the unhappiest people are those who see the world as something to be manipulated, who take without giving. Mr. Anon gives all he has without expectation of receiving what he wants, Miss M.'s love. *Memoirs of a Midget* is more than a story of a social outcast's view of society; it is a depiction of spiritual conflict and revelation.

De la Mare was a seeker, a questioner, and an observer; the endings of his novels are suggestive but provide few answers. A skilled and demanding craftsman, he never failed to entertain his readers, but he employed his storyteller's gift in the service of the lifelong spiritual quest that animated all of his works.

Kirk H. Beetz

OTHER MAJOR WORKS

SHORT FICTION: *Story and Rhyme: A Selection*, 1921; *The Riddle, and Other Stories*, 1923; *Ding Dong Bell*, 1924; *Broomsticks, and Other Tales*, 1925; *Miss Jemima*, 1925; *Readings*, 1925-1926 (2 volumes); *The Connoisseur, and Other Tales*, 1926; *Old Joe*,

1927; *Told Again: Traditional Tales,* 1927; *On the Edge,* 1930; *Seven Short Stories,* 1931; *The Lord Fish,* 1933; *The Nap, and Other Stories,* 1936; *The Wind Blows Over,* 1936; *Animal Stories,* 1939; *The Picnic,* 1941; *The Best Stories of Walter de la Mare,* 1942; *The Old Lion, and Other Stories,* 1942; *The Magic Jacket, and Other Stories,* 1943; *The Scarecrow, and Other Stories,* 1945; *The Dutch Cheese, and Other Stories,* 1946; *Collected Stories for Children,* 1947; *A Beginning, and Other Stories,* 1955; *Ghost Stories,* 1956; *Short Stories, 1895-1926,* 1996 (Giles de la Mare, editor); *Short Stories, 1927-1956,* 2001 (Giles de la Mare, editor).

PLAY: *Crossings: A Fairy Play,* pr. 1919.

POETRY: *Songs of Childhood,* 1902; *Poems,* 1906; *A Child's Day: A Book of Rhymes,* 1912; *The Listeners, and Other Poems,* 1912; *Peacock Pie: A Book of Rhymes,* 1913; *The Sunken Garden, and Other Poems,* 1917; *Motley, and Other Poems,* 1918; *Flora: A Book of Drawings,* 1919; *Poems 1901 to 1918,* 1920; *Story and Rhyme,* 1921; *The Veil, and Other Poems,* 1921; *Down-Adown-Derry: A Book of Fairy Poems,* 1922; *Thus Her Tale,* 1923; *A Ballad of Christmas,* 1924; *Stuff and Nonsense and So On,* 1927; *Self to Self,* 1928; *The Snowdrop,* 1929; *News,* 1930; *Poems for Children,* 1930; *Lucy,* 1931; *Old Rhymes and New,* 1932; *The Fleeting, and Other Poems,* 1933; *Poems, 1919 to 1934,* 1935; *This Year, Next Year,* 1937; *Memory, and Other Poems,* 1938; *Haunted,* 1939; *Bells and Grass,* 1941; *Collected Poems,* 1941; *Collected Rhymes and Verses,* 1944; *The Burning-Glass, and Other Poems,* 1945; *The Traveller,* 1946; *Rhymes and Verses: Collected Poems for Young People,* 1947; *Inward Companion,* 1950; *Winged Chariot,* 1951; *O Lovely England, and Other Poems,* 1953; *The Complete Poems,* 1969.

NONFICTION: *Rupert Brooke and the Intellectual Imagination,* 1919; *The Printing of Poetry,* 1931; *Lewis Carroll,* 1932; *Poetry in Prose,* 1936; *Pleasures and Speculations,* 1940; *Chardin, J.B.S., 1699-1779,* 1948; *Private View,* 1953.

EDITED TEXTS: *Come Hither,* 1923; *The Shakespeare Songs,* 1929; *Christina Rossetti's Poems,* 1930; *Desert Islands and Robinson Crusoe,* 1930; *Stories from the Bible,* 1930; *Early One Morning in the Spring,* 1935; *Animal Stories,* 1939; *Behold, This Dreamer!,* 1939; *Love,* 1943.

BIBLIOGRAPHY

Campbell, James. "A Kind of Magic." *The Guardian,* June 10, 2006. Profile of de la Mare, written on the fiftieth anniversary of his death, focuses primarily on the writer's life but provides some information on his poetry and novels. Notes that although de la Mare's use of language was "at odds with the realism of his contemporaries," he became one of England's "best-loved poets and storytellers."

Hopkins, Kenneth. *Walter de la Mare.* Rev. ed. London: Longmans, Green, 1957. Slim volume touches on de la Mare's life as well as his prose and verse writings, providing a useful introduction to the author. Hopkins, an ardent admirer of de la Mare, briefly examines all of his major works. Supplemented by a select bibliography.

McCrosson, Doris Ross. *Walter de la Mare*. New York: Twayne, 1966. Presents a good critical introduction to de la Mare. Examines at length his total literary output, concentrating particularly on the novels, which McCrosson argues are not only neglected but also contain the clearest statement of his vision of life. Points out that de la Mare's fascinating quest into the mysteries of life never coalesced into a coherent vision. Complemented by a chronology and a select bibliography.

Manwaring, Randle. "Memories of Walter de la Mare." *Contemporary Review* 264 (March, 1994): 148-152. Reminiscence by a longtime acquaintance of de la Mare comments on his style and his influence. Reflects de la Mare's childish delight in simple things that is so often reflected in his fiction.

Megroz, R. L. *Walter de la Mare: A Biographical and Critical Study*. London: Hodder & Stoughton, 1924. Classic work—more an appreciation than a critical examination—is the first book-length study of de la Mare's work. Megroz professes deep admiration for de la Mare, sketches a brief biography, comments on personal impressions, and then devotes the rest of his discussion to de la Mare's poetry.

Wagenknecht, Edward. *Seven Masters of Supernatural Fiction*. Westport, Conn.: Greenwood Press, 1991. Chapter on de la Mare includes a brief biographical sketch and discusses his fiction in the context of the English literary tradition. Addresses both the short and the long fiction, providing a succinct overview of de la Mare's body of work in prose.

Whistler, Theresa. *The Life of Walter de la Mare*. London: Duckworth, 2003. Interesting biography draws on previously unavailable information about the author. Includes discussion of de la Mare's novels; Whistler argues that de la Mare's work is deserving of serious critical reevaluation.

ANITA DESAI

Born: Mussoorie, India; June 24, 1937
Also known as: Anita Mazumbar

PRINCIPAL LONG FICTION
Cry, the Peacock, 1963
Voices in the City, 1965
Bye-Bye, Blackbird, 1971
Where Shall We Go This Summer?, 1975
Fire on the Mountain, 1977
Clear Light of Day, 1980
In Custody, 1984
Baumgartner's Bombay, 1988
Journey to Ithaca, 1995
Fasting, Feasting, 1999
The Zigzag Way, 2004

OTHER LITERARY FORMS

In addition to her novels, Anita Desai (duh-SI) has published many short stories. Her first story was published in 1957, when she was twenty years old. Since then, she has contributed stories to various magazines and periodicals, including the London publication *Envoy*; Indian periodicals *Quest*, *The Illustrated Weekly of India*, and *Miscellany*; and the American magazine *Harper's Bazaar*. Some of her stories have been collected in *Games at Twilight, and Other Stories* (1978) and *Diamond Dust: Stories* (2000). Desai has also written three books for children, *The Peacock Garden* (1974), *Cat on a Houseboat* (1976), and *The Village by the Sea: An Indian Family Story* (1982). Two of her works have been adapted to film: *The Village by the Sea* in 1992 and *In Custody* in 1993.

ACHIEVEMENTS

Anita Desai is among the more prominent Indian English novelists of the late twentieth and early twenty-first centuries. With her first novel, *Cry, the Peacock* (1963), she added a new psychological dimension to Indian English fiction. Desai was probably the first Indian English novelist to be concerned primarily with the inner lives of her characters—their fleeting moods, wisps of memory, subtle cerebrations. In her novels, Desai succeeds in capturing these evanescent moments of consciousness, preserving them from oblivion and investing them with the permanence of art. The result is that Desai not only creates something of value for herself out of the endless flux of her own psyche but also provides for readers the opportunity to share this rich inner life through her characters.

Desai's stylistic accomplishment is noteworthy as well. Unlike many other Indian

English novelists, Desai does not find it necessary to experiment with language. In her novels, no clash between English, her medium of expression, and the Indian subject matter is apparent. Indeed, her use of the language is natural and unselfconscious. Her writing is both supple and precise. Though each sentence is carefully crafted, the overall manner is easy, not precious or labored. Stylistically, Desai is thus in the mainstream of twentieth century English novelists.

Desai is a writer of considerable achievement, perhaps the best contemporary Indian English woman novelist. Critical interest in her work has grown steadily since her first novel was published. She received the Royal Society of Literature Winifred Holtby Prize in 1978 and the Sahitya Akademi of India Award in 1979; she has been a member of the Sahitya Akademi English Board since 1972, a fellow of the Royal Society of Literature since 1978, a fellow of Girton College, Cambridge, and a visiting fellow at Balliol College, Oxford. For *The Village by the Sea* she received the Guardian Award for children's fiction in 1982. Her novels *Clear Light of Day, In Custody,* and *Fasting, Feasting* were all short-listed for the Booker Prize.

Biography

Anita Mazumbar was born in Mussoorie, India, and grew up in Delhi. Her father, D. N. Mazumdar, was a Bengali businessman, and her mother, Toni, was German. Her parents met when her father was a student in Germany; they married and then moved to India in the late 1920's. As a child, Desai spoke German at home and Hindi to her friends and neighbors. She then learned English once she started school. She grew up during the World War II years of the late 1930's and early 1940's, sensing the anxiety in her mother about the situation in Germany. Fearing the devastation and change wrought by the war, Desai's mother never returned to Germany, a fact that probably inspired some of the facets of the character Hugo Baumgartner in Desai's novel *Baumgartner's Bombay.*

Desai was educated at Queen Mary's School, Delhi, and then at Miranda House at the University of Delhi. At Miranda House she studied English literature, receiving her B.A. in 1957. Her studies helped to fuel her passion for writing, a compulsion that began at the age of seven. After working for a year in Max Muller Bhavan, Calcutta (now known as Kolkata), she married Ashwin Desai, a business executive, in 1958. Since then, she has lived in Kolkata, Mumbai (formerly known as Bombay), Chandigarh, Delhi, and Pune. She and her husband had four children: Rahul, Tani, Arjun, and Kiran.

Desai's writing came to be respected worldwide, and she became a fellow of the Royal Society of Literature in London and of the American Academy of Arts and Letters in New York, as well as a fellow of Girton College, Cambridge. Desai has taught writing at both Smith College and Mount Holyoke College in the United States. In 1993 she became a professor of writing at Massachusetts Institute of Technology.

ANALYSIS

Anita Desai's novels reveal certain recurring patterns in plots, settings, and character-izations. The plots of her novels fuse two opposing propensities—one toward the gothic mystery and the other toward the philosophical novel. The gothic orientation, which Desai probably derived from Emily Brontë's *Wuthering Heights* (1847), is evident in varying degrees in all her novels. *Fire on the Mountain*, the novel that comes closest to being purely a psychological thriller, ends with a half-insane, reptilelike child setting fire to the forest surrounding her house; in *Cry, the Peacock*, Maya, the neurotic heroine, kills her husband, thereby fulfilling the prophecy of an albino sorcerer; in *Voices in the City*, Monisha, an unsettled, manic-depressive housewife, pours kerosene over herself and burns herself to death. On the other hand, most of Desai's novels also contain a deep-rooted, philosophical concern about the meaning of life. From Maya to Matteo, most of Desai's protagonists, dissatisfied with their routine existence, search for a more meaning-ful life. Such a spiritual orientation is reminiscent of similar concerns in novels such as E. M. Forster's *Howards End* (1910) and Virginia Woolf's *Between the Acts* (1941).

Desai's novels also evolve a typical setting or "world" of their own. Most are set in the city, which comes to represent the undesirable, unimaginative reality; most also have a ro-mantic counterpoint to the city in a hill station or an island that seems to represent the re-mote, romantic, ideal but is revealed to be an unreal or unsatisfying delusion. At the hearts of the novels are usually big, old houses with several verandas, green shutters, gardens, servants, and pets. The garden is extremely important in Desai's world because her char-acters show an unusual sensitivity to it. Trees, creepers, tendrils, flowers, fruits, seasons, pets—the concerns of the so-called woman's world—are more vividly perceived in Desai's novels than anywhere else in Indian English fiction. Also part of Desai's world is a brooding, Faulknerian obsession with the past; the present is usually seen by the charac-ters as a decadent remnant, a husk of a glamorous past. Finally, the characters are all mem-bers of the upper class who belong to once-affluent, now-decaying families. The city, the hill station, the big house with a garden, a decadent family, an obsession with the past—these make up the typical world of a Desai novel.

Desai's protagonists can be divided into essentially two types: One type possesses a neurotic, hypersensitive, artistic sensibility; the other is cynical, tough, and acerbic. Maya, Monisha, Sarah, Sita, Tara, and Matteo belong to the first category, while Nirode, Amla, Dev, Nanda, Bim, and Sophie belong to the second. In addition to these are two types of supporting characters: the old, ugly, sterile crone, who has been a failure, and the mysteri-ous, insulated character, intriguing but ultimately inscrutable. The best example of the for-mer is Ila Das of *Fire on the Mountain*; of the latter, Dharma of *Voices in the City*. The rest of the characters are the common crowd against whom the protagonist defines him- or herself: They have given up trying to make their lives meaningful and have accepted the full mediocrity of a futile existence. Against such a backdrop, Desai's protagonists strug-gle to come to terms with their lives. They are usually in a state of conflict, either with themselves or with their environment. The results of this basic conflict are murder, insanity, suicide, compromise, death, or, in the rare instance of Desai's best novel, *Clear Light of Day*, balance, reconciliation, rich acceptance of reality, and a resolution of the conflict.

In the mid-1980's, Desai started to look more closely at the lives of the less privileged. *In Custody* is an ironic story told with humor about literary traditions and academic illusions in a world dominated by men. The central characters are Nur, an Urhi poet, who has fallen on hard times, and Deven, a professor of Hindi. In *Baumgartner's Bombay*, Desai goes back to her parental heritage as she zeroes in on a German Jew who seeks refuge in India. *Journey to Ithaca* is much like *Baumgartner's Bombay* in that it also approaches India through Europeans who are attracted to the mystic India.

Desai's novels since the mid-1990's have continued to explore a concern with imagery built on places, cities that affect her characters who are uprooted or alienated, living away from their homelands and disturbed by their own inner conflicts. In *Fasting, Feasting*, Desai contrasts the American and Indian cultures as well as male and female roles, as Arun leaves India to study in Massachusetts while his sister Uma lives in a small provincial city in India. In *The Zigzag Way*, Desai departs from her familiar territories, setting her story of self-discovery in twentieth century Mexico.

CRY, THE PEACOCK

Cry, the Peacock, Desai's first novel, is divided into three sections: a short introduction and conclusion in objective, third-person narrative, and a long subjective middle section narrated by the neurotic heroine, Maya. In Maya's narrative, Desai employs stream of consciousness to fill in details of Maya's past and to chronicle the progressive deterioration of both Maya's relationship with her husband, Gautama, and her own mental poise and sanity. In the climax, Maya, a slave to the fate she has feared, kills Gautama in accordance with the prophecy of an astrologer. The novel ends with her total mental collapse.

Maya is the sensitive, poetic, intuitive, and unstable type of personality that appears consistently in Desai's fiction. She is extremely sensitive to the beauty around her—the flowers and fruits in the garden, the trees and plants, the sky and the seasons, her pets and other animals—in brief, the whole gamut of nature. Gautama, her husband, is her opposite: He is insensitive to transient beauty; a pure rationalist, he is concerned only with absolutes. The characters' names themselves epitomize their irreconcilability: Maya means "illusion," and Gautama is the name of the Buddha, who was able to rend the veil of maya. Thus, while Maya revels in the world of the senses, Gautama rejects it entirely. According to the astrologer's prophecy, one of them must die. Maya decides to kill Gautama because, in her view, he has rejected all that makes life worth living; hence, to her, he is already "dead." Unable to resolve her conflict with Gautama, Maya pushes him from a terrace, thereby terminating her struggle.

VOICES IN THE CITY

Desai's second novel, *Voices in the City*, is more ambitious than her first but also noticeably flawed. The narrative centers on the effect of Calcutta on Nirode and his two sisters, Monisha and Amla. The novel is divided into three sections: "Nirode," "Monisha," and "Amla." Nirode is the first of Desai's tough, cynical protagonists, a type that finds fruition in Bim, the heroine of *Clear Light of Day*, fifteen years later. Nirode, realizing that his uncreative job at a respectable newspaper will never allow him to live meaningfully, quits. He refuses support from his rich, widowed mother, who lives in the hills; instead, he sinks from failure to failure, cynically awaiting the bottom. He starts a magazine that fails after a brief run; his subsequent attempts to be a writer fail, too, when his brutally honest play is rejected by a theater group. Nirode envisions himself as fighting Calcutta, the city of Kali, the city that destroys all that is worthwhile in its denizens. Surrounded by quitters, he refuses to compromise, to succumb to an existence he despises.

Monisha, Nirode's elder sister, is the sensitive, neurotic type, like Maya in *Cry, the Peacock*. Married into a traditional Bengali family, she has, to all appearances, accepted the compromise of a routine existence. In fact, however, Monisha leads a secretive inner life that is inviolate despite the ugliness of her surroundings. For example, her inability to bear a child symbolizes her refusal to allow another life into what is, to her, a meaningless and loathsome world. Her section of the novel—a sort of compressed version of Maya's long narrative in *Cry, the Peacock*—takes the form of a diary. Amla, the youngest sibling, is a muted version of Nirode. Beneath the surface, all three characters struggle against Calcutta, fighting to preserve their inner integrity. Of the three, Amla seems the most likely to succeed because she has neither the excessive cynicism of Nirode nor the neurosis of Monisha.

An interesting minor character is Dharma ("righteousness"), the unflappable painter who has left Calcutta but who, upon discovering an ideal model in Amla, returns, following a drastic revolution in his painting. Though Dharma is shown to be the only character who has survived against Calcutta, his inscrutability renders him incomprehensible to Nirode and Amla, as well as to the reader.

The novel has a sensational climax and a somewhat contrived ending. Monisha triumphs by burning herself to death in her bathroom. Her death brings her mother down to Calcutta from the hills. Nirode has a vision of his mother as Kali, the preserver and the destroyer; apparently, his conflict is thus resolved. Nirode, therefore, becomes the initiate, and Amla's more promising efforts at wisdom are sidestepped. In fact, Amla is the only character out of the three whose spiritual growth is utterly convincing; after her encounter with Dharma, she becomes more reconciled to Calcutta. Disregarding the triviality of her job in an advertising agency, she manages to do something that truly satisfies her—making sketches for Professor Bose's translations from the *Panchatantra*. Amla's progress, however, is not allowed fruition; it is neglected in favor of the more artificial vision of Nirode. Part of the problem lies in Desai's definition of the central conflict in the novel; by pitting three individuals against an entire city, the novelist, in effect, disallows the possibility of a single creative, balanced, and happy person in the whole city. Such an opposition is precarious because the reader questions the stance of the protagonists instead of accepting the destructiveness of their environment. Thus, when Nirode's very ordinary mother, who has retreated to the hills, is suddenly revealed to be the goddess Kali, Nirode's vision and the novel's resolution seem to be mere impositions of the novelist.

BYE-BYE, BLACKBIRD

In Desai's third novel, *Bye-Bye, Blackbird*, the action shifts to England. The novel, like the two earlier works, has a tripartite structure: arrival, "Discovery and Recognition," and "Departure." The three main characters are Dev, who has recently arrived in London from India when the novel begins, his friend Adit, with whom he is staying, and Adit's British wife, Sarah. All three characters are in conflict with their environment. Sarah is an unstable wife (in the tradition of Maya and Monisha) who finds herself playing two roles, that of an Indian at home and that of a Britisher outside; all the while, she questions who she really is. Dev and Adit are, in a sense, doubles like Nirode and Amla. Dev is the more cynical and aggressive of the two, while Adit, though essentially the same, is muted at the beginning. The novel follows a pattern like that of Henry James's *The Ambassadors* (1903): Adit, who thought he had felt at home in England, returns to India, while Dev, the militant cynic who has reviled Adit for staying, takes Adit's place after his departure, accepting a job in Adit's firm and moving to Adit's apartment.

Bye-Bye, Blackbird is a satisfying novel partly because Desai builds an inevitability into the narrative; characters are subordinated to pattern and rhythm. Dev's and Adit's decisions, hence, do not have to be fully explained. Their conflicts are not resolved so much as exchanged; the pleasure at the end is as much formal as it is emotional.

WHERE SHALL WE GO THIS SUMMER?

In Desai's fourth novel, *Where Shall We Go This Summer?*, all of her pervasive themes return: the neurotic heroine, the dissatisfaction with the here and now, the obsessive search for the meaning of existence. Sita, the wife of an industrialist, is disgusted with her indifferent husband, her meaningless life in their Bombay flat, and her selfish, uncaring children. Her memory of an idyllic childhood with her father on a nearby island, Manori, keeps haunting her as a reminder of what life can be. After becoming pregnant with a fifth child, she decides not to continue the charade; she visits the island again to regain the secret magic of life that she had experienced as a child. To her dismay, she realizes that her father, instead of being the great leader she has thought him to be, was really a charlatan. She has glamorized the past, and she now realizes that her memory has deceived her. Completely disillusioned, she waits for her drab husband to take her back to Bombay.

Toward the close of the novel, Sita's conflict appears to have found its solution when she recalls a verse from D. H. Lawrence that has eluded her for a long time. With the recollection, she feels she knows all the answers and can explain everything to her husband.

This euphoria, however, is short-lived, ending with her realization that she cannot connect psychologically with her husband. The novel thus ends with a compromise after a false resolution; Sita is back where she began. Commenting that if she had been younger when she wrote the novel she might have ended it with Sita's suicide, Desai has explained that her less melodramatic conclusion is more in keeping with the realities of middle age. Hence, although Sita continues living, her conflict is not resolved; instead, she accepts defeat and compromise.

FIRE ON THE MOUNTAIN

In *Fire on the Mountain* Desai reverts to the psychological thriller form exemplified by her first novel. In this work the narrative builds to a superb pitch of suspense and tension, only to end in sensational melodrama: the rape and murder of an old, ugly woman and a forest fire started by a demented child. Embittered by the indifference and infidelity of her husband, worn out from the rearing of several children and grandchildren, and now abandoned by her relatives, Nanda Kaul lives alone in her mountaintop cottage in Kasauli, surrounded by a pine forest. She tries to conceal her bitterness and loneliness behind a facade of cold, cynical aloofness, pretending that she does not need anyone, that she is living in Kasauli out of choice, and that she is in happy retirement after a rich and fulfilling life. When Raka, her great-granddaughter, comes to live with her, Nanda's craving for contact is revived. She tries to win the child by various devices, telling her wild stories, going for walks with her, and bribing her with food. Raka, who is as inscrutable and self-sufficient as a reptile, rebuffs the old woman. Into this situation steps Ila Das, Nanda's childhood friend, a complete failure, a pathetic harridan who has descended into desperate poverty after the ruin of her once-rich, decadent family. It is only when Ila is raped and murdered that Nanda is willing to acknowledge the lie at the core of her life; just then, Raka, the strange, half-crazy child, informs her that she has set the forest on fire.

Fire on the Mountain is superbly narrated but does not aim at being much more than a thriller. Nanda's quest for a meaningful life is subordinated to the demands of the plot. The novel is interesting, however, for at least two reasons. First, the hill station, usually the romantic contrast to the anticreative life of the city, here becomes a horrifying place of ghosts, mad dogs, demented women, impoverished hags, lonely great-grandmothers living in illusions, and demented children; the fantasy has turned into a nightmare. To the Kasauli of *Fire on the Mountain*, even the Calcutta of *Voices in the City* seems preferable. Second, Ila and Raka are two of Desai's most disturbing characters: Both are consistently sketched in animal and reptile imagery, and both are, in a sense, unhinged. They represent the extremes of the fondness for the bizarre that lurks in all of Desai's fiction.

CLEAR LIGHT OF DAY

Clear Light of Day is one of Desai's most accomplished novels. In it, the typical elements of her art merge to create a unique artistic triumph. The plot, for example, is a fine blend of the gothic and the philosophical, each strengthening the other. The mysterious well in the back, the drowned cow, Mira Masi's alcoholic disintegration, Tara's fear that her mother was murdered by her father, Baba's idiocy—all these contribute to the final resolution of the novel. One by one, these events are put into their place by the two heroines, Bim and Tara; the mystery, horror, or shame enveloping these events is slowly peeled away, and the past emerges in a new light of clarity and understanding.

The setting of *Clear Light of Day* has the typical Desai elements—the ugly city, the large house with verandas, the garden, the servants' quarters, upper-class characters, and decadent families. These elements, however, are augmented by acute social observation and particularity of place and time. Not only the inner life of the characters but also their milieu is fully developed. Perhaps no other English novel so successfully immortalizes mid-twentieth century Delhi and its locales—Civil Lines, the old Delhi convent school, the Jamuna, Connaught Circus, Hindu College, Darya Ganj, Chandni Chowk, the Ridge, and the Lodi Gardens. *Clear Light of Day* is thus also valuable as a sociohistorical document, a feat rare in Desai's canon.

Desai's main concern, of course, remains with the characters and their conflicts. Bim is the tough, cynical heroine, the one who refuses to compromise. Tara is her softer, more sensitive, counterpart. Raja, the deserter, their brother, is Bim's double. Mira Masi and the sisters next door are the hags. Bakul, Tara's husband, is a shallower, stupider version of Gautama. Bim, Tara, and Raja share the same determination to live meaningfully, without compromise. At the beginning of the novel, when Tara returns to the old house, both sisters are equally distant from resolving their conflicts: While Tara is too weak, Bim is too harsh, too bitter. Both are uncertain about their past, about their relationships to each other and Raja, about the meaningfulness of their lives. Together, they slowly relive their entire past, which leads to a marvelous reconciliation in the last few pages of the novel. Bim, to her astonishment, realizes that Tara—despite her marriage to Bakul and several mundane years as the wife of a diplomat—whom she has always despised, is just like her, and that Tara, too, has managed to preserve her integrity. Tara and Bim reach a new understanding for the first time; through Tara, Bim at last relinquishes her grudge against Raja, reconciling herself to him again.

After Tara's departure, Bim and Baba listen to Mulk and his Guru; Mulk is not after all merely a slothful drunkard as Bim has thought—he *can* sing, he is an artiste. Bim realizes that she does not have to degenerate into another Mira Masi; she fathoms the truth of T. S. Eliot's line from *Four Quartets* (1943): "Time the destroyer is also time the preserver." Bim's conflict ceases, dissolves; she transcends her duality and her contradictions. She can face reality without bitterness or neurosis. Her fancy ceases to cheat her; her imagination no longer makes her despise the reality around her. Instead, she realizes that ordinary life has its moments of fulfillment too. *Clear Light of Day* thus ends in balance, harmony, reconciliation, and resolution, not in murder, suicide, death, insanity, or compromise, as do all of Desai's earlier novels and as does *Baumgartner's Bombay*.

BAUMGARTNER'S BOMBAY

In *Baumgartner's Bombay*, the main character is neither Indian nor English—he is a German Jew. The story follows Hugo Baumgartner from childhood in pre-World War II Germany to his death in Bombay, India. The novel, however, starts with the ending (though the reader cannot realize it until the actual end of the book) and then jumps to the middle of the story. Baumgartner's past is relayed in a series of flashbacks from his time in India.

Baumgartner is forced to leave Germany when the Nazis' rise to power can no longer be ignored. Indeed, by the time Baumgartner leaves, his father has already committed suicide after being sent to a concentration camp, though he was later released. Interestingly, Desai has said about *Baumgartner's Bombay* that she "wasn't writing about the Nazis. I was writing about random evil." Baumgartner himself never expresses much feeling about the injustices done to him; about his six years in a British internment camp for German nationals, Baumgartner protests that "they were not such bad days."

Baumgartner's escape from Germany takes him to Venice, where he is to catch a boat for India. Venice remains in Baumgartner's mind as a kind of paradise, despite the troubles he has there and the fact that he is in the city for less than a week. These fabled and probably half-imagined qualities of Venice contrast sharply with the squalor and degradation of Bombay and of Baumgartner's life there. In fact, he spends most of his time going from restaurant to restaurant trying to find scraps for the multitude of cats with which he shares his dingy little flat. Ironically, Baumgartner does die at the hands of a German, though not a Nazi; rather, a German junkie whom Baumgartner has offered a place to stay kills him for his silver trophies.

Baumgartner's Bombay marks a return for Desai to the twin themes of hopelessness and despair. Baumgartner, his aging friend Lotte, Julius Roth—all are stranded in India; none can return to Germany because the old Germany is gone forever, and they do not fit into the new Germany. Indeed, it is the new Germany that becomes the death of Baumgartner in the shape of the brutal junkie. Desai's picture of foreigners, or *firanghi*, as the Indians label these outcasts, is that they can never fit into Indian society no matter how hard they try. It is Desai's great talent, however, to be able to make these characters compelling despite their obvious fate, which is to be forgotten. They leave no mark or memory when they die, though Desai ensures that they remain with the reader long past the end of the novel.

JOURNEY TO ITHACA

Desai's ninth novel, *Journey to Ithaca*, continues certain structures and themes of the earlier novels. It, too, has three parts: prologue, text (divided into chapters), and epilogue. The characters' search for spiritual meaning prompts the action of the story. The title is an allusion to the Greek island home of Homer's Odysseus, who made one of fiction's greatest journeys.

Set in the 1970's, the story is about Sophie and Matteo, two wealthy Italian young people who travel to India on a lark. Matteo, the more emotionally sensitive of the two, is quickly swept up in the spirituality of India, and eventually the couple find themselves in an ashram run by a spiritual leader called Mother. The conflicts created by the personal nature of a journey to enlightenment are manifest as Sophie and Matteo produce two children. Matteo is drawn into the rhythms and beliefs of Mother's ashram, but Sophie, the more practical and cynical of the pair, cannot fathom the attraction, let alone the squalor and deprivation she experiences. Upset, she leaves India and returns to Italy with the children.

In time, Sophie is summoned back to India because Matteo is deathly ill; she leaves the children to go to him. Sick as he is, Matteo is an unrepentant follower of Mother and wishes only to continue his spiritual studies. Shocked and angered, Sophie begins her own journey to understand him. She literally traverses the world to learn who Mother is and how she came to command such devotion. She discovers that Mother was once a young Egyptian girl named Laila and that even as a child Laila sought deeper meaning in life. While attending school in Paris, Laila encountered a troupe of Indian dancers and was taken into the group by the charismatic male lead dancer, Krishna. Through the troupe she learned to employ her dance as a means to spirituality. The story of Laila and her ultimate arrival in India is interwoven with Sophie's search for her, and it introduces the third journey in the novel.

Journey to Ithaca relates the experiences of three people seeking enlightenment. Desai's contribution to this type of literature is that she illustrates the consequences of a spiritual journey, which by its very nature must be personal if not solitary. For the seeker, the arduousness of the search is a reward in itself. Moments of illumination, large or small, are worth striving for. On the journey, however, others are excluded. Matteo's devotion to Mother leaves no room for his family. Sophie at one point recognizes that she has abandoned her children in an obsessive search to discover the truth about Mother. Mother steps on the careers of others and abandons Krishna to seek God in the Himalayas. The journey to Ithaca is a difficult and sorrowful one.

The novel's construction emulates a journey to spiritual enlightenment; it does not follow a simple chronological pattern. The story begins when Sophie has been summoned back to India because Matteo is sick. It then returns to their children, Isabel and Giacomo, in Italy. Then it reverts to Matteo's childhood, his marriage to Sophie, and their trip to India. Next, the action returns to Italy, then back to India, followed by Sophie's pursuit of Mother, retracing her history from Egypt to Europe to the United States and finally back to India. The path to spirituality is a jagged one, sometimes moving forward, sometimes moving backward or even sideways.

FASTING, FEASTING

Desai's tenth novel, *Fasting, Feasting*, deals with themes of suppression and escape. It also deals with oppression and the objectification of women in a sensitive and thoughtful way. The story contrasts the cultures of the United States and India, particularly male and female roles in the two countries. The parents of the two main characters do not consider the possibility that their children have their own lives to live; daughter Uma is a victim of patriarchy, and son Arun is trapped in the education meant to liberate him. The title *Fasting, Feasting* signifies deprivation and abundance, whether of food or of emotional sustenance. Uma is deprived of attention, and Arun is deprived of his freedom of choice. Feasting can be identified in the excesses and opulence in the American lifestyle to which Arun is exposed.

The story depicts the struggles of Arun and his older sister Uma as the siblings attempt to strike a balance between their parents' expectations and their own. Arun studies in Massachusetts while Uma lives in a small provincial Indian city with their parents, to whom she refers collectively as "MamaPapa." Structured in two parts, the story is told first from Uma's point of view, then from Arun's. The first part takes place in India and tells the story of Uma, the eldest daughter of an educated Indian family; the father is a lawyer, but he is provincial and traditional at heart. Uma is not necessarily ugly but she is awkward; her younger sister, Aruna, is the pretty and vivacious one who makes a successful marriage. Uma's celebrated younger brother, Arun, makes it to the United States to study. Meanwhile, Uma stays at home to serve their parents, embarrassed by one failed attempt after another to marry her off; Uma's every chance to find some freedom and space is thwarted by her possessive parents. Even if Uma is not smart, she has a kind heart and a strong willpower, and she grows immensely in spirit throughout the life-changing events in her life, so that by the end of the novel she finds a place for herself in Indian society where she can show her individuality.

The second part of the book focuses on Arun, Uma's younger brother who is attending college in Massachusetts. During the summer, when school is out, he stays with a local family, the Pattons. This section of the book comments on American society through the Patton family, particularly the diminishment of the family structure in the United States and the American obsession with materialism. It also touches on the issue of eating disorders. Arun's childhood was one of oppression—he has been constantly coached and pushed by a domineering father, and initially when he was sent to the United States, his life was still farmed out to family friends through an arrangement made back in India. Arun changes and grows through his experiences in the United States, however. At the American university, Arun finds himself isolated in every way from his peers and from his culture, even others from India. His isolation is more or less his own choice; after his oppressive upbringing, he wants space and freedom. His isolation echoes Uma's as she escapes to the privacy of her room in India—the siblings are in different cultures, but they are equally sad.

Makarand Paranjape; Judith L. Steininger
Updated by Tel Asiado

OTHER MAJOR WORKS

SHORT FICTION: *Games at Twilight, and Other Stories*, 1978; *Diamond Dust: Stories*, 2000.

SCREENPLAY: *In Custody*, 1993 (adaptation of her novel; with Shahrukh Husain).

CHILDREN'S LITERATURE: *The Peacock Garden*, 1974; *Cat on a Houseboat*, 1976; *The Village by the Sea: An Indian Family Story*, 1982.

BIBLIOGRAPHY

Afzal-Khan, Fawzia. *Cultural Imperialism and the Indo-English Novel: Genre and Ideology in R. K. Narayan, Anita Desai, Kamala Markandaya, and Salman Rushdie*. University Park: Pennsylvania State University Press, 1993. Scholarly examination of postcolonial Indian fiction places Desai's work in historical context.

Bande, Usha. *The Novels of Anita Desai: A Study in Character and Conflict*. New Delhi: Prestige Books, 1988. Briefly surveys the critical material written on Desai and then provides detailed discussion of each of her novels up to *In Custody*.

Budholia, O. P. *Anita Desai: Vision and Technique in Her Novels*. Delhi: B. R., 2001. Presents a formalistic analysis of Desai's work.

Choudhury, Bidulata. *Women and Society in the Novels of Anita Desai*. New Delhi: Creative Books, 1995. Focuses on Desai's treatment of female characters and their circumstances.

Dash, Sandhyarani. *Form and Vision in the Novels of Anita Desai*. New Delhi: Prestige, 1996. Examines the style of Desai's writing and the themes that recur throughout her works. Includes bibliographical references and an index.

Jena, Seema. *Voice and Vision of Anita Desai*. New Delhi: Ashish, 1989. Concentrates on the place of Desai among female Indian novelists, with discussion of the individual novels' plots and characters.

Khanna, Shashi. *Human Relationships in Anita Desai's Novels*. New Delhi: Sarup & Sons, 1995. Offers a thoughtful examination of Desai's characters and their relationships. Includes bibliographical references.

Prasad, V. V. N. Rajendra. *Five Indian Novelists: B. Rajan, Raja Raa, R. K. Narayan, Arun Jashi, Anita Desai*. Oxford, England: Advent Books, 1997. Presents a study of the self, family, and society in the novels of the five authors.

Rege, Josna. "Codes in Conflict: Post-independence Alienation in Anita Desai's Early Novels." *Journal of Gender Studies* 5, no. 3 (November, 1996): 317-329. Provides a detailed discussion of *Cry, the Peacock*, *Voices in the City*, and *Where Shall We Go This Summer?* in the context of the conflict between the interests of Indian nationalists and women's interests in the postindependence era.

Tandon, Neeru. *Anita Desai and Her Fictional World*. New Delhi: Atlantic, 2008. Examines Desai's contributions to Indian English fiction, assessing the individual novels through *The Zigzag Way*.

DAPHNE DU MAURIER

Born: London, England; May 13, 1907
Died: Par, Cornwall, England; April 19, 1989
Also known as: Lady Daphne Browning

OTHER LITERARY FORMS

In addition to her many novels, Daphne du Maurier (dew MOHR-ee-ay) wrote and edited biographies, collections of letters, travel books, plays, and short stories. Her biographical works include *Gerald: A Portrait* (1934), the life story of her actor father; *The du Mauriers* (1937), the inside story of her famous family of actors, dramatists, and novelists; and *The Young George du Maurier: A Selection of His Letters, 1860-1867* (1951), a collection of her caricaturist-novelist grandfather's letters. She earned a place among playwrights with *The Years Between* (pr. 1944) and *September Tide* (pr. 1948). Her travel book *Vanishing Cornwall* (1967) describes the rugged coastal area of southwestern England, where she set so many of her novels and stories. Often weaving elements of the supernatural into her tales of mystery and romance, du Maurier produced several notable volumes of short stories, including *Echoes from the Macabre* in 1976 and *Classics of the Macabre* in 1987.

ACHIEVEMENTS

The theatrical quality of Daphne du Maurier's novels is evidenced by the frequency and reported ease with which her works have been adapted for the big screen. Alfred Hitchcock directed film versions of *Jamaica Inn* (1939) and her best-selling gothic novel *Rebecca* (1940). The latter won an Academy Award for Best Picture. Paramount Pictures released *Frenchman's Creek* in 1944, and Universal Pictures released a film adaptation of *Hungry Hill* in 1947, for which du Maurier herself wrote the first draft of the screenplay. *My Cousin Rachel* became a Twentieth Century Fox production in 1952, and Metro-Goldwyn-Mayer released *The Scapegoat* in 1959. Hitchcock turned her story "The Birds" into a highly successful motion picture of the same title in 1963, and her story "Don't Look Now" became a hit film in 1973.

Rebecca won an award from the American Booksellers' Association in 1939. In 1969, du Maurier was named a Dame Commander of the Order of the British Empire.

BIOGRAPHY

Daphne du Maurier was born to a theatrical family. Her father, Gerald, was an actor and manager; her mother, Muriel Beaumont, was an actor. Du Maurier was educated in both England and France. Plagued from childhood by feelings of self-doubt and inadequacy, she turned to writing to achieve the solitude she desperately craved. She preferred fantasy to reality and shunned social engagements. She began writing stories and poems in her teens. By the time she was in her twenties, she was selling regularly to magazines such as *The Bystander* and the *Sunday Review.*

She wrote her first novel, *The Loving Spirit*, when she was only twenty-two years old. This romantic family saga earned both critical acclaim and best-seller status. It so impressed a major in the Grenadier Guards that he arranged a meeting with its author. The two soon developed an attachment, and in 1932 du Maurier married Major Frederick Arthur Montague Browning, whom she called Tommy. He later earned the rank of lieutenant general, became Chancellor of the Exchequer in the household of Princess Elizabeth, and became treasurer to the Duke of Edinburgh. The couple had three children: daughters Flavia and Tessa and son Christian. Browning died in 1965.

In 1943, du Maurier fulfilled a childhood dream and moved into Menabilly, a seventy-room manor house in Cornwall that inspired Manderley, the eerie setting for *Rebecca*. She adored the reputedly haunted house, asserting that it whispered its secrets to her in the solitude of midnight. Never one for social life, she preferred solitary walks in the woods to bustling cities and glittering social gatherings. Her family life was seldom serene, with du Maurier's troubled and erratic spirit manifesting itself in frequently problematic ways; in addition, Browning was plagued with psychological problems and poor physical health, both associated with his chronic abuse of alcohol.

A rocky marriage was only one of the writer's torments. Biographer Margaret Forster asserts that du Maurier's stories and novels reflected severe emotional turbulence. Du Maurier had, according to Forster, a stifling relationship with her father, a complicated extramarital affair, and a lesbian relationship with actor Gertrude Lawrence. The details of daily life troubled her, and she frequently retreated from family and friends to find solace in make-believe. Twice she faced plagiarism charges and endured the agonies of court hearings as a result of claims that she had stolen the second-wife theme used in *Rebecca*. Although she was acquitted in both instances, the publicity wearied and shamed her, and she grew increasingly reclusive in later life. Du Maurier died in Cornwall, England on April 19, 1989.

ANALYSIS

Daphne du Maurier came naturally by her dramatic bent. Having eschewed a career in acting, she turned instead to writing, creating the settings of her novels as a vivid stage on which her melodramas could unfold. Most often, she wrote about what she knew: the craggy, tempestuous coasts and climate of Cornwall. With the playwright's flare, she elicited as much suspense from her setting as from her characters and plots. Du Maurier yearned to write light romance, but it was not in her nature. "I may determine to write a gay, light romance. But I go for a walk on a moor and see a twisted tree and a pile of granite stones beside a deep, dark pool, and *Jamaica Inn* is born," she told *Current Biography* in 1940. Du Maurier's readers can only be glad for the writer's solitary walks, for *Jamaica Inn* and the writer's many other haunting novels and stories rank among the finest spine-tingling page turners ever written. Her books contain passion, jealousy, evil, and murder, with surprise heaped upon surprise.

While du Maurier's works may not probe the depths of human experience, they create worlds and peoples that haunt long after the books are finished. Du Maurier believed in her own brand of predestination, a reincarnation of the human spirit. Evil is inevitable, in her view, but not insurmountable. People are, however, condemned by their very nature to a vision that exceeds their grasp. Du Maurier's interest in character took a backseat to her fascination with personality types symbolic of abstract qualities of good and evil. She told Barbara Nichols in an interview for *Ladies' Home Journal*,

> I am not so much interested in people as in types—types who represent great forces of good or evil. I don't care very much whether John Smith likes Mary Robinson, goes to bed with Jane Brown and then refuses to pay the hotel bill. But I *am* [emphasis in original] passionately interested in human cruelty, human lust, and human avarice—and, of course, their counterparts in the scale of virtue.

Although critics have complained about her melodrama, plot contrivances, shallow characterization, romanticism, sentimentality, vague motivations, and moralizing, such commentary probably misses the point. Du Maurier's unfailing appeal to her readers is fundamental: She tells a good story, and she tells it well. Unsurpassed as a teller of gothic tales tinged with horror or the supernatural, she is worth studying if only for her pacing, which moves from plot twist to plot twist with consummate ease. A romance writer in the best sense of the label, she creates engaging heroines blessed with immense inner strength. Her heroes helped to establish the model for modern romances: dark of complexion, dark of spirit, silent, enigmatic, harboring some unspeakable secret. Her settings evoke the foreboding ambience of Cornwall's precipitous cliffs and misty moors, the perfect backdrop for the dramatic events that so astonish and delight du Maurier's readers.

REBECCA

Among the most memorable opening lines in English literature is the first sentence of du Maurier's best-known work, *Rebecca*: "Last night I dreamt I went to Manderley again." In a landscape of words, du Maurier takes her readers to Manderley to hear the rustle of leaves, smell the flowers in the garden, luxuriate in the opulence of the estate's drawing room. As ominous waves pound the Cornish coast, the dark tale unfolds. Maxim de Winter, the brooding, detached master of Manderley, marries in haste while abroad and brings his new bride home to Cornwall. The new Mrs. de Winter (whose given name is never revealed) recounts her tale entirely in flashback, compelling the reader to stay with her as the reason for her departure from Manderley is slowly brought to light.

What begins as a Cinderella story—this young girl of modest means swept off her feet by a wealthy, powerful gentleman—soon turns sinister. The narrator is haunted by the lingering influence of Maxim's first wife, Rebecca, who died in a sailing accident. Rebecca's presence is perpetually felt; even the name of Rebecca's boat, *Je reviens* (French for "I return"), suggests its owner will not depart, either in body or in spirit. Manderley itself seems keeper of Rebecca's mystique, with its forbidden halls, haunted rooms, and secret passages accidentally discovered. Beautiful, witty, flirtatious, and strong, Rebecca looms large—her power all the greater, even as a memory, for its contrast to the reticent nature of de Winter's diffident second bride. The narrator imagines she can hear Rebecca calling to the dogs and Rebecca's evening dress rustling on the stairs. The housekeeper, Mrs. Danvers, exhibits fierce loyalty to the first Mrs. de Winter and sullen contempt for the second. She plots to displace the narrator from Manderley and drive a wedge between its master and mistress.

The ensuing labyrinth of deceptions, betrayals, and revelations spellbinds readers and proves that the new Mrs. de Winter is not without resources. Determined to uncover the truth and break free of Rebecca's legacy, she counters the housekeeper's wicked lies and her husband's silent brooding with a resolute search for the truth. In a surprise ending, she rises whole and victorious, her nightmare ended and justice served. Manderley was great and corrupt, just as was Max's dead wife. Readers find it satisfying to learn that love can be deep and enduring enough to overcome an adversary as powerful as Rebecca.

JAMAICA INN

Critics praised *Jamaica Inn* as a tale nineteenth century adventure writer Robert Louis Stevenson would have been proud to write, and du Maurier admitted it was similar to—and inspired by—his *Treasure Island* (1883). The rain-swept Cornish coast in raw November portends danger, but orphan Mary Yellan is determined to keep the promise she made to her dying mother—to make her home with her victimized Aunt Patience and brutish Uncle Joss. Working at the dilapidated Jamaica Inn, where thieves and smugglers come to divide their spoils and pirates plot their next raids, Mary discovers a secret about her father's death. Alone and afraid, Mary feels a sexual (although not romantic) attraction to Jem Merlyn, Joss's younger brother and a domineering ruffian not above violence. In the background lurks the mysterious vicar of Altarnum, who hides a few secrets of his own. With its twisted motives, midnight crimes, smugglers, and secrets, this is du Maurier at her best. Although depicting a rather pessimistic view of the plight of women as helpless and subservient, the fast-paced adventure gains fresh popularity with each new generation of readers who discover it.

THE HOUSE ON THE STRAND

In du Maurier's penultimate novel, *The House on the Strand* (the last among five du Maurier books featuring a male protagonist), the narrator, Dick, travels back to fourteenth century England, his journeys made possible by an experimental drug concocted by his scientist friend and mentor, Magnus. A stereotypical "nice guy," Dick marries an American who is already mother to two sons. Dick is no fan of women (including his wife), judging the feminine point of view trivial and restrictive, but he changes his mind when he becomes entranced with Isolda, a woman of the fourteenth century who is saddled with a faithless husband. Dick develops as a pathetic character who longs for perceived glories of the past but can find no fulfillment in any epoch, past or present.

Combining historical fact with psychological analysis, the book paints the same haunting atmosphere so apparent in du Maurier's earlier works, this time using the Kilmarth house in Cornwall and its rich history as both setting and theme. Dick's unwillingness to be pulled away from his time travels reflects du Maurier's own total immersion in her fantasy worlds. When writing, she lost herself in the lives of her characters, finding real life little more than a distraction and an annoyance.

Faith Hickman Brynie

OTHER MAJOR WORKS

SHORT FICTION: *Come Wind, Come Weather*, 1940; *Happy Christmas*, 1940; *The Apple Tree: A Short Novel and Some Stories*, 1952 (also known as *The Birds, and Other Stories* and as *Kiss Me Again, Stranger: A Collection of Eight Stories*); *Early Stories*, 1955; *The Breaking Point*, 1959 (also known as *The Blue Lenses, and Other Stories*); *The Treasury of du Maurier Short Stories*, 1960; *Not After Midnight, and Other Stories*, 1971 (also known as *Don't Look Now*); *Echoes from the Macabre*, 1976; *The Rendezvous, and Other Stories*, 1980; *Classics of the Macabre*, 1987.

PLAYS: *Rebecca: A Play in Three Acts*, pr. 1940 (adaptation of her novel); *The Years Between*, pr. 1944; *September Tide*, pr. 1948.

NONFICTION: *Gerald: A Portrait*, 1934; *The du Mauriers*, 1937; *The Infernal World of Branwell Brontë*, 1960; *Vanishing Cornwall*, 1967; *Golden Lads: Sir Francis Bacon, Anthony Bacon, and Their Friends*, 1975; *The Winding Stair: Francis Bacon, His Rise and Fall*, 1976; *Growing Pains: The Shaping of a Writer*, 1977 (also known as *Myself When Young: The Shaping of a Writer*); *The Rebecca Notebook, and Other Memories*, 1980; *Letters from Menabilly: Portrait of a Friendship*, 1994 (Oriel Malet, editor).

EDITED TEXTS: *The Young George du Maurier: A Selection of His Letters, 1860-1867*, 1951; *Best Stories of Phyllis Bottome*, 1963.

BIBLIOGRAPHY

Auerbach, Nina. *Daphne du Maurier, Haunted Heiress*. Philadelphia: University of Pennsylvania Press, 1999. Auerbach discusses her literary passion for du Maurier and demonstrates how du Maurier's work has been inaccurately categorized as romance fiction. Includes a chapter on du Maurier's family that examines how du Maurier's fiction was a reaction to her male heritage.

Cook, Judith. *Daphne: A Portrait of Daphne du Maurier*. London: Bantam Books, 1991. Thorough biography offers perceptive insights into du Maurier's life and work.

Du Maurier, Daphne. *Letters from Menabilly: Portrait of a Friendship*. Edited by Oriel Malet. New York: M. Evans, 1994. Presents a selection of du Maurier's correspondence with writer Oriel Malet, which took place for about thirty years beginning in the 1950's.

Forster, Margaret. *Daphne du Maurier: The Secret Life of the Renowned Storyteller*. New York: Doubleday, 1993. A candid, meticulous, and riveting biography, prepared with cooperation of the du Maurier family after du Maurier's death. Focuses on the motivations behind the author's works.

Horner, Avril, and Sue Zlosnik. *Daphne du Maurier: Writing, Identity, and the Gothic Imagination*. New York: St. Martin's Press, 1998. Evaluates du Maurier's fiction from historical, cultural, geographic, and female gothic literary perspectives. In addition to a discussion of *Rebecca*, presents analyses of her lesser-known novels, including *I'll Never Be Young Again* and *The Flight of the Falcon*.

Kelly, Richard Michael. *Daphne du Maurier*. Boston: Twayne, 1987. Provides a solid introduction to the author's works. Includes bibliography and index.

Leng, Flavia. *Daphne du Maurier: A Daughter's Memoir*. Edinburgh: Mainstream, 1994. In recounting her childhood, Leng provides a powerful portrait of her mother, Daphne du Maurier. Describes du Maurier's love for Cornwall and her estrangement from family and friends.

Taylor, Helen, ed. *The Daphne du Maurier Companion*. London: Virago, 2007. Collection of essays presents a reassessment of du Maurier's work, with essays examining her novels, short stories, and biographies. Includes analyses of the film adaptations of her works, such as director Alfred Hitchcock's films *Rebecca* and *The Birds*.

L. P. HARTLEY

Born: Whittlesea, England; December 30, 1895
Died: London, England; December 13, 1972
Also known as: Leslie Poles Hartley

PRINCIPAL LONG FICTION

Simonetta Perkins, 1925
The Shrimp and the Anemone, 1944
The Sixth Heaven, 1946
Eustace and Hilda, 1947
The Boat, 1949
My Fellow Devils, 1951
The Go-Between, 1953
A Perfect Woman, 1955
The Hireling, 1957
Facial Justice, 1960
The Brickfield, 1964
The Betrayal, 1966
Poor Clare, 1968
The Love-Adept, 1969
My Sisters' Keeper, 1970
The Harness Room, 1971
The Collections, 1972
The Will and the Way, 1973

OTHER LITERARY FORMS

L. P. Hartley published, in addition to eighteen novels, six collections of short stories: *Night Fears* (1924), *The Killing Bottle* (1932), *The Traveling Grave* (1948), *The White Wand* (1954), *Two for the River* (1961), and *Mrs. Carteret Receives* (1971). Reprinted in *The Complete Short Stories of L. P. Hartley* (1973), with the exception of ten apprentice pieces from *Night Fears*, the stories reveal Hartley's reliance on the gothic mode. At their least effective, they are workmanlike tales utilizing conventional supernatural machinery. At their best, however, they exhibit a spare symbolic technique used to explore individual human personalities and to analyze the nature of moral evil. The best of Hartley's ghost and horror stories include "A Visitor from Down Under," "Feet Foremost," and "W. S.," the last dealing with an author murdered by a character of his own creation. "Up the Garden Path," "The Pampas Clump," and "The Pylon" deal more directly with the theme central to Hartley's major fiction: the acquisition, on the part of an innocent, even morally naïve, protagonist, of an awareness of the existence of evil.

A frequent lecturer, and a reviewer for such periodicals as *The Observer*, *Saturday Review*, and *Time and Tide* from the early 1920's to the middle 1940's, Hartley published a volume of essays titled *The Novelist's Responsibility: Lectures and Essays* (1967), in which he deplored the twentieth century devaluation of a sense of individual moral responsibility. These essays explain Hartley's fictional preoccupation with identity, moral values, and spiritual insight. His choice of subjects, particularly the works of Jane Austen, Emily Brontë, Nathaniel Hawthorne, and Henry James, suggests the origins of the realistic-symbolic technique he employs in both his short stories and his novels.

ACHIEVEMENTS

While L. P. Hartley's novels from *Simonetta Perkins* to *Facial Justice* were published in the United States, they did not enjoy the popularity there that they earned in England. *The Go-Between*, for example, continued to be in print in England since its publication in 1953, and the *Eustace and Hilda* trilogy—comprising *The Shrimp and the Anemone*, *The Sixth Heaven*, and *Eustace and Hilda*—was given a radio dramatization by the British Broadcasting Corporation (BBC). In the course of a literary career of roughly fifty years, Hartley came to be a noted public figure, and his work received favorable attention from Lord David Cecil, Walter Allen, and John Atkins. Only in the United States, however, did his novels receive detailed critical attention. The three full-length studies of his fiction— Peter Bien's *L. P. Hartley* (1963), Anne Mulkeen's *Wild Thyme, Winter Lightning: The Symbolic Novels of L. P. Hartley* (1974), and Edward T. Jones's *L. P. Hartley* (1978)—are all American, as are the notable treatments of Hartley's work by James Hall and Harvey Curtis Webster.

BIOGRAPHY

Born on December 30, 1895, near Whittlesea in Cambridgeshire, Leslie Poles Hartley was named for Sir Leslie Stephen, the father of Virginia Woolf and himself a noted late Victorian literary man. According to Edward T. Jones, whose book *L. P. Hartley* contains the most complete biographical account, Hartley's mother, Mary Elizabeth Thompson, was the daughter of a farmer named William James Thompson of Crawford House, Crowland, Lincolnshire. His father, H. B. Hartley, was a solicitor, justice of the peace, and later director of the successful brickworks founded by the novelist's paternal grandfather. This information figures as part of the background to Hartley's *The Brickfield* and *The Betrayal*.

Hartley was the second of his parents' three children; he had an older sister, Enid, and a younger, Annie Norah. None of the three ever married. Reared at Fletton Tower, near Peterborough, Hartley was educated at Harrow and Balliol College, Oxford, his stay at the latter interrupted by military service as a second lieutenant in the Norfolk Regiment during World War I. He was discharged for medical reasons and did not see action in France. In Oxford after the war, Hartley came into contact with a slightly younger generation of men, among them Anthony Powell, Graham Greene, and Evelyn Waugh. His closest literary friend at this period, however, may have been Lord David Cecil. After leaving Balliol with a second honours degree in 1921, Hartley worked as a reviewer for various periodicals, wrote the stories later collected in *Night Fears* and *The Killing Bottle*, and cultivated friendships with members of both bohemian Bloomsbury and British society. His novella *Simonetta Perkins*, a Jamesian story of a young American woman's inconclusive passion for a Venetian gondolier, was published in 1925.

Hartley made many trips to Venice. From 1933 to 1939, he spent part of each summer and fall there, and he drew on this experience for parts of *Eustace and Hilda*, *The Boat*, and *My Fellow Devils*. Returning to England just before the start of World War II, Hartley started work on the series of novels that earned for him a place in the British literary establishment. Given the James Tait Black Memorial Prize for *Eustace and Hilda* in 1947 and the Heinemann Foundation Prize for *The Go-Between* in 1953, he served as head of the British Association of Poets, Playwrights, Editors, Essayists and Novelists (PEN) and on the management committee of the Society of Authors. In 1956, he was created a Commander of the British Empire by Queen Elizabeth II. In his later years, Hartley gave frequent talks, most notably the Clark lectures delivered at Trinity College, Cambridge, in 1964. Joseph Losey won the Grand Prize at Cannes, France, in 1971 for a film version of *The Go-Between*, for which Harold Pinter wrote the script, and in 1973, Alan Bridges's film of *The Hireling*, from a script by Wolf Mankowitz, won the same prize. Hartley died in London on December 13, 1972.

ANALYSIS

Indebted to Bloomsbury, as shown by a concern with personal conduct and a highly impressionistic style, L. P. Hartley betrays affinities with D. H. Lawrence, Aldous Huxley, and George Orwell in a more fundamental concern with larger social and moral issues. His best books argue for the existence of a spiritual dimension to life and demonstrate that recognition of its motive force, even union of oneself with its will, is a moral imperative. In this emphasis on connection, his novels recall those of E. M. Forster, but unlike his predecessor, Hartley insists that the nature of the motive force is supernatural, even traditionally Christian. In his most successful books, Hartley draws upon elements of both novel and romance, as Richard Chase defines them in *The American Novel and Its Tradition* (1957), and the uniqueness of the resulting hybridization precludes comparisons with the work of most of his contemporaries.

Hartley's moral vision, revealed by the gradual integration of realism and symbolism in his novels, is the most striking characteristic of his long fiction. In a book such as *The Go-Between*, he shows that all people are subject to the power of love, even when they deny it, and that achievement of insight into love's capabilities is a prerequisite of achieving moral responsibility. This pattern of growth at the center of Hartley's novels is conventionally Christian in its outlines. The protagonist of each book, beginning with Eustace

Cherrington in the *Eustace and Hilda* trilogy, accepts his status as a "sinner" and experiences, if only briefly and incompletely, a semimystical transcendence of his fallen state.

The epiphanic technique Hartley develops in the trilogy to objectify these moments of insight recurs in various forms in all of his novels, coming in time to be embodied not in symbolism but in the pattern of action in which he casts his plots. Without suggesting that Hartley's fiction is about theology, it is clear that his concern with the subject of morality cannot avoid having religious overtones. Like Nathaniel Hawthorne, he traces the process of spiritual growth in innocent, morally self-assured, and thereby flawed personalities who experience temptation, even commit sins, and eventually attain spiritual kinship with their fellow people. These encounters, in a book such as *Facial Justice*, occur in settings symbolic of traditional religious values, and so while Hartley's novels may be read from psychoanalytic or mythic points of view, they are more fully comprehended from a metaphysical vantage point.

There is a thematic unity to all of Hartley's longer fiction, but after 1960, there is a marked decline in its technical complexity. In one sense, having worked out his thematic viewpoint in the process of fusing realism and symbolism in his earlier books, Hartley no longer feels the need to dramatize the encounter of good and evil and to set it convincingly in a realistic world. His last novels are fables, and in *The Harness Room*, the most successful of them, the lack of realism intensifies his treatment of the psychological and sexual involvement of an adolescent boy and his father's slightly older chauffeur. This book brings Hartley's oeuvre full circle, back to the story of the American spinster and the Venetian gondolier he produced in *Simonetta Perkins* at the start of his career.

EUSTACE AND HILDA TRILOGY

The three novels constituting the *Eustace and Hilda* trilogy—*The Shrimp and the Anemone, The Sixth Heaven*, and *Eustace and Hilda*—objectify a process of moral growth and spiritual regeneration to be found in or behind all of Hartley's subsequent fiction. The process is not unlike that which he describes, in the Clark lectures reprinted in *The Novelist's Responsibility*, as characteristic of Hawthorne's treatment of the redeeming experience of sin in *The Marble Faun* (1860). The epiphanic moments Hartley uses to dramatize his protagonist's encounters with Christ the Redeemer reveal truths that can be read on psychological, sociological, and theological levels.

In *The Shrimp and the Anemone*, Hartley depicts the abortive rebellion of Eustace Cherrington, aged nine, against the moral and psychological authority of his thirteen-year-old sister, Hilda. Set in the summers of 1905 and 1906, the novel reveals young Eustace's intimations of a spiritual reality behind the surface of life. Unable to act in terms of these insights, for they are confused with his aesthetic sense, Eustace feeds his romantic inclination to construct an internal fantasy world and refuses to see the moral necessity of action.

In *The Sixth Heaven*, Hartley details Eustace's second effort to achieve his freedom from Hilda, this time by engineering a socially advantageous marriage for her with Dick Staveley, a war hero and rising young member of Parliament. This novel focuses on a visit the Cherringtons make in June, 1920, to the Staveleys, acquaintances who live near their childhood home at Anchorstone. Eustace's adult epiphanic experiences are more insistent. Less tied to his childish aestheticism, they emerge in the context of the novel as hauntingly ambiguous intimations of a moral and spiritual realm that he unconsciously seeks to avoid acknowledging.

In *Eustace and Hilda*, the final novel in the trilogy, Hartley brings his protagonist face-to-face with Christ during the Venetian Feast of the Redeemer, the third Sunday in July, 1920. This encounter leads to Eustace's return to Anchorstone and acceptance of moral responsibility for the emotionally induced paralysis Hilda experienced at the end of her love affair with Dick Staveley. Back in his childhood home, Eustace learns the lesson of self-sacrificial love in Christ's example, and he effects a cure for Hilda by staging a mock accident for her at the edge of Anchorstone Cliff. Because of the strain this involves, he suffers a fatal heart attack, and the novel ends. His death signals the genuineness of the moral growth and spiritual regeneration that had begun in Venice. The interpenetration of realistic narrative and symbolic subtext that occurs by the end of the *Eustace and Hilda* trilogy objectifies Hartley's vision of the world.

THE BOAT

Hartley's equivalent of Ford Madox Ford's and Evelyn Waugh's treatments of men at war, *The Boat* presents the mock-epic struggle of Timothy Casson, a forty-nine-year-old bachelor writer, to gain permission to use his rowing shell on the fishing stream that runs through Upton-on-Swirrell. Timothy, settling back in England in 1940 after an eighteen-year stay in Italy, consciously attempts to isolate himself from the effects of the war in progress in the larger world. He devotes himself to collecting china, to cultivating friends, to raising a dog, and to forcing the village magnates to allow him to row on the Swirrell. In the process, Timothy violates his own self-interest, as well as that of his nation and his class, but he is not the tragicomic figure that Eustace Cherrington becomes in the trilogy. In Hartley's hands, Timothy achieves only a degree of the self-awareness that Eustace does, and this enables the novelist to label him the "common sinner" that all people are, a figure both sinned against and sinning.

Timothy's desire to take his boat out on the river is an assertion of individuality that polarizes the community. His attachment to his boat becomes a measure of his moral and political confusion, for Timothy is torn between the influences of Vera Cross, a Communist secret agent sent to Upton-on-Swirrell to organize unrest among the masses, and Volumnia Purbright, the wife of the Anglican vicar and an unconventional, perhaps mystical, Christian. The emblematic names suggest the comic possibilities Hartley exploits in his treatment of the two, but *The Boat* is a serious novel. Vera represents a social disharmony resultant upon the advocacy of ideology, while Volumnia reflects both social harmony and personal tranquillity resulting from sacrifice of self. Indeed, when Timothy persists in his protest against the prohibition against rowing and sets forth on the flooded Swirrell with two children and his dog as passengers, Volumnia confronts Vera on the riverbank. Vera attacks the vicar's wife, and the two women tumble into the water. When Vera drowns in the Devil's Staircase, Volumnia blames herself for the younger woman's death and subsequently dies from exposure and pneumonia. When at the end of *The Boat* Timothy, who had to be rescued from the river when his boat capsized in the flooded stream, dreams he receives a telephone call from Volumnia inviting him to tea, he hears Vera's voice as well as Volumnia's, and the two women tell him that they are inseparable, as are the moral and ethical positions they represent.

Near the end of the novel, Timothy prepares to leave Upton-on-Swirrell in the company of two old friends, Esther Morwen and Tyrone MacAdam. The two discuss the prospects for Timothy's acceptance of himself as an ordinary human being. At the time of the boating accident, he had managed to rescue one of the children with him, but he needed the fortuitous help of others to rescue the second child and to reach safety himself. Timothy is clearly partially responsible for the deaths of Vera Cross and Volumnia Purbright, and the "true cross" he must bear is an acceptance of moral complexity. Whether he will achieve this insight is an open question at the end of *The Boat*, and Hartley's refusal to make the book a neat statement reinforces its thematic point.

THE GO-BETWEEN

Hartley's *The Go-Between*, arguably his finest novel, is the only one with a first-person narrator as protagonist. Leo Colston, like the focal characters of the *Eustace and Hilda* trilogy and *The Boat*, frees himself from psychological constraints and achieves a measure of moral insight. Indeed, Leo's story amounts to a rite of passage conforming to the pattern of initiation characteristic of the bildungsroman. More significantly, *The Go-Between* is a study of England on the verge of its second Elizabethan Age, and the patterns of imagery that Hartley uses to reveal the personality of Leo suggest indirectly that the Age of Aquarius will be a golden one.

These linguistic patterns, introduced into the novel by Leo himself, derive from the signs of the zodiac. On one hand, they are a pattern manufactured by Leo as a schoolboy and utilized to explain his conviction that the start of the twentieth century, which he dates incorrectly as January 1, 1900, is the dawn of a second Golden Age. On the other hand, the zodiac motifs, as associated with Leo and other characters in the novel, underscore Hartley's thematic insistence on the power of self-sacrificial love to redeem both individuals and society from error.

At the start of the novel in 1951 or 1952, Leo is an elderly man engaged in sorting through the accumulated memorabilia of a lifetime. Coming upon his diary for the year 1900, inside the cover of which are printed the zodiac signs, he recalls his experiences at Southdown Hill School and his vacation visit to a schoolmate, Marcus Maudsley. In the body of the novel, the account of that nineteen-day visit to Brandham Hall, the narrative voice is split between that of the thirteen-year-old Leo of 1900 and that of the aged man with which the book begins. Used by Marcus's sister Marian to carry messages to her lover, the tenant farmer Ted Burgess, Leo finds himself faced with the dubious morality of his actions when Marcus tells him that Marian is to marry Viscount Trimingham, the owner of Brandham Hall and a scarred veteran of the Boer War.

In Leo's mind, Marian is the Virgin of the zodiac, Trimingham the Sagittarian archer, and Burgess the Aquarian water-carrier. Determined to break the bond between Marian and Ted and to restore her to Viscount Trimingham, Leo resorts to the schoolboy magic with which he had handled bullies at school. He plans a spell involving the sacrifice of an *atropa belladonna* or deadly nightshade growing in a deserted outbuilding, but the ritual goes awry and he finds himself flat on his back with the plant on top of him. The next day, his thirteenth birthday, Leo is forced to lead Marian's mother to the spot where the girl meets her lover, and they discover the pair engaged in sexual intercourse. For Leo, whose adult sexuality has just begun to develop, this is a significant shock, and he feels that he has been defeated by the beautiful but deadly lady, both the deadly nightshade and Marian herself.

In the epilogue to *The Go-Between*, the elderly Leo Colston returns to Norfolk to find out the consequences of the mutual betrayal. Encountering Marian, now the dowager Lady Trimingham, once more, he undertakes again to be a messenger. This time he goes to her grandson Edward in an effort to reconcile him to the events of the fateful year 1900, to the fact that his father was really the son of Ted Burgess. This action on Leo's part embodies the theme of all of Hartley's fiction: The only evil in life is an unloving heart. At the end of his return journey to Brandham Hall, Leo Colston is a more vital man and a more compassionate one. Having faced the evil both inside and outside himself, he is open to love, and the Age of Aquarius can begin. That it will also be the age of Elizabeth II, given the political and sociological implications of the central action, gives Hartley's *The Go-Between* its particular thematic rightness.

Robert C. Petersen

OTHER MAJOR WORKS

SHORT FICTION: *Night Fears*, 1924; *The Killing Bottle*, 1932; *The Traveling Grave*, 1948; *The White Wand*, 1954; *Two for the River*, 1961; *Mrs. Carteret Receives*, 1971; *The Complete Short Stories of L. P. Hartley*, 1973.

NONFICTION: *The Novelist's Responsibility: Lectures and Essays*, 1967.

BIBLIOGRAPHY

Bien, Peter. *L. P. Hartley*. University Park: Pennsylvania State University Press, 1963. The first book on Hartley's fiction, important for its Freudian analysis of his novels; its identification of his indebtedness to Nathaniel Hawthorne, Henry James, and Emily

Brontë; and its examination of Hartley's literary criticism. At its best when discussing the novels about the transition from adolescence to adulthood.

Bloomfield, Paul. *L. P. Hartley.* 1962. Rev. ed. Harlow, England: Longman, 1970. Bloomfield, a personal friend of Hartley, focuses on character analysis and thematic concerns, providing a brief discussion of Hartley's novels. Laudatory, perceptive, and very well written.

Fane, Julian. *Best Friends: Memories of Rachel and David Cecil, Cynthia Asquith, L. P. Hartley, and Some Others.* London: Sinclair-Stevenson and St. George's Press, 1990. Fane writes about his friendship with Hartley and others, which helps to situate Hartley's fiction in terms of his sensibility and his time.

Hall, James. *The Tragic Comedians: Seven Modern British Novelists.* Bloomington: Indiana University Press, 1963. Claims that the Hartley protagonist possesses an inadequate emotional pattern that leads inevitably to failure. This neurotic behavior is discussed in his major fiction: *The Boat, Eustace and Hilda, My Fellow Devils,* and *The Hireling.* In these novels, Hartley demonstrates that confidence is accompanied by a contradictory desire to fail.

Jones, Edward T. *L. P. Hartley.* Boston: Twayne, 1978. An excellent analysis of Hartley's literary work, particularly of his novels, which are conveniently grouped. Also contains a chronology, a biographical introductory chapter, a discussion of Hartley's literary criticism, and an excellent annotated bibliography. Of special interest is Jones's definition of the "Hartleian novel."

Mulkeen, Anne. *Wild Thyme, Winter Lightning: The Symbolic Novels of L. P. Hartley.* Detroit, Mich.: Wayne State University Press, 1974. Focuses on Hartley's fiction until 1968, stressing the Hawthornian romance elements in his early novels. Particularly concerned with his adaptations of the romance and how his characters are at once themselves and archetypes or symbols.

Webster, Harvey Curtis. *After the Trauma: Representative British Novelists Since 1920.* Lexington: University Press of Kentucky, 1970. The chapter on Hartley, entitled "Diffident Christian," concerns his protagonists' struggles to distinguish between God's orders and society's demands. Discusses *Facial Justice, Eustace and Hilda, The Boat,* and *The Go-Between* extensively.

Wright, Adrian. *Foreign Country: The Life of L. P. Hartley.* London: A. Deutsch, 1996. A good biography of Hartley for the beginning student, providing a balanced account of Hartley's life and information about his novels and other works. Includes a bibliography and an index.

York, R. A. " L. P. Hartley: *The Go-Between.*" In *The Rules of Time: Time and Rhythm in the Twentieth-Century Novel.* Madison, N.J.: Fairleigh Dickinson University Press, 1999. York's examination of Hartley's book and novels by other authors focuses on the rhythm and pace of reading, maintaining that these elements affect readers' perception of time—a conspicuous presence in all twentieth century fiction.

NATHANIEL HAWTHORNE

Born: Salem, Massachusetts; July 4, 1804
Died: Plymouth, New Hampshire; May 19, 1864
Also known as: Nathaniel Hawthorne, Jr.; Nathaniel Hathorne

PRINCIPAL LONG FICTION
Fanshawe: A Tale, 1828
The Scarlet Letter, 1850
The House of the Seven Gables, 1851
The Blithedale Romance, 1852
The Marble Faun: Or, The Romance of Monte Beni, 1860
Septimius Felton, 1872 (fragment)
The Dolliver Romance, 1876 (fragment)
The Ancestral Footstep, 1883 (fragment)
Doctor Grimshawe's Secret, 1883 (fragment)

OTHER LITERARY FORMS

Many of Nathaniel Hawthorne's short stories were originally published anonymously in such magazines as the *Token* and the *New England Magazine* between 1830 and 1837. Several collections appeared during his lifetime, including *Twice-Told Tales* (1837; expanded 1842), *Mosses from an Old Manse* (1846), and *The Snow-Image, and Other Twice-Told Tales* (1851). Houghton Mifflin published the complete works in the Riverside edition (1850-1882) and the Old Manse edition (1900). Hawthorne also wrote stories for children, collected in *Grandfather's Chair* (1841), *Biographical Stories for Children* (1842), *True Stories from History and Biography* (1851), *A Wonder-Book for Boys and Girls* (1852), and *Tanglewood Tales for Boys and Girls* (1853). With the help of his sister, Elizabeth, he edited the *American Magazine of Useful and Entertaining Knowledge* (1836) and *Peter Parley's Universal History* (1837) and, as a favor to would-be president Franklin Pierce, wrote a biography for the presidential campaign. His last completed work was *Our Old Home* (1863), a series of essays about his sojourn in England. At the time of his death, he left four unfinished fragments: *Septimius Felton, The Dolliver Romance, The Ancestral Footstep*, and *Doctor Grimshawe's Secret*.

ACHIEVEMENTS

Few other American authors, with the possible exception of Henry James, have engaged in so deliberate a literary apprenticeship as Nathaniel Hawthorne. After an initial period of anonymity during his so-called solitary years from 1825 to 1837, he achieved an unfaltering reputation as an author of short stories, romances, essays, and children's books. He is remembered for not only furthering the development of the short-story form

Nathaniel Hawthorne
(Library of Congress)

but also distinguishing between the novel and the romance. The prefaces to his long works elucidate his theory of the "neutral ground"—the junction between the actual and the imaginary—where romance takes place. He is noted for his masterful exploration of the psychology of guilt and sin; his study of the Puritan heritage contributed to the emerging sense of historicity that characterized the American Renaissance of the mid-nineteenth century.

Hawthorne is unrivaled as an allegorist, especially as one whose character typologies and symbols achieve universality through their psychological validity. While he has been faulted for sentimentality, lapses into archaic diction, and gothicism, Hawthorne's works continue to evoke the "truth of the human heart" that is the key to their continuing appeal.

BIOGRAPHY

Nathaniel Hawthorne was born in Salem, Massachusetts, on July 4, 1804. On his father's side, Hawthorne was descended from William Hathorne, who settled in Massachusetts in 1630 and whose son, John, was one of the judges in the 1692 Salem witchcraft trials. Hawthorne's father, a sea captain, married Elizabeth Clarke Manning in 1801. His mother's English ancestors immigrated to the New World in 1679; her brother, Robert, a successful businessman, assumed responsibility for her affairs after Captain Hathorne died of yellow fever in Suriname in 1808.

After his father's death, Hawthorne, his two sisters, Elizabeth Manning and Maria Louisa, and his mother moved into the populous Manning household, a move that on one hand estranged him from his Hathorne relatives and on the other provided him with an attentive family life, albeit an adult one, for the eight aunts and uncles living there were unmarried at that time. Perhaps the adult company accounted in part for his literary tastes, as did his less than regular education. Although he attended a school taught by Joseph Emerson Worcester, a renowned philologist of the time, Hawthorne led a sedentary existence for almost three years after being lamed at the age of nine. During his enforced inactivity, he spent long afternoons reading Edmund Spenser, John Bunyan, and William Shakespeare, his favorite authors.

When Hawthorne was twelve years old, his mother moved the family temporarily to Raymond, Maine, where the Mannings owned a tract of land. The outdoor activity occasioned by nearby Lake Sebago and the surrounding forest land proved beneficial to Hawthorne; quickly recovering his health, he became an able marksman and fisherman. During these years, interrupted by schooling with the Reverend Caleb Bradley, a stern man not to Hawthorne's liking, Hawthorne accumulated Wordsworthian memories of the wilderness and of village life that were to be evoked in his fiction. Recalled to Salem, he began in 1820 to be tutored for college by lawyer Benjamin Lynde Oliver, working, in the meantime, as a bookkeeper for his Uncle Robert, an occupation that foreshadowed his later business ventures. He continued his reading, including such authors as Henry Fielding, Sir Walter Scott, William Godwin, Matthew "Monk" Lewis, and James Hogg, and produced a family newspaper, *The Spectator*, characterized by humorous notices and essays and parodies of sentimental verse.

The first member of his family to attend college, Hawthorne was sent to Bowdoin, where he graduated eighteenth in a class of thirty-eight. Known for his quietness and gentle humor, he disliked declamations, was negligent in many academic requirements, and, indeed, was fined for playing cards. His fellow students at Bowdoin included Henry Wadsworth Longfellow and Franklin Pierce, who later was elected president of the United States.

Hawthorne had determined early on a career in letters. Returning to Salem upon graduation, he began a self-imposed apprenticeship, the solitary years. During this time, Hawthorne privately published *Fanshawe*, a work that he so thoroughly repudiated that his wife, Sophia, knew nothing of it; he published many short stories anonymously and unsuccessfully attempted to interest publishers in such collections as *Seven Tales of My Native Land*, *Provincial Tales*, and *The Storyteller*. As a means of support he edited the *American Magazine of Useful and Entertaining Knowledge* and compiled *Peter Parley's*

Universal History. Not until the publication of *Twice-Told Tales* under the secret financial sponsorship of his friend, Horatio Bridge, did Hawthorne's name become publicly known.

The label "solitary years" is somewhat of a misnomer, for, as his journals indicate, Hawthorne visited with friends, went for long walks and journeys, and, most important, met Sophia Peabody, the daughter of Dr. Nathaniel Peabody. For Hawthorne, Sophia was the key by which he was released from "a life of shadows" to the "truth of the human heart." Four years passed, however, before they could marry—four years in which Hawthorne became measurer in the Boston Custom House, which he called a "grievous thraldom," and then, although not sympathetic to the burgeoning transcendental movement, joined the utopian community Brook Farm (April, 1841), investing one thousand dollars in an attempt to establish a home for himself and Sophia.

After little more than six months, Hawthorne gave up the communal venture and, settling in the Old Manse at Concord, married Sophia on July 19, 1842. His financial difficulties were exacerbated by the birth of Una in 1844; finally, in 1846, when his son, Julian, was born and *Mosses from an Old Manse* was published, he was appointed surveyor of the Salem Custom House, a post he held from 1846 to 1849, when a political upset cost him his job. With more time to write and with the pressure to support a growing family, Hawthorne began a period of intense literary activity; his friendship with Herman Melville dates from that time. *The Scarlet Letter*, whose ending sent Sophia to bed with a grievous headache, was finished in February, 1850. *The House of the Seven Gables* appeared in 1851, the year Hawthorne's daughter, Rose, was born; by the end of the next year, Hawthorne had completed *The Blithedale Romance*, two volumes of children's tales, *The Life of Franklin Pierce*, and a collection of stories, *The Snow-Image, and Other Twice-Told Tales.*

From 1853 to 1857, Hawthorne served as American consul in Liverpool, England, a political appointment under President Pierce. After four years of involvement with the personal and financial problems of stranded Americans, Hawthorne resigned and lived in Rome and Florence from 1857 to 1858, where he acquired ideas for his last romance, *The Marble Faun.* After returning with his family to the United States, Hawthorne worked on four unfinished romances, *Doctor Grimshawe's Secret, Septimius Felton, The Dolliver Romance,* and *The Ancestral Footstep,* in which two themes are dominant: the search for immortality and the American attempt to establish title to English ancestry. His carefully considered essays on the paucity of American tradition, the depth of British heritage, and the contrast between democracy and entrenched class systems were first published in *The Atlantic Monthly* and then collected as *Our Old Home.* After a lingering illness, he died at Plymouth, New Hampshire, on May 19, 1864, during a trip with Pierce. Hawthorne was buried at Sleepy Hollow Cemetery in Concord, Massachusetts.

ANALYSIS

Central to Nathaniel Hawthorne's romances is his idea of a "neutral territory," described in the Custom House sketch that precedes *The Scarlet Letter* as a place "somewhere between the real world and fairy-land, where the Actual and the Imaginary may meet, and each imbue itself with the nature of the other." A romance, according to Hawthorne, is different from the novel, which maintains a "minute fidelity . . . to the probable and ordinary course of man's experience." In the neutral territory of romance, however, the author may make use of the "marvellous" to heighten atmospheric effects, if he or she also presents "the truth of the human heart." As long as the writer of romance creates characters whose virtues, vices, and sensibilities are distinctly human, he or she may place them in an environment that is out of the ordinary—or that is, in fact, allegorical. Thus, for example, while certain elements—the stigma of the scarlet letter, or Donatello's faun ears—are fantastical in conception, they represent a moral stance that is true to nature. Dimmesdale's guilt at concealing his adultery with Hester Prynne is, indeed, as destructive as the wound on his breast, and Donatello's pagan nature is expressed in the shape of his ears.

A number of recurring thematic patterns and character types appear in Hawthorne's novels and tales, as Randall Stewart suggests in the introduction to *The American Notebooks* (1932). These repetitions show Hawthorne's emphasis on the effects of events on the human heart rather than on the events themselves. One common motif is concern for the past, or, as Hawthorne says in the preface to *The House of the Seven Gables*, his "attempt to connect a bygone time with the very present that is flitting away from us." Hawthorne's interest in the Puritan past was perhaps sparked by his "discovery," as a teenager, of his Hathorne connections; it was certainly influenced by his belief that progress was impeded by inheritance, that "the wrong-doing of one generation lives into the successive ones, and . . . becomes a pure and uncontrollable mischief." For Hawthorne, then, the past must be reckoned with, and then put aside; the eventual decay of aristocratic families is not only inevitable, but desirable.

Hawthorne's understanding of tradition is illustrated in many of his works. In *The Scarlet Letter*, for example, he explores the effect of traditional Puritan social and theological expectations on three kinds of sinners: the adultress (Hester), the hypocrite (Dimmesdale), and the avenger (Chillingworth), only to demonstrate that the punishment they inflict on themselves far outweighs the public castigation. Hester, in fact, inverts the rigidified Puritan system, represented by the scarlet letter, whose meaning she changes from "adultress" to "able." Probably the most specific treatment of the theme, however, is found in *The House of the Seven Gables*, in which the Pyncheon family house and fortune have imprisoned both Hepzibah and Clifford, one in apathy and one in insanity; only Phoebe, the country cousin who cares little for wealth, can lighten the burden, for not only her relatives but also Holgrave, a descendant of the Maules who invoked the original curse. In *The Marble Faun*, Hawthorne goes to Italy for his "sense of the past," although

Hilda and Kenyon are both Americans. The past in this novel is represented not only in the setting but also in Donatello's pagan nature; at the end, both Miriam and the faun figure engage in a purgatorial expiation of the past.

Another recurring theme is that of isolation. Certainly Hawthorne himself felt distanced from normal social converse by his authorial calling. The firsthand descriptions of Hawthorne extant today present him more as an observer than as a participant, a stance over which he himself agonized. In writing to Longfellow about his apprenticeship years, he complained that he was "carried apart from the main current of life" and that "there is no fate in this world so horrible as to have no share in either its joys or sorrows. For the last ten years, I have not lived, but only dreamed about living." For Hawthorne, Sophia was his salvation, his link to human companionship. Perhaps that is why he wrote so evocatively of Hester Prynne's isolation; indeed, Hester's difficult task of rearing the elfin child Pearl without help from Dimmesdale is the obverse of Hawthorne's own happy domestic situation. Almost every character that Hawthorne created experiences some sense of isolation, sometimes from a consciousness of sin, sometimes from innocence itself, or sometimes from a deliberate attempt to remain aloof.

According to Hawthorne, this kind of isolation, most intense when it is self-imposed, frequently comes from a consciousness of sin or from what he calls the "violation of the sanctity of the human heart." For Hawthorne, the "unpardonable sin" is just such a violation, in which one individual becomes subjected to another's intellectual or scientific (rather than emotional) interest. Chillingworth is a good example; as Hester's unacknowledged husband, he lives with Dimmesdale, deliberately intensifying the minister's hidden guilt. In *The Blithedale Romance*, Coverdale's voyeurism (and certainly his name) suggests this kind of violation, as does Westervelt's manipulation of Priscilla and Hollingsworth's of Zenobia. Certainly, Clifford's isolation in insanity is the fault of Judge Pyncheon. There is also the implication that the mysterious model who haunts Miriam in *The Marble Faun* has committed the same sin, thereby isolating both of them. One of the few characters to refuse such violation is Holgrave, who, in *The House of the Seven Gables*, forbears to use his mesmeric powers on Phoebe.

Such a set of recurring themes is bolstered by a pervasive character typology. While literary works such as those by Edmund Spenser, John Milton, William Shakespeare, and John Bunyan form the historical context for many of Hawthorne's characters, many are further developments of his own early character types. *Fanshawe*, for example, introduced the pale, idealistic scholarly hero more fully developed in Dimmesdale. Others, personifications of abstract qualities, seem motivated by purely evil ends. Westervelt is one type; sophisticated and learned in mesmerism, he takes as his victim the innocent Priscilla. Chillingworth, whose literary ancestry can probably be traced to Miltonic devil figures, is old and bent but possesses a compelling intellect that belies his lack of physical strength. Finally, the worldly Judge Pyncheon manifests a practical, unimaginative streak that connects him to Peter Hovenden of Hawthorne's short story "The Artist of the Beautiful." As for Hawthorne's heroines, Hilda and Phoebe embody the domesticity that Hawthorne admired in Sophia; Priscilla, like Alice Pyncheon before her, is frail and easily subjugated; and Hester, Zenobia, and Miriam exhibit an oriental beauty and intellectual pride.

FANSHAWE

Three years after Hawthorne graduated from Bowdoin College, he anonymously published the apprenticeship novel *Fanshawe* at his own expense. While he almost immediately repudiated the work, it remains not only a revealing biographical statement but also a testing ground for themes and characters that he later developed with great success.

"No man can be a poet and a bookkeeper at the same time," Hawthorne complained in a letter he wrote while engaged in his Uncle Robert's stagecoach business before college. Just such a dichotomy is illustrated in *Fanshawe*, in which the pale scholar fails to rejoin the course of ordinary life and, in effect, consigns himself to death, while the active individual, Edward Walcott, wins the heroine, Ellen Langton, and so becomes, to use Hawthorne's later words, part of "The magnetic chain of humanity." To be sure, Fanshawe is an overdrawn figure, owing, as Arlin Turner points out, something to Gorham Deane, a Bowdoin schoolmate, and much to Charles Robert Maturin's gothic novel *Melmoth the Wanderer* (1820), from which Ellen's guardian, Dr. Melmoth, takes his name. In repudiating the book, however, Hawthorne is less repudiating the gothic form than he is an early, faulty conception of a writer's life. Certainly, Hawthorne recognized the tension between the intellectual and the practical lives, as his letters and journals suggest, especially when he was at the Boston and Salem Custom Houses and at the consulate in Liverpool.

Moreover, as Frederick Crews notes, Fanshawe and Walcott are "complementary sides," together fulfilling Hawthorne's twin desire for "self-abnegation" and "heroism and amorous success." Nevertheless, as the pattern of his own life makes clear, Hawthorne did not retire (as did Fanshawe) to an early grave after the solitary apprenticeship years; rather, he married Sophia Peabody (fictionally prefigured in Ellen Langton) and, in becoming involved in the ordinary affairs of life, merged the figures of Fanshawe and Walcott.

The plot of the novel—the abduction of Ellen by the villainous Butler—introduces Hawthorne's later exploration of the misuse of power, while the configuration of characters foreshadows not only the scholar figure but also two other types: the dark villain, whose sexual motivation remains ambiguous, and the innocent, domestic young heroine, later developed as Phoebe and Hilda. That Fanshawe should rescue Ellen, appearing like Milton's Raphael over the thickly wooded valley where Butler has secluded her, suggests that he is able to enter the world of action; but that he should refuse her offer of marriage, saying, "I have no way to prove that I deserve your generosity, but by refusing to take advantage of it," is uncharacteristic in comparison with Hawthorne's later heroes such as Holgrave and Kenyon. It may be that after his marriage to Sophia, Hawthorne could not conceive of a triangle existing when two "soul mates" had found each other, for in similar character configurations in *The House of the Seven Gables* and *The Marble Faun*, both Holgrave and Kenyon have no rivals to fear for Phoebe and Hilda.

In setting, however, *Fanshawe* is a precursor to the later novels, as well as an unformulated precedent for Hawthorne's famous definition of romance. Probably begun while Hawthorne was enrolled at Bowdoin, the novel has as its setting Harley College, a picturesque, secluded institution. Formal classroom tutoring is not the novel's central interest, however, just as it was not in Hawthorne's own life; nor is the novel completely a roman à clef in which actual people and places are thinly disguised. Rather, as is the case in the later novels in which Salem itself, Brook Farm, and Rome are the existing actualities on which Hawthorne draws, so in *Fanshawe* the setting is an excuse for the psychological action. To be sure, the later, sophisticated, symbolic effects are missing, and the interpenetration of the actual by the imaginary is not as successful as in, for instance, *The Scarlet Letter.* Nevertheless, although what later becomes marvelous is here simply melodramatic, the imagination plays a large, if unformulated, role in the novel's success.

THE SCARLET LETTER

Begun as a tale and completed shortly after Hawthorne's dismissal from the Salem surveyorship, *The Scarlet Letter* is prefaced by an essay titled "The Custom House" in which Hawthorne not only gives an imaginative account of his business experience but also presents a theory of composition. The essay is thus a distillation of the practical and the imaginative. It includes scant praise for the unimaginative William Lee, the antediluvian permanent inspector whose commonplace attitude typified for Hawthorne the customs operation. In writing, however, Hawthorne exorcised his spleen at his political dismissal, which, coupled with charges of malfeasance, was instigated by the Whigs who wanted him replaced; as Arlin Turner comments, "The decapitated surveyor, in becoming a character in a semifictional account, had all but ceased to be Hawthorne." The writer, in short, had made fiction out of his business experiences. He also had speculated about the preconceptions necessary for the creator of romances; such a man, he decided, must be able to perceive the "neutral territory" where the "actual" and the "imaginary" meet. The result of that perception was *The Scarlet Letter.*

In the prefatory essay to the book, Hawthorne establishes the literalism of the scarlet letter, which, he says, he has in his possession as an old, faded, tattered remnant of the past. Just as Hawthorne is said by Terence Martin to contemplate the letter, thus generating the novel, so the reader is forced to direct his or her attention to the primary symbol, not simply of Hester's adultery or of her ability, but of the way in which the restrictions of the Puritan forebears are transcended by the warmth of the human heart. Through this symbol, then, and through its living counterpart, Pearl, the daughter of Hester and Dimmesdale, Hawthorne examines the isolating effects of a sense of sin, using as his psychological setting the Puritan ethos.

With Hester's first public appearance with the infant Pearl and the heavily embroidered scarlet letter on her breast, the child—Hester's "torment" and her "joy"—and the letter become identified. Hester's guilt is a public one; Dimmesdale's is not. To admit to his share in the adultery is to relinquish his standing as the minister of the community, and so, initially too weak to commit himself, he pleads with Hester to confess her partner in the sin. She does not do so, nor does she admit that Chillingworth, the doctor who pursues Dimmesdale, is her husband. Three solitary people, then, are inexorably bound together by the results of the sin but are unable to communicate with one another.

The Puritan intention of bringing the sinner into submission has the opposite effect upon Hester, who, with a pride akin to humility, tenaciously makes a way for herself in the community. As an angel of mercy to the suffering, the sick, and the heavy of heart, she becomes a living model of charity that the townspeople, rigidly enmeshed in their Puritan theology, are unable to emulate. In addition, she exercises a talent for fine embroidery, so that even the bride has her clothing embellished with the sinner's finery. Hester's ostracization hardens her pride until, as she says to Dimmesdale in the forest, their act has a "consecration of its own." The adultery, in short, achieves a validation quite outside the letter of the Puritan law, and Hester finds no reason not to suggest that Dimmesdale run away with her in a repetition of the temptation and the original sin.

In the meantime, Dimmesdale has not had the relief of Hester's public confession. As veiled confessions, his sermons take on an ever growing intensity and apparent sincerity, gaining many converts to the church. Under Chillingworth's scrutiny, however, Dimmesdale's concealed guilt creates a physical manifestation, a scarlet letter inscribed in his flesh. While Hester's letter has yet to work its way inward to repentance, Dimmesdale's is slowly working its way outward. Chillingworth himself, initially a scholar, becomes dedicated to the cause of intensifying the minister's sufferings. Although Chillingworth eventually takes partial responsibility for Hester's sin, admitting that as a scholarly recluse he should not have taken a young wife, he inexorably causes his own spiritual death. He joins a line of scientist-experimenters who deprive their victims of intellectual curiosity, violating "the truth of the human heart" and severing themselves from "the magnetic chain of humanity." He becomes, as Harry Levin notes, the lowest in the hierarchy of sinners, for while Hester and Dimmesdale have at least joined in passion, Chillingworth is isolated in pride.

As Terence Martin suggests, the scaffold scenes are central to the work. For Dimmesdale, public abnegation is the key: Standing as a penitent on the scaffold at midnight is insufficient, for his act is illuminated only by the light of a great comet. His decision to elope with Hester is also insufficient to remove his guilt; what he considers to be the beginning of a "new life" is a reenactment of the original deed. In the end, the scaffold proves the only real escape from the torments devised by Chillingworth, for in facing the community with Hester and Pearl, the minister faces himself and removes the concealment that is a great part of his guilt. His "new life" is, in fact, death, and he offers no hope to Hester that they will meet again, for to do so would be to succumb to temptation again. Only Pearl, who marries a lord, leaves the community permanently; as the innocent victim, she in effect returns to her mother's home to expiate her mother's sin.

Like Fanshawe, then, Dimmesdale causes his own demise, but he is provided with motivation. In Pearl, Hawthorne was influenced perhaps by the antics of Una, his first child, but even her name, which is reminiscent of the medieval Pearl-Poet's "pearl of great price"—his soul—indicates that she is emblematic. Likewise, the minister's name is indicative of the valley of the shadow of death, just as Chillingworth's suggests his cold nature. The successful meshing of the literal and allegorical levels in this tale of the effects of concealed sin and the universality of its theme continue to lend interest to the work.

THE HOUSE OF THE SEVEN GABLES

As Hawthorne notes in his preface to *The House of the Seven Gables*, he intends to show the mischief that the past causes when it lives into the present, particularly when coupled with the question of an inheritance. Hawthorne's mood is similar to that of Henry David Thoreau when, in *Walden* (1854), he makes his famous plea to "simplify," evoking the image of Everyman traveling on the road of life, carrying his onerous possessions on his back. The family curse that haunts Hepzibah and Clifford Pyncheon, the hidden property deed, and even Hepzibah's dreams of an unexpected inheritance are so centered on the past that the characters are unable to function in the present. In fact, says Hawthorne, far more worrisome than the missing inheritance is the "moral disease" that is passed from one generation to the next.

This "moral disease" results from the greed of the family progenitor, Colonel Pyncheon, who coveted the small tract of land owned by one Matthew Maule. Maule's curse—"God will give him blood to drink"—comes true on the day the new Pyncheon mansion, built on the site of Maule's hut, is to be consecrated. The Colonel dies, presumably from apoplexy but possibly from foul play, and from that day, Hawthorne says, a throwback to the Colonel appears in each generation—a calculating, practical man, who, as the inheritor, commits again "the great guilt of his ancestor" in not making restoration to the Maule descendants. Clifford, falsely imprisoned for the murder of his uncle, Jaffrey Pyncheon, the one Pyncheon willing to make restitution, is persecuted after his release by Judge Pyncheon, another of Jaffrey's nephews and Jaffrey's real murderer, for his presumed knowledge of the hiding place of the Indian deed giving title to their uncle's property.

In contrast to these forces from the past, Hawthorne poses Phoebe, a Pyncheon country cousin with no pretensions to wealth but with a large fund of domesticity and a warm heart. Almost certainly modeled on Sophia, Phoebe, like Hilda in *The Marble Faun*, possesses an unexpected power, a "homely witchcraft." Symbolically, as Crews suggests, she neutralizes the morbidity in the Pyncheon household and eventually stands as an "ideal parent" to Hepzibah and Clifford. Indeed, Phoebe brings her enfeebled relatives into the circle of humanity.

If Phoebe represents the living present, Holgrave, the daguerreotypist and descendant of the Maules, represents the future. Like Clifford, however, who is saved by his imprisonment from an aesthetic version of the unpardonable sin, Holgrave runs the risk of becoming merely a cold-blooded observer. Like Hawthorne, Holgrave is a writer, boarding at the House of the Seven Gables to observe the drama created as the past spills into the present and turning Pyncheon history into fiction. He is, nevertheless, a reformer. In an echo of Hawthorne's preface, he would have buildings made of impermanent materials, ready to be built anew with each generation; likewise, he would merge old family lines into the stream of humanity. While Holgrave's progressive views become mitigated once he marries Phoebe, he is rescued from becoming a Chillingworth by his integrity, his conscience, and his reverence for the human soul. Although he unintentionally hypnotizes Phoebe by reading her his story of Matthew Maule's mesmerism of Alice Pyncheon, he eschews his power, thereby not only saving himself and her from a Dimmesdale/Chillingworth relationship but also breaking the chain of vengeance that was in his power to perpetuate. The chain of past circumstances is also broken by the death of Judge Pyncheon, who, unlike Holgrave, intended to exercise his psychological power to force Clifford to reveal where the Indian deed is hidden. Stricken by apoplexy (or Maule's curse), however, the Judge is left in solitary possession of the house as Clifford and Hepzibah flee in fear.

Holgrave's integrity and death itself thus prevent a reenactment of the original drama of power and subjection that initiated the curse. As Holgrave learns, the Judge himself murdered his bachelor uncle and destroyed a will that gave the inheritance to Clifford. Although exonerated, Clifford's intellect cannot be recalled to its former state, and so he remains a testimonial to the adverse effects of "violation of the human heart."

During Hepzibah and Clifford's flight from the scene of the Judge's death, Phoebe, representing the present, and Holgrave, the future, pledge their troth, joining the Pyncheon and Maule families. Hawthorne's happy ending, although deliberately prepared, surprised many of his critics, who objected that Holgrave's decision to "plant" a family and to build a stone house were motivated only by the dictates of the plot. F. D. Matthiessen, for example, suggests that Hawthorne's democratic streak blinded him to the implication that Holgrave was simply setting up a new dynasty. On the other hand, for Martin, the decision is foreshadowed; Holgrave's is a compromise position in which he maintains the importance of the structure of society while suggesting that the content be changed, just as a stone house might be redecorated according to its owners' tastes. In marrying Holgrave, Phoebe incorporates Pyncheon blood with the "mass of the people," for the original Maule was a poor man and his son a carpenter.

THE BLITHEDALE ROMANCE

The only one of Hawthorne's romances to be told by a first-person narrator, *The Blithedale Romance* is grounded in Hawthorne's abortive attempt to join the utopian

Brook Farm. Like Hawthorne, Miles Coverdale notes the disjunction between a life of labor and a life of poetry; like Hawthorne, he never wholeheartedly participates in the community. In fact, to Crews, the work displays "an inner coherence of self-debate." Coverdale is the isolated man viewed from inside; as a self-conscious observer, he is the most Jamesian of all of Hawthorne's characters. As Martin notes, Hawthorne sacrifices certain aesthetic advantages in allowing Coverdale to tell his own story. Although his name is as evocative as, for example, Chillingworth's, Coverdale loses symbolic intensity because many of his explanations—his noting, for example, that his illness upon arriving at Blithedale is a purgatory preparing him for a new life—sound like figments of an untrustworthy narrator's imagination.

As in his other romances, Hawthorne begins with a preface. While he points out the realistic grounding of the romance, he maintains that the characters are entirely imaginary. He complains that since no convention yet exists for the American romance, the writer must suffer his characters to be compared to real models; hence, says Hawthorne, he has created the Blithedale scenario as a theatrical device to separate the reader from the ordinary course of events (just as the gothic writer did with his medieval trappings). In effect, Coverdale, isolated as he is, serves as the medium who moves between two worlds.

Coverdale's destructive egocentrism is evident throughout the work. His unwillingness to grant a favor to Old Moodie loses him an early acquaintanceship with Priscilla; he cements his position as an outsider by belittling Priscilla and by spying on Zenobia; finally, seeing the intimacy that develops between Priscilla and Hollingsworth after Zenobia's suicide, he retires to enjoy his self-pity. As a minor poet, an urban man who enjoys his cigars and fireplace, he is out of place in the utopian venture; in fact, after his purgatorial illness, he wakes up to death-in-life rather than to reinvigoration. As he moves from Blithedale to the city and back again, his most active participation in the events is his searching for Zenobia's body.

Zenobia herself harks back to Hester, another in the line of Hawthorne's exotic, intellectual women. Like Miriam in *The Marble Faun*, Zenobia has a mysterious past to conceal. She is dogged by Westervelt, her urbane companion whose mesmeric powers become evident in his attempted despoliation of Priscilla. Coverdale imagines her as an orator or an actor; indeed, she is a female reformer whose free and unexpected rhetoric seems to bypass convention. Priscilla, on the other hand, is a frail version of Phoebe and Hilda; she is pliant, domestic, and biddable—hence her susceptibility to Westervelt's powers and her brief tenure as the Veiled Lady. Like Zenobia (whose sister she is revealed to be), she believes in Hollingworth's reformism, but less as a helpmate than as a supporter. In coming to Blithedale, Priscilla really does find the life that is denied to Coverdale, but in falling in love with Hollingsworth, she finds spiritual death.

Hollingsworth is related to Hawthorne's scientist figures. With Holgrave he wants to change society, but his special interest is in criminal reformation. It is Zenobia who, at the end of the novel, realizes that Hollingsworth has identified himself so closely with his plan that he has *become* the plan. Hollingsworth encourages Zenobia's interest in him because of her wealth; he spurns Coverdale's friendship because Coverdale objects to devoting himself entirely to the monomaniacal plan. It is, however, Hollingsworth who rescues Priscilla from Westervelt, exercising the power of affection to break mesmerism, but with him Priscilla simply enters a different kind of subjection.

Indeed, all the main characters suffer real or metaphorical death at the end of the book. Westervelt, like Chillingworth, is frustrated at his victim's escape; Zenobia's suicide has removed her from his power. Priscilla becomes a handmaiden to the ruined ideal of what Hollingsworth might have been, and Hollingsworth becomes a penitent, reforming himself—the criminal responsible for Zenobia's death. Even Coverdale relinquishes a life of feeling; his final secret, that he loves Priscilla, seems only to be fantasizing on the part of the poet who was a master of missed opportunities and who was more comfortable observing his own reactions to a lost love than in pursuing her actively himself.

THE MARBLE FAUN

In *The Marble Faun*, the product of a sojourn in Rome, Hawthorne seems to have reversed a progressively narrowing treatment of the effect of the past. In *The Scarlet Letter*, he deals with Puritan theology; in *The House of the Seven Gables*, a family curse; and in *The Blithedale Romance*, the effects of Coverdale's self-created past. In his last completed work, however, he takes the past of all Rome; in short, he copes with a length of time and complexity of events unusual in his writing experience. Hawthorne's reaction to Rome, complicated by his daughter Una's illness, was mixed. While he objected to the poverty, the dirt, and the paradoxical sensuality and spirituality of Rome, he never, as he put it, felt the city "pulling at his heartstrings" as if it were home.

Italy would seem to present to Hawthorne not only the depth of the past he deemed necessary for the flourishing of romance but also a neutral territory, this time completely divorced from his readers' experience. It can be said, however, that while *The Marble Faun* is Hawthorne's attempt to come to terms with the immense variety of the Italian scene, he was not completely successful. In his preface, he once again declares that the story is to be "fanciful" and is to convey a "thoughtful moral" rather than present a novelistic, realistic picture of Italian customs. He inveighs against the "commonplace prosperity" and lack of "antiquity" in the American scene, a lack that satisfies the kind of reforming zeal pictured in Holgrave but militates against the writer of romance.

Hawthorne broadens his canvas in another way as well; instead of presenting one or two main characters, he gives the reader four: Donatello, presumably the living twin of the sculptor Praxiteles' marble faun; Miriam Schaeffer, the mysterious half-Italian painter pursued by the ill-fated Brother Antonio; Kenyon, the American sculptor; and Hilda, the New England copyist. Donatello's double is not found elsewhere in the romances; in fact, he seems to be a male version of both Phoebe and Hilda. Unlike the two women, however, he comes in actual contact with evil and thereby loses his innocence, whereas Hilda's and

Phoebe's experiences are vicarious. Perhaps the nearest comparison is Dimmesdale, but the minister is portrayed after he chooses to hide his guilt, not before he has sinned. In Donatello's case, Hawthorne examines the idea of the fortunate fall, demonstrating that Donatello grows in moral understanding after he murders the model, a movement that seems to validate Miriam's secular interpretation of the fall as necessary to the development of a soul more than it validates Hilda's instinctive repudiation of the idea.

For some critics, such as Hyatt Waggoner and Richard Fogle, the *felix culpa*, or fortunate fall, is indeed the theme of *The Marble Faun*; Crews, however, emphasizes Hawthorne's unwillingness to confront the problem, noting that Kenyon is made to accept Hilda's repudiation without question. In the final analysis, Hawthorne does indeed seem reluctant to examine the ramifications of the theme.

Like Zenobia and Hester, Miriam is presented as a large-spirited, speculative woman whose talents are dimmed by a secret past, symbolized by the blood-red jewel she wears. Supposedly, Miriam (unlike Hester), has run away from a marriage with a much older man, but, Hawthorne suggests, her family lineage reveals criminal tendencies. She is followed by Brother Antonio, a wandering devil figure whom she meets in the catacomb of St. Calixtus and whom she employs as a model. The crime that links Miriam to Donatello is not, in this case, adultery, but rather murder. Donatello, who accompanies Miriam everywhere, throws the model from the Tarpeian Rock, the traditional death-place for traitors, saying later that he did what Miriam's eyes asked him to do. Linked in the crime and initially feeling part of the accumulated crimes of centuries, they become alienated from each other and must come separately to an understanding of their own responsibility to other human beings. During this time, Donatello retires to Monte Beni, the family seat, to meditate, and Miriam follows him, disguised.

Just as Miriam and Donatello are linked by their complicity, Kenyon and Hilda are linked by a certain hesitation to share in the other pair's secrets, thereby achieving an isolation that Hawthorne might earlier have seen as a breaking of the magnetic chain of humanity. Unnoticed as she observes the murder, Hilda nevertheless becomes a vicarious participant. She rejects Miriam's friendship, maintaining that she has been given an unspotted garment of virtue and must keep it pristine, but she does agree to deliver a packet of Miriam's letters to the Palazzo Cenci. For his part, Kenyon compensates for his earlier coldness to Miriam by effecting a reconciliation between her and Donatello. Visiting Monte Beni, he is struck by Donatello's air of sadness and maturity and believes that the pagan "faun," whose power to talk to animals was legendary, has come to an understanding of good and evil and has thereby escaped the possibility of a sensual old age to which the throwback Monte Beni eventually succumbs. Kenyon encourages his friend to work out his penitence in the sphere of human action and reunites him with Miriam under the statue of Pope Julius III in Perugia.

In the meantime, Hilda, suffering the pains of guilt for the murder as if she were the perpetrator, paradoxically gains comfort from confession in St. Peter's. Once she goes to the Palazzo Cenci to deliver Miriam's letters, however, she is incarcerated as a hostage for Miriam. Her disappearance is the novel's analogue to Donatello's self-imposed isolation; her experience in the convent, where she is detained, convinces her of her need for Kenyon. In searching for Hilda, Kenyon undergoes his own purgation, meeting the changed Donatello and Miriam in the Compagna and learning about Miriam's past. On Miriam's advice, he repairs to the Courso in the height of the carnival; it is there that he is reunited with Hilda. Her freedom means the end of Miriam and Donatello's days together, for Donatello is imprisoned for the murder of Brother Antonio. As did Sophia for Hawthorne, Hilda becomes Kenyon's guide to "home"; she is Hawthorne's last full-length evocation of the New England girl on whose moral guidance he wished to rely.

Patricia Marks

OTHER MAJOR WORKS

SHORT FICTION: *Twice-Told Tales*, 1837 (expanded 1842); *Mosses from an Old Manse*, 1846; *The Snow-Image, and Other Twice-Told Tales*, 1851

NONFICTION: *Life of Franklin Pierce*, 1852; *Our Old Home*, 1863; *The American Notebooks*, 1932; *The French and Italian Notebooks*, 1980; *Letters of Nathaniel Hawthorne*, 1984-1987 (4 volumes); *Selected Letters of Nathaniel Hawthorne*, 2002 (Joel Myerson, editor).

CHILDREN'S LITERATURE: *Grandfather's Chair*, 1841; *Biographical Stories for Children*, 1842; *True Stories from History and Biography*, 1851; *A Wonder-Book for Boys and Girls*, 1852; *Tanglewood Tales for Boys and Girls*, 1853.

EDITED TEXT: *Peter Parley's Universal History*, 1837.

MISCELLANEOUS: *Complete Works*, 1850-1882 (13 volumes); *The Complete Writings of Nathaniel Hawthorne*, 1900 (22 volumes); *The Centenary Edition of the Works of Nathaniel Hawthorne*, 1962-1997 (23 volumes).

BIBLIOGRAPHY

Bell, Millicent, ed. *Hawthorne and the Real: Bicentennial Essays*. Columbus: Ohio State University Press, 2005. Commemorates the bicentennial of Hawthorne's birth, exploring the concepts of "the real" and "reality" in his writing. Includes discussions of Hawthorne and politics, slavery, feminism, moral responsibility, and "the problem of American fiction."

Fogle, Richard Harter. *Hawthorne's Fiction: The Light and the Dark*. Rev. ed. Norman: University of Oklahoma Press, 1964. Fogle examines four of Hawthorne's mature novels and eight short stories in detail, concluding that Hawthorne's fiction is both clear ("light") and complex ("dark"). Fogle is particularly adept, although perhaps overly ingenious, in explicating Hawthorne's symbolism.

Mellow, James R. *Nathaniel Hawthorne and His Times*. Boston: Houghton Mifflin, 1980. In this substantial, readable, and illustrated biography, Mellow provides a number of insights into Hawthorne's fiction. Refreshingly, the author presents Sophia Hawthorne as not only the prudish, protective wife of the Hawthorne legend but also a woman with an artistic sensibility and talent of her own. Suitable for students and general readers.

Miller, Edward Havilland. *Salem Is My Dwelling Place: A Life of Nathaniel Hawthorne.* Iowa City: University of Iowa Press, 1991. A large biography of more than six hundred pages, illustrated with more than fifty photographs and drawings. Miller has been able to draw on more manuscripts of family members and Hawthorne associates than did his predecessors and also developed his subject's family life in more detail.

Millington, Richard H. *The Cambridge Companion to Nathaniel Hawthorne.* New York: Cambridge University Press, 2004. Essays analyze various aspects of Hawthorne's work, including Hawthorne and American masculinity and the question of women. Discusses his major novels.

Moore, Margaret B. *The Salem World of Nathaniel Hawthorne.* Columbia: University of Missouri Press, 1998. Moore explores the relationship between Salem, Massachusetts, and its most famous resident, demonstrating how Hawthorne's association with the city influenced his fiction. She discusses the role of Hawthorne's ancestors in the city's colonial history and examines how the author was affected by Salem's religion and politics.

Pennell, Melissa McFarland. *Student Companion to Nathaniel Hawthorne.* Westport, Conn.: Greenwood Press, 1999. An introductory overview of Hawthorne's life and work designed for high school students and general readers. Includes a discussion of Hawthorne's contribution to American literature, analyses of his four major novels, a bibliography, and an index.

Person, Leland S. *The Cambridge Introduction to Nathaniel Hawthorne.* New York: Cambridge University Press, 2007. An accessible introduction to the author's life and works designed for students and general readers. It includes analysis of Hawthorne's fiction, with separate chapters on the major novels, a brief survey of Hawthorne scholarship, and a bibliography.

Scharnhorst, Gary. *The Critical Response to Hawthorne's "The Scarlet Letter."* New York: Greenwood Press, 1992. Includes chapters on the novel's background and the history of its composition, the contemporary American and early British receptions, the growth of Hawthorne's reputation after his death, modern criticism, and stage and screen adaptations of the novel.

Weldon, Roberta. *Hawthorne, Gender, and Death: Christianity and Its Discontents.* New York: Palgrave Macmillan, 2008. Weldon analyzes how Hawthorne depicts death and his characters' reactions to death in his four major novels and "The Custom House." Includes notes, a bibliography, and an index.

Wineapple, Brenda. *Hawthorne: A Life.* New York: Alfred A. Knopf, 2003. A meticulously researched, even-handed analysis of Hawthorne's often contradictory life that proposes that much of Hawthorne's fiction was autobiographical. Includes more than one hundred pages of notes, a bibliography, and an index.

E. T. A. HOFFMANN

Born: Königsberg, East Prussia (now Kaliningrad, Russia); January 24, 1776
Died: Berlin, Prussia (now in Germany); June 25, 1822
Also known as: Ernst Theodor Wilhelm Hoffmann

PRINCIPAL LONG FICTION

Die Elixiere des Teufels: Nachgelassene Papiere des Bruders Medardus, eines Kapuziners, 1815-1816 (*The Devil's Elixirs: From the Posthumous Papers of Brother Medardus, a Capuchin Friar*, 1824)
Lebensansichten des Katers Murr, nebst fragmentarischer Biographie des Kapellmeisters Johannes Kreisler in zufälligen Makulaturblättern, 1819-1821 (*The Life and Opinions of Kater Murr, with the Fragmentary Biography of Kapellmeister Johannes Kreisler on Random Sheets of Scrap Paper*, 1969; also known as *The Educated Cat*)

OTHER LITERARY FORMS

For most of his life, E. T. A. Hoffmann (HAWF-mahn) cherished the hope that he would one day be remembered as a composer, and it was only late in his career as an artist that literary preoccupations began to outweigh his interest in music. By the time of his death, Hoffmann had nevertheless produced a considerable literary oeuvre that included two novels and more than seventy tales. Hoffmann gathered most of the tales into three collections. He published the first under the title *Fantasiestücke in Callots Manier* (1814-1815; *Fantasy Pieces in Callot's Manner*, 1996). Included in this collection are Hoffmann's important first story, "Ritter Gluck: Eine Erinnerung aus dem Jahr 1809" ("Ritter Gluck"), as well as his most famous fairy tale, "Der goldene Topf: Ein Marchen aus der neuen Zeit" ("The Golden Flower Pot"). Hoffmann's second collection, *Nachtstücke* (1817; night pieces), contains his most ghostly, even ghoulish, creations. Its opening story, "Der Sandmann" ("The Sandman"), still served Sigmund Freud in 1919 as a case study of the human sense of the uncanny. Into the four volumes of *Die Serapionsbrüder* (1819-1821; *The Serapion Brethren*, 1886-1892) Hoffmann incorporated "Rat Krespel" ("Councillor Krespel"), "Die Bergwerke zu Falun" ("The Mines of Falun"), and—immortalized by Peter Ilich Tchaikovsky in 1892 as *The Nutcracker Suite*—the fairy tale "Nussknacker und Mausekönig" ("Nutcracker and the King of Mice"). The first detective story in European literature and Hoffmann's most popular tale during his lifetime, "Das Fräulein von Scudéri" ("Mademoiselle de Scudéri"), also appeared in *The Serapion Brethren*.

During the last three years of his life, Hoffmann wrote three lengthy, complex tales in which he tried to achieve a unique blend of fairy tale, social satire, and aesthetic speculation: *Klein Zaches, genannt Zinnober* (1819; *Little Zaches, Surnamed Zinnober*, 1971), *Prinzessin Brambilla: Ein Capriccio nach Jakob Callot* (1821; *Princess Brambilla: A*

E. T. A. Hoffmann
(Library of Congress)

"Capriccio" in the Style of Jacques Callot, 1971), and *Meister Floh: Ein Märchen in sieben Abenteuern zweier Freunde* (1822; *Master Flea: A Fairy Tale in Seven Adventures of Two Friends*, 1826). Hoffmann's letters and diaries were published in the four-volume *Tagebücher* in 1971, and a volume of his letters was published in English in 1977.

ACHIEVEMENTS

In his own day, E. T. A. Hoffmann became a successful writer in a remarkably short time. His ghost and horror stories were received with favor by critics and with enthusiasm by the general reading public. Still, few would have considered Hoffmann to be more than an admittedly original and masterful entertainer. With his mixture of the miraculous, the fantastic, and the horrible, he clearly catered to his generation's fascination with the occult and his readers' thirst for the thrill of a spine-chilling story.

After Hoffmann's death, his reputation as a writer diminished rapidly and was finally destroyed by a formidable opponent from abroad. In 1827, Sir Walter Scott published in *Foreign Quarterly Review* a scathing attack against the excessive employment of supernatural elements in fiction titled "On the Supernatural in Fictitious Composition; and Particularly on the Works of Ernest Theodore William Hoffmann." Using the works of Hoffmann to make his point, Scott concluded that only an opium-inflamed mind could have conceived such frightful chimeras. Scott's assault on Hoffmann's reputation proved fatal, because Johann Wolfgang von Goethe then made it his personal mission to recommend Scott's indictment of the unsavory Hoffmann to the sane sensibilities of his German compatriots.

That Hoffmann's writings survived this Olympian disapproval is largely the result of their success in France. Though none of Hoffmann's works had been translated into a foreign language during his life, French translations of several of his tales appeared shortly after his death and were quickly followed by a veritable Hoffmann vogue among France's most distinguished writers. Honoré de Balzac and Charles Baudelaire showed themselves to be greatly impressed, and in 1836, Gérard de Nerval summarized the French conception of Germany's literary pantheon by speaking of Germany as the land of Friedrich Schiller, Goethe, and Hoffmann. Stimulated by the French reception, enthusiasm for Hoffmann caught fire in Russia as well. Indeed, no major Russian writer of the nineteenth century—from Alexander Pushkin and Nikolai Gogol to Fyodor Dostoevski and Leo Tolstoy—failed to acknowledge Hoffmann's impact on his work.

In the Anglo-Saxon world, by contrast, Scott's article squelched whatever interest there might have been in the achievements of Hoffmann. Still, as if by an ironic twist, it is in that world that Hoffmann doubtless found his most congenial successor, Edgar Allan Poe. The precise nature and extent of Hoffmann's influence on Poe, however, remains a much-debated and apparently elusive issue among literary historians.

Hoffmann would certainly have derived special gratification from the fact that, while his own musical compositions did not bring him fame, composers throughout the nineteenth century set his literary inspirations to music. Thus, for a wide and international audience, Hoffmann's name is often linked, if not identified, with the names of his greatest musical admirers. Robert Schumann's *Kreisleriana* (1838; eight fantasies for keyboard devoted to Kreisler, the hero of Hoffmann's second novel), Jacques Offenbach's opera *Les Contes d'Hoffmann* (1881; *The Tales of Hoffmann*), and Tchaikovsky's ballet *The Nutcracker Suite* are only the best known of many musical offerings to the genius of Hoffmann.

In the twentieth century, Hoffmann finally emerged, even in Germany, as one of that country's most brilliant writers of fiction. He became especially valued as a fearless explorer of the labyrinthine qualities of the human psyche in its desperate search for inner order in the face of instinctual lust and aggression. Hoffmann's works definitely began to cast their spell again, although more than ever before readers often found themselves feeling ambivalent about what is charm and what is curse within that spell's obsessive power.

BIOGRAPHY

Ernst Theodor Wilhelm Hoffmann—who in later life replaced his third baptismal name with Amadeus, in honor of Wolfgang Amadeus Mozart—was born in Königsberg, then the capital of East Prussia, now a Russian city known as Kaliningrad. The disastrous marriage between his father, an alcoholic lawyer, and his mother, a mentally unstable recluse, was dissolved when Hoffmann was only three years old. He subsequently grew up under the pedantic tutelage of a bachelor uncle. The precocious boy spent a loveless and lonely childhood from which only his instructions in music and painting provided some much-needed relief.

At the age of sixteen, Hoffmann enrolled as a student of law at the University of Königsberg. Three years later, he passed his examinations with great distinction. He then joined the legal branch of Prussia's civil service and was employed in various capacities in Glogau (1796-1798), Berlin (1798-1800), Posen (1800-1802), Plock (1802-1804), and Warsaw (1804-1806). All through these years, Hoffmann combined a punctilious execution of his official duties with an increasing interest in music as well as a wild bachelor existence in which the consumption of alcohol played an increasingly significant part. Hoffmann's marriage in 1802 to Michalina Rohrer, the daughter of a minor Polish civil servant, was entered into almost casually and seems to have been of little consequence to Hoffmann for the rest of his life.

It was in Warsaw that Hoffmann seriously started to cultivate a second career as composer and conductor. When, in 1806, the collapse of Prussia's Polish empire under the Napoleonic onslaught deprived him of his position and livelihood in Warsaw, he decided to embark on a musical career. For more than a year, he tried to establish himself in Berlin—an impossible task, as it turned out, in the defeated and impoverished capital of Prussia. He finally accepted a position as music director at the theater and opera house of Bamberg, a small town in northeastern Bavaria.

Hoffmann began his career in music with great expectations and, in spite of an almost immediate disenchantment with the new occupation, remained in Bamberg for four and a half years, supplementing his frequently uncertain income by giving music lessons to members of patrician families in town. His hopeless passion for the gifted vocal student Julia Marc was to become the most embittering experience of his stay. In 1813, Hoffmann joined an opera company that traveled between Leipzig and Dresden, yet this change only caused his professional frustrations to reach new heights. When an influential friend, Theodor Gottlieb von Hippel, managed to have him reinstated in Prussia's legal service in 1814, Hoffmann eagerly jumped at the chance. He returned to his beloved Berlin, where he was to reside until his death in 1822.

In 1814, Hoffmann was thirty-eight years old. Until that time, little in his life suggested that during the eight years left to him he was to become one of the most prominent writers of his age. In the preceding ten years, he had made a concerted effort to establish himself as a composer. By 1814, the list of his compositions included several operas, two masses, and one symphony as well as a considerable quantity of vocal and instrumental music, yet it was only with the publication of his first collection of tales, during the same year, that Hoffmann finally gained the recognition that had eluded him in all of his musical productivity. Obviously exhilarated by the experience of success, Hoffmann set out to write with single-minded fervor. Publishers sought him out, and so did the literary salons of Berlin. The publishers Hoffmann tried to satisfy; the literary salons, however, he more and more regularly exchanged for the wine cellar of Lutter and Wegener, where he and his alter ego, the famous actor Ludwig Devrient, drank themselves into states of fantastic exaltation.

In spite of his private excesses, Hoffmann's professional career—he was to become vice president of the Supreme Court of Prussia—and literary career proceeded with unimpeded speed until his body gave way under the triple strain. In 1821, Hoffmann began to suffer from a rapidly advancing paralysis, perhaps the result of a syphilitic infection. Writing—finally dictating—at a feverish pace, Hoffmann died several months later, at the age of forty-six.

ANALYSIS

E. T. A. Hoffmann's literary work constitutes a compelling and insightful expression of the prevailing anxieties of a deeply unsettled age. The rational improvement of the private self and the enforced stability of the social self were severely shaken by the upheavals of the French Revolution and the rise of Napoleon I's will to power. The heroes of this restless time revealed to the perceptive observer unexpectedly atavistic passions compared to which all existing social and ethical norms proved exceedingly insubstantial. People came to the realization that they had hardly known themselves to that point and that it was critical for them to learn more about what was asserting itself so menacingly in their lives. Interest in marginal, even pathological, states of the mind—in hypnosis, telepathy, magnetism, somnambulism, dreams, and trances—became a widespread obsession. In the wake of this trend, there arose the specter of a human existence threatened from within by chaotic instincts and threatened from without by capricious turns of events.

Probably more than any other writer of his time, Hoffmann delved into the vicissitudes that the defenseless psyche undergoes as it finds itself in the grip of conflicting demands that it can neither adjudicate nor deny. To introduce the reader to the torture chambers of the mind, Hoffmann employed an arsenal of literary devices that his audience knew well from gothic horror stories. Madness, witchery, cloak-and-dagger intrigues, secret passageways, mysterious doubles, incest, rape, and human sacrifice follow one another with baffling speed in mystifying plots that disorient readers until they can no longer tell what is real and what is imagined, what is mere wish and what is accomplished fact.

THE DEVIL'S ELIXIRS

In *The Devil's Elixirs*, the plot of which was clearly inspired by Matthew Gregory Lewis's gothic novel *The Monk: A Romance* (1796; also known as *Ambrosio: Or, The*

Monk), the Capuchin friar Medardus recounts the story of his rebellious flight from the monastery and his repentant return to it. Medardus is born within the precincts of a monastery, grows up in the vicinity of a nunnery, and promptly resolves to live a religious life himself. After having become an extraordinarily successful preacher at his monastery, he suddenly experiences a breakdown of his rhetorical abilities and is desperate for a cure from the mysterious ailment. He knows that among the monastery's sacred relics is preserved a flask filled with a potent elixir that the Devil had once offered to the hermit Saint Anthony during his temptations in the desert. Medardus takes a drink from the flask and finds his powers restored, but he also senses new and ominous passions rushing through his veins. Medardus's superior, concerned about the peace of the monastic community, soon finds himself forced to send the agitated and arrogant monk on a mission to Rome.

From the moment Medardus leaves the monastery, the reader is hard put to assess the actual nature of the monk's frenzied adventures. Torn between contradictory desires, Medardus's personality repeatedly breaks apart, integral elements battling one another as life-size enemies. Presented with a chance to assume another identity—which in fact appeals to everything he has suppressed during his years as a monk—Medardus wantonly enters an adulterous affair with a baroness while, at the same time, falling in love with her angelic stepdaughter, Aurelie. The resulting emotional turmoil culminates in a scene of horror in which Medardus poisons the baroness and tries to rape Aurelie. Momentarily exorcised from his evil self by the enormity of the crime, he hurries away in frantic fear of his own passions.

After further wanderings, Medardus meets Aurelie again. This time, he is determined to court her with genuine love and devotion, yet the demoniac compulsion to subjugate and destroy the love he awakens never completely leaves him. On their wedding day, the indomitable strain in Medardus's soul flares up with renewed ferocity. As he sees his alter ego carted off to execution, he refuses to let it die, rejects Aurelie and everything noble in himself, and runs off, his satanic double on his back, until rage and frustration deprive him of his senses. Several months later, Medardus revives, finding himself in an Italian insane asylum. He proceeds to submit his body to a rigorous course of penance, and, after many additional adventures, he returns to the monastery from which he had set out. He arrives the day before Aurelie is to take her religious vows in a nearby convent. Overwhelmed by the coincidence, Medardus feels rent apart again. He claims Aurelie for himself and slays her on the steps of the altar. Having thus destroyed the object of his passion, Medardus is at last free to reject the call of instinct and to reenter the tranquillity of monastic life.

The Devil's Elixirs can be read on at least two levels. Late in the novel, the reader is told that the main characters are, unbeknown to themselves, members of one family that for several generations has lived under a curse resulting from a sacrilege committed by an ancestor. That curse can be laid to rest only if the remaining members of the family renounce earthly love and thus mark the family for extinction. Medardus and Aurelie, the last of the unholy clan, embrace the necessary self-denial and break the chain of sin and guilt. The notion of an inherited curse was the stock-in-trade of the gothic novel. The introduction of supernatural agencies allowed authors to explain the many otherwise inexplicable coincidences needed to sustain the suspense of their stories. The real impact of *The Devil's Elixirs*, therefore, does not arise from Hoffmann's belated revelations about Medardus's guilt-ridden family but rather from his relentless depiction of a man's fearful struggle with instincts that lie, in stubborn and hostile cynicism, beyond the reach of his moral self.

Medardus, of course, does put an end to the curse, not only for his family but also for his own troubled self. *The Devil's Elixirs*, after all, is his autobiography; it contains his retrospective creation of a continuous self and signals a significant victory over his chaotic past. The success with which Medardus has managed to construct—from the fragmented impulses of his psyche—the notion of a responsible personality shows that he has established for himself a basis for moral behavior. Still, he has stabilized his personality at a high price: the exclusion of all instinct, the truncating of his very life. Secure as Medardus's self now might be, a unified self it is not, and no amount of Catholic pageantry can disguise the pessimism of that conclusion.

THE LIFE AND OPINIONS OF KATER MURR

Hoffmann's second novel, *The Life and Opinions of Kater Murr*, remained a fragment, a fact that—considering the less-than-convincing end of *The Devil's Elixirs*—rather enhances its effectiveness. In contrast to *The Devil's Elixirs*, which in spite of its confusing plot follows the traditional technique of a chronological narration, *The Life and Opinions of Kater Murr* surprises the reader with one of the most amusingly original structures in German literature. The novel is composed of two distinct narratives bewilderingly conflated: the autobiography of a tomcat (Murr) and the biography of a musician (Kreisler). Murr, so the editor apologizes, had, while writing his memoirs, torn up the biography of Kreisler in order to use its pages as writing pad and blotting paper. When Murr had his work published, the printer mistakenly thought the sheets from Kreisler's life to be part of the tomcat's autobiography, so that in the finished product two very dissimilar stories interrupt each other with maddening regularity.

In Murr's account, Hoffmann parodies the educational novel, the bildungsroman, of his day. Murr, a smugly egotistical tomcat, pompously details the stages by which he planned to advance himself in the world. With all the naïveté of his inflated ego, he tells how he first embarked on an academic career, then felt free to pursue romantic love, became involved in the political arena, and finally aspired to be recognized as a true gentleman. At the end, the reader is informed that the splendid cat has unfortunately died, a fate common to those who achieve too much at too early an age.

That Murr's penmanship at least left much to be desired might be gathered from the fact that about two-thirds of all pages in the book were apparently needed as blotting paper. These pages tell of the life of Johannes Kreisler. The story opens at the small court of Sieghartsweiler, where for some time now the former mistress of Prince Irenäus has spun an intrigue that is to lead to a marriage between Irenäus's half-witted son Ignaz and her own daughter, the beautiful and sensitive Julia.

The plot gets under way as the eccentric musician Kreisler joins the tedious life at the miniature court. He soon is asked to give Julia and Hedwiga, Prince Irenäus's only daughter, music lessons, and the two girls are quickly attracted to Kreisler by the strange powers that his curiously extravagant behavior reveals. Their idyllic association is destroyed by the news that Hedwiga is to marry the handsome but unscrupulous Prince Hektor. Hektor, assured that in time he will possess Hedwiga, promptly sets out to seduce Julia. For a while, Kreisler manages to foil Hektor's plans, until an attempt on Kreisler's life forces the musician to flee from court. He takes up residence in a nearby Benedictine abbey and there resumes work as composer and music director. Unfortunately, Kreisler has barely achieved peace in his new surroundings when an urgent letter from Sieghartsweiler implores him to return to court, where a double wedding joining Hektor and Hedwiga as well as Ignaz and Julia is about to take place. Whether Kreisler was able to prevent this impending misfortune remains unclear, as the novel breaks off in the middle of a sentence.

Throughout the story, evidence accumulates suggesting that Kreisler, whose identity is the central mystery of the plot, may well be the victim of a long-standing court intrigue. The attraction that Kreisler's character exerts, however, seems to depend even less on the unraveling of a web of fateful family relations than does the account of the friar Medardus. What the torn-out pages of Kreisler's biography tell about the torn-up life of its hero, no clandestine schemes could possibly bind together. Kreisler's existential rootlessness is ultimately the result not of clever machinations from without but of his own self-lacerating quest for human perfection in a petty environment. Sheltering a highly idealistic and highly vulnerable personality behind masks of cynicism and eccentricity, Kreisler is plagued by the sudden shifts of an artistic vision that shows the trivial to be sublime as often as it shows the sublime to be trivial. Thus barred from any consistent perspective on world or self, he is forced to vacillate between ecstatic joy and despondent frustration: ecstatic joy at the world's grandeur, despondent frustration at its inevitable depreciation at the hands of unresponsive men. In contrast to Medardus, who could still reconstruct his divided will from the secure vision of an undisputed faith, Kreisler's divided perception finds no such security; even his monastic retreat offers him hardly more than a brief respite from his self-tormented life.

It would be inaccurate, however, to think of *The Life and Opinions of Kater Murr* as a thoroughly pessimistic novel. It must not be forgotten that Hoffmann chained Kreisler's volatile idealism to the pedestrian common sense of the tomcat Murr. If the musician unmasks the cat's vain shallowness, Murr, too, provides a mocking mirror for Kreisler's pursuit of perfection at the Lilliputian court of Sieghartsweiler. How serious Hoffmann was about seeing the perspectives of the conformist animal and of the nonconformist artist as complementary becomes clear when Murr ends his memoirs with the remark that henceforth he will live with a new master, the concertmaster Kreisler.

Murr's death, of course, leaves it to the reader to imagine what the unlikely companions could have meant to each other. For Hoffmann, the outcome of their partnership cannot be in doubt. Whenever people admit to being part self-serving cat and part self-effacing idealist, self-irony—the tolerant smile at one's own incongruous personality—will turn the menace of a divided ego into the promise of a healthily deflated, less commanding but also less aggressive self. Although Hoffmann's creatures have not yet attained their creator's humorous wisdom, the reader understands and is invited to rise to its challenge.

Joachim Scholz

OTHER MAJOR WORKS

SHORT FICTION: *Fantasiestücke in Callots Manier*, 1814-1815 (*Fantasy Pieces in Callot's Manner*, 1996); *Nachtstücke*, 1817; *Klein Zaches, genannt Zinnober*, 1819 (*Little Zaches, Surnamed Zinnober*, 1971); *Die Serapionsbrüder*, 1819-1821 (4 volumes; *The Serapion Brethren*, 1886-1892); *Prinzessin Brambilla: Ein Capriccio nach Jakob Callot*, 1821 (*Princess Brambilla: A "Capriccio" in the Style of Jacques Callot*, 1971); *Meister Floh: Ein Märchen in sieben Abenteuern zweier Freunde*, 1822 (*Master Flea: A Fairy Tale in Seven Adventures of Two Friends*, 1826); *Four Tales*, 1962; *The Best Tales of Hoffmann*, 1967; *Selected Writings of E. T. A. Hoffmann*, 1969 (2 volumes); *The Golden Pot, and Other Tales*, 1992.

NONFICTION: *Briefwechsel*, 1967-1969 (3 volumes; correspondence); *Tagebücher*, 1971 (4 volumes; diaries); *Selected Letters*, 1977.

MUSICAL COMPOSITIONS: *Liebe und Eifersucht: Oper*, 1807; *Trois Canzonettes*, 1808; *Arlequinn: Ballett*, 1811; *Undine*, 1816; *Musikalische Werke*, 1922-1927.

BIBLIOGRAPHY

Chantler, Abigail. *E. T. A. Hoffmann's Musical Aesthetics*. Burlington, Vt.: Ashgate, 2006. Hoffmann was a music critic and composer as well as a writer, and this book describes his aesthetic ideas about music, placing them within the context of late eighteenth and early nineteenth century philosophy. Also discusses the significance of Hoffmann's literary works.

Daemmrich, Horst S. *The Shattered Self: E. T. A. Hoffmann's Tragic Vision*. Detroit, Mich.: Wayne State University Press, 1973. Important study of Hoffmann's literary work begins with an introduction that places Hoffmann in historical context and outlines critical appraisals of his work. Analysis of Hoffmann's major themes and motifs finds in the author's work a portrayal of "the disintegration of the individual in a world of uncontrolled forces." Includes extensive notes, bibliography, and index.

Hewett-Thayer, Harvey W. *Hoffmann: Author of the Tales*. Princeton, N.J.: Princeton University Press, 1938. Classic work, intended as an introduction for both students and general readers, that provides a comprehensive biography of Hoffmann and discussion of his works, with very readable story analyses. Informative footnotes include suggestions for further reading as well as the original German for many passages when these appear in English translation in the main text. Supplemented by a listing of Hoffmann's literary works with dates of publication, a bibliography, and an index of names and works.

Kohlenbach, Margarete. "Women and Artists: E. T. A. Hoffmann's Implicit Critique of Early Romanticism." *Modern Language Review* 89, no. 3 (July, 1994): 659-673. Examines the Romantic philosophy of love in the novel *The Life and Opinions of Kater Murr* and in Hoffmann's other works. Argues that the character Johannes Kreisler expresses ideas about love that are at variance with Hoffmann's writings as a whole and explains the significance of this divergence.

McGlathery, James M. *E. T. A. Hoffmann.* New York: Twayne, 1997. Interesting introduction to Hoffmann's life and work analyzes his major works of fiction and also discusses the critical reception of Hoffmann's writings and Hoffmann's own works of criticism.

Negus, Kenneth. *E. T. A. Hoffmann's Other World: The Romantic Author and His "New Mythology."* Philadelphia: University of Pennsylvania Press, 1965. Very readable monograph focuses on Hoffmann's development of a coherent body of myth in his fantasy world—a "new mythology" founded on an inner spiritual (or psychological) world but extending to form a "cosmic myth." Examines all of Hoffmann's major literary works as well as many of his minor works with a view to laying a critical foundation for his narrative art. Includes select bibliography and index.

Riou, Jeanne. *Imagination in German Romanticism: Re-thinking the Self and Its Environment.* New York: Peter Lang, 2004. Examines the works of Hoffmann and other German writers and philosophers to explore the Romantic concept of the imagination and the imagination's critique of reason.

VICTOR HUGO

Born: Besançon, France; February 26, 1802
Died: Paris, France; May 22, 1885
Also known as: Victor-Marie Hugo

Principal long fiction

Han d'Islande, 1823 (*Hans of Iceland*, 1845)
Bug-Jargal, 1826 (*The Noble Rival*, 1845)
Le Dernier Jour d'un condamné, 1829 (*The Last Day of a Condemned*, 1840)
Notre-Dame de Paris, 1831 (*The Hunchback of Notre Dame*, 1833)
Claude Gueux, 1834
Les Misérables, 1862 (English translation, 1862)
Les Travailleurs de la mer, 1866 (*The Toilers of the Sea*, 1866)
L'Homme qui rit, 1869 (*The Man Who Laughs*, 1869)
Quatre-vingt-treize, 1874 (*Ninety-Three*, 1874)

Other literary forms

Victor Hugo (YEW-goh) dominates nineteenth century literature in France both by the length of his writing career and by the diversity of his work. Indeed, it is difficult to think of a literary form Hugo did not employ. Lyric, satiric, and epic poetry; drama in verse and prose; political polemic and social criticism—all are found in his oeuvre. His early plays and poetry made him a leader of the Romantic movement. His political writing included the publication of a newspaper, *L'Événement*, in 1851, which contributed to his exile from the Second Empire. During his exile, he wrote vehement criticism of Napoleon III as well as visionary works of poetry. His poetic genius ranged from light verse to profound epics; his prose works include accounts of his travels and literary criticism as well as fiction.

Achievements

The complete works of Victor Hugo constitute more nearly a legend than an achievement. In poetry, Hugo had become a national institution by the end of his life. He was a member of the Académie Française, an officer of the Légion d'Honneur, and a Peer of France under the monarchy of Louis-Philippe. When he died, he was accorded the singular honor of lying in state beneath Paris's Arc de Triomphe before his burial in the Panthéon.

During his lifetime, Hugo's novels accounted for much of his popularity with the public. Both sentimental and dramatic, they were excellent vehicles for spreading his humanitarian ideas among large numbers of people. His two most famous novels are *The Hunchback of Notre Dame* and *Les Misérables*. The former is an example of dramatic historical romance, inspired in France by the novels of Sir Walter Scott. It is said to have created in-

Victor Hugo
(Library of Congress)

terest in and ensured the architectural preservation of the Notre Dame cathedral in Paris. It is also a study in Romanticism, with its evocation of the dark force of fate and the intricate intertwining of the grotesque and the sublime.

Les Misérables testifies to Hugo's optimistic faith in humanitarian principles and social progress. The intricate and elaborate plot confronts both social injustice and indifference. It is typical of many nineteenth century attitudes in its emphasis on education, charity, and love as powerful forces in saving the unfortunate creatures of the lower classes from becoming hardened criminals. *Les Misérables* is a novel on an epic scale both in its historical tableaux and as the story of a human soul. Thus, even though Hugo's achievements in the novel are of a lesser scale than his poetry and drama, they are enduring and worthy monuments to the author and to his century.

BIOGRAPHY

Victor-Marie Hugo was born in Besançon, France, in 1802, the third son of Joseph-Léopold-Sigisbert Hugo and Sophie-Françoise Trébuchet. His father had been born in Nancy and his mother in Nantes. They met in the Vendée, where Léopold Hugo was serving in the Napoleonic army. His military career kept the family on the move, and it was during Major Hugo's tour of duty with the Army of the Rhine that Victor-Marie was born in Besançon.

Léopold and Sophie did not have a happy marriage, and after the birth of their third son, they were frequently separated. By 1808, Léopold had been promoted to general and was made a count in Napoleon I's empire. During one reunion of Hugo's parents, Victor and his brothers joined General Hugo in Spain, a land that fascinated Victor and left its mark on his poetic imagination.

In spite of their father's desire that they should study for entrance to the École Polytechnique, Victor and his next older brother, Eugène, spent their free time writing poetry, hoping to emulate their master, François-René de Chateaubriand. In 1817, Victor earned the first official recognition of his talent by winning an honorable mention in a poetry competition sponsored by the Académie Française. Because he was only fifteen, the secretary of the Académie asked to meet him, and the press displayed an interest in the young poet.

Eugène and Victor received permission from their father to study law in 1818 and left their boarding school to live with their mother in Paris. Sophie encouraged them in their ambition to become writers and never insisted that they attend lectures or study for examinations. Victor continued to receive recognition for his poems, and the brothers founded a review, *Le Conservateur littéraire*, in 1819. Unfortunately, the two brothers also shared a passion for the same young woman, Adèle Foucher. In love as well as in poetry, Eugène took second place to his younger brother. Adèle and Victor were betrothed after the death of Madame Hugo, who had opposed the marriage. The wedding took place in 1822. At the wedding feast, Eugène went insane; he spent nearly all the rest of his life in institutions.

Hugo's early publications were favorably received by the avant-garde of Romanticism, and by 1824, Hugo was a dominant personality in Charles Nodier's Cénacle, a group of Romantic poets united in their struggle against the rules of French classicism. The year 1824 also marked the birth of Léopoldine, the Hugos' second child and the first to survive infancy. She was always to have a special place in her father's heart. In 1827, the Hugos had another child, Charles.

The Hugos were acquainted with many of those writers and artists who are now considered major figures in the Romantic movement, among them Alexandre Dumas, *père*, Alfred de Vigny, and Eugène Delacroix. The sculptor David d'Angers recorded Hugo's youthful appearance on a medallion. (Decades later, sculptor Auguste Rodin would also preserve his impression of the aged poet.) The influential critic Charles-Augustin Sainte-Beuve also became a frequent visitor to the Hugos' apartment.

Momentum was building for the Romantic movement, and in December, 1827, Hugo published a play, *Cromwell* (English translation, 1896), the preface to which became the manifesto of the young Romantics. Two years later, his verse drama *Hernani* (pr., pb. 1830; English translation, 1830) would provide the battleground between Romanticism and classicism. In the meantime, General Hugo had died in 1828, and a son, François-Victor, had been born to Victor and Adèle.

The famous "battle of *Hernani*" at the work's premiere on January 10, 1830, was an outcry against outmoded conventions in every form of art. Artists sympathetic to Romanticism had been recruited from the Latin Quarter in support of Hugo's play, which breaks the rules of versification as well as the three unities of classical drama (time, place, and action). They engaged in a battle for modern artistic freedom against the "authorities" of the past. *Hernani* therefore had political significance as well: The restoration of the Bourbons was in its final months.

Stormy performances continued at the Théâtre-Français for several months, and, by the end, the tyranny of classicism had been demolished. In addition to artistic freedom for all, *Hernani* brought financial well-being to the Hugos. It also brought Sainte-Beuve increasingly into their family circle, where he kept Adèle company while Hugo was distracted by the *Hernani* affair.

In July of 1830, Victor and Adèle's last child, Adèle, came into the world to the sound of the shots of the July Revolution, which deposed Charles X, the last Bourbon "king of France." The new monarch was Louis-Philippe of the Orléans branch of the royal family, who called himself "king of the French." There was now a deep attachment between Madame Hugo and Sainte-Beuve. Although Adèle and Victor were never to separate, their marriage had become a platonic companionship.

In 1832, the Hugos moved to the Place Royale (now called the Place des Vosges), to the home that would later become the Victor Hugo museum in Paris. Scarcely a year passed without a publication by Hugo. By that time, he was able to command enormous sums for his work in comparison with other authors of his day. He was already becoming a legend, with disciples rather than friends. His ambition had always been fierce, and he was beginning to portray himself as a bard, a seer with powers to guide all France. Only in his family life was he suffering from less than complete success.

At the time, *Lucrèce Borgia* (pr., pb. 1833; *Lucretia Borgia*, 1842) was in rehearsal, and among the cast was a lovely young actor, Juliette Drouet. Soon after opening night, she and Hugo became lovers, and they remained so for many years. Juliette had not been a brilliant actor, but she abandoned what might have been a moderately successful career to live the rest of her life in seclusion and devotion to Hugo. In *Les Chants du crépuscule* (1835; *Songs of Twilight*, 1836), Hugo included thirteen poems to Juliette and three to Adèle, expressing the deep affection he still felt for his wife.

Critics were beginning to snipe at Hugo for what seemed to be shallow emotions and facile expressions. (Sainte-Beuve deplored Hugo's lack of taste, but Sainte-Beuve was hardly a disinterested critic.) The fashion for Hugo seemed to be somewhat on the wane, although adverse criticism did not inhibit the flow of his writing. The publication of *Les Rayons et les ombres* (1840) marked the end of one phase of Hugo's poetry. The splendor of the language and the music in his verse as well as the visual imagery were richer than ever, but Hugo was still criticized for lacking genuine emotion. He had by this time decided, however, to devote himself to his political ambitions.

He was determined to become a Peer of France, having been made an officer of the Légion d'Honneur several years before. In order to obtain a peerage, a man of letters had to be a member of the Académie Française. After presenting himself for the fifth time, he was elected to the Académie in 1841, and in the spring of 1845 he was named a Peer of France, a status that protected him from arrest the following summer, when police found him in flagrante delicto with the wife of Auguste Biard. Léonie Biard was sent to the Saint-Lazare prison, but Hugo's cordial relations with King Louis-Philippe helped calm the scandal, and Léonie retired to a convent for a short while before resuming her affair with Hugo.

An event of much deeper emotional impact had occurred in 1843, when Hugo's eldest daughter, Léopoldine, had married Charles Vacquerie. Hugo had found it difficult to be separated from his child, who went to live in Le Havre. That summer, in July, he paid a brief visit to the young couple before leaving on a journey with Juliette. In early September, while traveling, Hugo read in a newspaper that Léopoldine and Charles had been drowned in a boating accident several days before. Grief-stricken, Hugo was also beset by guilt at having left his family for a trip with his mistress. He published nothing more for nine years.

Eventually, the political events of 1848 eclipsed Hugo's complex relationship with his wife and two mistresses. During the Revolution of 1848, Louis-Philippe was forced to abdicate. The monarchy was rejected outright by the provisional government under the leadership of the Romantic poet Alphonse de Lamartine. The peerage was also abolished, and although Hugo sought political office, he was generally considered to be too dramatic and rhetorical to be of practical use in government. More than a few of his contemporary politicians viewed him as a self-interested opportunist. He seems to have longed for the glory of being a statesman without the necessary political sense.

On June 24, 1848, militant insurgents had occupied the Hugo apartment on the Place Royal. The family had fled, and Adèle had refused to live there again. One of the first visitors to their new apartment was Louis-Napoleon Bonaparte, nephew of Napoleon I. He was seeking Hugo's support of his candidacy for president of the new republic. Thereafter, Louis-Napoleon was endorsed in Hugo's newspaper, *L'Événement*, which he had founded that summer and which was edited and published by his sons.

Louis-Napoleon became president in December of 1848, but he did not long remain on good terms with Hugo. Hugo and *L'Événement* increasingly took leftist political positions as the new government was moving toward the Right. Freedom of the press was increasingly limited, and, in 1851, both of Hugo's sons were imprisoned for violating restrictions on the press and for showing disrespect to the government.

It was in this year that Juliette and Léonie attempted to force Hugo to choose between them. In the end, politics resolved the conflict. On December 2, 1851, Louis-Napoleon dissolved the National Assembly and declared himself prince-president for ten years. When Hugo learned of the coup d'état, he attempted to organize some resistance. There was shooting in the streets of Paris. Juliette is given credit for saving him from violence. She hid him successfully while a false passport was prepared, and on December 11, he took the train to Brussels in disguise and under a false name. Juliette followed him into exile.

From exile, the pen was Hugo's only political weapon, and he wrote *Napoléon le petit* (1852; *Napoleon the Little*, 1852) and *Histoire d'un crime* (1877; *The History of a Crime*, 1877-1878). Having been authorized to stay in Belgium for only three months, Hugo made plans to move to Jersey, one of the Channel Islands. His family joined him, and Juliette took rooms nearby. He began work on *Les Châtiments* (1853), poems inspired by anger and pride. France remained his preoccupation while he was in exile. Indeed, it has been said that exile renewed Hugo's career. Certainly, his fame suffered neither from his banishment nor from the tone of righteous indignation with which he could thus proclaim his contempt for the empire of Napoleon III.

There was a group of militant exiles on the island, and when, in 1855, they attacked Queen Victoria in their newspaper for visiting Napoleon III, Jersey officials informed them that they would have to leave. The Hugos moved to Guernsey, where they eventually purchased Hauteville House. At about the same time, in the spring of 1856, *Les Contemplations* was published, marking Hugo's reappearance as a lyric poet. Juliette moved to a nearby house that she called Hauteville-Féerie, where the lawn was inscribed with flowers forming a bright "V H." Although Hugo's prestige benefited immensely from his exile, his family suffered from their isolation, especially his daughter Adèle, who was in her early twenties. Eventually, she followed an army officer, Albert Pinson, to Canada, convinced that they would marry. After nine years of erratic, senseless wandering, she was brought home to end her life in a mental institution.

For her father, exile was a time to write. The first two volumes of *La Légende des siècles* (1859-1883; *The Legend of the Centuries*, 1894) was followed by *The Toilers of the Sea* and *The Man Who Laughs*, among other works. In 1859, Napoleon III offered amnesty of Republican exiles, but Hugo refused to accept it, preferring the grandeur of defiance and martyrdom on his rocky island.

After Adèle's flight, the island became intolerable for Madame Hugo. In 1865, she left for Brussels with the younger son, François-Victor, and spent most of her time there during the remainder of Hugo's exile. In his isolation, Hugo continued his work.

On the occasion of the Paris International Exposition in 1867, the imperial censors permitted a revival of *Hernani* at the Théâtre-Français. Adèle traveled to Paris to witness the great success of the play and the adulation of her husband. Another visitor to the Paris Exposition would be instrumental in ending Hugo's self-imposed banishment. Future German Chancellor Otto von Bismarck came to Paris ostensibly on a state visit from Prussia but secretly taking the measure of French armaments. Adèle died in Brussels the following year. Her sons accompanied her body to its grave in France; Hugo stopped at the French border and soon returned to Guernsey with Juliette.

One of Hugo's dreams had always been a United States of Europe, and in Lausanne in 1869, he presided over the congress of the International League for Peace and Freedom. Early in 1870, he was honored by the Second Empire with a revival of *Lucretia Borgia* and a recitation of his poetry before the emperor by Sarah Bernhardt. On July 14 of that year, the poet planted an acorn at Hauteville House. The future tree was dedicated to "the United States of Europe." By the following day, France and Prussia were at war.

The Franco-Prussian War brought an end to the Second Empire and to Hugo's nineteen years of exile. He returned in time to participate in the siege of Paris and to witness the cataclysmic events of the Commune. His own politics, however, although idealistically liberal and Republican, did not mesh with any political group in a practical way. He refused several minor offices that were offered to him by the new government and resigned after only a month as an elected deputy for Paris to the new National Assembly.

The following years were marked by family sorrows. Soon following Hugo's resignation from active politics, his elder son, Charles, died of an apoplectic stroke. Hugo was to remain devoted to his son's widow, Alice, and to his grandchildren, Jeanne and Georges. In 1872, Adèle was brought home from Barbados, insane. The following year, his younger son, François-Victor, died of tuberculosis. Only the faithful Juliette remained as a companion to Hugo in his old age.

He continued to write unceasingly in Paris, but in 1878 he suffered a stroke. This virtually brought his writing to an end, although works he had written earlier continued to be published. On his birthday in 1881, the Republic organized elaborate festivities in his honor, including a procession of admirers who passed beneath his window for hours. In May, the main part of the avenue d'Eylau was rechristened the avenue Victor-Hugo.

Juliette died in May of 1883. On his birthday in 1885, Hugo received tributes from all quarters as a venerated symbol of the French spirit. He became seriously ill in May, suffering from a lesion of the heart and congestion of the lungs. He died on May 22, 1885. Hugo's funeral was a national ceremony, the coffin lying in state beneath the Arc de Triomphe. He was the only Frenchman to be so honored before the Unknown Soldier after World War I. While Napoleon III lay buried in exile, the remains of Victor Hugo were ceremoniously interred in the Panthéon, France's shrine to her great men of letters.

ANALYSIS

The earliest published full-length fiction by Victor Hugo was *Hans of Iceland*, begun when he was eighteen years old, although not published until three years later. In part a tribute to Adèle Foucher, who was to become his wife, it is a convoluted gothic romance in which it is not clear where the author is being serious and where he is deliberately creating a parody of the popular gothic genre. It is worthwhile to begin with this youthful work, however, because it contains many themes and images that were to remain important in Hugo's work throughout his life.

HANS OF ICELAND

The characters in *Hans of Iceland* are archetypes rather than psychologically realistic figures. In a sense, it is unfair to criticize Hugo for a lack of complexity in his characterizations, because he is a creator of myths and legends—his genius does not lie in the realm of the realistic novel. This is the reason his talent as a novelist is eclipsed by the other great novelists of his century, Stendhal, Honoré de Balzac, Gustave Flaubert, and Émile Zola. Hugo's last novels were written after Flaubert's *Madame Bovary* (1857; English translation, 1886) and after Zola's first naturalistic novels, yet Hugo's late books remain closer in tone to *Hans of Iceland* than to any contemporary novel.

It is thus more useful to consider *Hans of Iceland* as a romance, following the patterns of myths and legends, rather than as a novel with claims to psychological and historical realism. Although tenuously based on historical fact, set in seventeenth century Norway, the plot of *Hans of Iceland* closely resembles that of the traditional quest. The hero, Ordener Guldenlew (Golden Lion), disguises his noble birth and sets out to rescue his beloved, the pure maiden Ethel, from the evil forces that imprison her with her father, Jean Schumaker, Count Griffenfeld. Ordener's adventures take him through dark and fearsome settings where he must overcome the monster Hans of Iceland, a mysterious being who, although a man, possesses demoniac powers and beastly desires.

As in traditional romance, the characters in *Hans of Iceland* are all good or evil, like black and white pieces in a chess game. Ethel's father is the good former grand chancellor who has been imprisoned for some years after having been unjustly accused of treason. His counterpart is the wicked Count d'Ahlefeld, who, with the treacherous countess, is responsible for Schumaker's downfall. Their son Frédéric is Ordener's rival for Ethel's love. The most treacherous villain is the count's adviser, Musdoemon, who turns out to be Frédéric's real father. Opposed to everyone, good or evil, is the man-demon Hans of Iceland, who haunts the land by dark of night, leaving the marks of his clawlike nails on his victims.

Ordener's quest begins in the morgue, where he seeks a box that had been in the possession of a military officer killed by Hans. The box contains documents proving Schumaker's innocence. Believing it to be in Hans's possession, Ordener sets off through storms and danger to recover the box.

As the adventure progresses, Hugo begins to reveal his personal preoccupations and thus to depart from the traditional romance. Hans's ambiguous nature, grotesque as he is, has some unsettling sympathetic qualities. One begins to feel, as the story progresses and as the social villains become more devious and nefarious, that Hans, the social outcast, is morally superior in spite of his diabolically glowing eyes and his tendency to crunch human bones. Hugo appears to suggest the Romantic noble savage beneath a diabolic exterior. Because Ordener is a strangely passive hero, who fails to slay Hans or even to find the box, the reader's interest is transferred to Hans. In this monster with redeeming human qualities, it is not difficult to see the prefiguration of later grotesques such as Quasimodo in *The Hunchback of Notre Dame*.

The social commentary that is constant in Hugo's narratives has its beginning here in the figure of Musdoemon, the true evil figure of the work. This adviser to the aristocracy, whose name reveals that he has the soul of a rat, betrays everyone until he is at last himself betrayed and hanged. The executioner turns out to be his brother, delighted to have revenge for Musdoemon's treachery toward him years before.

At one point, Musdoemon tricks a group of miners (the good common people) into rebelling against the king in Schumaker's name. Ordener finds himself in the midst of the angry mob as they battle the king's troops. Hans attacks both sides, increasing the confusion and slaughter. Later, at the trial of the rebels on charges of treason, Ordener takes full responsibility, thus diverting blame from Schumaker. Given the choice of execution or marriage to the daughter of the wicked d'Ahlefeld, he chooses death. He and Ethel are married in his cell and are saved by the chance discovery of the documents. Hans gives himself up and dies by his own hand.

By comparing *Hans of Iceland* with another early novel, *The Noble Rival*, the reader can trace the preoccupations that led to *The Hunchback of Notre Dame* and *Les Misérables*. *The Noble Rival* is the story of a slave revolt in Santo Domingo, Dominican Republic. The hero of the title is a slave as well as the spiritually noble leader of his people. The Romantic hero is Léopold, a Frenchman visiting his uncle's plantation. Like Ordener, Léopold is pure but essentially passive. The heroic energy belongs to the outcast from society, Bug-Jargal. In both novels, Hugo's sympathy for the "people" is apparent. The miners and the slaves point directly to the commoners of Paris in *The Hunchback of Notre Dame*.

THE HUNCHBACK OF NOTRE DAME

At the center of *The Hunchback of Notre Dame* is the theme of fatality, a word that the author imagines to have been inscribed on the wall of one of the cathedral towers as the Greek *anankè*. The cathedral is the focus of the novel, as it was the heart of medieval Paris. It is a spiritual center with an ambiguous demoniac-grotesque spirit within. Claude Frollo, the priest, is consumed by lust for a Gypsy girl, Esmeralda. Quasimodo, the bell ringer, a hunchback frighteningly deformed, is elevated by his pure love for Esmeralda, whom he attempts to save from the pernicious Frollo. In an image central to the novel and to Hugo's entire work, Frollo watches a spider and a fly caught in its web. The web, however, stretches across a pane of glass so that even if the fly should manage to escape, it will only hurl itself against the invisible barrier in its flight toward the sun. The priest will be the spider to Esmeralda but also the fly, caught in the trap of his own consuming desire. All the characters risk entrapment in the web prepared for them by fate. Even if they somehow break free of the web, the glass will block escape until death releases them from earthly concerns.

Esmeralda believes she can "fly to the sun" in the person of the handsome military captain Phoebus, but he is interested in her only in an earthly way. Frollo's destructive passion leads him to set a trap for Esmeralda. For a fee, Phoebus agrees to hide Frollo where he can watch a rendezvous between Phoebus and Esmeralda. Unable to contain himself, the priest leaves his hiding place, stabs Phoebus, and leaves. Esmeralda is, of course, accused of the crime.

Quasimodo saves her from execution and gives her sanctuary in the cathedral, but she is betrayed again by Frollo, who orders her to choose between him and the gallows. Like the fly, Esmeralda tears herself away from the priest to collapse at the foot of the gibbet. Phoebus, who did not die of his wound, remains indifferent to her plight, but Quasimodo pushes Frollo to his death from the tower of Notre Dame as the priest gloats over Esmeralda's execution. Quasimodo, the grotesque, gains in moral stature throughout the novel, just as Frollo falls from grace. Two years later, a deformed skeleton is found in a burial vault beside that of the virtuous Esmeralda.

The Hunchback of Notre Dame and *Les Misérables* are justly Hugo's most famous novels because they combine the exposition of his social ideas with an aesthetically unified structure. By contrast, *The Last Day of a Condemned*, written in 1829, is basically a social treatise on the horrors of prison life. In the same way, *Claude Gueux*, a short work of 1834, protests against the death penalty. In both works, the writer speaks out against society's injustice to man, but it was with *Les Misérables* that the reformer's voice spoke most effectively.

LES MISÉRABLES

Les Misérables tells of the spiritual journey of Jean Valjean, a poor but honorable man, driven in desperation to steal a loaf of bread to feed his widowed sister and her children. Sent to prison, he becomes an embittered, morally deformed creature, until he is redeemed by his love for the orphan girl Cosette. The plot of the novel is quite complex, as Jean rises to respectability and descends again several times. This is true because, as a convict, he must live under an assumed name. His spiritual voyage will not end until he can stand once more as Jean Valjean. His name suggests the French verb *valoir*, "to be worth." Jean must become worthy of Jean; he cannot have value under a counterfeit name.

His first reappearance as a respectable bourgeois is as Monsieur Madeleine, Mayor of Montreuil-sur-Mer. He is soon called upon, however, to reveal his true identity in order to save another from life imprisonment for having been identified as Jean Valjean, parole breaker. He descends into society's underworld, eluding capture by his nemesis, the policeman Javert. In Hugo's works, the way down is always the way up to salvation. Just as Ordener descended into the mines, Jean must now pass through a valley (*Val*) in order to save Jean. Here, as in *The Hunchback of Notre Dame*, moral superiority is to be found among the lowly.

In order to save himself, Jean must be the savior of others. He begins by rescuing Cosette from her wicked foster parents. Later, he will save Javert from insurrectionists. His greatest test, however, will be that of saving Marius, the man Cosette loves and who will separate Jean from the girl who is his paradise. This episode is the famous flight through the sewers of Paris, a true descent into the underworld, whence Jean Valjean is re-born, his soul transfigured, clear, and serene. He still has one more trial to endure, that of regaining his own name, which, through a misunderstanding, brings a painful estrange-ment from Cosette and Marius. He begins to die but is reconciled with his children at the last moment and leaves this life with a soul radiantly transformed.

THE TOILERS OF THE SEA

Les Misérables was written partly in exile, and certain episodes begin to show a prefer-ence for images of water. *The Toilers of the Sea*, written on Guernsey in 1864 and 1865, is a novel dominated by the sea. The text originally included an introductory section titled "L'Archipel de la Manche" ("The Archipelago of the English Channel"), which Hugo's editor persuaded him to publish separately at a later date (1883). The two parts reveal that Hugo has separated sociology from fiction. It would seem that, at odds with the predomi-nant novelistic style of his time, Hugo preferred not to communicate his social philosophy through the imagery and structure of his novels. Thus, the prologue contains Hugo's doc-trine of social progress and his analysis of the geology, customs, and language of the Channel Islands. The larger section that became the published novel is once again the story of a solitary quest.

The hero, Gilliatt, is a fisherman who lives a simple, rather ordinary life with his el-derly mother on the island of Guernsey. In their house, they keep a marriage chest contain-ing a trousseau for Gilliatt's future bride. Gilliatt loves Déruchette, niece of Mess Lethierry, inventor of the steamboat *Durande*, with which he has made his fortune in com-merce. When the villain, Clubin, steals Lethierry's money and wrecks his steamer, Gilliatt's adventures begin.

Like the king of myth or legend, Lethierry offers his niece's hand in marriage to whomever can salvage the *Durande*. Gilliatt sets out upon the sea. Ominously missing are the magical beasts or mysterious beings who normally appear to assist the hero as he sets off. Even Ordener, for example, had a guide, Benignus Spiagudry, at the beginning of his quest. It is entirely unaided that Gilliatt leaves shore.

He now faces nature and the unknown, completely cut off from human society. He sur-vives a titanic struggle for the ship against the hurricane forces of nature, but he must still descend into an underwater grotto, where he is seized by a hideous octopus. Gilliatt is, in

Hugo's words, "the fly of that spider." The language of the passage makes it clear that in freeing himself from the octopus, Gilliatt frees himself from evil.

Exhausted, Gilliatt prays, then sleeps. When he wakes, the sea is calm. He returns to land a savior, bringing the engine of the ship as well as the stolen money. When he learns that Déruchette wishes to marry another, he gives her his own marriage chest and leaves to die in the rising tide. *The Toilers of the Sea* is considered by many to be the finest and purest expression of Hugo's mythic vision.

THE MAN WHO LAUGHS

Almost immediately after *The Toilers of the Sea*, Hugo turned his attention back to history. In 1866, he began work on the first novel of what he intended to be a trilogy focusing in turn on aristocracy, monarchy, and democracy. The first, *The Man Who Laughs*, is set in England after 1688; the second would have taken place in prerevolutionary France; and the third is *Ninety-three*, a vision of France after 1789. The role of fate is diminished in these last two novels because Hugo wished to emphasize man's conscience and free will in a social and political context.

In *The Man Who Laughs*, the disfigured hero, Gwynplaine, chooses to leave his humble earthly paradise when he learns that he had been born to the aristocracy. Predictably, the way up leads to Gwynplaine's downfall. Noble society is a hellish labyrinth (another type of web) from which Gwynplaine barely manages to escape. A wolf named Homo helps him find his lost love again, a blind girl named Déa. When she dies, Gwynplaine finds salvation by letting himself sink beneath the water of the Thames.

NINETY-THREE

Hugo's vivid portrayal of a demoniac aristocratic society justified the cause of the French Revolution in 1789, preparing the way for his vision of an egalitarian future as described in his last novel, *Ninety-three*. By choosing to write about 1793 instead of the fall of the Bastille, Hugo was attempting to deal with the Terror, which he considered to have deformed the original ideals of the Revolution.

Rather than the familiar love interest, Hugo places the characters Michelle Fléchard and her three children at the center of the novel. In Hugo's works, kindness to children can redeem almost any amount of wickedness. The monstrous Hans of Iceland, for example, is partially excused because he was avenging the death of his son. It is therefore not surprising to find in *Ninety-three* that each faction in the Revolution is tested and judged according to its treatment of Michelle and her children.

The extreme positions in the violent political clash are represented by the Marquis de Lantenac, the Royalist leader, and his counterpart, Cimourdain, a former priest and fanatic revolutionary. Both men are inflexible and coldly logical in their courageous devotion to their beliefs. The violent excesses of both sides are depicted as demoniac no matter how noble the cause. Human charity and benign moderation are represented in Gauvain, a general in the revolutionary army. He is Lantenac's nephew and the former pupil of Cimourdain. He is clearly also the spokesman for Hugo's point of view.

In the course of events, Lantenac redeems his inhumanity by rescuing Michelle's children from a burning tower. He is now Gauvain's prisoner and should be sent to the guillotine. Gauvain's humanity, however, responds to Lantenac's act of self-sacrifice, and Gauvain arranges for him to escape. It is now Cimourdain's turn, but he remains loyal to his principles, condemning to death his beloved disciple. Before his execution, Gauvain expounds his (Hugo's) idealistic social philosophy in a dialogue with Cimourdin's pragmatic view of a disciplined society based on strict justice.

In this final novel, Hugo's desire to express his visionary ideology overwhelms his talents as a novelist. At the age of seventy, he had become the prophet of a transfigured social order of the future. He would create no more of his compelling fictional worlds. It was time for Hugo the creator of legends to assume the legendary stature of his final decade.

Jan St. Martin

OTHER MAJOR WORKS

PLAYS: *Cromwell*, pb. 1827 (verse drama; English translation, 1896); *Amy Robsart*, pr. 1828 (English translation, 1895); *Hernani*, pr., pb. 1830 (verse drama; English translation, 1830); *Marion de Lorme*, pr., pb. 1831 (verse drama; English translation, 1895); *Le Roi s'amuse*, pr., pb. 1832 (verse drama; *The King's Fool*, 1842; also known as *The King Amuses Himself*, 1964), *Lucrèce Borgia*, pr., pb. 1833 (*Lucretia Borgia*, 1842), *Marie Tudor*, pr., pb. 1833 (English translation, 1895); *Angelo, tyran de Padoue*, pr., pb. 1835 (*Angelo, Tyrant of Padua*, 1880); *Ruy Blas*, pr., pb. 1838 (verse drama; English translation, 1890); *Les Burgraves*, pr., pb. 1843 (*The Burgraves*, 1896); *Inez de Castro*, pb. 1863 (wr. c. 1818; verse drama); *La Grand-mère*, pb. 1865; *Mille Francs de Recompense*, pb. 1866; *Les Deux Trouvailles de Gallus*, pb. 1881; *Torquemada*, pb. 1882 (wr. 1869; English translation, 1896); *Théâtre en liberté*, pb. 1886 (includes *Mangeront-ils?*); *The Dramatic Works*, 1887; *The Dramatic Works of Victor Hugo*, 1895-1896 (4 volumes); *Irtamène*, pb. 1934 (wr. 1816; verse drama).

POETRY: *Odes et poésies diverses*, 1822, 1823; *Nouvelles Odes*, 1824; *Odes et ballades*, 1826; *Les Orientales*, 1829 (*Les Orientales: Or, Eastern Lyrics*, 1879); *Les Feuilles d'automne*, 1831; *Les Chants du crépuscule*, 1835 (*Songs of Twilight*, 1836); *Les Voix intérieures*, 1837; *Les Rayons et les ombres*, 1840; *Les Châtiments*, 1853; *Les Contemplations*, 1856; *La Légende des siècles*, 1859-1883 (5 volumes; *The Legend of the Centuries*, 1894); *Les Chansons des rues et des bois*, 1865; *L'Année terrible*, 1872; *L'Art d'être grand-père*, 1877; *Le Pape*, 1878; *La Pitié suprême*, 1879; *L'Âne*, 1880; *Les Quatre vents de l'esprit*, 1881; *The Literary Life and Poetical Works of Victor Hugo*, 1883; *La Fin de Satan*, 1886; *Toute la lyre*, 1888; *Dieu*, 1891; *Les Années funestes*, 1896; *Poems from Victor Hugo*, 1901; *Dernière Gerbe*, 1902; *Poems*, 1902; *The Poems of Victor Hugo*, 1906; *Océan*, 1942.

NONFICTION: *La Préface de Cromwell*, 1827 (English translation, 1896); *Littérature et philosophie mêlées*, 1834; *Le Rhin*, 1842 (*The Rhine*, 1843); *Napoléon le petit*, 1852 (*Napoleon the Little*, 1852); *William Shakespeare*, 1864 (English translation, 1864); *Actes et paroles*, 1875-1876; *Histoire d'un crime*, 1877 (*The History of a Crime*, 1877-1878); *Religions et religion*, 1880; *Le Théâtre en liberté*, 1886; *Choses vues*, 1887 (*Things Seen*, 1887); *En voyage: Alpes et Pyrénées*, 1890 (*The Alps and Pyrenees*, 1898); *France et Belgique*, 1892; *Correspondance*, 1896-1898.

MISCELLANEOUS: *Œuvres complètes*, 1880-1892 (57 volumes); *Victor Hugo's Works*, 1892 (30 volumes); *Works*, 1907 (10 volumes).

BIBLIOGRAPHY

Bloom, Harold, ed. *Victor Hugo*. New York: Chelsea House, 1988. Collection of twelve essays discusses all aspects of Hugo's career. Two essays are devoted to analysis of *Les Misérables*. Includes introduction, chronology, and bibliography.

Brombert, Victor. *Victor Hugo and the Visionary Novel*. Cambridge, Mass.: Harvard University Press, 1984. Study by one of the most distinguished scholars of modern French literature includes an especially informative chapter on *Les Misérables*. Provides detailed notes and bibliography.

Frey, John Andrew. *A Victor Hugo Encyclopedia*. Westport, Conn.: Greenwood Press, 1999. Comprehensive guide to the works of Hugo includes introductory and biographical material. Addresses Hugo as a leading poet, novelist, artist, and religious and revolutionary thinker of France. The balance of the volume contains alphabetically arranged entries discussing his works, characters, and themes as well as relevant historical persons and places. Includes a general bibliography.

Grossman, Kathryn M. *"Les Misérables": Conversion, Revolution, Redemption*. New York: Twayne, 1996. Examination of the novel, aimed at students and general readers, recounts the historical events leading up to the novel's publication, discusses the importance of the book, describes how Hugo's political and philosophical ideas are expressed in the work, and analyzes the character of protagonist Jean Valjean. Includes bibliographical references and index.

Maurois, André. *Olympio: The Life of Victor Hugo*. Translated by Gerard Hopkins. New York: Harper & Row, 1956. This work, originally published in French in 1954, is probably as close an approach as possible to an ideal one-volume biography dealing with both the life and the work of a monumental figure such as Hugo. Of the sparse illustrations, several are superb; the bibliography, principally of sources in French, provides a sense of Hugo's celebrity and influence, which persisted well into the twentieth century.

_____. *Victor Hugo and His World*. London: Thames and Hudson, 1966. The 1956 English translation of Maurois's text noted above was edited to conform to the format of a series of illustrated books. The result is interesting and intelligible, but rather schematic. In compensation for the vast cuts in text, a chronology and dozens of well-annotated illustrations have been added.

Porter, Laurence M. *Victor Hugo*. New York: Twayne, 1999. Study of Hugo and his works provides a biography, separate chapters analyzing *The Hunchback of Notre Dame* and *Les Misérables*, and discussions of Hugo's plays and poetry. Includes bibliography and index.

Raser, Timothy. *The Simplest of Signs: Victor Hugo and the Language of Images in France, 1850-1950*. Newark: University of Delaware Press, 2004. Analyzes the relationship of Hugo's works to French architecture and other visual arts, examining how Hugo used language to describe time, place, and visual details, his aesthetics and politics, and the language and methods of French art criticism.

Richardson, Joanna. *Victor Hugo*. New York: St. Martin's Press, 1976. Well-written, scholarly biography of Hugo is divided into three sections: "The Man," "The Prophet," and "The Legend." Includes detailed notes, extensive bibliography, and index.

Robb, Graham. *Victor Hugo*. New York: W. W. Norton, 1998. Thorough biography reveals many previously unknown aspects of Hugo's long life and literary career. Robb's introduction discusses earlier biographies. Includes detailed notes and bibliography.

Vargas Llosa, Mario. *The Temptation of the Impossible: Victor Hugo and "Les Misérables."* Princeton, N.J.: Princeton University Press, 2007. Provides a fascinating look at Hugo's writing of *Les Misérables*, including an examination of the work's structure and narration. Includes comparisons to modern novels and critics' reactions to the novel in Hugo's day.

JOSEPH SHERIDAN LE FANU

Born: Dublin, Ireland; August 28, 1814
Died: Dublin, Ireland; February 7, 1873
Also known as: Joseph Thomas Sheridan Le Fanu

PRINCIPAL LONG FICTION

The Cock and Anchor, 1845
The Fortunes of Colonel Torlogh O'Brien, 1847
The House by the Churchyard, 1863
Uncle Silas: A Tale of Bartram-Haugh, 1864
Wylder's Hand, 1864
Guy Deverell, 1865
All in the Dark, 1866
The Tenants of Malory: A Novel, 1867 (3 volumes)
Haunted Lives, 1868
A Lost Name, 1868
The Wyvern Mystery, 1869
Checkmate, 1871
The Rose and the Key, 1871
Willing to Die, 1872-1873 (3 volumes)
Morley Court, 1873

OTHER LITERARY FORMS

Joseph Sheridan Le Fanu (LEHF-uhn-yew) is better known today as a short-story writer than as a novelist. His many tales first appeared in periodicals, later to be combined into collections. In addition to having genuine intrinsic merit, the stories are important to an understanding of Le Fanu the novelist, for in them he perfected the techniques of mood, characterization, and plot construction that make his later novels so obviously superior to his early efforts. Indeed, Le Fanu seems to have recognized little distinctive difference between the novel and the tale; his novels are often expansions of earlier stories, and stories reissued in collections might be loosely linked by a frame created to give them some of the unity of a novel. The major collections, *Ghost Stories and Tales of Mystery* (1851), *Chronicles of Golden Friars* (1871), *In a Glass Darkly* (1872), and *The Purcell Papers* (1880), reveal an artist who ranks with Edgar Allan Poe, Ambrose Bierce, M. R. James, and Algernon Blackwood as one of the masters of supernatural fiction in the English language. One story from *In A Glass Darkly*, "Carmilla," is reprinted in almost every anthology of horror stories and has inspired numerous film versions, the most famous being Carl Theodore Dreyer's *Vampyr* (1932).

Le Fanu wrote verse throughout his literary career. While unknown as a poet to modern audiences, in his own day at least one of his compositions achieved great popularity in both Ireland and the United States. "Shamus O'Brien" (1850) is a fine ballad that relates the adventures of the title character in the uprising of 1798.

ACHIEVEMENTS

In the preface to his most famous novel, *Uncle Silas*, Joseph Sheridan Le Fanu rejects the claim of critics that he is a mere writer of "sensational novels." Pointing out that the great novels of Sir Walter Scott have sensational elements of violence and horror, he denies that his own work, any more than Scott's, should be characterized by the presence of such elements; like Scott, Le Fanu, too, has "moral aims."

To see the truth in this self-appraisal requires familiarity with more than one of Le Fanu's novels. Singly, each of the major works overwhelms the reader with the cleverness of its plot, the depravity of its villain, the suspense evoked by its carefully controlled tone. Several novels together, however, recollected in tranquillity, reveal a unity of theme. Moreover, each novel can then be seen as not merely a variation on the theme but also as a deliberate next logical step toward a more comprehensive and definitive statement. The intricacies of plot, the kinds of evil represented by the villains, the pervasive gothic gloom are to Le Fanu more than story elements; they are themselves his quite serious comment on the nature of human existence, driven by natural and social forces that leave little room for the effective assertion of free will toward any beneficial end.

In Le Fanu's short stories, more often than in his novels, those forces are embodied in tangible supernatural agents. "Carmilla," for example, is the tale of a real female vampire's attack on a young woman, but seen in the context of the larger theme, it is more than a bit of occult fiction calculated to give its readers a scare. With her intense sexuality and lesbian tendencies, the vampire is depicted as nothing less than the embodiment of a basic human drive out of control, and that drive—like the others that move society: self-preservation, physical comfort—can quite unpredictably move toward destruction. Le Fanu's most significant achievement as a novelist was to show how the horror genre could be used for serious purposes—to show that monsters are not as horrible as minds that beget monsters, and that ghosts are not as interesting as people who are haunted.

BIOGRAPHY

Joseph Thomas Sheridan Le Fanu was descended from a Huguenot family that had left France for Ireland in the seventeenth century. Both his grandfather, Joseph, and great uncle, Henry, had married sisters of the famous playwright, Richard Brinsley Sheridan. His father, Philip Le Fanu, was a noted scholar and clergyman who served as rector at the Royal Hibernian School, where Le Fanu was born, and later as dean of Emly. His mother was from all accounts a most charming and gentle person, an essayist on philanthropic subjects and a leader in the movement for humane treatment of animals. With loving and indulgent parents and the excitement of life at school, Le Fanu's childhood was a happy one.

In 1826, the family moved to Abington in county Limerick. Le Fanu and his brother, William, were not sent to a formal school but were tutored by their father with the help of an elderly clergyman, who gladly excused the boys from their lessons so he could pursue the passion of his life: fishing. Walking tours through the wild Irish countryside, conversations with friendly peasants, who told of fairies and pookhas and banshees, shaped very early the imagination of the boy who would become the creator of so many tales of the mysterious and supernatural. The Tithe Wars of 1831 and the resulting animosity of the peasants to the Le Fanus, who were seen as representative of the Anglo-Irish establishment, forced the young Le Fanu to examine his own Irishness. On one hand, he was intellectually supportive of the union and convinced that British rule was in the best interests of the Irish people; on the other, the courage and sacrifices of the bold Irish nationalists filled him with admiration and respect.

In 1837, Le Fanu graduated from Trinity College, Dublin. He took honors in classics and was well known for his fine orations before the College Historical Society. Called to the Irish bar in 1839, he never practiced law but entered a productive career in journalism. His first published work, "The Ghost and the Bonesetter," appeared in the *Dublin University Magazine* in January, 1838. That magazine was to publish serially eight of Le Fanu's fourteen novels after he became its owner and editor in 1861. During the early 1840's, Le Fanu became proprietor or part-owner of a number of journals, including *The Warder, The Statesman, The Protestant Guardian*, and the *Evening Mail*.

In 1844, Le Fanu married Susan Bennett. The union was a happy one; the Le Fanus had two sons and two daughters. One son, George, became an artist and illustrated some of his father's works. Le Fanu's novels published in the 1840's, *The Cock and Anchor* and *Torlogh O'Brien*, received poor reviews, and Le Fanu turned from writing fiction to concentrate on his journalistic work. With the death of his beloved wife in 1858, he withdrew from society and became a recluse. Only a few close friends were allowed to visit "the invisible prince" at his elegant home at Merrion Square, Dublin. Emerging only occasionally to visit booksellers for volumes on ghosts and the occult, Le Fanu established a daily routine he was to follow for the remaining years of his life: writing in bed by candlelight from midnight till dawn, rising at noon, and writing all afternoon at a prized, small desk once owned by Richard Brinsley Sheridan. In this manner was produced the greatest share of a literary canon that rivals in quantity the output of the most prolific authors of the Victorian age.

At the end, under treatment for heart disease, troubled by nightmares—especially one recurring scene of a gloomy, old mansion on the verge of collapsing on the terrified dreamer—Le Fanu refused the company of even his closest friends. On the night of February 7, 1873, his doctor found him in bed, his arms flung wide, his unseeing eyes fixed in terror at something that could no longer do him harm. "I feared this," the doctor said; "that house fell at last."

ANALYSIS

After writing two novels that failed to impress the critics, Joseph Sheridan Le Fanu left that genre for approximately fifteen years. In his reclusive later life, he returned to long fiction to produce the fine work for which he is remembered. Le Fanu's career as a novelist reveals a marked change in his perception of humanity and the very nature of the universe itself. The development of the author's major theme can be illustrated by a survey of the major novels in his quite extensive canon.

THE COCK AND ANCHOR

The early works, *The Cock and Anchor* and *Torlogh O'Brien*, are both historical novels dealing with the Ireland of the late seventeenth and early eighteenth centuries, the turbulent time of the Williamite Wars (1689-1691). *The Cock and Anchor* presents a slice of Irish life that cuts across events and persons of real historical significance and the personal misfortunes of one fictional couple, Mary Ashewoode and Edmund O'Connor. The story of these ill-fated lovers has nothing special to recommend it. Mary is kept from Edmund first by her father, Sir Richard, who would marry her for a fortune to Lord Aspenly, a conventional fop, and then by her brother, Henry, who would see her wed to one Nicholas Blarden, a conventional villain. Mary escapes these nefarious designs and flees to the protection of Oliver French, the conventional benevolent uncle. There is, however, no happy ending: Mary dies before Edmund can reach her. The designing Sir Richard suffers a fatal stroke; brother Henry finally finds the destiny for which he was born, the hangman's noose; and even Edmund's unlucky life ends on the battlefield of Denain in 1712.

More interesting to the modern reader are the historical characters. The haughty Lord Warton, Viceroy of Dublin, personifies power and Machiavellian self-interest. Joseph Addison and young Jonathan Swift are also here in well-drawn portraits that demonstrate considerable historical research. Still, the novel is at best uneven, the work of an author with promise who has more to learn about his craft.

The technical obstructions, however, cannot hide Le Fanu's message: The problems of Ireland are profound and rooted deep in a history of conflict. The Anglo-Irish establishment, represented by the Ashewoode family, has lost sight of the values needed to end the strife and move the society toward peace and prosperity, values such as personal responsibility, compassion, and even love within the family. Le Fanu was unwilling to risk clouding his theme by allowing the happy marriage of Mary and Edmund, the conventional ending to which the conventional plot could be expected to lead. They die to prove the point. The Ashewoodes's decay is really Ireland's decay, and the wage is death.

TORLOGH O'BRIEN

Torlogh O'Brien, Le Fanu's second novel and the last he was to write for sixteen years, is set a few years before *The Cock and Anchor*, during the Williamite War. Again, most critics have found little to admire in the work. The historical scenes and characters show that once more Le Fanu thoroughly researched his subject, but the fictional characters reveal little improvement in their creator's art. The plot, except for some unusually violent scenes, would hold no surprises for a reader of romances. The villainous Miles Garret, a traitor to the Protestant cause, wishes to take Glindarragh Castle from Sir Hugh Willoughby, a supporter of William of Orange. Arrested on false charges created by Garret, Sir Hugh and his daughter, Grace, are taken to Dublin for trial. Their escort is Torlogh O'Brien, a soldier in the army of King James II, whose family originally held the estate. O'Brien and Sir Hugh, both honorable men, rise above their political differences to gain mutual respect. Finally, it is O'Brien who intervenes to save the Willoughbys from the designs of Garret, and of course his bravery is rewarded by the love of Grace.

From the first novel to the second, villainy—Nicholas Blarden or Miles Garret—remains a constant, and the agony of a torn Ireland is the common background against which Edmund O'Connor and Torlogh O'Brien act out their parts. The social cancer that blighted the love of Mary and Edmund is, however, allowed a possible cure in *Torlogh O'Brien*. As the deaths of the lovers in the first novel showed Ireland as a sterile wasteland, so the union of the Willoughbys and O'Briens in the second promises restoring rain, but when after the long hiatus Le Fanu returned to novel writing, he chose to let the promise go unfulfilled.

THE HOUSE BY THE CHURCHYARD

Held by many critics to be Le Fanu's finest work, *The House by the Churchyard*, the first novel of his later period, appeared in the *Dublin University Magazine* in 1861; two years later, it was published in London as a book.

The story is set in late eighteenth century Chapelizod, a suburb of Dublin. As in the earlier historical romances, there are villains, lovers, and dispossessed heirs. A major plot concerns the righting of an old wrong. Eighteen years after the death of Lord Dunoran, executed for a murder he did not commit, his son, using the name Mr. Mervyn, returns to the confiscated family lands hoping to establish his father's innocence. The real murderer, Charles Archer, has also returned to Chapelizod under the alias of Paul Dangerfield. He is soon recognized by a former accomplice, Zekiel Irons, and a witness, Dr. Barnaby Sturk. Sturk attempts blackmail, only to have Archer beat him severely. His victim in a coma, Archer plays benefactor and arranges for a surgeon he knows to be incompetent to perform a brain operation, supposedly to restore Sturk to health. To Archer's surprise, the operation gives Sturk a period of consciousness before the expected death. Irons joins Sturk in revealing Archer as the murderer, Lord Dunoran's lands and title are restored to Mervyn, and the family name is cleared at last.

This, however, is only one of several interrelated plots that make *The House by the Churchyard* a marvel of Victorian complexity. To label the Archer mystery as the major story line would be to mislead the reader who has yet to discover the book. More accurately, the novel is about Chapelizod itself. The discovery of a murderer stands out in the plot as, to be sure, it would in any small community, but Le Fanu is reminding his readers that what immediately affects any individual—for example, Mervyn's need to clear his father's name—no matter how urgently, is of limited interest to other individuals, who are in turn preoccupied with their own concerns. Mrs. Nutter has her own problem with protecting her inheritance from wicked Mary Matchwell. Captain Devereux and Lilias Walsingham have their doomed romance to concern them, as, on a more humorous note, Captain Cuffe is preoccupied with his love for Rebecca Chattesworth, who is finally joined with Lieutenant Puddock, the former suitor of Gertrude Chattesworth, who in turn has a secret romance with Mervyn. Indeed, the unsolved murder cannot totally dominate even the life of Lord Dunoran's son.

Some of the characters serve a comic purpose, and with so many complex entanglements, the comic could easily slide into complete farce. Le Fanu avoids caricature, however, by providing each comic figure with some other distinguishing quality—wit, compassion, bravery. In *The House by the Churchyard*, Le Fanu, already a master of description and mood, added the one needed skill so obviously absent in his early novels, the art of characterization.

The characterization of Archer, alias Dangerfield, is by itself sufficient to demonstrate Le Fanu's growth as a novelist. Dangerfield is almost supernatural in his evil; he describes himself as a corpse and a vampire, a werewolf and a ghoul. He is incapable not only of love but also of hate, and he calmly announces before his suicide that he "never yet bore any man the least ill will." He has had to "remove two or three" merely to ensure his own safety. The occult imagery used to define Dangerfield also links him to the microcosm of Chapelizod, for Mervyn's Tiled House is reputedly haunted; the specter of a ghostly hand has frightened more than one former resident. Le Fanu allows Mervyn, like Torlogh O'Brien, his happy ending, but so powerful is the hold of Dangerfield on the novel that the possibility of colossal evil that he personifies is not totally exorcised even by his death. That he was not really supernatural but was the embodiment of human depravity in no way diminishes the horror.

WYLDER'S HAND

With his fourth novel, *Wylder's Hand*, Le Fanu left historical romances and social panoramas to study evil with a closer eye. The story, certainly Le Fanu's finest mystery, concerns the strange disappearance of young Mark Wylder, a lieutenant in the navy and rival of Captain Stanley Lake for the hand of Dorcas Brandon, a rich heiress. From several locations in Europe, Wylder has sent letters containing instructions for the conduct of his business and releasing Dorcas to marry Lake. The suspicions of Larkin, a family attorney, are aroused by a problem with the dating of certain letters, but then Wylder returns to Brandon Hall, where he is actually seen in conversation with Lake. The very next day, however, Lake is thrown from his horse as the animal is startled by the pointing hand of Mark Wylder's corpse protruding from the ground, exposed by a heavy rain. Dying, Lake confesses to having murdered his rival and arranging for the posting of forged letters. In fact, it was not Wylder who appeared the preceding night at Brandon but one James Dutton, the unwitting accomplice who had posted the letters and who happens to resemble Wylder. Only one person knew of Wylder's fate, having witnessed his midnight burial: Rachel Lake, the murderer's sister. Devotion to her brother and to Dorcas Brandon, who really loves Lake, compelled her silence.

The plot is a masterpiece of suspense, but still more impressive are the characterizations. Each figure is finely drawn and fits into a mosaic of human types that together portrays a species ill equipped to deal with evil. Wylder is a swaggering braggart, crude, unfeeling, with a general air of disreputability that seems to promise some future act of monstrous brutality had not a violent death cut short his career. Like two vicious dogs claiming the same territory, Wylder and Lake cannot exist in the same world without one destroying the other. Lake's evil, however, is of a quite different nature. In many respects, he is Le Fanu's most interesting study. Wylder's is a rather directionless evil; it could as easily manifest itself in one abhorrent action as another. Dangerfield was simply amoral. Born without any sense of restraint, his natural selfishness led to murder for convenience. Lake's evil is weakness. Greed for property and position seems almost an outside force, a part of human society that can compel even murder in those who lack the strength to resist. He experiences guilt and fear and never is able to derive satisfaction from his villainy.

Considering that the murdered man was certainly no credit to the human race, the reader may actually feel sympathy for Lake. In him, Le Fanu presents the criminal as victim, but the consequences of Lake's weakness affect others as well. Rachel's knowledge of the secret and Dorcas's ignorance isolate them from the man they love, much as Lake is himself isolated. Gloom, a sense of a scheme of things not quite right, permeates the texture of the entire novel. There is no happy ending. Years later, Rachel and Dorcas are seen in Venice, sad and alone.

UNCLE SILAS

In *Uncle Silas*, Le Fanu continued his investigation of the terrible yet tragic evil represented by Lake. Two earlier tales, "An Episode in the Secret History of an Irish Countess" (1838) and "The Murdered Cousin" (1851) provided a basic plot structure for the study, and in 1864, the same year that *Wylder's Hand* was published, a bound edition in three volumes with the full title *Uncle Silas: A Tale of Bartram-Haugh* appeared. Considered by most critics Le Fanu's finest novel, it brings all the skill acquired over a productive career to a definitive study of the themes that interested its author most: the nature of evil, and the hereditary aristocracy as a paradigm for the effects of that destructive force. As usual, the study is conducted through carefully drawn characters and a plot filled with mystery and suspense.

In compliance with the will of the deceased Austin Ruthyn, his daughter, Maud, is made the ward of Austin's brother, Silas, a sinister man suspected but never convicted of a past murder. The suspicions are well founded, for Uncle Silas will stop at nothing to gain full ownership of Maud's estate. When an arranged marriage between Maud and Silas's son, Dudley, proves impossible—the scoundrel is discovered to be already married—murder seems the only solution. Dudley botches the job, however, and kills Madame de la Rougierra, another of Silas's agents, by mistake. Maud flees to a kindly relative; Dudley flees to Australia; and Uncle Silas dies that same night from an overdose of opium.

Le Fanu called *Uncle Silas* a "tragic English romance," and indeed the novel does depict a truly tragic situation. The Ruthyns stumble blindly through situations and realities they can hardly perceive, much less understand. Austin Ruthyn, heedless of the suspicions surrounding his brother, sends his daughter into the wolf's lair. Dudley, purposeless and crude, sees only the moment, and this he addresses with instinct rather than intelligent consideration of consequences. Even Maud Ruthyn, the heroine and narrator, is unaware of her perilous situation until it is almost too late. Gothic heroines are expected to be naïve, and Le Fanu uses that trait in his narrator to good advantage. Maud often tells more than she realizes, and the reader sensitive to the unspoken messages that careful diction can convey sees the closing circle of predators before she does. The rhetorical effect is a sense of foreboding, a tension that charges the entire novel.

Despite his avoidance of prosecution for an earlier crime and his careful designs for his niece's downfall, Silas is as blind as any of the lesser characters. His lust for wealth and property is virtually inherited: Similar drives have directed his family for generations. His body a slave to narcotics, his mind to religious fanaticism, he is the aristocracy in decay. Le Fanu surrounds him with appropriate death imagery, and his loutish son, Dudley, married without Silas's knowledge to a barmaid, is final evidence of the collapse of the Ruthyn line. Silas's first murder victim had been a Mr. Charke, to whom he owed gambling debts, but with the planned murder of Maud, the violence turns in upon the Ruthyns themselves. Austin's blind trust puts Maud in harm's way, and Silas's blind greed would destroy her; *Uncle Silas* is ultimately nothing less than a portrait of the aristocratic class cannibalizing itself. Maud survives and eventually marries a young lord, but her concluding words speak more of hope for happiness than happiness realized, and the death of her first child, sorrowfully remembered, strikes at the last the same note sounded throughout the novel.

WILLING TO DIE

That note of futility is heard most clearly in Le Fanu at the end of his career as a novelist. *Willing to Die*, first published serially in *All the Year Round* (1872-1873), is by no means his finest effort. The story, while complex, lacks the gothic excitement of the works for which he is remembered. Still, the novel is important in a thematic study.

Ethel Ware, the heroine, is allowed to sample a full range of life's possibilities. Poverty, loneliness, love, all contribute to the growth of her character; she surmounts all obstacles to achieve great material wealth and an understanding of the meaning of life. This is a new picture; in Ethel, the reader does not meet yet another aristocrat beaten by an ignorance of the forces at work in human society. Ethel wins, in the sense that Silas Ruthyn and Stanley Lake would have liked to win, but the mature vision that comes with the material victory only shows that the quest is pointless and the victory hollow. Isolated in her accomplishment as the protagonists of earlier novels were most often isolated in their failures, Ethel sees that the human struggle is manipulated by forces of society and chance, and whether the struggle culminates in a moment that might be called success or failure is finally irrelevant, for the last force to take part in the struggle, death, affects the Wares and the Ruthyns alike.

The novels of Le Fanu are the record of an artist exploring social structures and individual minds in quest of horrors natural and supernatural. With his final entry in that often brilliant record, *Willing to Die*, he penetrated at last to the very heart of darkness to discover the ultimate horror: the utter futility of it all.

William J. Heim

OTHER MAJOR WORKS

SHORT FICTION: *Ghost Stories and Tales of Mystery*, 1851; *Chronicles of Golden Friars*, 1871; *In a Glass Darkly*, 1872; *The Purcell Papers*, 1880; *The Watcher, and Other Weird Stories*, 1894; *A Chronicle of Golden Friars, and Other Stories*, 1896; *Madam Crowl's Ghost, and Other Tales of Mystery*, 1923 (M. R. James, editor); *Green Tea, and Other Ghost Stories*, 1945; *Best Ghost Stories of J. S. Le Fanu*, 1964; *Ghost Stories and Mysteries*, 1975.

POETRY: *The Poems of Joseph Sheridan Le Fanu*, 1896.

BIBLIOGRAPHY

Begnal, Michael H. *Joseph Sheridan Le Fanu*. Lewisburg, Pa.: Bucknell University Press, 1971. Although this volume is only an essay-length discussion of Le Fanu's works, it is valuable in providing general commentary about Le Fanu's intellectual and artistic interests, especially his sensitive understanding of women.

Browne, Nelson. *Sheridan Le Fanu*. London: Arthur Barker, 1951. This short critical exposition places emphasis on Le Fanu's "essentially Gothick quality." The author believes Le Fanu to be at his best in his short fiction, advancing familiar objections to his novels' prolixity. Dated in tone and attitude, but a pioneering study.

McCormack, William J. *Dissolute Characters: Irish Literary History Through Balzac, Sheridan Le Fanu, Yeats, and Bowen*. New York: Manchester University Press, 1993. The section on Le Fanu discusses his relationship to the English novel, the development of his fiction, his treatment of characters, and his drawing on history. Includes notes but no bibliography.

_____. *Sheridan Le Fanu and Victorian Ireland*. New York: Oxford University Press, 1980. The standard work on Le Fanu. The author's approach is twofold. First, this study is a detailed biography of Le Fanu; second, it locates, with much intellectual sophistication, Le Fanu's life in his times, giving historical significance to its biographical data. A second, enlarged edition of this important work was issued in 1991.

Melada, Ivan. *Sheridan Le Fanu*. Boston: Twayne, 1987. Melada's approach is chronological, proceeding from Le Fanu's early short fiction to the major novels with which his career ends. The critical emphasis sees Le Fanu as a writer of popular fiction, the quality of which entitles him to serious academic consideration. Includes a chronology and bibliography.

Sage, Victor. *Le Fanu's Gothic: The Rhetoric of Darkness*. New York: Palgrave Macmillan, 2004. This work examines Le Fanu's stylistic development and includes extensive analyses of *Uncle Silas* in addition to rarely discussed unpublished romances. Includes a bibliography and an index.

Sullivan, Kevin. "*The House by the Churchyard*: James Joyce and Sheridan Le Fanu." In *Modern Irish Literature: Essays in Honour of William York Tindall*, edited by Raymond J. Porter and James D. Brophy. New Rochelle, N.Y.: Iona College Press, 1972. Le Fanu's novel *The House by the Churchyard* has some of its significant scenes set in the village of Chapelizod, a few miles west of Dublin and at the western end of Phoenix Park. James Joyce's *Finnegans Wake* (1933) contains numerous important allusions to both these Dublin settings. This essay traces the presence of the earlier work in the later. The undertaking is both an academic rehabilitation of Le Fanu's novel and an illustrative instance of Joyce's method in *Finnegans Wake*.

Walton, James. *Vision and Vacancy: The Fictions of J. S. Le Fanu*. Dublin: University College Dublin Press, 2007. An examination of Le Fanu's fiction, discussing his philosophy and literary influences. Walton places Le Fanu's work within the context of Victorian English and Continental novels and shows how his horror writing stands apart from traditional ghost stories of the Victorian era.

MATTHEW GREGORY LEWIS

Born: London, England; July 9, 1775
Died: At sea, near Jamaica; May 14, 1818
Also known as: Monk Lewis

OTHER LITERARY FORMS

Matthew Gregory Lewis's work in genres other than fiction deserves more critical attention than it has generally received. In his own day, his reputation as a dramatist almost equaled his fame as the author of *The Monk*. *The Castle Spectre* (pr. 1797), a gothic drama, was a major success. Clearly the work of the author of *The Monk*, the drama is populated by stock characters who move through an intricate plot decorated with ghosts and spectacle. *The Castle Spectre* allowed Lewis to show what *The Monk* would only let him describe. *Alfonso, King of Castile* (pb. 1801), a tragedy, was much hailed by critics, and helped establish Lewis's reputation as a major figure in the literary world of the early nineteenth century.

Lewis also wrote poetry. Some of his finer pieces appear in the text of *The Monk*. One, "Alonzo the Brave and the Fair Imogine," is still read as an excellent example of the then-popular gothic ballad and is included in *The Oxford Book of Eighteenth Century Verse* (1926). Lewis is also highly respected as a writer of nonfiction. *Journal of a West India Proprietor, Kept During a Residence in the Island of Jamaica* (1834) is a detailed and vivid account of Jamaica in the days of slavery and of the reactions of a genuinely humane person to this environment.

ACHIEVEMENTS

Matthew Gregory Lewis's outstanding achievement is his famous novel, *The Monk*. Often mentioned but seldom read today, this work helped to define a particular type of gothic novel that is still popular today. Rather than merely suggesting a dangerous supernatural presence by the careful use of tone, *The Monk* relies upon graphic description and bold action. Lewis's imagination worked with clear visual images rather than with hints and elusive impressions. Indeed, he has contributed more to the gothic conventions of stage and cinema than he has to later horror fiction. The great gothic writers of the nineteenth century—Nathaniel Hawthorne, Edgar Allan Poe, Emily Brontë—relied more on psychological effects and less on graphic horror than did Lewis. Lewis's true successors are contemporary novelists such as Stephen King and Peter Straub, who have taken the graphic depiction of horror to new extremes.

Among the countless readers of *The Monk*, perhaps none has enjoyed the book so thor-

Matthew Gregory Lewis
(Library of Congress)

oughly as Lewis himself. In September, 1794, he announced in a letter to his mother that he had produced "a romance of between three and four hundred pages octavo" in a mere ten weeks. With the outrageous immodesty of youth, he proclaimed, "I am myself so pleased with it, that, if the Booksellers will not buy it, I shall publish it myself." Two years later, the novel was published with a preface in imitation of Horace: "Now, then, your venturous course pursue,/ Go, my delight! dear book, adieu!" *The Monk*'s course has been "venturous" indeed. An immediate success, it went into a second edition the same year it was published, and by 1800, readers were buying the fifth edition. The first edition had been published anonymously; the second, however, not only bore the proud author's name but also his title of MP (member of Parliament).

While the earliest reviews of *The Monk* had been generally favorable—the book was deemed artful, skillful, interesting—the second wave of criticism brought judgments less kind. *The Monk* was "a poison for youth, and a provocative for the debauchee," said poet Samuel Taylor Coleridge in the *Critical Review* for February, 1797. Moreover, the poison had been brewed by a member of Parliament, the critics were fond of noting. Such criticism did no harm to the sale of the book, but an embarrassed Lewis expurgated later editions of *The Monk*.

BIOGRAPHY

Matthew Gregory Lewis was the oldest of four children born to Matthew Lewis and Frances Maria Sewell. Both families were quite prominent: Frances was the daughter of Sir Thomas Sewell, master of the rolls, and Matthew, born in Jamaica to a landed family, was deputy-secretary at war. They were an ill-matched pair, the elder Matthew being distant and austere, his wife delighting in gay times and the company of musical and literary people. The marriage failed, and the Lewises separated. While loyal to both parents, young Lewis was his mother's favorite, and he returned her affection in full.

From an early age, Lewis showed a great love for music and drama. At the age of fifteen, he submitted a farce to the Drury Lane Theatre; it was rejected, but this did nothing to curb his industry. He sent his mother numerous songs and poems and outlined his plan to write a two-volume novel, burlesquing popular novels of sensibility. His father intended for him to have a diplomatic career, and in preparation, Lewis spent school vacations in Europe, where he soon mastered German. Through his father, he received a position as an attaché to the British embassy in Holland. While in The Hague, he completed *The Monk.* Lewis returned to England, and his novel was published in March, 1796.

Still in his early twenties, "Monk" Lewis became one of the most popular writers in England. In the following few years, this popularity was reinforced by some noteworthy successes on the stage. *The Castle Spectre* enjoyed a long run at Drury Lane; *Alfonso, King of Castile* played to enthusiastic audiences at Covent Garden. In the later years of his short life, Lewis turned away from literary effort. Having achieved great prominence at an early age, he seems to have found little reason to continue in an activity that could bring him no greater fame and that he did not need to pursue for a livelihood. "The act of composing has ceased to amuse me," he wrote in the preface to the play *Venoni: Or, the Novice of St. Mark's* (pr. 1808).

Lewis's father provided more than adequate support, and after his death in 1812, the son inherited substantial fortune and property. Modest in his own needs and habits, he was known to his friends (who included poets Percy Bysshe Shelley, Lord Byron, and Sir Walter Scott) as a man of generosity and deep concern for the oppressed. In 1815, he sailed for Jamaica to do all he could to improve the conditions of the slaves on his estates. He was responsible for important reforms and improvements, including a hospital and a humane code regulating punishments for crimes. After a brief return to England and then to Italy to visit Shelley and Byron, Lewis sailed again for Jamaica. During a five-month stay, he continued to work for better conditions for slaves. He left the island on May 4, 1818.

Already sick with yellow fever, Lewis's health declined over the next several days. He died on board ship, on May 14, and was buried at sea. According to witnesses, the coffin was wrapped in a sheet with sufficient ballast to make it sink. The plunge caused the weights to fall out, however, and the loose sheet caught the wind. The body of Lewis, the author of one of the most fantastic books in the English language, was last seen in a sailing coffin headed for Jamaica.

ANALYSIS: THE MONK

While *The Monk* is seldom read today, few students of English literature have not heard of this scandalous example of the gothic novel. While the modern devotee of popular gothic literature and film whose sensitivity has long since been dulled by graphic, technicolor horrors may find *The Monk* mild stuff indeed, the novel is not without excitement, and its relation to modern gothic cinema is closer than that of most other classic gothic novels, especially those of Ann Radcliffe. Radcliffe would not allow her imagination to break free from eighteenth century rationalism; the supernatural, in the end, had to be given a natural explanation. Matthew Gregory Lewis's gothic vision looked toward nineteenth century Romanticism. He endowed certain characters with total confidence in tangible reality only to deflate their skepticism with head-on encounters with the supernatural that defy reason's best efforts at explanation. Magic works in *The Monk*; the ghosts are real and interfere with human destiny; demons interact with humans, and Satan himself, as a deus ex machina, finally resolves the plot.

The plot of *The Monk*, like the plot of most classic gothic novels, is not easily summarized. Father Ambrosio, a renowned priest and orator of Madrid who symbolizes all that is chaste and holy, falls in love with Antonia, an innocent girl in his congregation. He is, at the same time, pursued by the bolder Matilda, who enters the order disguised as a novice to be near Ambrosio. She and Ambrosio become passionate lovers, and Matilda, seeing that Ambrosio still pines for the young Antonia, promises to grant her to him by the aid of magic. Ambrosio bungles the staged seduction, kills Antonia's mother, Elvira, by mistake, and is forced to abduct Antonia to the dungeon of the monastery, where he drugs and rapes her. Seized with remorse and fear of exposure, he drives a knife in her heart when she returns to consciousness and begins to cry out. Imprisoned and faced with an inquisitional investigation, he yields to Matilda's entreaties to sell his soul to the Devil in exchange for release from prison. He soon bitterly realizes that he faces far worse punishment at the Devil's hands than he would have, had he faced the inquisitors, who were preparing to pardon him.

A subplot of the novel involves Agnes, a youthful nun who has given birth to the child of her lover, Raymond. She and the child are condemned to languish without food or water in the deepest part of the dungeon. In the final chapters of the book, she is discovered, half-dead, and restored to Raymond.

Perhaps the most important thing to remember about Lewis the novelist is that he was also a successful playwright for the popular stage. Readers of *The Monk* do not have to concern themselves with questions of interpretation; they need not be bothered with understanding complex characters and subtle motivations. Lewis has made all the important decisions, principally that the supernatural is not only real but also a controlling force in human affairs, and with that decision, complex characterization becomes impossible and unnecessary. While Lewis denied his creation some of the elements that make a novel great, he added enough action to produce a good story.

Critics in Lewis's time generally agreed that the disreputable member of Parliament who authored *The Monk* had indiscriminately heaped immoral action upon blasphemous action to create a plot utterly devoid of moral purpose. Such a charge is not entirely fair, for *The Monk* obviously teaches a number of moral lessons. Antonia demonstrates that innocence alone is no defense against evil. The adventures of Agnes could hardly be said to promote promiscuity, and the decline and fall of Ambrosio, the monk, provides the major theme: Pride is a vice that can pervert all virtues, even religious piety.

Nevertheless, those early critics were not altogether unfair in their severe judgment, for Lewis's morality is only shallowly rooted in his plot. Antonia, a model of virtue, is forcibly raped and then stabbed to death by the panic-stricken monk. Agnes, in the heat of passion, gives herself to Raymond; her reward, after suffering the loss of her child and imprisonment in a subterranean crypt, is finally to be united in matrimony with her dashing and well-to-do lover. Ambrosio is proud of the spirituality and dedication to priestly celibacy that sets him above men bound to the flesh. A truly tragic Ambrosio would finally come to understand that his pride was misplaced, for, indeed, he is a man like his fellows. In fact, the events of the book viewed in the light of the revelations at the conclusion may even support Ambrosio's original pride. The monk is enticed to damnation by the personal attention of the Devil himself, who is apparently unwilling to trust this prize to the temptations that are sufficient to damn normal men.

Until the final two or three pages of the novel, Ambrosio seems quite capable of damning himself with no outside help, and more than one sentence would be helpful in understanding why this particular monk is deserving of such special demoniac effort. Lust, perfidy, rape, and murder so much direct his actions that the reader is at a loss to understand how Ambrosio has ever been considered virtuous. Those last pages, however, cast the preceding four hundred pages in a quite different light. After revealing that Elvira and Antonia (the murdered mother and daughter) were, in fact, Ambrosio's own mother and sister, the Devil goes on to brag,

> "It was I who threw Matilda in your way; it was I who gave you entrance to Antonia's chamber; it was I who caused the dagger to be given you which pierced your sister's bosom; and it was I who warned Elvira in dreams of your designs upon her daughter, and thus, by preventing your profiting by her sleep, compelled you to add rape as well as incest to the catalogue of your crimes."

The prior existence of that virtue is suddenly given credibility by this surprise revelation of the total manipulation that was necessary for its destruction.

These concluding revelations come as such a surprise that some critics regard them as merely tacked on to the action of the novel. In particular, the revelation of Matilda's true nature suggests that the conclusion was a kind of afterthought. Early in the novel, disguised as a young monk, she wins the friendship of Ambrosio. When she reveals her true sex, friendship turns to lustful love, and when Ambrosio's lust cools, her love becomes utter dedication to satisfying his every desire, even his desire for Antonia. Matilda is, in some ways, the most interesting and complex character in the novel. In the conclusion, however, Lewis does his readers the dubious favor of unraveling her complexity by having the Devil finally announce that she is not a woman at all but a lesser demon in human form, whose every action has followed the Devil's own blueprint for Ambrosio's destruction. This is especially puzzling for the careful reader, who remembers that in earlier pages, Matilda professed love for Ambrosio while thinking him asleep, and that on more than one occasion, even the narrator presented her affection as sincere.

The Monk's conclusion, then, both damages the credibility of the narrator and clouds whatever moral might be found in the fall of Ambrosio. More accurately, he does not fall; he is pushed. Those late eighteenth and early nineteenth century critics for whom morality was a measure of artistic accomplishment had some cause for their attack on *The Monk*. A more generous interpretation will allow that Lewis did not construct his plot or characters to illustrate morals; he only tried to salvage what morality he could from a plot that was allowed to go its own way in search of excitement and adventure.

While there was much in *The Monk* to surprise and shock readers of the day, the novel was, in many ways, highly conventional. For example, the death of Antonia was demanded by convention. Once "deflowered," an unmarried female character was useless as a symbol of virtue. Although the woman was raped against her will, her very participation in an extramarital sex act destroyed her aura of purity for eighteenth century audiences. If the association of purity with that particular character was still needed to move the plot or motivate other characters, as Antonia's purity is clearly still needed as a contrast to Ambrosio's final sin, the selling of his soul, then something must be done to remove the taint of sex and reestablish the woman in her former symbolic role. She must pay for her unintentional sin through sacrifice, and Lewis's audience expected the ultimate sacrifice: death. After her rape, Antonia, alive, is of no use to the novel; her marriage to her sweetheart, Lorenzo, a man of wealth and breeding, would be unthinkable. Dead, however, her purity is restored and can effectively serve as a foil to Ambrosio's depravity. Antonia's fate could not have been otherwise.

Romantic conventions also demanded a happy ending for the characters left alive. Lorenzo's all too rapid recovery from the loss of his beloved Antonia and his speedy attachment to Virginia, a minor character introduced late in the plot as an obvious replacement, is perhaps Lewis's most awkward attempt to satisfy convention.

Lewis's handling of Agnes, the other major female character, is considerably more skillful. In a cast of one-dimensional characters, Agnes stands out, if only as a slightly more believable human being. She displays moral frailty without becoming a caricature of lust; she is possessed of a sense of humor and at least enough intelligence to remind the reader that the quality is generally lacking among the other characters. Agnes, like Antonia, loses her virginity. That she does so with her own true love, Raymond, whom she hopes to marry, helps only a little. Lewis recognized that it would be awkward indeed to kill off Agnes in addition to Antonia. He would then be forced to end his story with a miserable Raymond or to find some way to kill him as well. Either solution would detract from the utter misery of the monk, whose fate is seen as all the more wretched in contrast to the final happiness of the other characters. Another Virginia created in the last pages to help Raymond forget his lost love would be more than even a reader of romances could accept. Forced by his plot to allow Agnes to live, Lewis at least attempted to satisfy his audience's predictable indignation at her indiscretion by bringing her as close to death as possible.

Before her happy reunion with Raymond, Agnes passes through a purgatory as horrible as any in literature. Thought dead by all but a very few, the pregnant Agnes is imprisoned by the evil prioress in a hidden dungeon under the convent's crypt. There, alone, with barely enough bread and water to sustain her, she gives birth. The child soon dies, and the nearly insane Agnes is left to lavish a mother's love on its putrefying corpse until her rescue by Lorenzo. Lewis was certainly aware that here he was walking a fine line between pity and disgust. If the audience reacts with repugnance, Agnes would acquire a new taint that would make her happy union with Raymond unacceptable. To avoid this, Lewis carefully chooses his words when Lorenzo comes upon the despairing Agnes. The dead baby is only a "bundle" with which Agnes refuses to part, and while the bundle's contents is obvious, Lewis wisely—and uncharacteristically—renders the scene vague and withholds description. Several pages later, a fully recovered and quite sane Agnes is allowed to tell her own story, and she tells it with such sensitivity and self-understanding as to convince the audience that she has passed through the fire, learned from the experience, and is now a proper wife for Raymond.

The destinies of the individual characters—Antonia, Lorenzo, Agnes, the monk himself—show that Lewis was not naïve. He knew what his readers demanded to satisfy their moral expectations and sense of justice, and as far as was convenient, he was willing to comply, but if popular expectation conflicted with his own sense of what made a good story—adventure, graphic detail, action rather than characterization, and no rationalization of the fantastic—then he was committed to disappointing expectation.

William J. Heim

OTHER MAJOR WORKS

PLAYS: *Village Virtues*, pb. 1796; *The Castle Spectre*, pr. 1797; *The East Indian*, pr. 1799; *The Twins: Or, Is It He or His Brother?*, pr. 1799 (adaptation of Jean François Regnard's *Les Ménechmes: Ou, Les Jumeaux*); *Adelmorn the Outlaw*, pr., pb. 1801; *Alfonso, King of Castile*, pb. 1801; *The Captive*, pr. 1803 (dramatic monologue); *The Harper's Daughter: Or, Love and Ambition*, pr. 1803 (adaptation of his translation *The Minister*); *Rugantino: Or, The Bravo of Venice*, pr., pb. 1805 (two acts; revision of *The Bravo of Venice*); *Adelgitha: Or, The Fruits of a Single Error*, pb. 1806; *The Wood Daemon: Or, "The Clock Has Struck,"* pr. 1807; *Venoni: Or, the Novice of St. Mark's*, pr. 1808 (adaptation of Jacques Marie de Monvel's play *Les Victimes cloîtrées*); *Temper: Or, The Domestic Tyrant*, pr. 1809 (adaptation of Sir Charles Sedley's translation, *The Grumbler*, of David Augustin Brueys and Jean Palaprat's play *Le Grondeur*); *One O'Clock: Or, The Knight and the Wood Daemon*, pr., pb. 1811 (music by Michael Kelly and Matthew Peter King; revision of *The Wood Daemon*); *Timour the Tartar*, pr., pb. 1811; *Rich and Poor*, pr., pb. 1812 (music by Charles Edward Horn; adaptation of Lewis's *The East Indian*).

POETRY: *The Love of Gain: A Poem Initiated from Juvenal*, 1799; *Tales of Wonder*, 1801 (with Sir Walter Scott, Robert Southey, and John Leyden); *Monody on the Death of Sir John Moore*, 1809; *Poems*, 1812; *The Isle of Devils: A Metrical Tale*, 1827.

NONFICTION: *Journal of a West India Proprietor, Kept During a Residence in the Island of Jamaica*, 1834 (also known as *Journal of a Residence Among the Negroes in the West Indies*, 1861).

TRANSLATIONS: *The Minister*, 1797 (of Friedrich Schiller's play *Kabale und Liebe*); *Rolla: Or, The Peruvian Hero*, 1799 (of August von Kotzebue's play *Die Spanier in Peru: Oder, Rollas Tod*); *The Bravo of Venice: A Romance*, 1805 (of J. H. D. Zschokke's novel *Aballino der Grosse Bandit*); *Feudal Tyrants: Or, The Counts of Carlsheim and Sargans: A Romance, Taken from the German*, 1806 (4 volumes; of Christiane Benedicte Eugénie Naubert's novel *Elisabeth, Erbin von Toggenburg: Oder, Geschichte der Frauen in der Schweiz*).

EDITED TEXTS: *Tales of Terror*, 1799 (also known as *An Apology for Tales of Terror*; includes work by Sir Walter Scott and Robert Southey); *Tales of Wonder*, 1801 (2 volumes; includes work by Scott, Southey, Robert Burns, Thomas Gray, John Dryden, and others).

MISCELLANEOUS: *Romantic Tales*, 1808 (4 volumes; includes poems, short stories, and ballads); *Twelve Ballads, the Words and Music by M. G. Lewis*, 1808; *The Life and Correspondence of M. G. Lewis, with Many Pieces Never Before Published*, 1839 (2 volumes; Margaret Baron-Wilson, editor).

BIBLIOGRAPHY

Blakemore, Steven. "Matthew Lewis's Black Mass: Sexual, Religious Inversion in *The Monk*." *Studies in the Novel* 30, no. 4 (Winter, 1998): 521-539. This analysis of *The Monk* examines Lewis's views as they manifested themselves in this work. In analyzing the novel, Blakemore also sheds light on Lewis's dramatic works.

Ellis, Markman. "Revolution and Libertinism in the Gothic Novel." In *The History of Gothic Fiction*. Edinburgh, Scotland: Edinburgh University Press, 2000. Ellis devotes an entire chapter to *The Monk*, discussing the novel's "compositional politics" as well as Lewis and the French Revolution and criticism and censorship of the novel.

Euridge, Gareth M. "The Company We Keep: Comic Function in M. G. Lewis's *The Monk*." In *Functions of the Fantastic: Selected Essays from the Thirteenth International Conference on the Fantastic in the Arts*, edited by Joe Sanders. Westport, Conn.: Greenwood Press, 1995. Euridge takes exception to previous psychoanalytical studies of *The Monk*, arguing that Lewis's book, which may be the "apotheosis" of the gothic novel, contains many ironic and comic elements that critics have neglected.

Howard, Jacqueline. "Anticlerical Gothic: Matthew Lewis's *The Monk*." In *Reading Gothic Fiction: A Bakhtinian Approach*. Oxford, England: Clarendon Press, 1994. Howard discusses the German influences on Lewis's novel and its relationship to eighteenth century writings. Recommended for advanced students with some grounding in literary theory.

Irwin, Joseph James. *M. G. "Monk" Lewis*. Boston: Twayne, 1976. Provides information on the life and writings of Lewis, with a concluding overview of his achievements. Focuses on *The Monk*, which brought Lewis fame and notoriety and set the standard for tales of terror. Includes notes, an annotated bibliography, and an index.

Macdonald, David Lorne. *Monk Lewis: A Critical Biography*. Buffalo, N.Y.: University of Toronto Press, 2000. A biography in which Macdonald discusses all of Lewis's works and their connections to his personal life, particularly his position as a slave owner and a probable homosexual. Includes a bibliography and an index.

Peck, Louis F. *A Life of Matthew G. Lewis*. Cambridge, Mass.: Harvard University Press, 1961. This first modern full-length biography of Lewis uses materials not available to earlier biographers, such as diaries, memoirs, and the correspondence of Lewis's contemporaries. Contains a collection of selected letters, a list of his principal works, a bibliography of works cited, notes, and an index.

Reno, Robert Princeton. *The Gothic Visions of Ann Radcliffe and Matthew G. Lewis*. New York: Arno Press, 1980. Reno focuses on *The Monk* and the gothic works of Ann Radcliffe, and he also provides valuable information on Lewis's life and dramatic works. Includes a bibliography.

CHARLES ROBERT MATURIN

Born: Dublin, Ireland; September 25, 1780
Died: Dublin, Ireland; October 30, 1824
Also known as: Dennis Jasper Murphy

PRINCIPAL LONG FICTION

Fatal Revenge: Or, The Family of Montorio, 1807 (as Dennis Jasper Murphy)
The Wild Irish Boy, 1808 (as Murphy)
The Milesian Chief, 1812 (as Murphy)
Women: Or, Pour et Contre, 1818
Melmoth the Wanderer, 1820
The Albigenses, 1824

OTHER LITERARY FORMS

In addition to his novels, Charles Robert Maturin (MAT-choo-rihn) also wrote plays, three of which were performed and published during his lifetime: *Bertram: Or, The Castle of St. Aldobrand, a Tragedy* (pr., pb. 1816), *Manuel* (pr., pb. 1817), and *Fredolfo* (pr., pb. 1819). A fourth, *Osmyn, the Renegade: Or, The Siege of Salerno, a Tragedy*, written some-time between 1817 and 1821, was produced in Dublin in 1830. It was never published in its entirety; excerpts were printed in *The Edinburgh Literary Journal* (April 24, 1830). Of these plays, only *Bertram* was financially successful. When it first appeared, it was one of the most talked about plays of the season, and today it is noted for being one of the first dramatic portrayals of the brooding, sinned against, and sinning figure who has come to be called the Byronic hero.

Two short fictional pieces were published posthumously: "Leixlip Castle: An Irish Family Legend" appeared in *The Literary Souvenir: Or, Cabinet of Poetry and Romance* of 1825, and "The Sybil's Prophecy: A Dramatic Fragment" was printed in the 1826 edition of the same publication. Both these pieces are in the gothic style.

ACHIEVEMENTS

Charles Robert Maturin is best known for *Melmoth the Wanderer*, the fifth of his six novels. Although, when it first appeared, many critics viewed it merely as an unfortunate attempt to revive the gothic novel, a form earlier made popular by such authors as Ann Radcliffe and Matthew Gregory Lewis, scholars now consider *Melmoth the Wanderer* one of the finest examples of its genre. It is judged to be not only a culmination of the gothic novel but also a forerunner of the psychological novels of such writers as Fyodor Dostoevski and Franz Kafka. Although Maturin's handling of narrative structure is often awkward and confusing, and although he borrowed so closely from the works of others that he can be accused of plagiarism, his novels are original in their depiction of extreme

Charles Robert Maturin
(Library of Congress)

states of mind, especially those engendered by fear. Maturin himself was aware of his major strength. In the prefatory pages of *The Milesian Chief*, he wrote

> If I possess any talent, it is that of darkening the gloomy, and of deepening the sad; of painting life in extremes, and representing those struggles of passion when the soul trembles on the verge of the unlawful and the unhallowed.

His settings of mazelike madhouses and dungeons lead the reader into the dark places of the human soul. This particular aspect of his novels fascinated and influenced many other authors. Edgar Allan Poe, Robert Louis Stevenson, Oscar Wilde, Christina and Dante Gabriel Rossetti, Honoré de Balzac, and Charles Baudelaire were all impressed by Maturin's attempt to penetrate the mystery of evil.

Critical attention also has been given to Maturin's role in Irish literary history. In such novels as *The Milesian Chief* and *The Wild Irish Boy*, descriptions of Irish settings and character play an important part. More study needs to be done to evaluate fully this contribution to the development of the Irish regional novel; whatever the outcome, Maturin's place among the significant writers of the English gothic novel is assured.

BIOGRAPHY

Charles Robert Maturin was born in 1780, one of several children born to William Maturin and Fidelia Watson. The Maturin family was of French descent. One of their ancestors was a Huguenot priest who was forced to leave France because of religious persecution during the reign of Louis XIV. This aspect of his family history strongly impressed the young Maturin, and throughout his life he was fond of relating how his ancestors had suffered for their faith. He himself was strongly anti-Catholic and especially opposed to the rule of monastic life, which he considered dangerously repressive. His novels contain many scenes and descriptions of monasteries as sadistic places where virtue turns to vice.

When in Ireland, Maturin's family became closely connected with the Anglican Church. Maturin's great-grandfather, Peter Maturin, was dean of Killala from 1724 to 1741, and his grandfather, Gabriel James Maturin, succeeded Jonathan Swift as dean of St. Patrick's in Dublin in 1745. Following this tradition, Maturin entered Trinity College in 1795 to study theology, and in 1803 he took holy orders. In the same year, he married Henrietta Kingsbury, a daughter of the archdeacon of Killala. From all reports, the couple were well suited and happily married. After ordination, Maturin served as curate in Loughrea, Galway, for two years. He then returned to Dublin to become curate of St. Peter's, a position he held for the rest of his life. His small income from this curacy was insufficient to support his family, especially after his father was accused of fraud and dismissed from his position with the Irish post office in 1809. Later, he was cleared and given another position, but for a time, the family struggled in severe poverty. In fact, Maturin was continually troubled by financial difficulties. To supplement his income, he ran a school to prepare boys for college, and later he turned to novel writing.

The prefaces of his novels and the styles of romance he chose to employ indicate that he wanted very much to become a popular writer. Because he realized that many of his parishioners and superiors might not approve of a minister writing novels, he used the pseudonym Dennis Jasper Murphy, publishing three novels under that name. When it was discovered that he was the author of the play *Bertram*, a play involving adultery and an amoral hero, he was for a time in danger of losing his curacy. Apparently, friends intervened to soothe the necessary bishops. After this incident, since his identity was known, he published his next novels and plays under his own name. It is quite possible that his literary activities did prevent his advancement in the clerical profession. There were those who interpreted the beliefs of his characters, some of which were atheistic and heretical, as Maturin's own.

Maturin's novels did gain him one very influential friend, Sir Walter Scott. In 1810, Scott wrote a generally favorable review of *Fatal Revenge* for *The Quarterly Review*. Encouraged, Maturin wrote to him, and a correspondence was begun that lasted until Maturin's death. Although the two never actually met, Scott did assist Maturin with encouragement and advice, and he was instrumental in Maturin's one financial success; he recommended *Bertram* to Lord Byron, who was then responsible for play selection at Drury Lane Theatre. Byron was favorably impressed, and the famous actor Edmund Kean agreed to play the lead. The play's success earned Maturin one thousand pounds, most of which paid a relative's debt. Earlier, Maturin had been able to sell the copyright of his third novel, *The Milesian Chief,* for eighty pounds (the first two novels he had printed at his own expense), and later he was advanced five hundred pounds for *Melmoth the Wanderer,* but his literary efforts never brought the long-sought and often desperately needed financial stability.

Up until his death, Maturin continually tried to write in a style that would sell. *The Albigenses* is a historical romance, a type Scott had established and made quite popular. This novel was the first in what was to be a trilogy depicting European manners in ancient, medieval, and modern times. Soon after *The Albigenses* was completed, Maturin died in his home on October 30, 1824, apparently after a long period of ill health. The exact cause of his death is not known. He left his wife and four children, who were still in desperate need of financial assistance.

ANALYSIS

In his preface to *Fatal Revenge*, Charles Robert Maturin stresses the fear of the unknown as essential in the emotional and spiritual lives of humans:

> It is *not* the weak and trivial impulse of the nursery, to be forgotten and scorned by manhood. It is the aspiration of a spirit; 'it is the passion of immortals,' that dread and desire of their final habitation.

In one of his sermons, he focuses on the same theme:

> The very first sounds of childhood are tales of another life—foolishly are they called tales of superstition; for, however disguised by the vulgarity of narration, and the distortion of fiction, they tell him of those whom he is hastening from the threshold of life to join, the inhabitants of the invisible world, with whom he must soon be, and be for ever.

These quotations indicate a major aspect of Maturin's perception of human existence; the haunted and the sacred are interwoven and share a common ground. Human fascination with the supernatural, the world of demons and ghosts, springs from the same source as the desire to believe in salvation and a return to paradise. In fact, the road to salvation leads through the dark places of the soul where individuals must admit their fallen state, their own guilt.

The theme of guilt is common in all of Maturin's novels. His major characters must struggle with the serpents in their own hearts, their own original sin. In keeping with this theme, the settings of his novels are generally those of a fallen world; dungeons and underground passages are common backgrounds for the action. Even in those novels that contain descriptions of more natural surroundings, storms and earthquakes are common occurrences, always reminding people that they have been exiled from paradise. Harmony with nature, with humanity, and with God has been lost.

Maturin develops this theme of guilt, which brings exile and separation, through his handling of character. The divided nature of humanity is represented by the pairing of characters, especially brothers: Ippolito and Annibal in *Fatal Revenge*, Connal and Desmond in *The Milesian Chief*, Paladour and Amirald in *The Albigenses*. These brothers are described in such a way as to suggest one identity fragmented into two opposing selves. Ippolito is passionate, Annibal rational; Desmond is the soft flower, Connal the proud oak. Often a character is torn in two opposing directions and does not know how to reconcile them: Connal between his Irish pride and his realization that the Irish peasants are not yet ready to govern themselves; Charles in *Women* between his love for Eva, a shy quiet girl, and Zaira, a worldly and more accomplished woman. At times, a character seems pursued by a dark, sinister double: Montorio by Schemoli in *Fatal Revenge*; Alonzo by the parricide in *Melmoth the Wanderer*. By far the most striking and powerful example of this is the character of the wanderer himself. Melmoth represents the potential for evil that can be found in all humans. In developing Melmoth's character, Maturin echoes the warning in Genesis against too much curiosity about the tree of knowledge of good and evil. Melmoth has sold his soul for increased knowledge; his sin is one of "pride and intellectual glorying," the sin of Lucifer and of the first mortals.

As Maturin's characters wander in a fallen world, little guidance is provided. Especially weak and ineffective are the parental figures. In fact, a distinguishing trait of this fallen world is the disintegration of the family. In all of Maturin's six novels, there are parents who are woefully irresponsible. They are often self-centered, putting their own greedy desires before their children's welfare, or they seek to expiate their own guilt by placing the burden of their sin upon their children. This selfish turning inward and transference of guilt to another is also found in Maturin's representations of larger structures of authority, especially the Catholic Church. As the divided soul wanders in a fallen world, parent and church offer little hope.

Maturin reserves the role of spiritual guide for the female characters who either love or are loved by the hero (such love is not always fulfilled or requited). Often his women are idealized creatures who can reconcile within themselves all conflicting opposites: in *Melmoth the Wanderer*, Immalee embodies passion and purity; in *The Albigenses*, Genevieve is a "mixture of strength and purity that is never to be found but in woman." Even if a woman finds herself hurled into a world of experience and corruption, as Zaira is in *Women*, her heart remains pure. At times, Maturin uses his female characters to symbolize self-sacrificing love that, although never placing the beloved before God, does place the beloved before the self. Despite Maturin's emphasis on such redeeming love, however, when domestic happiness is found by his characters it seems contrived and imposed upon them by others. Maturin is undoubtedly at his best when depicting people lost and searching for wholeness, not in actually finding it.

FATAL REVENGE

Maturin titled his first novel *The Family of Montorio*, but the publisher changed the title to *Fatal Revenge*, hoping to attract readers who would be interested in a gothic tale. The novel is definitely written in the style of Radcliffe—one of its central figures, a ghostlike monk who calls himself Schemoli, is clearly patterned on Radcliffe's Schoedoni in 1797's *The Italian*—but Maturin uses what he borrows to develop his own characteristic theme with originality. Although he follows Radcliffe's technique of revealing the supernatural events as merely the result of disguise and charade, his descriptions of aberrant states of mind, to which all are subject, go beyond her handling of evil, and beyond the mere cataloging of grotesque horrors used by those writers who chose to imitate the more sensational style of Matthew Gregory Lewis. Annibal concludes after a brief period of solitary confinement that an "inward acquaintance" delights one not with tranquillity but, on the contrary, with "the grave of the mind." In describing the anguish of his guilt, Montorio cries, "the worm within me never dieth; and every thought and object it converts into its own morbid food." In Maturin, the evil within is quite real.

The plot of this novel is complicated, and Maturin's narrative is at times twisted and confusing. The tale relates the vengeful machinations of Schemoli, the once noble Count Montorio. He is seeking revenge for the wrongs his younger brother committed against him by manipulating Ippolito and Annibal, two young men he believes are his brother's sons, into believing that they are fated to murder their father. In part, the novel's convoluted structure works to Maturin's advantage, for it helps create a nightmare quality that suits this theme of revenge and guilt. By the end of the novel, after several brutal crimes, it is clear that the words of Ippolito to the Inquisition accurately represent human nature as portrayed in the novel:

> There is no human being fully known to another. . . . To his own consciousness and recollection, a man will not dare to reveal every thought that visits his mind; there are some which he almost hopes are concealed from the Deity.

THE WILD IRISH BOY

Maturin's second novel, *The Wild Irish Boy*, although often following the style of the sentimental, regional novel, still has some of the same motifs and themes as those of the gothic *Fatal Revenge*. The novel does have many flaws and is probably Maturin's poorest work: There are long pointless digressions, a decidedly awkward handling of point of view, and an ineffective mixture of literary techniques. Nevertheless, when Maturin touches upon those subjects that most fascinated him, he does so with some success. The novel's most interesting character is Lady Montrevor, a strong, compelling woman who through her own foolish vanity allows herself to be trapped into a loveless marriage, thus sacrificing the sincere love of a good man. She must bear the anguish of her loss and the knowledge of her guilt. She does so grandly, wanting no man's pity. Maturin often alludes to John Milton's fallen angel when describing her: She is "no less than archangel ruined." In many ways, she is a female Byronic hero who knows that evil is more than appearance. This type of female character clearly interested Maturin. Zaira in *Women* and Armida in *The Milesian Chief* are similarly delineated, and all three are quite unlike the sentimental heroines so typical of the other novelists of the day.

THE MILESIAN CHIEF

In Maturin's third novel, *The Milesian Chief*, his interest in the anguish of the proud heart reveals itself in his portrayal of the hero as well as of the heroine. Connal, the Irish rebel, is the once-great angelic chief fallen among lesser spirits, an appropriate male partner for the melancholy Armida, who is shaded by a "proud dejection, like that of an abdicated monarch." The novel is set in Ireland during an uprising against the British in 1798. As the plot unfolds, it becomes clear that Maturin is more successful in handling narrative structure and point of view than in his previous works, and although the final scene, in which the four major characters (Connal, Armida, Desmond, and Ines) all die more or less at the same time in the same place, seems contrived, it is psychologically appropriate. Throughout the novel, these four personalities have been interwoven. Connal and Desmond function as opposites linked in one identity, and each female character both mirrors and complements her male counterpart. Again, even when trying to write a regional novel, Maturin shows that his main interest lies in depicting the individual lost and searching for a way back to some longed-for paradise.

WOMEN

In his preface to *Women*, Maturin writes that he believes his previous novels failed to win popular approval because they lacked reality. He indicates that in this novel he has fashioned his characters to resemble those of "common life." This intention does not, however, cause any significant change in his major theme. Again, through his three central characters, Maturin depicts human nature as torn and guilt ridden. Charles vacillates between his love for Eva, a shy innocent girl, and Zaira, the older, more accomplished woman. He is never able to commit himself fully to loving one or the other until it is too late. Only when Eva is dying of consumption brought on by Charles's abandoning her for Zaira does he desert Zaira to return to Eva.

Throughout the novel, Eva has struggled with her love for Charles, for in her heart it conflicts with her love for God. On her deathbed, she rejects Charles completely, refusing even to see him, and she dies at peace with God. Zaira undergoes a similar ordeal after Charles abandons her. She turns to God, hoping for consolation, yet she continues to see Charles's image before her eyes. After Eva's death, Charles dies from fever and madness. As the novel closes, Zaira becomes the primary figure of guilt. She lives on, always holding her hand to her heart, accusing herself of having murdered her daughter. She has discovered that Eva was the child taken from her at birth, the child she has been trying to find.

This discovery is not made until it is too late to remedy the painful consequences of the mother and daughter loving the same man. Maturin concludes the novel with an image typical of his style: "The serpents that devour us, are generated out of our own vitals."

MELMOTH THE WANDERER

Although Maturin's preface to *Melmoth the Wanderer* suggests that what follows will show the reader the enemy of humankind in the form of Satan, the tales within tales that constitute the novel show instead that this enemy lies within each individual. By combining the qualities of Faust, Mephistopheles, and the Wandering Jew, Maturin fashioned a hero-villain suitable for leading the reader through the maze of tales that takes him into the obscure recesses of the human soul.

Melmoth is Maturin's most compelling and powerful character; he is an embodiment of the dark side of each human being, the shadow that each person casts. Thus, it is particularly appropriate that in the narrative frame of these tales of human malignity, John Melmoth, who bears the same name as the mysterious wanderer, inherits the task of dealing with the molding manuscript that will set him on his own journey into the mystery of evil. His withdrawal at midnight into a closed room, sealed off from society, to read the manuscript, disregarding his uncle's warning that perhaps he should destroy it unread, suggests a type of original sin. Indeed, as he pursues knowledge of the wanderer's life, he learns that all humans are potential agents of Satan. After all, Melmoth the Wanderer did not spring from the fires of hell, but from his own family.

The hope that Maturin offers in his guilty state is to be found in self-sacrificing love; yet to love in this manner one must believe in the potential for goodness in humankind, the possibility of redemption. Melmoth is finally damned not because of his original bargain to sell his soul but because of his own misanthropy. He believes in nothing but the hostility and evil of human nature. Immalee, the island maiden who learns of suffering by loving him, was his hope. If he had chosen to trust in her love, seeing in it the essence of the greater self-sacrificing love of Christ, he might have been saved.

THE ALBIGENSES

Maturin's last work, *The Albigenses*, is a historical novel that focuses on the crusade in 1208 against the Albigenses, a Manichaean sect declared heretical by the Catholic Church. Maturin, however, follows the historical facts only roughly, altering events and chronology to suit plot and character. Again, he portrays two brothers, Paladour and Amirald, and their two loves, Isabelle and Genevieve. Although the theme of the fragmented self is not as predominant as in his previous novels, it is present. Paladour and Amirald were separated at birth, and for most of the novel neither knows the other is his brother; they are characterized in such a way as to suggest differing aspects of one personality. Paladour is associated with iron and Amirald with flowers, yet they are bound together through suffering. In choosing their brides, they also reveal complementary personality traits: Paladour marries the noble Lady Isebelle, and Amirald chooses the simple peasant girl Genevieve. When the novel ends, the reader is left with the impression that all four live together in absolute harmony.

Such an easy resolution does seemed contrived, for *The Albigenses* begins with Paladour's sinister encounter with a seemingly demoniac lady of the lake. He believes there is a curse upon him and that he is fated to murder his bride on their wedding night. When the effects of these dark tones are no longer wanted, Maturin quickly resolves all with rational explanations. Paladour is then free to live as a very natural husband. Part of the dissatisfaction the reader feels with this happy ending may be accounted for by the fact that the novel bristles with gothic motifs that are not smoothly integrated into the historical aspects of the novel.

Despite Maturin's own belief that the day of the gothic novel had already passed when he began writing, and his repeated attempts to use whatever narrative form might suit the reading public, he was continually drawn to the techniques of the gothic tale. Whether it be a mysterious monk haunting underground passages or a madwoman raving prophetic truths, all his novels have gothic elements. The gothic novel provided him with a literary world suitable for the images of evil and suffering that populated his own mind, a mind repeatedly drawn to the problems of human guilt and the divided soul. Maturin's work, although uneven, offers ample proof of his ability to shape these dark themes with power and originality.

Diane D'Amico

OTHER MAJOR WORKS

SHORT FICTION: "Leixlip Castle: An Irish Family Legend," 1825 (in *The Literary Souvenir: Or, Cabinet of Poetry and Romance*); "The Sybil's Prophecy: A Dramatic Fragment" 1826 (in *The Literary Souvenir*).

PLAYS: *Bertram: Or, The Castle of St. Aldobrand, a Tragedy*, pr., pb. 1816; *Manuel*, pr., pb. 1817; *Fredolfo*, pr., pb. 1819; *Osmyn, the Renegade: Or, The Siege of Salerno, a Tragedy*, pr. 1830.

BIBLIOGRAPHY

Bayer-Berenbaum, Linda. *The Gothic Imagination: Expansion in Gothic Literature and Art*. Rutherford, N.J.: Fairleigh Dickinson University Press, 1982. A sympathetic study of gothicism, the essence of which is its confrontation with evil and feelings of doom. Contains chapters on literary gothicism and Gothic art's relationship to literature as well as focused analyses of particular works of literature. Maturin is given considerable attention, including an extensive analysis of *Melmoth the Wanderer.*

Jeffares, A. Norman, and Peter van de Kamp. *Irish Literature: The Nineteenth Century*. Dublin: Irish Academic Press, 2006-2007. A three-volume reference set that contains critical essays about the lives and works of numerous Irish writers. Includes an essay on Maturin in the first volume.

Johnson, Anthony. "Gaps and Gothic Sensibility: Walpole, Lewis, Mary Shelley, and Maturin." In *Exhibited by Candlelight: Sources and Developments in the Gothic Tradition*, edited by Valeria Tinkler-Villani, Peter Davidson, and Jane Stevenson. Amsterdam: Rodopi, 1995. This study of gothic literature includes Johnson's learned and clear discussion of how Maturin handles the gaps in reality that are exploited in gothic fiction.

Kiely, Robert. *The Romantic Novel in England*. Cambridge, Mass.: Harvard University Press, 1972. An important book about Romantic prose fiction, including Maturin's gothic romances, which analyzes twelve Romantic novels. *Melmoth the Wanderer* is covered in detail; this novel is found to be more emotionally involved with Catholicism and rebellion against authoritarian political systems than other gothic fiction.

Kosok, Heinz. "Charles Robert Maturin and Colonialism." In *Literary Inter-Relations: Ireland, Egypt, and the Far East*, edited by Mary Massoud. Gerrards Cross, England: C. Smythe, 1996. Kosok's paper, initially delivered in 1993 at a conference examining Ireland's literary relationships with countries in the Middle and Far East, focuses on Maturin's representation of colonialism.

Kramer, Dale. *Charles Robert Maturin*. New York: Twayne, 1973. Analyzes Maturin's personality, describes the conditions of his life, and indicates his innovations in the gothic tradition. Includes a chronology, notes and references, a selected annotated bibliography, and an index.

Lougy, Robert E. *Charles Robert Maturin*. Lewisburg, Pa.: Bucknell University Press, 1975. An insightful review of Maturin's life and writings, dividing his career into early, middle, and later years. Includes a chronology and a selected bibliography of primary and secondary works.

Moynahan, Julian. "The Politics of Anglo-Irish Gothic: Charles Robert Maturin, Joseph Sheridan Le Fanu, and the Return of the Repressed." In *Anglo-Irish: The Literary Imagination in a Hyphenated Culture*. Princeton, N.J.: Princeton University Press, 1995. Moynahan's analysis of gothic literature by the two authors is included in his study of literary works written by Anglo-Irish authors during the nineteenth century.

Norton, Rictor, ed. *Gothic Readings: The First Wave, 1764-1840*. London: Leicester University Press, 2000. This study of gothic literature includes an excerpt from *Melmoth the Wanderer*, which is defined as belonging to "the German school of horror," and two contemporary reviews of the novel, including one by Sir Walter Scott. Useful for placing Maturin within the larger context of the gothic and Romantic novel.

JOYCE CAROL OATES

Born: Lockport, New York; June 16, 1938
Also known as: Rosamond Smith

PRINCIPAL LONG FICTION

With Shuddering Fall, 1964
A Garden of Earthly Delights, 1967 (revised 2003)
Expensive People, 1968
them, 1969
Wonderland, 1971
Do with Me What You Will, 1973
The Assassins: A Book of Hours, 1975
Childwold, 1976
The Triumph of the Spider Monkey, 1976
Son of the Morning, 1978
Cybele, 1979
Unholy Loves, 1979
Bellefleur, 1980
Angel of Light, 1981
A Bloodsmoor Romance, 1982
Mysteries of Winterthurn, 1984
Solstice, 1985
Marya: A Life, 1986
Lives of the Twins, 1987 (as Rosamond Smith)
You Must Remember This, 1987
American Appetites, 1989
Soul/Mate, 1989 (as Smith)
Because It Is Bitter, and Because It Is My Heart, 1990
I Lock My Door upon Myself, 1990
Nemesis, 1990 (as Smith)
The Rise of Life on Earth, 1991
Black Water, 1992
Snake Eyes, 1992 (as Smith)
Foxfire: Confessions of a Girl Gang, 1993
What I Lived For, 1994
You Can't Catch Me, 1995 (as Smith)
Zombie, 1995
First Love, 1996
We Were the Mulvaneys, 1996

Man Crazy, 1997

My Heart Laid Bare, 1998

Broke Heart Blues, 1999

Starr Bright Will Be with You Soon, 1999 (as Smith)

Blonde, 2000

Middle Age: A Romance, 2001

The Barrens, 2001 (as Smith)

Beasts, 2002

I'll Take You There, 2002

Rape: A Love Story, 2003

The Tattooed Girl, 2003

The Falls, 2004

Missing Mom, 2005

Black Girl/White Girl, 2006

The Gravedigger's Daughter, 2007

My Sister, My Love: The Intimate Story of Skyler Rampike, 2008

OTHER LITERARY FORMS

Joyce Carol Oates's first work for the stage, *Miracle Play*, appeared in 1974, and others opened later to appreciative audiences. In addition, Oates has published collections of short stories with regularity. These began with *By the North Gate* (1963), which predated her first novel, and continued with collections such as *Upon the Sweeping Flood* (1966), *The Wheel of Love* (1970), *Marriages and Infidelities* (1972), *Where Are You Going, Where Have You Been?* (1974), *The Poisoned Kiss* (1975), *The Seduction* (1975), *Crossing the Border* (1976), *All the Good People I've Left Behind* (1978), *A Sentimental Education* (1980), *Raven's Wing* (1986), *The Assignation* (1988), *Where Is Here?* (1992), *Faithless: Tales of Transgression* (2001), *The Female of the Species: Tales of Mystery and Suspense* (2006), and *Wild Nights! Stories About the Last Days of Poe, Dickinson, Twain, James, and Hemingway* (2008). In the early years of the twenty-first century, Oates added literature for children and young adults to her repertoire. These works include *Big Mouth and Ugly Girl* (2002), *Freaky Green Eyes* (2003), *After the Wreck, I Picked Myself Up, Spread My Wings, and Flew Away* (2006), and *Naughty Chérie* (2008).

While Oates is often recognized as one of the primary American writers of imaginative literature, she also is a highly respected reviewer and critic. Some of Oates's best literary criticism and writing about her work has been collected in such volumes as *New Heaven, New Earth: The Visionary Experience in Literature* (1974); *(Woman) Writer: Occasions and Opportunities* (1988), *Where I've Been, and Where I'm Going: Essays, Reviews, and Prose* (1999), and *The Faith of a Writer: Life, Craft, Art* (2003). In addition, Oates has edited several anthologies of the short fiction and nonfiction of other authors, including *Night Walks: A Bedside Companion* (1982), *First Person Singular: Writers on Their Craft*

Joyce Carol Oates
(Library of Congress)

(1983), *American Gothic Tales* (1996), *Snapshots: Twentieth Century Mother-Daughter Fiction* (2000; with Janet Berliner), and *The Best American Mystery Stories* (2005; with Otto Penzler). Oates's books of poems include *Anonymous Sins, and Other Poems* (1969), *Angel Fire* (1973), *Women Whose Lives Are Food, Men Whose Lives Are Money* (1978), *The Time Traveler* (1989), and *Tenderness* (1996). In 1974, Oates and her husband founded the literary journal *Ontario Review*.

ACHIEVEMENTS

As a writer and as a teacher, Joyce Carol Oates has collected numerous and varied prizes and honors. Among them are O. Henry Awards throughout the 1970's, 1980's, and 1990's, twelve Pushcart Prizes, the Richard and Hinda Rosenthal Award of the National Institute of Arts and Letters (1968), the National Book Award for 1970, and the Lotos Club Award of Merit (1975). In 1990, Oates received the Rea Award for the short story and the Alan Swallow Award for her 1988 short-story collection *The Assignation*. Oates has also been honored with the PEN/Malamud Award for Lifetime Achievement in the

Short Story (1996), the F. Scott Fitzgerald Award for Lifetime Achievement in American Literature (1998), the Thomas Cooper Medal for Distinction in the Arts and Sciences (2005), the Humanist of the Year Award (2007), and the Mary McCarthy Award (2008). She has also been the recipient of eight honorary degrees.

BIOGRAPHY

Joyce Carol Oates was born on June 16, 1938, in Lockport, New York. She received a modest education in a one-room schoolhouse and, as a child, had very little exposure to literature. This, however, did not quell her desire to write, and she spent much of her time as a child writing stories and short books. Even with all the writing and composing experience she had in her childhood, however, she did not publish her first story until 1959. While studying at Syracuse University, she won *Mademoiselle* magazine's college fiction competition with her short story "In the Old World." This would be the first of many public acknowledgments of the quality of her writing.

After receiving her B.A. from Syracuse in 1960, where she was valedictorian, Oates went on to receive her M.A. from the University of Wisconsin. During her term at Syracuse, she met her future husband, Raymond J. Smith. They married in 1961 and then moved to Beaumont, Texas, and Oates began to work on her Ph.D. at Rice University. She would never complete the degree; she and her husband moved to Michigan in 1962. While in Michigan, she taught English at the University of Detroit until 1967, when she and her husband began teaching at the University of Windsor in Ontario, Canada. During their tenure at the university, Smith and Oates cofounded the *Windsor Review*. After leaving the university in 1978, Oates went on to join the Princeton University Creative Writing Program. While a member of the program, she wrote not only fiction but also some brilliant essays on writers ranging from William Shakespeare to Norman Mailer.

Oates's teaching career has proved rich and rewarding. In 1987 she was appointed Roger S. Berlind Distinguished Professor in the Humanities at Princeton and published a monograph titled *On Boxing*, after which she became internationally known as an expert on the sport. In addition to serving on the faculty at Princeton, Oates has traveled extensively, often undertaking her journeys to bring attention to her most recently published novel or short-story collection. Throughout the years she has given many public readings of her works and has appeared as the keynote speaker at various national and international conferences. After joining the Princeton faculty she also toured Eastern Europe under the auspices of the U.S. Information Agency.

ANALYSIS

There have been few writers to match Joyce Carol Oates for sheer numbers—her novels, plays, short stories, and poems appear to multiply by themselves on library shelves. Even though the curse of quantity is often mediocrity, Oates consistently supplies a product of the highest quality, dense with meaning and filled with beautiful words and rich characters.

Oates's poor, unimaginative characters typically ply their swords through a fogged-in existence inflicted on them by a fatalistic creator. They cannot escape from the miasma they must breathe, and so they are poisoned by it, confused by muddled thoughts in an unkind world. The characters finally become enraged by their situation and so do bloody battle to extricate themselves from it. Sometimes as a result they resign themselves to the human condition of conflict; at other times, they experience a tragic lack of resolution.

WITH SHUDDERING FALL

In her first novel, *With Shuddering Fall*, Oates introduces a theme that has pervaded almost all the rest of her fiction works: the awful responsibility of freedom. Her characters struggle to divest themselves of their little lives in order to achieve personal freedom, but they are unable to cope with the consequences of their release from their former lives. They learn that they have abandoned not only their pasts but also their identities. Then they must struggle either to reclaim their selves or to forge new ones.

With Shuddering Fall is one character's reconciliation with her life, and this treaty gains for her a new appreciation of her history and that of her family. Karen must endure a sort of familiar ritual under the hands of her father, Hert, and her lover, Shar. At first Karen rejects her father's values. He is a legendary figure who wields great power and enjoys a close relationship with Karen; however, this is destroyed by the arrival of the violent, virile Shar, who deposes Hert. Shar is not a new ruler, however, but an anarchist who wishes only to topple kings, not replace them. He leaves, and Karen follows, not because she believes in him but because she seeks to escape Hert and "a life dominated by fathers." Once free from her father, Karen begins to feel uprooted, aimless and nameless. Without Hert, she has "nothing of herself but a face, a body, a set of emotions." She discovers that she needs her familial history to add meaning to her identity and so finally refuses the historyless Shar and his attempts at nihilism.

One of these trials is Shar's proclivity for race-car driving in the lowland town of Cherry River. Cherry River is a place that seems to exist for the edification of the summer tourists and little else. It offers appreciation of self-gratification but not of history. The high point of the summer seems to be when Shar commits suicide on the racetrack. Oates shows that in a community with no shared history, the only communal ties that exist are with shared acts of violence. The spokesman for the novel is Max, a self-centered businessman, who is the only one intelligent enough to share Oates's philosophy with the reader. He appears in many other novels as the maniacal oracle who tries to make Fate subservient to his will. He tries to cheat Karen of her birthright by confounding her with questions, but she eludes him and is, thus, saved. She returns to herself, her family.

EXPENSIVE PEOPLE

Expensive People opens with the fictional narrator explaining to the reader that he is telling the truth. Richard Everett begins by setting up a paradox because nothing he "tells" can ever be the truth since everything in the book is imagined. He goes on to explain that he is—or was—a child murderer in the sense that when he was young, he killed someone. *Expensive People* is written as a memoir, a memoir of someone who does not exist. In fact, Everett confesses that "it's possible that I'm lying without knowing it."

If *Expensive People* appears to be a parody of comic nihilism, of the nothingness of suburban life, it is. From Ernest Hemingway to John Barth, Oates pokes fun at those serious authors who proclaim the world to be formless and empty. Everett's mother, ironically nicknamed Nada, writes in her journal: "In any first-person narration there can be a lot of freedom. Certain central events—what the hell can they be?—leading up to the death." This is certainly a self-criticism of the very novel she is in as well as of those she despises for their negativism.

If Nada consoles herself with her own writing, poor Richard has little with which to comfort himself, unless it is the thought of his mother's death. He is convinced that she hates him, despite his near genius IQ, and wishes to stave off his affections with a series of unwanted puppies. Finally, Richard's fantasies of matricide become confused with reality. In the end, the newspapers show nothing of Nada, only of their house. Richard fades into closure of the book.

WONDERLAND

It is not chance that Lewis Carroll's child adventure and Oates's novel *Wonderland* bear the same word in the title. Oates considers the work of this nineteenth century English mathematician to ask the pertinent questions of life: Can all of life be just a game, and am I the only one who is not cheating? The protagonists of both novels—Alice and Jesse Harte—run and jump from square to square on a large, mostly unseen chessboard. Along the way they are both transmogrified into oddly sized versions of their original selves. Finally, in order to survive, Jesse and Alice regain their normal proportions and become resolved with their communities.

In the beginning of *Wonderland*, the newly orphaned Jesse travels from his grandfather's farm to an orphanage and finally to the home of Dr. Pedersen, a brilliant but unbalanced surrogate father. He is the first of a triumvirate of adoptive fathers whom Jesse must survive. His biological father's initial attack has given Jesse the strength to deal with these surrogates. His father has slaughtered his wife and their unborn child and wounded Jesse before killing himself. Jesse escapes to his grandfather's farm, where he recuperates until he must start his strange odyssey. Living with the Pedersen family, Jesse learns of things small and fantastic. He studies cell life and becomes involved in Dr. Pedersen's cancer research. The more he learns, the more he is confused by his father's view of life, which is overshadowed by death. At last, Pedersen grows impatient with Jesse and dismisses him from the family, saying, "You have no existence. You are nothing." Jesse must seek another, more receptive, lifestyle.

Jesse enters medical school, graduates, marries, and tries to forge a new family, a home, for himself. He keeps returning, however, to the site of his father's tragic demise in his dreams. His own children gradually start to shrink away like Carroll's Cheshire Cat. Michelle becomes Shelley and ultimately Shell, until Jesse can no longer grasp her—or the rest of his family—with any degree of certitude. Even Jesse's two father figures, Cady and Perrault, become in turn distant and disdainful. Dr. Cady will not acknowledge anything but the ethereal, and Dr. Perrault will not admit that the mind is anything but actual. These two opposing views further succeed in alienating Jesse from a "real" life. To offset these unrealistic real people, Jesse creates an unreal friend, or series of friends, but she only promises disharmony and death, so he eventually rejects her, too.

In the end of the novel, the action quickens, racing toward the now of the narrative, 1971. Jesse returns to his father's psyche and discovers the final, perfect answer: "A clean, pure, empty being, a void." It is only through the total destruction of the universe that a peaceful existence (or nonexistence) can be enjoyed.

CHILDWOLD

The setting of *Childwold* is again Eden Valley, scene of the action in *With Shuddering Fall* and *Wonderland*. The novel is peopled by a variety of characters and is narrated by several of them in turn, as each becomes the lover of the central figure's mother, Arlene Bartlett. Arlene's daughter, Laney Bartlett, is the unconscious catalyst for much of the violence in the novel.

The primary reaction between Laney and another character occurs between her and Fitz John Kasch, a fiftyish hermit who lives among the debris of his large but deceased family. In Laney, Kasch sees not only his failed marriage but also his repressed desires. She becomes for him both an icon and a Tantalus, love and passion. Unable to avail himself of her, Kasch woos and wins Arlene and becomes another in a lengthy retinue of lovers.

Arlene is a figure of the sex goddess, but, unlike so many untouchable figures, she is the small statue in the back of the church, worn down by the grasp of many hands. This, however, does not dismay her; indeed, it invigorates her. Where many single women would not welcome pregnancy, Arlene revels in it; her children reaffirm her existence in a world of many people. Kasch, on the other hand, is unable to enjoy the company of others. He secrets himself in a small part of what was once the family manse, now a museum. He blames his self-imposed isolation on his divorce, brought on by his former wife's infidelity. By retiring into his hermitage, however, he only amplifies his feelings of detachment from life. Although he seeks to redefine himself in various ways (as a voyeur, among others), he remains at one, in harmony with only himself. When he finally becomes reconciled to the Bartletts' violent way of life, he remains unfulfilled. He can satiate himself neither with the daughter nor with the mother.

Instead of an object of violence, of rape or murder, Laney becomes an object of Kasch's creation. It is at this point that *Childwold* most neatly resembles Vladimir

Nabokov's *Lolita* (1955)—the story of a middle-aged man's obsession with a nubile teenage girl. As does Humbert Humbert in *Lolita*, Kasch casts a spell about Laney, using art as a medium, but she eventually escapes, moving though the two-dimensional world of Kasch's photographs to the world of nature outside his museum/prison. She frees herself from the world he is doomed to inhabit.

It is a world that is of his own design. After Arlene has joined Kasch, her former lover, Earl Tuller, returns to threaten and bully her. In a rage, Kasch kills him and seals his fate as a prisoner. He has dreamed of being a murderer, but now that his fantasy has been accidentally made real, he is unable to bear the results. He has been defeated by his own desires mixed with the mindless tide of the universe. The novel ends with Arlene musing over the turn their lives have taken. Laney returns to Kasch's mansion, but he will not answer the door. Imagining that she sees him behind a curtained window, she calls out. She feels she is strong enough, has changed enough from the girl she was, to save him, and so in a flush of anticipation she waits for "a sign, a sign," but it never comes. Oates demonstrates in *Childwold* the tragic consequences of the conflict between humanity's ambitions and the machinations of the world.

BELLEFLEUR

In *Bellefleur*, Oates combines the gothic grotesque and a sense of realism to create a novel that, incredibly, has believable unhuman creatures. If this type of book seems out of character for her, it may be that she wishes to warn her audience that what seems extraordinary may, upon examination, be simply ordinary. In one episode, a huge rodent runs screaming into the house; the next morning, it is nothing but a cat. On the other hand, normality might suddenly become monstrous.

Bellefleur traces the history of the Bellefleur family through several generations and as many psychological aberrations. There are psychics in the family, a gnome who serves Leah Bellefleur, and several ghosts. Jedediah Bellefleur is the manifestation in this novel of the character who forces himself to exist against the will of nature. He is a recurring character in Oates's novels, and in *Bellefleur*, Jedediah is delightfully crazy. In the end, he is persuaded to continue the Bellefleur line despite his (and the reader's) misgivings.

The novel can be difficult for readers because it jumps back and forth from past to present. Another difficulty stems from the fact that the main character of interest, the telepathic Germaine Bellefleur, ages only four years from her birth during the entire action of the novel, while her father ages two or three decades. The setting of the novel itself—the Adirondack mountain range—ages thousands of years. In addition, the mountains and the people shrink or grow spasmodically. The final chapters contain spiritual references that, at first, seem disjointed. After Gideon's transformation into the skeletal Angel of Death, however, a Native American appears to the ancestral Jedediah and tells him to embrace the world that he has abandoned. This is Oates's final message to the reader, that only in a full and relished life is there union with God's body. Thus, as in her first novel, Oates's characters do battle with their own existences, their own beings. They struggle, escape, and wander only to return to their initial resting places within themselves and within the confines of their destinies.

MYSTERIES OF WINTERTHURN

The characters in *Mysteries of Winterthurn*, however, appear to have relinquished their resting places for ghostly—and ghastly—forays among the living. This gothic mystery novel has been hailed as a feminist dissertation, a charge that Oates has not refuted. Although the main character is male and the action in the novel is seen through his eyes, most of the victims are women and children, and it is to their plight that the narrator and the reader grow sympathetic. In *Mysteries of Winterthurn*, Oates discusses the existence of women in a male-dominated society, and a pitiable existence it is.

Even though Oates owes much of her presentation of the situation of nineteenth century women and children to several other popular authors, her interpretation is uniquely her own. Her victims are disposable pawns in a society that is more than willing to sacrifice them for its own (male) devices. Oates inserts the supernatural into the novel to allow her women a modicum of revenge on these perpetrators. If this seems to be impossible (the unreal attacking the real), Oates insists that once something is thought to be real, it becomes so whether it should be real or not. Thus the view of women as passive, thoughtless beings is true for the males in her novel, even though it is a false concept. The women victims in the novel are freed by this misconception to react violently to those who misuse them because they (the women) cannot have acted in such a manner within the male scheme of things.

To drive this point home, Oates repeats it three times during the novel. The first story, "The Virgin in the Rose-Bower," deals with a sadistic husband and father, Erasmus Kilgarven, who has a hand in the brutal deaths of his two wives and commits incest for several years with his daughter, Georgina, causing her to become pregnant several times. Georgina kills her infants but claims that they have been destroyed by angels painted on the ceiling of her bedroom. The narrator, young Xavier Kilgarven, sees one painted angel bleed, and this leads to the discovery of several other infant corpses, silent witnesses to Erasmus Kilgarven's hideous habit. By claiming supernatural murder (and rape), Georgina is able to evade guilt and exact a small amount of revenge on her father.

In the persona of Iphigenia, her pen name, Georgina is also able to free her female family members by publishing her poetry. The money she receives from this enterprise, until her father forbids it as unseemly, is later used to finance even more unfeminine exploits by the young Perdita. Perdita needs no spectral avenger; she takes matters into her own hands, although she is never seen as a murderer by anyone but the reader. The only people who are capable of violent acts in *Mysteries of Winterthurn* are male; the females are those upon whom these acts are perpetrated. An invisible shield is thus created around Perdita, enabling her to murder several people in order to achieve her goal, union with young Xavier.

The third sister, Thérèse, is able to profit from her sisters' cloaked deeds, and, indeed, there are indications that she may be involved in Perdita's violent crimes in a peripheral manner. This is only hinted at, however; outwardly, Thérèse appears to be a happy, modern woman. It is here that Oates's use of paradox—the woman who is both angel and demon, visible and invisible—culminates. All the women in the novel have been so seduced by the theory of their own guilt that they must violently oppose it in order to free themselves.

FOXFIRE

Another brilliantly innovative work encompassing Oates's feminist vision is *Foxfire: Confessions of a Girl Gang*. This novel, set in upstate New York in the 1950's, centers on five high school girls who seek and get revenge on the men who exploit them. By chronicling the exploits of the Foxfire gang, which comprises Legs Sadovsky, Goldie, Lana, Rita, and Maddy Wirtz, Oates reveals how class conflict and the exploitation of girls and women by men and boys consistently reinforce each other. Unlike the female characters in *Mysteries of Winterhurn*, the girl gang members are not paralyzed by fear, guilt, or insecurity. Finding strength in solidarity, the girls, all from low-income families who daily feel the sting of poverty and the humiliation of male chauvinism, resolve not to suffer at the hands of their exploiters, villains they cast as upper-class white men.

The girls, in a wild experiment of role reversal, aggressively seek out their own victims, men who have hurt one or all of them. They subsequently put these men "on trial," and all their victims are "sentenced" to some punishment. By inflicting physical pain or by causing irreversible damage to the men's reputations, the girls see to it that the guilty suffer for the psychic wounds they have caused. While Oates's sympathies clearly lie with the girls, she mitigates the gang's actions by providing the girls with an important insight. All the girls come to realize that evil is not strictly the province of men or the upper class; their own acts of violence clearly reveal to them that, tragically, the propensity for harming others exists in all human beings.

WHAT I LIVED FOR

In *What I Lived For*, Jerome "Corky" Corcoran, the main character, makes a discovery similar to that of the Foxfire gang. As Corky bounces from one volatile situation to another throughout the dense, highly intricate plot of the novel, he becomes the principal figure in a modern tragedy. The narrative, an account of the three most intense days of Corky's life, related by the protagonist himself, reveals his participation in situations and relationships that, as they disintegrate before his eyes, challenge all of Corky's beliefs in the innate goodness of humanity. They also force him to revise his opinion of others as well as his opinion of himself.

Finding himself entangled in these events, which are charged with class conflict, racial tension, political strife, and economic distress, Corky learns that the myths of success, the very myths that he has internalized and employed to sustain his dreams, are false and corrupt. This realization compels him to examine himself, body and soul. He concludes that he too is false and corrupt. He has worshiped the false gods of money and power and has neglected family, religion, and anything else that could have given real meaning and substance to his life. As the narrative proceeds to its tragic conclusion, Oates helps the reader perceive that Corky's flaws are particularly tragic because they are so universal.

MY HEART LAID BARE

Like Nabokov's *Lolita*, *My Heart Laid Bare* presents a panorama of a vast, gullible America, a jigsaw puzzle of independent states where people can change identities just by crossing boundary lines. The novel is a parodistic epic about a family of confidence artists in nineteenth and early twentieth century America whose careers are largely shaped by the political, financial, and sociological changes of that turbulent period. Oates's catchy (and somewhat misleading) title refers to a memoir that the protagonist, Abraham Licht, intends to write someday but leaves unfinished at his death. Readers who expect the novel to present a famous woman author's personal confession may feel confused when they find themselves involved with a complicated semihistorical, semigothic, partially tongue-in-cheek story reminiscent of Oates's *Bellefleur*, *A Bloodsmoor Romance*, and *Mysteries of Winterthurn*. Oates has called those popular books "parodistic," explaining that "they are not exactly parodies, because they take the forms they imitate quite seriously."

Abraham Licht is the quintessential laissez-faire social Darwinist of the late nineteenth century. He teaches his children that life is an endless struggle for survival, with every individual pitted against every other. Their only allegiance should be to the family, particularly to himself. Every outsider should be regarded as an enemy and potential victim.

Abraham's two oldest sons are temperamentally as different as Cain and Abel. Thurston is tall, handsome, and refined; Harwood is stocky, ugly, and vulgar. Harwood is the only member of the family who is vicious. When Thurston is scheming to make his fortune by marrying a wealthy society matron, the volatile Harwood creates a scene that exposes Thurston as a bounder and an impostor. When the deluded woman interposes between the quarreling brothers, Harwood inadvertently breaks her neck and flees. Thurston has no choice but to flee also—but in a different direction. Only Thurston is captured, and, true to his family's code of honor, he chooses to be hanged rather than point the finger at his brother. Ultimately, the wily Abraham saves his son by giving him a drug that makes the young man appear dead and spiriting him out of prison in a coffin.

Characters in the novel have a way of disappearing for years and reappearing under different names. Harwood comes back into the saga as Harmon Liges when he befriends Roland Shrikesdale III, a wealthy young tenderfoot vacationing in the Wild West. Harwood conceives a daring scheme based on the fact that he resembles his new friend so closely that they might be taken for twins. He lures his victim into the wilderness, commits a cold-blooded murder, then stumbles back into civilization wearing the dead man's clothing and pretending to be suffering from amnesia. The victim's mother unquestioningly accepts Harwood as her adored child. She has not long to live, and Harwood stands to inherit a large fortune; however, he overplays his hand by inviting Abraham to visit him so that he can show off his affluence and cleverness. The old woman's nephews, who will inherit the fortune if they can prove, as they suspect, that Harwood is an impostor and probably a murderer, investigate and discover the truth about the Lichts. Abraham finds it expedient to disappear when his son's dismembered body is delivered to him in a number of gift-wrapped containers.

In his old age, Abraham finally enters into his first legal marriage. His young bride, Rosamund, as might be expected, belongs to a socially prominent family and inherits a fortune. They have a daughter and lead a peaceful life at Muirkirk. Abraham no longer needs to obtain money illegally. He invests all of his own and his wife's capital in corporate stocks. His whole career has been affected by the invisible hand of history, and it ends in disaster with the great Wall Street crash of 1929. During the subsequent Great Depression, he becomes dependent on his son Darian, who ekes out a living as a music teacher and part-time musician. Then Abraham discovers that Darian and Rosamund have fallen in love. This new blow to his inflated ego changes him into a violent psychopath, but he turns his rage against himself, committing suicide in the treacherous marsh after setting the family home afire in a grand gothic finale.

MISSING MOM

Nikki Eaton, who finds her mother murdered and learns about herself as well as her mother during the grief process, is the protagonist of *Missing Mom*, a novel that takes the reader through Nikki's life, from her sibling rivalry and personality conflicts with her suburban perfectionist sister, Claire, to her affair with Wally Szalla, a married man.

In her thirties, Nikki is known as the rebel of the family. Single, with no children, and working as a reporter for the *Chautauqua Valley Beacon*, she lives what some might consider an alternative lifestyle, dying her spiked hair maroon and wearing miniskirts and thigh-high boots rather than the more conservative pantsuits that her sister, a mother and housewife, wears. Nikki's family disapproves of her affair with Wally. Her mother, Gwen, wishes that Nikki would "settle down" and regularly introduces her to "eligible bachelors."

Beginning with a Mother's Day party, the novel introduces Gwen, her family, and her friends. Readers learn that Gwen is popular in the neighborhood, appreciated for her skill and creativity in bread baking as well as her willingness to sacrifice herself for others. She is the shoulder that her friends and family lean on in times of trouble and has a hard time resisting "strays" of any type. This quality contributes to her murder, as it leads her to give a ride to a methamphetamine addict, Ward Lynch, who had formerly done odd jobs at Gwen's house in Mt. Ephraim, New York, as part of a prison rehabilitation program. After forcing her to drive to her house and burglarizing it, Lynch stabs Gwen and leaves her in the basement for dead.

After she finds her mother's body, Nikki endures the trauma of notifying the authorities, including Detective Ross Strabane, and her sister. Throughout the process of grieving over their mother's death, both Nikki and Claire make life changes. Nikki decides to stop seeing Wally after a meeting with his wife, Isabel, in which she learns that she is not the only "other woman."

After Claire and her husband, Rob, agree to a trial separation, Claire moves to Philadelphia, where a wealthy friend of hers has connections that will help her get into graduate school—a step she has put on hold since she "settled" for marriage to Rob and raising a family. Nikki feels abandoned and sad, and her sister's disapproval of Nikki's moving into their mother's home rather than selling it lingers. When Nikki learns that Ward Lynch has requested a trial, claiming innocence, she tries to manage her anger and prepare herself for the trauma of testifying; she then finds out from Detective Strabane that there will be no trial after all. In her profound relief and happiness when Strabane gives her the news, Nikki realizes her attraction to this man, who has been subtly pursuing her, repeatedly giving her his card and letting her know that she can call him any time of the day, for any reason; they become lovers. At the end of the first full year of her grief, Nikki finds that, although it has not ended, she does not have to go through it alone. From learning about the life of her mother, Nikki realizes that she can pay tribute to her mother's memory by settling for no less than love for herself.

BLACK GIRL/WHITE GIRL

Black Girl/White Girl centers on two roommates at Schuyler College: Genna Hewett-Meade, a young white woman whose relatives founded the all-women's school, and Minette Swift, an African American scholarship student. During their time together in 1975, Genna develops a deep loyalty to Minette, an unpopular preacher's daughter who holds herself apart from her fellow students and makes no attempts to befriend them. When Genna hears other students make fun of her roommate's middle-aged style of dress, her thick glasses, and her forceful way of speaking, she defends Minette, for which Minette shows little appreciation. When Minette has difficulties keeping her scholarship because her grades are poor, Genna encourages her to seek academic help and assures her that she can raise her grades if she wants to.

Genna, the daughter of a 1960's political radical and a mother with a history of drug and alcohol abuse and sexual promiscuity, with an investment banker brother from whom she is essentially estranged, feels like the most normal member of her family, but she is constantly on edge, waiting for news that her father has been arrested or her mother has had another emotional meltdown. As she tries to befriend Minette and earn her trust, she also finds herself in the role of confidant for her family members, classmates, and even a dean, who questions her when Minette becomes the target of a series of racially oriented incidents. Realizing that Minette herself has orchestrated the incidents (ranging from the defacement of her textbook to a racial slur scrawled on the door of their dorm room), possibly for attention, Genna recognizes Minette's instability but decides to show her loyalty and try to win her trust by keeping the information to herself while Minette gains more attention for the perceived attacks against her.

Feeling betrayed and abandoned when Minette leaves the dorm to live by herself in Stone Cottage, a historical building on campus where only a few students are privileged to live, Genna visits her on her birthday in a final attempt to seal their friendship. She is troubled by the number of candles Minette has carelessly placed around her room and its state of disarray and dirtiness, as well as by Minette's state of agitation. When Genna learns the next day that Minette has died in a fire caused by those candles, she blames herself for not having said anything to Minette about them for fear of incurring her wrath.

At about the same time, Genna finds out that her father has been arrested for aiding and abetting terrorists, and she starts to develop a new identity separate from her family, one in which she can insulate herself from her pain. She gains weight, darkens her hair, trims it short, and wears nondescript clothes. Having dropped out of Schuyler College, she earns a Ph.D. in later years and gains a faculty position. Secure professionally and financially, having inherited investments from her wealthy Meade grandparents, she gives away the interest (approximately $100,000 yearly) to causes and institutions she deems worthy, including Minette's father's church. Ending the novel with a visit to her father in prison, Genna shows how she has succeeded in spite of her dysfunctional family and friends but has sacrificed the vulnerability that might have allowed her to be loved herself.

Jennifer L. Wyatt; Traci S. Smrcka and Bill Delaney
Updated by Holly L. Norton

OTHER MAJOR WORKS

SHORT FICTION: *By the North Gate*, 1963; *Upon the Sweeping Flood*, 1966; *The Wheel of Love*, 1970; *Marriages and Infidelities*, 1972; *The Goddess and Other Women*, 1974; *The Hungry Ghosts: Seven Allusive Comedies*, 1974; *Where Are You Going, Where Have You Been?*, 1974; *The Poisoned Kiss*, 1975; *The Seduction*, 1975; *Crossing the Border*, 1976; *Night-Side*, 1977; *All the Good People I've Left Behind*, 1978; *The Lamb of Abyssalia*, 1979; *A Sentimental Education*, 1980; *Last Days*, 1984; *Raven's Wing*, 1986; *The Assignation*, 1988; *Heat, and Other Stories*, 1991; *Where Is Here?*, 1992; *Haunted: Tales of the Grotesque*, 1994; *Will You Always Love Me?*, 1994; *The Collector of Hearts*, 1998; *Faithless: Tales of Transgression*, 2001; *I Am No One You Know*, 2004; *The Female of the Species: Tales of Mystery and Suspense*, 2005; *High Lonesome: Stories, 1966-2006*, 2006; *The Museum of Dr. Moses: Tales of Mystery and Suspense*, 2007; *Wild Nights! Stories About the Last Days of Poe, Dickinson, Twain, James, and Hemingway*, 2008.

PLAYS: *Miracle Play*, pr. 1974; *Three Plays*, 1980; *I Stand Before You Naked*, pb. 1991; *In Darkest America: Two Plays*, 1991; *Twelve Plays*, 1991; *The Perfectionist, and Other Plays*, 1995; *New Plays*, 1998.

POETRY: *Women in Love*, 1968; *Anonymous Sins, and Other Poems*, 1969; *Love and Its Derangements*, 1970; *Angel Fire*, 1973; *The Fabulous Beasts*, 1975; *Women Whose Lives Are Food, Men Whose Lives Are Money*, 1978; *Invisible Woman: New and Selected Poems, 1970-1982*, 1982; *The Luxury of Sin*, 1984; *The Time Traveler*, 1989; *Tenderness*, 1996.

NONFICTION: *The Edge of Impossibility: Tragic Forms in Literature*, 1972; *The Hostile Sun: The Poetry of D. H. Lawrence*, 1973; *New Heaven, New Earth: The Visionary Experience in Literature*, 1974; *Contraries: Essays*, 1981; *The Profane Art: Essays and Reviews*, 1983; *On Boxing*, 1987; *(Woman) Writer: Occasions and Opportunities*, 1988; *George Bellows: American Artist*, 1995; *Where I've Been, and Where I'm Going: Essays, Reviews, and Prose*, 1999; *The Faith of a Writer: Life, Craft, Art*, 2003; *Uncensored: Views and (Re)views*, 2005; *Joyce Carol Oates: Conversations, 1970-2006*, 2006; *The Journal of Joyce Carol Oates, 1973-1982*, 2007 (Greg Johnson, editor).

CHILDREN'S/YOUNG ADULT LITERATURE: *Come Meet Muffin*, 1998; *Big Mouth and Ugly Girl*, 2002; *Freaky Green Eyes*, 2003; *Sexy*, 2005; *After the Wreck, I Picked Myself Up, Spread My Wings, and Flew Away*, 2006; *Naughty Chérie*, 2008.

EDITED TEXTS: *Scenes from American Life: Contemporary Short Fiction*, 1972; *The Best American Short Stories 1979* 1979 (with Shannon Ravenel); *Night Walks: A Bedside Companion*, 1982; *First Person Singular: Writers on Their Craft*, 1983; *The Best American Essays*, 1991; *The Oxford Book of American Short Stories*, 1992; *American Gothic Tales*, 1996; *The Best American Essays of the Century*, 2000 (with Robert Atwan); *Snapshots: Twentieth Century Mother-Daughter Fiction*, 2000 (with Janet Berliner); *The Best American Mystery Stories*, 2005 (with Otto Penzler); *The Ecco Anthology of Contemporary American Short Fiction*, 2008 (with Christopher R. Beha).

BIBLIOGRAPHY

Cologne-Brookes, Gavin. *Dark Eyes on America: The Novels of Joyce Carol Oates*. Baton Rouge: Louisiana State University Press, 2005. Presents analysis of selected significant works by Oates, with a focus on exposing her philosophical and cultural worldviews. Valuable addition to studies of Oates's work.

Creighton, Joanne V. *Joyce Carol Oates*. Boston: Twayne, 1979. Provides a penetrating exploration of the themes that dominate Oates's work, such as self-definition, isolation, and violent liberation. Includes chronology and annotated bibliography.

_____. *Joyce Carol Oates: Novels of the Middle Years*. New York: Twayne, 1992. Focuses on Oates's authorial voice, combining critical analysis of Oates's work with the author's own criticism of her work. Surveys fifteen novels written between 1977 and 1990, exploring their autobiographical elements, feminist subtexts, and realistic dimensions. Includes a selected bibliography.

Johnson, Greg. *Invisible Writer: A Biography of Joyce Carol Oates*. New York: Penguin Putnam, 1998. Provides a thorough analysis of Oates's work and life, drawing on a variety of sources, including Oates's private letters and journals.

_____. *Understanding Joyce Carol Oates*. Columbia: University of South Carolina Press, 1987. Good introduction to Oates for the general reader examines both her early major novels and some of her best-known stories. Includes some biographical material and a bibliography.

_____, ed. *Joyce Carol Oates: Conversations*. Princeton, N.J.: Ontario Review Press, 2006. Collection of previously published interviews with Oates spans the years 1970 to 2006. Topics covered include the author's thoughts on the art of fiction, her "lighter" side, and Marilyn Monroe, the subject of her novel *Blonde*. Includes a brief chronology of her life.

Oates, Joyce Carol. *The Journal of Joyce Carol Oates: 1973-1982*. Edited by Greg Johnson. New York: Ecco Press, 2007. Wide-ranging collection of thoughtful, reflective entries traces Oates's life from her time as a professor at the University of Windsor through her move to Princeton University. Oates describes the joys and frustrations of writing as well as her enjoyment of spending time with friends, including some famous writers, and family. Provides a record of her productivity as a writer as well as insight into her philosophical explorations and her views of the human condition.

Wagner, Linda, ed. *Critical Essays on Joyce Carol Oates*. Boston: G. K. Hall, 1979. Collection of twenty-eight reviews and essays includes discussions of particular works as well as analyses of Oates's general themes and stylistic considerations. Supplemented with a chronology and a bibliography as well as a short, refreshing preface by Oates herself.

Wesley, Marilyn. *Refusal and Transgression in Joyce Carol Oates's Fiction*. Westport, Conn.: Greenwood Press, 1993. Feminist analysis focuses on the family as portrayed in Oates's fiction. Contends that the young protagonists of many of Oates's stories and novels commit acts of transgression that serve as critiques of the American family.

JAMES PURDY

Born: Fremont, Ohio; July 17, 1914
Died: Englewood, New Jersey; March 13, 2009
Also known as: James Amos Purdy

PRINCIPAL LONG FICTION

Malcolm, 1959
The Nephew, 1960
Cabot Wright Begins, 1964
Eustace Chisholm and the Works, 1967
Jeremy's Version, 1970
I Am Elijah Thrush, 1972
The House of the Solitary Maggot, 1974
In a Shallow Grave, 1976
Narrow Rooms, 1978
Mourners Below, 1981
On Glory's Course, 1984
In the Hollow of His Hand, 1986
Garments the Living Wear, 1989
Out with the Stars, 1992
Gertrude of Stony Island Avenue, 1997

OTHER LITERARY FORMS

In addition to his novels, James Purdy wrote in a variety of genres, including poetry, the short story, and drama. The most important of these other works are *Sixty-three: Dream Palace* (1956); *Color of Darkness: Eleven Stories and a Novella* (1957); *Children Is All* (1961), a collection of ten stories and two plays; and a volume of poetry, *The Running Sun* (1971).

ACHIEVEMENTS

James Purdy is considered one of the most important of the postmodern American writers. Along with Thomas Pynchon, John Barth, and John Hawkes, Purdy is acknowledged as one of the best of the generation of post-Joycean experimental writers. His writing is unique and powerful, and his vision remains etched in the reader's mind. Like other postmodern writers, Purdy took delight in experimenting with the texts and subtexts of narratives and treated his themes with humor and irony. In essence, Purdy's characters are motivated by irrationality; his style is ornate and complex, and his themes are surreal. Purdy is a writer whose works must be examined if the textures and ideas of the postmodern novel are to be appreciated.

BIOGRAPHY

James Amos Purdy was born on July 17, 1914, near Fremont, Ohio. He attended the University of Chicago and the University of Puebla in Mexico. Later, he worked as an interpreter in Spain, Latin America, and France. From 1949 until 1953, he taught at Lawrence College in Appleton, Wisconsin. In 1953, he decided to devote himself to writing full time. Purdy received Guggenheim Fellowships in 1958 and 1962 and a Ford Fellowship in Drama in 1961. He took a teaching post at New York University and settled in Brooklyn Heights, New York. On March 13, 2009, Purdy died in New Jersey.

ANALYSIS

Because James Purdy was so hesitant to make public the details of his private life, it is impossible to correlate any of his works with his personal experiences. His works are hermetically sealed from his life and must be examined as entities in themselves. Purdy's themes, styles, and ideas change, develop, and expand from novel to novel, so it is not possible to delineate any one particular aspect of his work that is found consistently throughout. Certain preoccupations, however, are found, in varying degrees, in most of his works, and certain characteristics that are typical of postmodern fiction.

The characters in Purdy's novels are bizarre, grotesque, and governed by abnormal impulses and desires. Purdy uses his characters for purposes of symbolic manipulation rather than for the purpose of character development in the traditional sense. Many of his characters are physically or mentally mutilated, or both: They are tattooed, wounded, stabbed, raped, and, in one case, crucified. One of the major characteristics of all of his novels is his use of "unreal" characters whose thinking processes are "nonrealistic."

A primary concern of Purdy is the relationship of children to their parents; most of his novels include a domineering phallic woman, the search for a father, and the interrelationships within a family matrix. Many of his characters are orphans, illegitimate children, or children who have been abandoned by their parents. Along with these motifs, Purdy is preoccupied with the idea of being "grown-up" or mature. Within the quest for a father figure, the idea of becoming mature is interwoven into the text, and within this framework Purdy usually parodies the search for identity and its resultant ambivalence.

The interplay of sex, love, and violence occurs frequently throughout Purdy's writing. Virtually no love between man and woman appears in Purdy's novels—male-female relationships are either those of a prostitute and a man or a man who rapes women. Purdy does include a number of sexual affairs between men in his works, but these usually end in obsession and violence. In addition, many of the novels involve incest.

Also interwoven in the stories are themes of tyranny, freedom, dominance, and obsessive love. Frequently, the female characters are aggressive and domineering, and often the male characters are passive and dominated. Many of the characters are attempting to find their "freedom" from dominance, but the nature of obsessive love does not permit this.

Finally, in some manner or another, Purdy's novels all involve a writer within the narrative. In some books, this figure takes on more importance than in others; this device, typical of self-conscious "metafiction," serves to emphasize the autonomous reality of the fictive world.

MALCOLM

Many of the themes, motifs, and preoccupations of his subsequent novels are found in Purdy's first novel, *Malcolm*. The orphan motif that occurs so frequently in Purdy's works plays a vital part in *Malcolm*. Malcolm (no last name given), the reader is told, belongs nowhere and to nobody. His father has disappeared, and Malcolm's search for him forms the central psychological structure of the book. The fifteen-year-old Malcolm is sitting on a park bench outside the hotel where he is staying when Mr. Cox, an astrologer, takes an interest in him. He gives Malcolm a series of addresses in order to interest him in "things," and the ensuing visits to the people who live at the respective addresses form the core of the action in the novel. Malcolm becomes a parody of the picaro, for instead of acting he is acted upon. His main concern is to find his father, but his actions are governed by the tyrannical Mr. Cox and his circle of friends.

Within Mr. Cox's circle are Madame Girard and Girard Girard, an eccentric billionaire. At one point in the novel, Malcolm is offered a chance to be Girard Girard's son, but Malcolm tells him he has only one father and Girard Girard cannot take his place. Later, after Malcolm marries Melba, a famous black singer, he believes that he sees his father at a restaurant. Malcolm follows this man into the restroom. The man, however, denies that he is Malcolm's father and throws Malcolm down, causing Malcolm to hit his head. After this incident, Malcolm, who has deteriorated physically since his marriage, becomes too weak to get out of bed and eventually dies.

Thus, in this first novel, Purdy reveals many of his recurring preoccupations. In addition to the orphan's search for the father (paralleling the search for identity), Purdy explores the topic of tyranny and the theme of the fatality of a loveless marriage. A concern with the maturation process is also found in *Malcolm*. Gus, one of Melba's former husbands, is chosen to help Malcolm mature before his marriage. Gus's solution to helping Malcolm "mature" is to have Malcolm tattooed and to have him visit a prostitute.

In *Malcolm*, the characters are constantly questioning the substantiality of their existence; they are two-dimensional, almost comic-book figures. Malcolm is given addresses, not names, and consequently, places and events take primacy over the development of the personality. Malcolm himself has no last name, and when he dies there is no corpse in his coffin. All that is left of Malcolm are three hundred pages of manuscript that he had written, which Madame Girard attempts to organize.

THE NEPHEW

In *The Nephew*, Purdy turns to the small town of Rainbow Center for his setting and tells a story that superficially resembles a slice of small-town life. Underneath the seemingly placid exterior of Rainbow Center, however, as beneath the surface of the novel, much is happening. The text is surcharged with meanings, and the experience of reading this novel is similar to that of watching a film with the sound track slightly off.

The plot is simple and straightforward. Alma Mason and her brother, Boyd, receive news that their nephew Cliff is missing in action during the Korean War. Cliff, another of Purdy's orphans, had lived with the Masons. In order to alleviate some of the grief of his death, Alma decides to write a memorial honoring Cliff. The novel focuses on Alma's attempts to gather material for the writing of Cliff's memorial. During this process, she discovers many facets of Cliff's existence of which she had been unaware—particularly that Cliff had hated the town and that he had had a homosexual affair—which lead her to some revelations about herself and her relationship to Boyd and others in the community.

One of Purdy's concerns that can be noted throughout the novel is the inadequacy of judging people by their actions and their words. Communication is always inadequate and misinterpreted. Alma never does finish her memorial to Cliff, another indication that one can never fully understand another person. By the end of the story, however, Alma does become much more tolerant in her attitude toward what she considers the foibles of others.

CABOT WRIGHT BEGINS

Like *The Nephew*, *Cabot Wright Begins* concerns the attempt to write about another person—in this case, a businessman and rapist named Cabot Wright. Instead of one narrative voice, as in *The Nephew*, many emerge in *Cabot Wright Begins*, and this blending and confusion of narrative voices further demonstrate the impossibility of learning the true story about another person.

Purdy's third novel is an extremely pessimistic indictment and extended meditation on modern American culture. In *Cabot Wright Begins*, people are controlled by media-think, big business, and popular culture and by all the superficial aspects of modern existence. Feelings, emotions, and actions are all superficial, and even the rape scenes involving Cabot Wright are narrated in a dispassionate manner—much like secondhand violence seen on television or in the cinema. People exist on the screen of the text, and their ability to function in normal human terms is questioned.

Cabot Wright, another orphan, is twenty-six years old during the time of the novel. He is a stockbroker turned rapist. Bernie Gladhart, a used-car salesman, has been cajoled by his wife into writing the great American novel and has decided that a life history of Cabot Wright would be the perfect subject matter. In fact, the tentative title of Bernie's novel is "Indelible Smudge," which indicates Purdy's judgment about American culture at this time. Princeton Keith, the owner of a large publishing house, however, has commissioned Zoe Bickle to write the story in terms of popular fiction. Through a skylight, Zoe literally falls upon Cabot Wright himself, and Cabot offers to help her ghostwrite his biography. In the process of turning his life into popular fiction, however, he becomes alienated from himself. To him, the story does not portray his real self.

Cabot Wright seems to symbolize the attempt of modern men and women to assert their identity through violence. Only through the act of rape can Cabot penetrate the surface of another, but even then he becomes increasingly alienated and less alive. For Cabot, there are no answers.

EUSTACE CHISHOLM AND THE WORKS

In _Eustace Chisholm and the Works_, Purdy presents his concept of the sacrificial, violent, and grotesque aspects of love. In many horrific scenes he shows the results of obsessional love. The story revolves around the sexual love Daniel Hawes has for seventeen-year-old Amos Ratcliff. Amos, an illegitimate son, has been rejected by his father and has had incestuous relationships with his cousin (later revealed to be his mother). Daniel attempts to repress his feelings for Amos, but they finally become so overwhelming that he reenlists in the Army to escape. Instead of escaping, however, he permits his love for Amos to be brought to the surface and projected upon his commanding officer, Captain Stadger. During the affair between these two, Captain Stadger becomes increasingly more sadistic until finally he kills Daniel by disemboweling him, then commits suicide. This incident is the first in a series of homosexual blood sacrifices found in Purdy's novels.

Once again, as in all of Purdy's previous works, there is an author involved in an attempt to write the story. In this case, Eustace Chisholm is the writer who is attempting to incorporate the story of Amos and Daniel within the context of a larger epic poem that he is writing.

JEREMY'S VERSION

Purdy's next novel, _Jeremy's Version_, was written as part 1 of a projected trilogy called _Sleepers in the Moon-Crowned Valleys_. Although Purdy had dealt with orphans, the search for a father figure, and interrelationships within families in his previous works, this was his first novel in which the family matrix formed the basis for the entire work.

Again, there is a writer—in this case, Jeremy Cready—narrating the story being told to him by Uncle Matt. The basic story (which actually occurred more than fifty years before) involves the battle of wills between two strong women, Elvira Summerlad and Winifred Fergus; a divorce case; and the interrelationships of the three sons with one another and with their mother and father. Elvira Summerlad and Wilders Fergus were married, much against the wishes of his sister, Winifred, who thought the marriage was doomed. In a sense, Winifred was right, because Wilders abandoned Elvira and their sons. Winifred, however, goes to Wilders and tells him that since his sons are almost grown, he is needed at home. When he arrives, Elvira starts divorce proceedings against him.

The basic conflict is between Elvira and Winifred for custody of the children. Wilders is indifferent to the whole affair. One of Purdy's major themes—that of the son confronting the father—occurs during the divorce proceedings, when the gay oldest son, Rick, confronts Wilders. Rick demands that Wilders tell him the reason for his existence since his father has never been around before to teach him—he has only had his mother, who, he claims, has emasculated him. After Elvira wins the divorce case, her second son, Jethro, attempts to shoot her, but Matt saves her and is wounded. A similar shooting scene, between mother and son, occurs again in *The House of the Solitary Maggot*.

I AM ELIJAH THRUSH

I Am Elijah Thrush is a dreamlike, ornate, and highly stylized book, populated with strange characters and filled with unusual events. More than any of Purdy's other novels, this book exists in the realm of allegory and symbols. Among the major characters are a famous mime, Elijah Thrush; his great-grandson, a mute, called the Bird of Heaven; Millicent De Frayne, a tyrannical old dowager who retains her youth by drinking the seminal fluid of young men; and Albert Peggs, the black memoirist who tells the story and who, himself, has a bizarre "habit." In addition, the novel incorporates many elements of mythology in a comic manner, suggesting the debasement of culture in modern America.

As in many of Purdy's previous novels, the plot in *I Am Elijah Thrush* involves a person (in this case, Albert Peggs) being hired by someone to write the story. Millicent De Frayne hires Albert to recount the story of Elijah Thrush. Once again, this story involves a clash of wills between two strong people—Millicent and Elijah. For more than fifty years, she has been trying to gain control of Elijah and marry him. Eventually, she succeeds by manipulating Albert, the Bird of Heaven, and Elijah onto her boat, where she finally marries him. Late in the novel, Albert's "habit" is discovered: He sustains the life of a golden eagle by permitting the eagle to feed upon him. At the wedding feast of Millicent and Elijah, the eagle is served as the entree. After this incident, Albert "becomes" Elijah Thrush.

One of Purdy's major themes is that of confirming, or finding, an identity. In his novels, there is a plethora of name-changes, mistaken identities, disguises, masquerades, and other such motifs. The dreamlike structure of the narrative suggests that Albert Peggs is attempting to discover his identity by telling this story.

THE HOUSE OF THE SOLITARY MAGGOT

The House of the Solitary Maggot is part 2 of the series called *Sleepers in Moon-Crowned Valleys*. The story is reconstructed—this time on a tape recorder—by one of the characters, and, as in part 1 of the series, *Jeremy's Version*, the family matrix is the psychological focus in the novel. The story involves Mr. Skegg, the magnate (the "solitary maggot"); Lady Bythewaite; and their three illegitimate sons: Clarence, who is legally "acknowledged" by the father; Owen, who is acknowledged by the mother; and Aiken, who is not acknowledged by either parent until later in the book.

The novel takes place in a dying community called Prince's Crossing. Owen, the youngest son, hero-worships his brother, Clarence, who goes to New York to become a famous silent-film star. After Clarence leaves, Owen turns to the other older brother, Aiken, whom he also worships. The two become inseparable. Aiken, who himself has no acknowledged father or mother, serves as a father figure to Owen, helping him "mature" by giving him his first shave and taking him to visit a prostitute. After visiting her, Owen loses his sight. Aiken, who has finally been acknowledged by Lady Bythewaite as her long-lost son, buys the Acres, the showplace of the community. When Clarence returns and refuses to accept Aiken as his brother, Aiken, whose pride is hurt, burns down the house and marries the prostitute. This marriage is a failure, and Aiken decides to leave.

Although Aiken has been estranged from Owen, he loves him obsessively. When Aiken goes to say good-bye to Owen and their mother, Owen shoots him. Lady Bythewaite, one of Purdy's typical strong-willed, castrating women, then shoots Owen. In another of Purdy's characteristically grotesque scenes, Owen's eyeballs fall out and Aiken swallows them. While Aiken remains unconscious in the hospital, Clarence returns and wants to be acknowledged as Aiken's brother. When the unconscious Aiken cannot comply, Clarence slits his own throat. Eventually, Aiken comes to live with his mother. Mr. Skegg acknowledges him as his son and takes care of him in his illness. The story concludes with the death of Aiken, who, in a dreamlike sequence, tries to ride off on a horse with the dead Owen.

IN A SHALLOW GRAVE

The protagonist of Purdy's next novel, *In a Shallow Grave*, is Garnet Montrose, a war hero who has been so badly wounded that he is turned almost inside-out and is the color of mulberry juice. Garnet seeks "applicants" to take messages from him to the Widow Rance, whom he wishes to court, but the applicants are so appalled by Garnet's appearance that they cannot accept the job. Finally, Quintus, a black adolescent, shows up by accident at Garnet's house and accepts the position. Quintus's responsibilities are to read to Garnet and to rub his feet. Later, a man named Daventry shows up. Even though he is not an applicant, he takes the position of messenger to the Widow Rance. Within this narrative structure, Purdy pursues many of his recurring themes.

One of the primary scenes involves a communion among Garnet, Quintus, and Daventry. Garnet is about to have his property taken away, but Daventry says that he will save Garnet's land and property if Garnet will commune with him. Daventry takes his knife, slits open his chest, and the three of them drink his blood. Later, they discover that Garnet's property has been saved by the Veterans Administration, who heard of his plight and paid the mortgage. The wounding and shedding of blood, along with the religious connotations of the scene, seem to indicate that language is inadequate for portraying emotions, that the only way to "love" another person is to shed blood for him or her.

Again, homosexual love appears in the novel, for Daventry and Garnet fall in love. They consummate their love in the dance hall where Garnet goes to dance by himself and relive the moments in the past when he was "normal." With Garnet's permission, Daventry marries the Widow Rance, but on his wedding night, he is swept up by a strong wind, smashed against a tree, and killed.

NARROW ROOMS

Narrow Rooms is a story about the love-hate relationship between Roy Sturtevant (the renderer) and Sidney De Lakes. Roy Sturtevant had been in love with Sidney since the eighth grade, until Sidney slapped him publicly and humiliated him; from that time, Roy has been planning his revenge. The story opens after Sidney has returned from prison, where he served time for killing Brian McFee. He finds a job as keeper of Gareth Vaisey, who has been injured in a fall from a horse. Sidney and Gareth fall in love and have an affair, but Roy Sturtevant still exercises a strange power over them.

In the central scene in the novel, after Roy and Sidney have a sexual encounter, Roy commands Sidney to crucify him on the barn door and then bring the body of Brian McFee to view the crucifixion. Roy, still alive, is taken down from the barn door and carried into the house. Sidney and Roy then pledge their love for each other, and Gareth, jealous, shoots them both. Subsequently, Gareth also dies. Though the subject matter of *Narrow Rooms* is largely sensational, the novel continues Purdy's exploration of the destructive nature of obsessive love.

MOURNERS BELOW

In *Mourners Below*, Purdy returns to the theme of hero worship. Seventeen-year-old Duane Bledsoe is mourning the death of his two half brothers, Justin and Douglas, who have been killed in the war. Eugene Bledsoe, the father, with whom Duane lives, is aloof and psychologically distant. The central episode in the novel occurs when Duane goes to a fancy-dress ball at the mansion of Estelle Dumont (who had been Justin's lover), and Estelle seduces him. After the ball, another of Purdy's rape scenes occurs when Duane is sexually assaulted by two men along the roadside. During the brief affair between Duane and Estelle, Estelle conceives a child, also named Justin. At the end of the story, Duane is given the child to rear, and Eugene states that it is Duane's destiny to rear a son.

Although this novel incorporates many of Purdy's familiar conceptions, it appears to be much more optimistic about the human condition than his previous novels. For example, Eugene and Duane do become reconciled in many ways, and there are many indications that Duane will make a good parent for the child. Furthermore, many of the grotesque and sadistic aspects of love are absent in this book. The men and the women in the story are not the tyrannical types found in previous works; they exhibit much more normal motivation. *Mourners Below* seems to indicate a new phase in Purdy's development, for in this novel he emphasizes the hopeful qualities of love and human existence.

ON GLORY'S COURSE

The search for a lost son plays a crucial role in *On Glory's Course*. Adele Bevington, the main character in the novel, has had an illegitimate son taken away from her and placed for adoption. The rest of the novel revolves around her quest for her lost son. One of the wounded veterans living in Fonthill, the location of the novel, believes that he knows the identity of Adele's son—he is a soldier who has been gravely wounded in the war and is now residing at the Soldiers' Home, barely alive and unable to respond to any communication. Adele attempts to prove that this soldier, Moorbrook, is her son, but by the end of the novel, neither Adele nor the reader is certain about Moorbrook's identity. Once again, Purdy's recurring motif of the search for a father figure is woven into the text of the novel.

IN THE HOLLOW OF HIS HAND

In the Hollow of His Hand relates the kidnapping of a boy, Chad Coultas, by Decatur, an Ojibwa Indian. Decatur is actually the father of the boy and wishes to rear him as an Indian; however, Lew Coultas, the man who has brought up Chad, wishes to recapture him and take him "home." The mother of Chad, Eva Lewis, had not even realized that Decatur was the father until he returned home from the military and began taking Chad on rides after school. She then remembered that she had, indeed, had a one-day affair with Decatur years before the action in the novel begins.

During the attempt to find Chad, the town of Yellow Brook is awakened to its small town foibles and provincial attitudes, and once again Purdy reveals the darker side of small town life and values. This novel is darkly satiric and deals with Purdy's attempts to create an almost mythological construct of his obsession with the search for an identity within the context of the family. Yet *In the Hollow of His Hand* is also an extremely humorous novel, delving into the souls of small-town America and American culture.

GARMENTS THE LIVING WEAR

Set in Manhattan, *Garments the Living Wear* opens with Jared Wakeman, an actor and organizer of a theater group facing a desperate situation. Not only has his benefactor, Peg Shawbridge, almost run out of money, his actors have been decimated by acquired immunodeficiency syndrome (AIDS), which Purdy's characters refer to simply as the Plague. Even Des Cantrell, whom Jared refers to as his soul mate, shows the first signs of the illness. The situation radically changes when Edward Hennings, an aged financial wizard and Peg's former lover, arrives with his young androgynous bride, Estrallita. Edward desires Jared, luring him with the dual attractions of money for his theatrical endeavors and the mysterious Estrallita.

Purdy imbues the novel with an aura of myth and mystery as Edward seemingly cures Des. This atmosphere is reinforced by the appearance of Jonas Hakluyt, an ex-convict turned evangelist with messianic overtones. The novel combines humor and psychological realism, myth, and magic as Purdy's characters struggle to survive in a world where both people and events are unpredictable and reality is frequently overshadowed by illusion.

OUT WITH THE STARS

Out with the Stars revolves around a group of socially intertwined figures. Abner Blossom, with the support of his talented protégé, Val Sturgis, has emerged from his retirement to compose an opera based on a mysterious libretto that was found in a "parlor" where young men indulge in orgies. The libretto is based on the life of Cyrus Vane, a photographer who specialized in nude studies of young African American men. Vane's wife, Madame Petrovna, is bitterly opposed to production of the opera and will go to any lengths to stop it. A secondary theme in the novel deals with corruption and the loss of innocence of Sturgis and his roommate, Hugh, as they drift deeper into the exotic world of Vane and Blossom. Purdy vividly explores both racial and sexual prejudice in *Out with the Stars*.

GERTRUDE OF STONY ISLAND AVENUE

In *Gertrude of Stony Island Avenue*, Carrie Kinsella, an elderly woman who has lived a dull and uneventful existence, attempts to understand the life and death of her daughter, Gertrude, a famous and flamboyant artist. During this search, she encounters a series of eccentric characters who influenced and were influenced by Gertrude. Purdy explores the nature of love and relationships as Carrie struggles to accept the fact that she and Gertrude failed to love each other. Like most of Purdy's novels, *Gertrude of Stony Island Avenue* presents a shadowy world full of pretense and ambiguity. Purdy's language and symbolism mirror this world, which is often distorted, hiding more than it reveals.

Earl Paulus Murphy
Updated by Mary E. Mahony

OTHER MAJOR WORKS

SHORT FICTION: *Don't Call Me by My Right Name, and Other Stories*, 1956; *Sixty-three: Dream Palace*, 1956; *Color of Darkness: Eleven Stories and a Novella*, 1957; *The Candles of Your Eyes*, 1985; *The Candles of Your Eyes, and Thirteen Other Stories*, 1987; *Sixty-three: Dream Palace—Selected Stories, 1956-1987*, 1991; *Moe's Villa, and Other Stories*, 2000.

PLAYS: *Mr. Cough Syrup and the Phantom Sex*, pb. 1960; *Cracks*, pb. 1962; *Wedding Finger*, pb. 1974; *Clearing in the Forest*, pr. 1978; *True*, pr. 1978; *A Day After the Fair*, pb. 1979; *Now*, pr. 1979; *Two Plays*, 1979 (includes *A Day After the Fair* and *True*); *What Is It, Zach?*, pr. 1979; *Proud Flesh: Four Short Plays*, 1980; *Strong*, pb. 1980; *The Berry-Picker*, pb. 1981; *Scrap of Paper*, pb. 1981; *In the Night of Time, and Four Other Plays*, 1992 (includes *In the Night of Time*, *Enduring Zeal*, *The Paradise Circus*, *The Rivalry of Dolls*, and *Ruthanna Elder*); *The Rivalry of Dolls*, pr., pb. 1992.

POETRY: *The Running Sun*, 1971; *Sunshine Is an Only Child*, 1973; *She Came Out of the Mists of Morning*, 1975; *Lessons and Complaints*, 1978; *The Brooklyn Branding Parlors*, 1986.

MISCELLANEOUS: *Children Is All*, 1961 (stories and plays); *An Oyster Is a Wealthy Beast*, 1967 (story and poems); *Mr. Evening: A Story and Nine Poems*, 1968; *On the Rebound: A Story and Nine Poems*, 1970; *A Day After the Fair: A Collection of Plays and Stories*, 1977.

BIBLIOGRAPHY

Adams, Stephen D. *James Purdy.* New York: Barnes & Noble Books, 1976. Adams examines Purdy's major work from the early stories and *Malcolm* up through *In a Shallow Grave.* Of particular interest is Adams's discussion of the first two novels in Purdy's trilogy *Sleepers in Moon-Crowned Valleys.*

Canning, Richard. *Gay Fiction Speaks: Conversations with Gay Novelists.* New York: Columbia University Press, 2000. This book's extensive interview focuses primarily on Purdy's identity as a gay novelist. Purdy also discusses his plays, acknowledging his interest in and debt to the Jacobean theater of early seventeenth century England.

Chupack, Henry. *James Purdy.* Boston: Twayne, 1975. This introductory overview contains a biography, an introductory chapter on what Chupack terms the "Purdian trauma," and analyses of Purdy's works. Includes a bibliography and an index.

Guy-Bray, Stephen. "James Purdy. In *The Gay and Lesbian Literary Heritage: A Reader's Companion to the Writers and Their Works, from Antiquity to the Present,* edited by Claude J. Summers. New York: Henry Holt, 1995. In this short article, Guy-Bray tries to identify some of Purdy's most pervasive themes, including the betrayal of love, the use of violence to resolve inner conflict, and the malevolence of fate.

Lane, Christopher. "Out with James Purdy: An Interview." *Critique* 40 (Fall, 1998): 71-89. Purdy discusses racial stereotypes, sexual fantasy, political correctness, religious fundamentalism, gay relationships, and the reasons he has been neglected by the literary establishment.

Schwarzchild, Bettina. *The Not-Right House: Essays on James Purdy.* Columbia: University of Missouri Press, 1968. A collection of Schwarzchild's incisive essays on Purdy's work, primarily focusing on his novels.

Tanner, Tony. Introduction to *Color of Darkness* and *Malcolm.* New York: Doubleday, 1974. Tanner's introductory essay discusses Purdy's novel *Malcolm* and the short-story collection *Sixty-Three: Dream Palace.* It also compares Purdy's effects with those achieved by the Russian realist Anton Chekhov.

Whitaker, Rick. "James Purdy." In *The First Time I Met Frank O'Hara: Reading Gay American Writers.* Photographs by Iannis Delatolas. New York: Four Walls Eight Windows, 2003. Whitaker examines the lives and works of Purdy and other gay writers, focusing on how their literary styles and perspectives were influenced by their sexuality.

Woodhouse, Reed. "James Purdy's *Narrow Rooms.*" *Unlimited Embrace: A Canon of Gay Fiction, 1945-1995.* Amherst: University of Massachusetts Press, 1998. Woodhouse devotes a chapter to Purdy in his evaluation of fifty years of fiction written for, by, and about gay men. He views Purdy's works as an exploration of the ethics of gay life.

ANN RADCLIFFE

Born: London, England; July 9, 1764
Died: London, England; February 7, 1823
Also known as: Ann Ward

PRINCIPAL LONG FICTION

The Castles of Athlin and Dunbayne, 1789
A Sicilian Romance, 1790
The Romance of the Forest, 1791
The Mysteries of Udolpho, 1794
The Italian: Or, The Confessional of the Black Penitents, 1797
Gaston de Blondeville, 1826

OTHER LITERARY FORMS

In addition to her novels, Ann Radcliffe published *A Journey Made in the Summer of 1794 Through Holland and the Western Frontier of Germany* (1795). It recounts a continental journey made with her husband and includes copious observations of other tours to the English Lake District. The work became immediately popular, prompting a second edition, *The Journeys of Mrs. Radcliffe*, published the same year. Following a common practice of romance writers, Radcliffe interspersed the lengthy prose passages of her novels with her own verses or with those from famous poets. An anonymous compiler took the liberty of collecting and publishing her verses in an unauthorized edition titled *The Poems of Ann Radcliffe* (1816). This slim volume was reissued in 1834 and 1845. Radcliffe's interest in versifying was increasingly evident when her husband, in arranging for the posthumous publication of *Gaston de Blondeville*, included with it a long metrical romance, *St. Alban's Abbey* (1826). Radcliffe also wrote an essay, "On the Supernatural in Poetry," which was published in *New Monthly Magazine* (1826). The record of her literary achievement still remains available, as all of her novels and the poems are in print.

ACHIEVEMENTS

Ann Radcliffe's fame as a novelist in modern times in no way compares to the popularity she enjoyed in the 1790's. With the publication of her third novel, *The Romance of the Forest*, this relatively unknown woman established herself as the best-selling writer of the period, receiving rave reviews from the critics and increasing demand for her works from circulating libraries.

Radcliffe's five gothic romances, published between 1789 and 1797, owed a portion of their motivation to Horace Walpole's *The Castle of Otranto* (1765) and two earlier gothic writers, Sophia Lee and Clara Reeve. The gothic tale reached its full development with Radcliffe's ability to manipulate the emotions of love and fear in such a manner as to provoke terror in her characters and readers alike. Though managing an effective use of the little understood complexities of the imagination, she offered her readers stereotyped plots, characters, and settings. Her disguises of foreign characters and lands were as thin as the supernatural illusions that often seemed anticlimactic in their emotional appeal. These weaknesses did not deter Radcliffe's public, who remained fascinated by her distinctive brand of romanticism, which combined the gloomy darkening vale of the more somber poets of the graveyard school, the extremes of imaginative sensibility (as in Henry Mackenzie's *The Man of Feeling*, 1771), and the medieval extravagance of the Ossianic poems of James Macpherson, as well as the pseudoarchaic fabrications of Thomas Chatterton's Rowley poems (1777).

Radcliffe nurtured this cult of melancholy, primitivism, sentimentalism, exoticism, and medievalism in her novels, becoming the epitome of the gothic genre to her contemporaries. *The Mysteries of Udolpho*, her best-known work, was satirized by Jane Austen in *Northanger Abbey* (1818) as representative of the entire mode.

Radcliffe's later importance was seen in a number of major Romantic writers who read her romances in their childhood. Percy Bysshe Shelley's *Zastrozzi* (1810), an extravagant romance, was a youthful answer to the genre. Lord Byron's *Manfred* (1817) appears as a gothic villain committing spiritual murder in a landscape of "sublime solitudes." Matthew Gregory Lewis and Mary Wollstonecraft Shelley clearly benefited from Radcliffe's strengths as a novelist of suspense, mystery, and the picturesque. In America, Washington Irving's, Edgar Allan Poe's, and Nathaniel Hawthorne's tales of terror, along with Charles Brockden Brown's *Edgar Huntly: Or, Memoirs of a Sleep-Walker* (1799), were suggested by Radcliffe's work.

As the most popular and perhaps most important novelist between the eighteenth century masters and Austen and Sir Walter Scott, Radcliffe continues to claim the attention of academicians. Psychological, feminist, folklorist, and the more traditional thematic studies have proved the strengths of her art. In 1980, Devendra P. Varma (*The Gothic Flame*, 1957) began serving as advisory editor for the Arno Press series Gothic Studies and Dissertations, which has published dozens of texts dealing with Radcliffe's literary output; of those texts, more than one dozen discuss Radcliffe's novels at length. It is clear that there is at present a remarkable revival of interest in the gothic and in Radcliffe's work.

BIOGRAPHY

Ann Radcliffe was born Ann Ward on July 9, 1764, in Holborn, a borough of central London, the only child of William Ward and Ann Oates Ward. Her father was a successful haberdasher who provided the family with a comfortable life, allowing Radcliffe access to a well-stocked library and the time to read the works of every important English author, as well as numerous popular romances.

This quiet, sheltered existence was enlivened by the visits of Radcliffe's wealthy and learned uncle, Thomas Bentley, who was the partner of Josiah Wedgwood, the potter.

Bentley's London home was a center for the literati; there, among others, the pretty but shy girl met Hester L. Thrale Piozzi, the friend and biographer of Samuel Johnson; Elizabeth Montagu, "Queen of the Blue-Stocking Club"; and "Athenian" Stuart.

In 1772, Radcliffe joined her parents at Bath, where her father had opened a shop for the firm of Wedgwood and Bentley. She remained sequestered in this resort until her marriage to the young Oxford graduate, William Radcliffe, in 1788. William had first decided to become a law student at one of the Inns of Court but abandoned this for a career in journalism. The couple moved to London soon thereafter, where William subsequently became proprietor and editor of the *English Chronicle*. The marriage was happy but childless, and the couple's circle of friends were primarily literary, which added encouragement to William's argument that his wife should begin to write.

With her husband away on editorial business, Radcliffe spent the evenings writing without interruption. Her first book, *The Castles of Athlin and Dunbayne*, was unremarkable, but her next two novels established her reputation as a master of suspense and the supernatural. *A Sicilian Romance* and *The Romance of the Forest* attracted the public's voracious appetite for romances. Both works were translated into French and Italian, and numerous editions were published, as well as a dramatization of *The Romance of the Forest*, performed in 1794. Radcliffe's success culminated in the appearance of *The Mysteries of Udolpho*; her decision to rely less on external action and more on psychological conflict produced ecstatic reviews. The excitement created by the book threatened the relative solitude of the Radcliffes, but the publisher's unusually high offer of five hundred pounds freed them to travel extensively on the Continent.

In the summer of 1794, the Radcliffes journeyed through Holland and along the Rhine River to the Swiss frontier. On returning to England, they proceeded north to the Lake District. While traveling, Radcliffe took complete notes concerning the picturesque landscape and included detailed political and economic accounts of the Low Countries and the Rhineland. These latter observations were probably contributed by her husband, though both Radcliffes found the devastation of the Napoleonic Wars appalling. *A Journey Made in the Summer of 1794 Through Holland and the Western Frontier of Germany* appeared in 1795.

Radcliffe's interest in the human misery of these regions and the legends and superstitions of the great fortresses and Roman Catholic churches of the Rhineland suggested her next work, *The Italian: Or, The Confessional of the Black Penitents*. As a romance of the Inquisition, it explored character motivation in great detail, while action became a method of dramatizing personalities and not a simple vehicle for movement from one adventure to another. *The Italian*, though not as popular as *The Mysteries of Udolpho*, was translated immediately into French and even badly dramatized at the Haymarket on August 15, 1797.

At the age of thirty-three, Radcliffe was at the height of her popularity; though she had never decided on writing as a potential source of income, her means by this time had become quite ample. With the deaths of her parents between 1798 and 1799, she found herself independently wealthy. Whether it was because of her secure financial condition or her displeasure with the cheap imitations of her novels, Radcliffe withdrew from the public domain and refrained from publishing any more works in her lifetime. Innumerable reports surfaced that she was suffering from a terminal illness, that the terrors of which she had written in her novels had driven her mad, or that she had mysteriously died. These reports were without substance; in fact, she wrote another novel, a metrical romance, and an extensive diary.

After her death, Radcliffe's husband found among her papers a novel, *Gaston de Blondeville*, which he arranged to have published. Written after Radcliffe's visit to the ruins of Kenilworth Castle in 1802, it came near to comparing with the historical romances of Sir Walter Scott but lost itself in a preoccupation with historical precision, leaving action and character to suffer from a lack of emphasis. The narrative poem, *St. Alban's Abbey*, appeared posthumously with this last novel; though Radcliffe had been offered an early opportunity for publication, she broke off negotiations with the publisher.

Content with retirement and relative obscurity, Radcliffe wrote in her last years only diary entries concerning the places she and her husband had visited on their long journeys through the English countryside. From 1813 to 1816, she lived near Windsor and probably at this time began suffering from bouts of asthma. From all reports, she enjoyed the company of friends, maintained a ready wit and a sly humor, but insisted on delicacy and decorum in all things. Shortly before her final illness, she returned to London; she died there on February 7, 1823, in her sixtieth year. The "Udolpho woman" or "the Shakespeare of romance writers," as one contemporary reviewer called her, has achieved a secure place in the history of English literature.

ANALYSIS

The novels of Ann Radcliffe serve as a transition between the major English novelists of the eighteenth century and the first accomplished novelists of the nineteenth century. In the years between 1789 and 1797, her five novels established a style that profoundly affected English fiction for the next twenty-five years and had a considerable impact in translation as well. From the negligible first novel, *The Castles of Athlin and Dunbayne*, to the sophisticated romances, *The Mysteries of Udolpho* and *The Italian*, Radcliffe demonstrated an ability to enrich the motives, methods, and machineries of each succeeding work. Manipulating the conventions of the gothic while introducing new thematic concerns and experiments with narrative techniques, Radcliffe became a master of her craft.

Improved control over the complex atmosphere of the gothic romance proved an early factor in Radcliffe's success. She went beyond the traditional gothic devices of lurking ghosts and malevolent noblemen torturing innocent girls to an interest in natural description. This delight with nature's sublime scenery gave tone and color to her settings while emphasizing the heightened emotions and imagination that were produced in reaction to the landscape. A skillful use of numerous atmospheric factors such as sunsets, storms, winds, thunderclaps, and moonlight, intensified the romantic tendencies of her time.

A scene typifying the Radcliffe concept of landscape portraiture has a ruined castle in silhouette, arranged on a stern but majestic plain at nightfall. This view does not depend on precision of outline for effect but instead on an ominous vagueness, creating in the reader an odd mixture of pleasure and fear. Her delight in the architecture of massive proportions and in the picturesque derived in part from her reading of the nature poets and her study of the paintings of Claude Lorrain, Nicolas Poussin, and Salvator Rosa. She reflected a mid-eighteenth century English passion in cultivating an acute sensibility for discovering beauty where before it had not been perceived. While she made landscape in fiction a convention, it was her combining of beauty in horror and the horrible in the beautiful that reflected the Romantic shift away from order and reason toward emotion and imagination.

Radcliffe's novels rely not only on strategies of terror but also on the psychology of feelings. The novels of sensibility of the past generation offered her alternatives to the gothic trappings made familiar in Walpole's *The Castle of Otranto*; those gothic aspects now became linked to various emotional elements in a total effect. By drawing on the poetry of Thomas Gray and Edward Young or the fiction of Oliver Goldsmith and Henry Mackenzie, Radcliffe created a minority of characters with complex natures who exhibited not only melancholy and doubt, love and joy, but also hate and evil intentions. She was one of the first English novelists to subject her characters to psychological analysis.

Of particular psychological interest are Radcliffe's villains. Cruel, calculating, domineering, relentless, and selfish, they are more compelling than her virtuous characters. Since their passions are alien to the ordinary person, she dramatically explores the mysteries of their sinister attitudes. Radcliffe's villains resemble those created by the Elizabethan dramatists, and their descendants can be found in the works of the great Romantics, Byron and Shelley.

At her best, Radcliffe manifested strengths not seen in her first two novels nor in her last. Her first novel, *The Castles of Athlin and Dunbayne*, exhibits the most obvious borrowings, from sources as well known as *The Castle of Otranto* to numerous other gothic-historical and sentimental novels. Though immature, the work offers her characteristic sense of atmosphere with the marvelous dangers and mysteries of feudal Scotland depicted to full advantage. Its weaknesses become evident all too soon, however, as stock characters populate strained, often confused incidents while mouthing rather obvious parables about morality. Didacticism seems the motivating principle of the work. As David Durant observes in *Ann Radcliffe's Novels* (1980), "The characters are so controlled by didactic interests as to be faceless and without personality." The rigid obligations of *The Castles of Athlin and Dunbayne* to the morality of sentimental novels, the uniformity of a neoclassical prose style, and the repetitious, predictable action of the romance plot, trap Radcliffe into a mechanical performance.

A SICILIAN ROMANCE

Radcliffe's second novel, *A Sicilian Romance*, has a new strategy, an emphasis on action and adventure while subordinating moral concerns. This approach, however, was not effective because of the obvious imbalance between the two methods, and characterization suffered before a mass of incident. The interest in fear was expanded throughout the tale as a long-suffering wife, imprisoned in the remote sections of a huge castle by a villainous nobleman (who has an attachment to a beautiful paramour), struggles helplessly until rescued, after much suspense, by her gentle daughter and the young girl's lover. The characters' shallowness is hidden by a chase sequence of overwhelming speed that prevents one from noticing their deficiencies. To dramatize the movement of plot, Radcliffe introduced numerous settings, offering the reader a complete vision of the Romantic landscape.

Though *A Sicilian Romance* lacks the sureness of technique of the later novels and remains a lesser product, it did establish Radcliffe's ingenuity and perseverance. It was followed by the three novels on which her reputation rests: *The Romance of the Forest, The Mysteries of Udolpho,* and *The Italian.* Radcliffe's last novel, the posthumous *Gaston de Blondeville,* which was probably never meant for publication, exhibits the worst faults of the two earliest romances. Lifeless characters abound in a narrative overloaded with tedious historical facts and devoid of any action. In reconstructing history, Radcliffe was influenced by Scott but clearly was out of her element in attempting to make history conform to her own preconceptions. The primary innovation was the introduction of a real ghost to the love story. This specter, the apparition of a murdered knight demanding justice, stalks the grounds of Kenilworth Castle at the time of the reign of King Henry III. Radcliffe detracts from this imposing supernatural figure when she resorts to explanations of incidents better left mysterious.

THE ROMANCE OF THE FOREST

With the publication of her third novel, *The Romance of the Forest,* Radcliffe moved from apprenticeship to mastery. Her technique had advanced in at least two important elements: The chase with its multitude of settings is scaled down to an exacting series of dramas set among a few extended scenes, and characterization of the heroine is improved with the reduction of external action. Though suspense is extended rather illegitimately in order to produce a glorious final surprise, the novel is a genuine exploration of the realm of the unconscious. This remarkable advance into modern psychology gave life to the standard situations of Radcliffe's stories, allowing the reader to create his own private horrors.

Radcliffe's new emphasis on internal action makes her protagonist, Adeline, more credible than the stock romantic heroines whom she in many ways resembles. Adeline suffers from a nervous illness after mysteriously being thrust upon the LaMotte family, who themselves have only recently escaped, under curious circumstances, from Paris. Soon the group discovers a Gothic ruin, which contains the requisite underground room, rotten tapestries, blood stains, and a general aura of mystery.

Instead of the familiar chase scenes, a series of unified set pieces portray the exploration of the ruin, the seduction of the heroine, and the execution of the hero. The entire plot depends on the actions of a vicious but dominating sadist, the Marquis Phillipe de Montalt, and his conspiratorial agent, Pierre de LaMotte, against the unprotected Adeline. Because of the uncertainty of her birth, the sexual implications of this situation involve the risk of incest. Among contemporary readers, *The Romance of the Forest* became an immediate success, owing to its well-constructed narrative, the charm of its description of Romantic landscapes, and a consummate handling of the principle of suspense.

THE MYSTERIES OF UDOLPHO

Radcliffe's next novel, *The Mysteries of Udolpho*, remains her best-known work. The sublimity of her landscapes and the control that she demonstrates in this novel mark an important change from her earlier novels; Radcliffe's handling of action and character also reached new levels of subtlety and success, moving the novel a step beyond the rather strict conventions of the sentimental mode to one of psychological inquiry.

The period of the novel is the end of the sixteenth century. The principal scenes are laid in the gloomy enclave of the Castle of Udolpho, in the Italian Apennines, but many glances are directed toward the south of France—Gascony, Provence, and Languedoc—and the brightness of Venice is contrasted with the dark horrors of the Apennines. Emily St. Aubert, the beautiful daughter of a Gascon family, is the heroine; she is intelligent and extraordinarily accomplished in the fine arts. Though revealing all the tender sensibilities of the characters associated with a hundred sentimental tales, Emily emerges as a credible figure who seems aware of the connections between the scenery around her and the characters who inhabit it. As a painter, she sees and thinks of life as a series of pictures. As Durant explains in *Ann Radcliffe's Novels* (1980), "She does not merely feel fright, but conjures up imaginary scenes which elicit it. . . . scenery inhabits the inner life of the heroine, as well as locating her actions."

A further element of Emily's characterization that adds to her credibility is her internalizing of the suspense produced by the action in the narrative. Her heightened sensibility reacts to fear and terror in an all-inclusive way; this acuteness of sensibility makes her easy prey for the villain, Signor Montoni. This sinister figure marries Emily's aunt for her money, and then conveys Emily and her unhappy aunt to the "vast and dreary" confines of the castle.

This impossible castle becomes a superbly appointed stage for the playing of the melodrama. As the melodrama has hopes of communicating a real sense of mystery, its action and characters remain subordinate to the environment, which pervades the entire texture of the work. Description of landscape is a major part of the book's concept, and Radcliffe pays homage to Rosa and Lorrain in emphasizing pictorial detail. The somber exterior of the castle prepares the reader for the ineffable horrors that lie within the walls and adumbrates the importance of landscape and massive architecture in the novel.

There are certain shortcomings in Radcliffe's method: Landscape description strangles action; the visual aspects of the novel have been internalized; and the device of the chase over great stretches of land has been subordinated by mental recapitulation of past scenes—action becomes tableaux. This internal action is slow-moving, tortuously so in a novel of 300,000 words. Critics have also objected to Radcliffe's penchant for a rational explanation of every apparent supernatural phenomenon she has introduced; others, however, point out that Radcliffe's readers enjoyed terror only if they were never forced into surrendering themselves.

The Mysteries of Udolpho brought new energy to the picturesque, the sentimental, and the gothic novel. Radcliffe alternated effectively between the picturesque vagueness of the landscape and the castle's hall of terrors. Her deft handling of sexual feeling, shown as antagonism between Montoni and Emily, is characteristic of her refusal to acknowledge sex overtly except as a frightening nameless power. The artificial terror, heightened sensibility, and pervading air of mystery produced a powerful effect on her readers, yet many felt cheated by her failure to satisfy fully the intense imaginative visions awakened by the book. These readers would have to wait for *The Italian*, probably Radcliffe's finest work and the high-water mark of gothic fiction.

THE ITALIAN

The unity, control, and concentration of *The Italian* display a superb talent. Radcliffe's narrative technique is more sophisticated than at any previous time, particularly in the subtle revelation of the unreliability of feelings based on first impressions rather than on rational judgment. The dramatic pacing remains rigorous throughout and relatively free from digressions. The story's impulse depends on the Marchesa di Vivaldi's refusal to allow her young son, Vincentio, to marry the heroine, Ellena di Rosalba, whose origins are in doubt. The Marchesa relies on the sinister machinations of her monk-confessor, Schedoni, who decides to murder Ellena. Radcliffe's antipathy to Roman Catholicism is evident in her account of the horrors of the Carmelite abbey and its order, including the labyrinthine vaults and gloomy corridors. A strange blend of fascination and disgust is evoked here and in the scenes of the trial in the halls of the Inquisition, the ruins of the Paluzzi, and in the prison of the Inquisition. Clearly, the gothic aspects of *The Italian* function as representations of a disordered and morally evil past.

The vividness continues through to the climax of the story, when Schedoni, dagger in hand, prepares to murder Ellena but hesitates when he recognizes the portrait miniature she wears. Believing the girl is his lost daughter, he tries to make amends for his crimes. Though the solution involves more complex developments, the excitement of the confrontation between these two figures remains exceptional. Ellena has been a paragon of virtue, displaying piety, sensibility, benevolence, constancy, and a love of nature. To this catalog, Radcliffe adds intelligence, courage, and ingenuity. As an idealized character, Ellena represents the strengths necessary to prevail in the Romantic conflict against external, malign forces.

Schedoni, the devil-priest, is a figure of strong and dangerous sexual desire, associated, as is often the case in Radcliffe's work, with incest. Radcliffe counters the passivity and weakness of Ellena's virtues with this masculine version of desire—the lust of unregulated ambition. She describes him thus:

> There was something terrible in his air, something almost superhuman. . . . His physiognomy . . . bore traces of many passions . . . his eyes were so piercing that they seemed to penetrate at a single glance into the hearts of men, and to read their most secret thoughts.

His pride, greed, and loneliness combine to form a demoniac figure vaguely suggesting John Milton's Satan.

Eino Railo, in *The Haunted Castle* (1964), believes *The Italian* and the central character, Father Schedoni, were created under the revivified Romantic impulse supplied by the tragic monastic figure in Matthew Gregory Lewis's *The Monk* (1796). According to Railo, the difference between Ambrosio and Schedoni is that the latter "is no longer a young and inexperienced saint preserved from temptations, but a person long hardened in the ways of crime and vice, alarmingly gifted and strenuous, hypocritical, unfeeling and merciless." Radcliffe was inspired by Monk Lewis to write a more impressive book than earlier conceived; her bias against sexual and sadistic impulses and toward heightened romantic effect wins out in *The Italian*. While Ambrosio's passions remain tangled and confused by his need for immediate satisfaction and his lack of any lasting goal, Schedoni has well-defined goals for power, wealth, and status. His Machiavellian inclinations blend with pride, melancholy, mystery, and dignity, making him Radcliffe's most fully realized character. Her protest against *The Monk* created a story of tragic quality that goes beyond the conventional gothic paraphernalia and toward the psychological novel.

Radcliffe remains the undisputed master of the gothic novel and a central figure in the gothic revival, beginning in the late 1950's, which has seen the resurrection of hordes of forgotten gothic novelists and their tales. The generous volume of Radcliffe criticism in the second half of the twentieth century has redefined her place in literary history, acknowledging the prodigious sweep of her influence. On first reading her works, one must remember to search behind the genteel exterior of the artistry to discover the special recesses of terror, subconscious conflict, and the psychology of feelings that played a major role in the evolution of dark Romanticism.

Paul J. deGategno

OTHER MAJOR WORKS

POETRY: *The Poems of Ann Radcliffe*, 1816; *St. Alban's Abbey*, 1826.

NONFICTION: *A Journey Made in the Summer of 1794 Through Holland and the Western Frontier of Germany*, 1795.

BIBLIOGRAPHY

Dekker, George. *The Fictions of Romantic Tourism: Radcliffe, Scott, and Mary Shelley.* Stanford, Calif.: Stanford University Press, 2005. Dekker examines novels and travel writing by Radcliffe, Mary Wollstonecraft Shelley, and Sir Walter Scott, showing the connections between the two genres within the broader context of English Romantic literature.

Gordon, Scott Paul. "Ann Radcliffe's *The Mysteries of Udolpho* and the Practice of Quixotism." In *The Practice of Quixotism: Postmodern Theory and Eighteenth-Century Women's Writing.* New York: Palgrave Macmillan, 2006. Radcliffe's novel is included in this study of how eighteenth century British women writers used quixotic motifs in unexpected ways. Includes bibliographical references and an index.

Kickel, Katherine E. "Seeing Imagining: The Resurgence of a New Theory of Vision in Ann Radcliffe's *The Mysteries of Udolpho.*" In *Novel Notions: Medical Discourse and the Mapping of the Imagination in Eighteenth-Century English Fiction.* New York: Routledge, 2007. Kickel describes how fiction by Radcliffe and other eighteenth century English writers reflected new medical discoveries about the area of the brain that spurred the imagination. Kickel argues that these authors similarly sought to map the area of the brain that was responsible for imagination by creating narrators who reflect on the process of writing.

McIntyre, Clara Frances. *Ann Radcliffe in Relation to Her Time.* 1920. Reprint. New York: Archon Books, 1970. A dated but still useful study of Radcliffe that reviews the facts of her life and surveys her work. Presents contemporary evaluations of her novels, considers their sources, and lists translations and dramatizations of them.

Miles, Robert. *Ann Radcliffe: The Great Enchantress.* New York: St. Martin's Press, 1995. Explores the historical and aesthetic context of Radcliffe's fiction, with separate chapters on her early works and mature novels. Miles also considers Radcliffe's role as a woman writer and her place in society. Includes notes and a bibliography.

Murray, E. B. *Ann Radcliffe.* New York: Twayne, 1972. Surveys Radcliffe's life, drawing from *A Journey Made in the Summer of 1794 Through Holland and the Western Frontier of Germany* to illustrate her novels' geography. Examines the background of the gothic, with its supernatural elements, sentiment and sensibility, and sense of the sublime and the picturesque. Includes notes, a selected annotated bibliography, and an index.

Norton, Rictor. *Mistress of Udolpho: The Life of Ann Radcliffe.* London: Leicester University Press, 1999. Norton provides a comprehensive account of Radcliffe's life, including her background as a dissenting Unitarian, and places her novels within the context of her life. Includes a bibliography, notes, an index, and illustrations.

Rogers, Deborah D., ed. *The Critical Response to Ann Radcliffe.* Westport, Conn.: Greenwood Press, 1994. A compilation of contemporary criticism of Radcliffe's individual novels, as well as general criticism published from 1798 until 1899 and written by such authors as Samuel Taylor Coleridge, William Hazlitt, and Sir Walter Scott. Also includes fourteen critical articles published during the twentieth century, including pieces by William Dean Howells and Virginia Woolf.

Smith, Nelson C. *The Art of the Gothic: Ann Radcliffe's Major Novels.* New York: Arno Press, 1980. Contains a valuable introduction that reviews the scholarship on Radcliffe between 1967 and 1980. Analyzes the narrative techniques used to craft the gothic tale and surveys the gothic writers who followed Radcliffe. Includes end notes for each chapter and a bibliography.

Tooley, Brenda. "Gothic Utopia: Heretical Sanctuary in Ann Radcliffe's *The Italian.*" In *Gender and Utopia in the Eighteenth Century: Essays in English and French Utopian Writing,* edited by Nicole Pohl and Brenda Tooley. Burlington, Vt.: Ashgate, 2007. Tooley's analysis of Radcliffe's novel is included in a study of the representation of women in eighteenth century utopian literature. Includes a list of works cited and an index.

ANNE RICE

Born: New Orleans, Louisiana; October 4, 1941
Also known as: Howard Allen Frances O'Brien; Anne Rampling; A. N. Roquelaure

OTHER LITERARY FORMS

Anne Rice is known primarily for her novels. In addition to her historical fiction and her well-known vampire and witch novel series, Rice has published several erotic novels. *The Claiming of Sleeping Beauty, Beauty's Punishment*, and *Beauty's Release* appeared under the pseudonym A. N. Roquelaure, while Rice used the pen name Anne Rampling for *Exit to Eden* and *Belinda*. Rice also wrote the screenplay for the 1994 film adaptation of her novel *Interview with the Vampire*.

ACHIEVEMENTS

For most of her career, Anne Rice has experimented with several different literary genres and has acquitted herself well in each: gothic horror, historical fiction, erotica, romance. The conventions of gothic fiction, however, best conform to Rice's early obsessions with eroticism, androgyny, myth, and the nature of evil. For critics and fans alike, the novels that constitute the Vampire Chronicles are her greatest achievement thus far. Gothic horror, like all popular fiction, is customarily slighted by commentators, who peg it as nothing more than a barometer of its own time, devoid of resonance. Paradoxically perhaps, Rice's success grew out of her ability to revamp the vampire, to update the hoary edifice first built by Horace Walpole in 1765 in *The Castle of Otranto*. She did more, however, than merely put her archetypal hero, the vampire Lestat, in black leather on a motorcycle; she made him, in all his selfishness and soul searching, emblematic of the waning days of the twentieth century.

With the publication in 2005 of the first of a projected four-part re-creation of the life of Jesus, Rice began mining a new literary vein. *Christ the Lord: Out of Egypt* and its sequel, *The Road to Cana*, draw on Rice's research into the Gospels and New Testament scholarship, but they also benefit from Rice's past experiments with historical fiction and—perhaps more surprising—her dexterity in creating fiction out of the supernatural.

BIOGRAPHY

Anne Rice was born Howard Allen Frances O'Brien on October 4, 1941, in New Orleans, Louisiana, to Howard O'Brien and Katherine Allen O'Brien. Howard O'Brien's reasons for bestowing his own name on his daughter remain obscure, but bearing a masculine name clearly had a profound effect on her. When she entered first grade, the little girl christened herself Anne. The name stuck, as did a lifelong obsession with androgyny.

The exotic, decadent, intoxicating atmosphere of her hometown must also be counted among Anne Rice's early influences—as must her mother's alcoholism. As she approached puberty, Anne devoted much of her time to reading in a darkened bedroom to the increasingly incapacitated Katherine. It was there, perhaps, that she acquired an affinity for vampires. She would later recall how her mother first explained alcoholism as a "craving in the blood" and then asked her to say the rosary. Anne watched her mother alternate between wild exhilaration and collapse and finally waste away, her body drained by addiction and an inability to eat. When Katherine died in 1956, the nexus of blood, religion, and death must have taken root in her young daughter's psyche.

Anne's father remarried when she was sixteen, and, after Anne's sophomore year in high school, he moved the family to Richardson, Texas, where Anne met Stan Rice. Stan was a year younger than Anne, and at first he did not seem to share her romantic feelings about their relationship. It was not until after Anne graduated and moved away to San Francisco that Stan finally realized his feelings. They were married on October 14, 1961, when Anne was twenty. The couple took up residence in the San Francisco Bay Area, where they would remain for the next twenty-seven years. Stan, a poet, completed his undergraduate education and began teaching creative writing. Anne, too, completed her B.A., majoring in political science. After receiving a master's degree in creative writing in 1972, she devoted herself full time to her writing career.

In the meanwhile, however, a momentous event had occurred in the Rices' lives. Their daughter, Michele, who was born in 1966, developed a rare form of leukemia and died two weeks before her sixth birthday. The trauma of this loss seems to have plunged Anne Rice into depression. The old association between blood and death had returned to haunt her, but she fought off her demons by submerging herself in her writing. The result was her first published novel, *Interview with the Vampire.*

In 1978, the Rices had a son, Christopher, and a decade later they moved to New Orleans. With the proceeds of many best-selling books and the lucrative sale of film rights, Anne Rice purchased a mansion in the Garden District, which later became the setting of one of her novels and the scene of such memorable parties as the 1995 Memnoch Ball. During the 1990's, the Rices purchased and restored a number of other New Orleans properties, including Anne's childhood home on St. Charles Avenue and St. Elizabeth's Orphanage.

In 1996, after decades of self-declared atheism, Anne returned to the Roman Catholic Church. Her husband's death in 2002 from brain cancer may have contributed to Rice's decision that year to write from that time forward only for and about Jesus Christ. In 2005, after completing *Christ the Lord: Out of Egypt,* Rice moved to southern California to be nearer her son, eventually settling in Rancho Mirage. *Christ the Lord: The Road to Cana,* a sequel to *Out of Egypt,* was published in 2008.

ANALYSIS

Anne Rice discovered her strong suit early. Written in five weeks, *Interview with the Vampire* introduced the themes of compulsion, exoticism, and eroticism that would inform her later works. Although she has explored these themes against a wide variety of backdrops, it is her revival of the gothic—and of the vampire in particular—that both brought her critical attention and transformed her into a popular cultural icon. In 2005, Rice took on a dramatically new approach in her work as she dedicated herself to explication, through historical fiction, of the life of Jesus.

VAMPIRE CHRONICLES

Interview with the Vampire is the first of the books that Rice produced in her series known as the Vampire Chronicles. The books in the series shift back and forth in time, from the prevampire life of Lestat in eighteenth century rural France to his escapades in twentieth century New Orleans and then, in *Memnoch the Devil*, to the time of the creation of heaven and hell.

Interview with the Vampire introduces Lestat through the narrative of Louis, a vampire Lestat has "made." Louis relates his story to Daniel, a young reporter. Even as Louis grieves for his mortal life, Daniel craves Louis's power and immortality. Daniel has to overcome his initial horror and skepticism before he can accept the truth of what Louis says, but by the end of Louis's long story, Daniel is begging to be made a vampire too.

In *The Vampire Lestat*, Lestat relates his own version of his life. Lestat's narrative, like Louis's, is published as a book. (Indeed, Lestat has written his in order to correct several errors he perceives in Louis's earlier account.) Lestat, always a show-off, revels in publicity, and he uses the book to launch his career as a rock star. Like so many of Lestat's grand schemes, however, this plan crashes, ending when Lestat barely escapes his fellow vampires' murderous attack as they seek revenge for his unpardonable publication of a book that reveals their secrets.

In *The Queen of the Damned*, Lestat becomes the consort of Akasha, the Egyptian ruler who became the mother of all vampires when a demon wounded and invaded her body, giving her immortality. Marius, an old Roman sage and vampire, has kept Akasha intact for more than two thousand years, but it is Lestat's energetic wooing that brings her out of her long stupor. She revives determined to rid the world of men, whose violence has made them unfit to survive. Only a remnant will endure for breeding purposes, she declares. Having partaken of her blood and fallen deliriously in love with her, Lestat nevertheless struggles against her insane project. He is finally saved from Akasha's wrath by Maharet and Mekare, witches who are also twin sisters and who destroy Akasha.

In *The Tale of the Body Thief*, Lestat, suffering from ennui, succumbs to the temptations of a body thief, Raglan James. The body thief offers Lestat a day of adventure in a mortal body in exchange for his own. Stupidly, Lestat accepts, even paying James twenty million dollars for the privilege of enjoying one day of mortality. James then absconds with both the money and Lestat's body, which Lestat is able to repossess only with the help of David Talbot, head of the Talamasca, a society dedicated to investigating the occult. Lestat, who is in love with David, then makes the resistant David into a vampire.

In *Memnoch the Devil*, a terrified Lestat discovers that he is being stalked by Satan, who calls himself Memnoch because he does not regard himself as a rebel angel or as God's accuser. Memnoch invites Lestat to become his lieutenant—not to gather souls for hell, but to redeem those awaiting enlightenment and salvation. Memnoch's argument is that he is offering God a grander creation, a purer vision of humankind, than God himself has conceived. In the end, Lestat repudiates Memnoch, doubting the devil's word and wondering if what he has "seen" is only what he has imagined.

With the Vampire Chronicles, Rice rejuvenates the conventions of gothic romance and the horror novel. Like earlier heroes, Lestat is a nobleman of surpassing courage and physical attractiveness. Indeed, the vampire elder Magnus makes him into a vampire because he has seen the handsome Lestat on the stage in Paris and admired his indomitable spirit. As in William Godwin's novel *Things as They Are: Or, The Adventures of Caleb Williams* (1794), Lestat is an insatiably curious protagonist attached to an older hero who represents both good and evil. Lestat must know the origins of vampirism, and he must follow his desires regardless of the cost to himself and others.

Lestat's eroticism also partakes of the gothic tradition. Reflecting Rice's abiding interest in androgyny, he finds himself attracted to both men and women—to the goddess Akasha and to the head of the Talamasca, David Talbot. Deeply devoted to his mother, Gabrielle, he takes her as his vampire lover. Incestuous and homoerotic elements that are veiled or only hinted at in earlier gothic fiction explode in Rice's chronicles. Rice also succeeds in making gothicism contemporary by making Lestat into a rock star, thus underscoring parallels between the cult of celebrity and the allure of the vampire.

MAYFAIR WITCHES SERIES

Rice conceived the first installment of the Mayfair Witches cycle, *The Witching Hour*, in 1985 after she finished writing *The Vampire Lestat*. She had generated some new characters that she at first envisioned as playing parts in the next volume of the Vampire Chronicles, but she soon reached the conclusion that these characters—a family of witches and their presiding spirit—deserved an entirely separate book, one set in New Orleans.

The protagonist of *The Witching Hour*, Michael Curry, is a successful forty-eight-year-old businessman who has his life blighted by a near-death experience. After nearly drowning in San Francisco Bay, he is rescued by a mysterious woman in a passing boat. He then discovers that simply by touching objects and people with his hands he has access to other lives and events. His insights, however, are fragmentary—as is his memory of an encounter with otherworldly beings during his drowning episode, when he promised to fulfill a mission for them.

One of Michael's doctors puts him in touch with his rescuer, who Michael believes will help him understand what he is meant to do. When he meets Dr. Rowan Mayfair, a thirty-year-old blond beauty and a superb surgeon, Michael falls in love with her. Like Michael, Rowan is searching for answers. She has the power both to hurt and to heal people. She can stop a patient's bleeding simply by a laying on of hands; she can also cause a heart attack or stroke if she does not control her rage. Her obsession with saving people is her effort at self-redemption. Just as Michael hopes that touching Rowan and her boat will bring back his sense of mission, Rowan hopes that Michael will help reveal her past, which remains a mystery to her.

Rowan and Michael realize that their fates are linked to New Orleans, where as a boy Michael developed a fixation on a Garden District mansion that turns out to be Rowan's ancestral home. There he saw a spectral man, the Mayfairs' presiding spirit. Michael's intense memories of his childhood are connected, he is sure, with his near-death experience. When Rowan's birth mother dies, Rowan is visited by a spectral man, and she decides that she must return to the Crescent City.

Hovering around this couple is Aaron Lightner, an agent of the Talamasca. Through Aaron, Michael learns that Rowan is the descendant of a matriarchal family of witches that has fascinated the Talamasca for nearly three hundred years. A strong woman, Rowan believes she can destroy Lasher, the spectral man who has maddened the Mayfairs in an attempt to possess them. Like the others, however, Rowan loses control of Lasher, who invades the cells of the fetus growing within her and emerges as a powerful boy-man.

Rowan is rather like a female Dr. Faustus, determined to conquer the secrets of nature. She wants to heal, but the extremity of her desire cuts her off from her own humanity. Like Faust, she risks damnation. She is in thrall to her Mephistopheles, Lasher. When Michael playfully calls his lover Dr. Mayfair, the epithet suggests not only Dr. Faustus but also Dr. Frankenstein. Indeed, although Rowan finds Lasher's proposal that they create a super-race seductive, once their offspring is born, she plans to submit its cells to laboratory tests, thus reducing it to the status of a research subject.

In *Lasher*, the second installment in the series, Rowan has begun to help Lasher fulfill his desire. Together they have a girl child, Emaleth. The central revelation of the book is that the Mayfairs can, by interbreeding, produce a genetic aberration—a legendary race of nearly immortal giants known as Taltos, of which Lasher is a member. The Talamasca believe that Lasher is possessed of a unique genome, so when at the end of the book Michael Curry destroys him and Rowan does away with her demoniac girl child, it seems that Lasher's kind is no more.

However, *Taltos*, the third installment of the series, features another Taltos, Ashlar Templeton, an eccentric and reclusive billionaire toy maker. Ashlar's profession indicates that his nature is far more benign than Lasher's. Indeed, he more closely resembles Rice's vampires than his own protean kind. Unlike Lasher, he is not devoured by a need to propagate his supernatural breed; instead, he yearns—as much as Louis and, in his weaker moments, Lestat—for integration with humanity.

CHRIST THE LORD SERIES

When asked about her motivations for writing *Christ the Lord: Out of Egypt*, Rice has answered with winning directness and simplicity: "I wrote this book to make Christ real to people who had never thought about Him as real." Similarly, one of the hallmarks of the first installment of her projected series about Jesus is Rice's unadorned prose. In fact, it could not be otherwise. *Out of Egypt* concerns one year in the life of the seven-year-old Jesus, and it is written in the first person. This approach to storytelling is one that Rice has employed to good effect before, but while taking readers into the mind of a vampire is a good trick, adopting the perspective of a young boy who is only beginning to understand what sets him apart from humanity requires remarkable skill.

Rice claims that she has taken few liberties when writing her life of Jesus, and to that end she concludes *Out of Egypt* with a lengthy author's note in which she sets forth the extensive historical and biblical research she conducted before writing the book. She has been obliged to cast her net widely in order to move in her subject's world, however. There is, for example, no real historical support for the novel's opening, which situates Jesus, Mary, and Joseph in Alexandria, Egypt, and Rice makes liberal use of apocryphal sources throughout the book. She does so with considerable success, creating a whole world for this extraordinary boy to inhabit. Jesus is pictured surrounded by an extended, very Orthodox Jewish family that includes not only his mother and father but also an array of aunts, uncles, and cousins. The city they inhabit is rich with detail and situated squarely within the larger framework that was the Roman Empire. Rice's historical accuracy might seem to be her paramount concern were it not for her protagonist's still inchoate sense of otherness.

Rice is not coy about Jesus' supernaturalness: The book opens with a scene in which his animosity kills another boy, who is then resurrected by Jesus' remorse. This seven-year-old, however, knows little and understands less about where he came from. He begins to understand more after Joseph (who Jesus knows is not his father) declares that now that Herod is dead, the family should go home to Nazareth. Once there, Jesus begins to discover what happened in Bethlehem the night he was born and to understand the meaning of his miraculous gifts. Although *Out of Egypt* is not on a par with James Joyce's 1916 novel *A Portrait of the Artist as a Young Man*, Rice's first-person rendition of Jesus' dawning self-awareness is itself something of a miracle.

The sequel to *Out of Egypt*, *The Road to Cana*, is arguably even more masterful in its realization of Jesus' dual nature. This second installment concerns the "lost" young adulthood of Jesus, about which the Bible is largely silent. Rice is concerned with filling in the particulars Jesus encounters along the way to becoming a public man. That concern takes the form of concentration on the human aspect of Jesus (or Yeshua, as he is called), as revealed, once more, in first-person narrative. In this book Jesus is a thirty-year-old, unmarried man who knows he will not marry and who is surrounded by a society that expects him to do so. Around him swirl both parochial rumors of the virgin birth and political tensions with Rome; within him, the all-too-human desire for the beautiful Avigail wars with his desire to do God's will. Rice's goal in this novel is to make this counterpoint sing while keeping it faithful to what is known about the historical Jesus and believed about the biblical son of God. Largely, she succeeds in making Jesus' transformation into a man capable of turning water into wine during the festival at Cana believable to his public and to her readers.

Lisa Paddock

OTHER MAJOR WORK

SCREENPLAY: *Interview with the Vampire*, 1994.

BIBLIOGRAPHY

Badley, Linda. *Writing Horror and the Body: The Fiction of Stephen King, Clive Barker, and Anne Rice.* Westport, Conn.: Greenwood Press, 1996. Examines horror fiction as a fantastic genre that distorts images of the body and the self. Argues that the approaches to horror taken by the three authors discussed constitute a dialogue on the anxieties of American culture.

Hoppenstand, Gary, and Ray B. Browne, eds. *The Gothic World of Anne Rice.* Bowling Green, Ohio: Bowling Green State University Press, 1996. Collection of essays by a number of important Rice critics addresses all aspects of her fiction, including the Vampire Chronicles and her other stories of the supernatural.

Keller, James R. *Anne Rice and Sexual Politics: The Early Novels.* Jefferson, N.C.: McFarland, 2000. Addresses Rice's early works in terms of the author's approaches to issues of gender identity and sexual matters. Includes bibliographical references and index.

Ramslund, Katherine M. *Prism of the Night: A Biography of Anne Rice.* New York: Dutton, 1991. One of the most complete sources of information about Rice available, written with her cooperation. Offers the first serious attempt to assess her work critically and in a broad context.

_____, ed. *The Anne Rice Reader.* New York: Ballantine, 1997. Comprehensive volume provides interviews with Rice, her personal essays, and articles about her life and career as well as literary critiques of her works, assessment of her contribution to the literature about vampires, and discussion of her relationship to the gothic tradition.

Riley, Michael. *Conversations with Anne Rice: An Intimate, Enlightening Portrait of Her Life and Work.* New York: Ballantine Books, 1996. In an extended interview format, Rice discusses her writing career, her emotional involvement with her work, and many other topics, including the various forms of literature to which she has contributed.

Roberts, Bette B. *Anne Rice.* New York: Twayne, 1994. Solid introductory study includes chapters on Rice's life and art, her relationship to the gothic tradition, her vampire series, her historical novels, and her erotic fiction.

Smith, Jennifer. *Anne Rice: A Critical Companion.* Westport, Conn.: Greenwood Press, 1996. Provides criticism and interpretation of Rice's work in the context of women and literature, fantasy fiction, horror tales, the gothic revival, witchcraft in literature, and vampires in literature. Includes bibliography and index.

Tomc, Sandra. "Dieting and Damnation: Anne Rice's *Interview with the Vampire*." In *Blood Read: The Vampire as Metaphor in Contemporary Culture*, edited by Joan Gordon and Veronica Hollinger. Philadelphia: University of Pennsylvania Press,

1997. Relates the vampire's transformation to contemporary female preoccupations with body image and self-abnegation.

Waxman, Barbara Frey. "Postexistentialism in the Neo-gothic Mode: Anne Rice's *Interview with the Vampire.*" *Mosaic* 25, no. 3 (Summer, 1992): 79-97. Explores the interrelationship of existentialism, postmodernism, and gothic fiction in Rice's Vampire Chronicles.

MARY WOLLSTONECRAFT SHELLEY

Born: London, England; August 30, 1797
Died: London, England; February 1, 1851
Also known as: Mary Wollstonecraft Godwin

OTHER LITERARY FORMS

Mary Wollstonecraft Shelley was a prolific writer, forced into copiousness by economic necessity. Punished by Sir Timothy Shelley, father of her husband, Percy Bysshe Shelley, for her violation of his moral codes with his son, Mary Shelley was denied access to the Shelley estate for a long time after her husband's death. Her own father, William Godwin, was eternally in debt himself and spared her none of his troubles. Far from helping her, Godwin threw his own financial woes in her lap. It fell to Mary to support her son by writing, in addition to her novels, a plethora of short stories and some scholarly materials. The stories were mainly available to the public in a popular annual publication called the *Keepsake*, a book intended for gift giving. Her stories were firmly entrenched in the popular gothic tradition, bearing such titles as "A Tale of Passion," "Ferdinand Eboli," "The Evil Eye," and "The Bride of Modern Italy." Her scholarly work included contributions to *The Lives of the Most Eminent Literary and Scientific Men* in *Lardner's Cabinet Encyclopedia* (1838). She attempted to write about the lives of both her father and her husband, although these efforts were never completed. She wrote magazine articles of literary criticism and reviews of operas, an art form that filled her with delight. She wrote two travel books, *History of a Six Weeks' Tour Through a Part of France, Switzerland, Germany, and Holland* (1817) and *Rambles in Germany and Italy* (1844). Shelley edited two posthumous editions of her husband's poetry (1824 and 1839), and she wrote several poetic dramas: *Manfred*, now lost, *Proserpine* (pb. 1922), and *Midas* (pb. 1922). She wrote a handful of poems, most of which were published in *Keepsake*.

ACHIEVEMENTS

Mary Wollstonecraft Shelley's literary reputation rests solely on her first novel, *Frankenstein*. Her six other novels, which are of uneven quality, are very difficult indeed to

Mary Wollstonecraft Shelley
(Library of Congress)

find, even in the largest libraries. Nevertheless, Shelley lays claim to a dazzling array of accomplishments. First, she is credited with the creation of modern science fiction. All subsequent tales of the brilliant but doomed scientist, the sympathetic but horrible monster, both in high and mass culture, owe their lives to her. Even Hollywood's dream factory owes her an imaginative and economic debt it can never repay.

Second, the English tradition is indebted to her for a reconsideration of the Romantic movement by one of its central participants. In her brilliant *Frankenstein* fantasy, Mary Shelley questions many of the basic tenets of the Romantic rebellion: the Romantic faith in humankind's blissful relationship to nature, the belief that evil resides only in the dead hand of social tradition, and the Romantic delight in death as a lover and restorer.

Finally, Shelley created one of the great literary fictions of the dialogue with the self. The troubled relationship between Dr. Frankenstein and his monster is one of the foundations of the literary tradition of "the double," doubtless the mother of all the doubles in Charles Dickens, Robert Louis Stevenson, and even in Arthur Conan Doyle and Joseph Conrad.

BIOGRAPHY

Born Mary Wollstonecraft Godwin, Mary Shelley lived the life of a great Romantic heroine at the heart of the Romantic movement. She was the daughter of the brilliant feminist Mary Wollstonecraft and the equally distinguished man of letters William Godwin. Born of two parents who vociferously opposed marriage, she was the occasion of their nuptials. Her mother died ten days after she was born, and her father had to marry for the second time in four years to provide a mother for his infant daughter. He chose a rather conventional widow, Mary Jane Clairmont, who had two children of her own, Jane and Charles.

In her childhood, Shelley suffered the torments of being reared by a somewhat unsympathetic stepmother; later, she led the daughter of this extremely middle-class woman into a life of notoriety. The separation traumas in her early years indelibly marked Shelley's imagination: Almost all of her protagonists are either orphaned or abandoned by their parents.

Shelley's stormy early years led, in 1812 and until 1814, to her removal to sympathetic "foster parents," the Baxters of Dundee. There, on May 5, 1814, when she was seventeen years old, she met Percy Bysshe Shelley, who was then married to his first wife, Harriet. By March 6, 1815, Mary had eloped with Shelley, given birth to a daughter by him, and suffered the death of the baby. By December 29, 1816, the couple had been to Switzerland and back, had another child, William, and had been married, Harriet having committed suicide. Mary Shelley was then nineteen years old.

By the next year, Mary's stepsister, Jane Clairmont, who called herself Claire Clairmont, had had a baby daughter by Lord Byron, while Mary was working on *Frankenstein*, and Mary herself had given birth to another child, Clara.

The network of intimates among the Shelley circle rapidly increased to include many literati and artists. These included, among others, Leigh and Marianne Hunt, Thomas Love Peacock, Thomas Jefferson Hogg, and John Polidori. The letters and diaries of the Shelleys from this period offer a view of life speeded up and intensified, life at the nerve's edge.

While the Shelleys were touring Switzerland and Italy, they sent frantic communications to their friends, asking for financial help. Mary issued frequent requests for purchases of clothing and household items such as thread. There were also legal matters to be taken care of concerning publishing, Percy Shelley's estate, and the custody of his children from his previous marriage.

The leaves of the letters and diaries are filled with urgent fears for the safety of the Shelley children and the difficulties of what was in effect an exile necessitated by the Shelleys' unorthodox lifestyle. In 1818, Clara Shelley died, barely a year old, and in 1819, William Shelley died at the age of three. Five months later, a son, Percy Florence, was born, the only child of the Shelleys who would grow to maturity.

In 1822, Mary Shelley's flamboyant life reached its point of desolation. Percy Shelley, while sailing with his close friend Edward Williams in his boat *Ariel*, drowned in the Gulf of Spezia. Mary's letters and diaries of the time clearly reveal her anguish, her exhaustion, and her despair. Her speeding merry-go-round suddenly and violently stopped.

Literary historians find themselves in debate over this point in Mary Shelley's life. Her letters and diaries record unambiguous desolation, and yet many scholars have found indications that Percy Shelley was about to leave her for Jane Williams, the wife of the friend with whom he drowned. There is also some suspicion that Mary's stepsister had recently given birth to a baby by Percy Shelley, a rumor that Mary Shelley denied. Because of Percy Shelley's mercurial nature, such speculations are at least conceivable. Against them stands Mary's diary, a purely private diary, which suggests that she would have no reason to whitewash her marriage among its confidential pages.

Mary's tragedy did not prompt warmth and help from her estranged father-in-law. He refused to support his grandson, Percy Florence, unless Mary gave the child to a guardian to be chosen by him. This she would not do, and she was rewarded for her persistence. Her son became heir to the Shelley estate when Harriet Shelley's son died in 1826. After the death, Mary's son became Lord Shelley. Just as important, however, was the warm relationship that he maintained with Mary until her death. Mary Shelley's life ended in the tranquil sunshine of family affection. Her son married happily and had healthy children. Mary seems to have befriended her daughter-in-law, and, at the last, believed herself to be a truly fortunate woman.

ANALYSIS

Mary Wollstonecraft Shelley's six novels are written in the gothic tradition. They deal with extreme emotions, exalted speech, the hideous plight of virgins, the awful abuses of charismatic villains, and picturesque ruins. The sins of the past weigh heavily on their plot structures, and often include previously unsuspected relationships.

Shelley does not find much use for the anti-Catholicism of much gothic fiction. Her nuns and priests, while sometimes troublesome, are not evil, and tend to appear in the short stories rather than in the novels. She avoids references to the supernatural so common in the genre and tends instead toward a modern kind of psychological gothic and futuristic fantasy. Like many gothic writers, she dwells on morbid imagery, particularly in *Frankenstein* and *The Last Man*. Graphic descriptions of the plague in the latter novel revolted the reading public that had avidly digested the grotesqueries of Matthew Gregory Lewis's *The Monk: A Romance* (1796; also known as *Ambrosio: Or, The Monk*).

With the exception of *Frankenstein*, Shelley's novels were written and published after the death of her husband; with the exception of *Frankenstein*, they appear to be attempting to work out the sense of desolation and abandonment that she felt after his death. In most of her novels, Shelley creates men and particularly women who resign themselves to the pain and anguish of deep loss through the eternal hope of love in its widest and most encompassing sense. Reconciliation became Shelley's preponderant literary theme.

FRANKENSTEIN

Frankenstein is Shelley's greatest literary achievement in every way. In it, she not only calls into the world one of the most powerful literary images in the English tradition, the idealistic scientist Victor Frankenstein and his ironically abominable creation, but also, for the one and only time, she employs a narrative structure of daring complexity and originality.

The structure of *Frankenstein* is similar to a set of Chinese boxes, of narratives within narratives. The narrative frame is composed of the letters of an arctic explorer, Robert Walton, to his sister, Mrs. Saville, in England. Within the letters is the narrative of Victor Frankenstein, and within his narrative, at first, and then at the end within Walton's narrative, is the firsthand account of the monster himself. Walton communicates to England thirdhand then secondhand accounts of the monster's thoroughly unbelievable existence. Here, it would seem, is the seminal point of Joseph Conrad's much later fiction, *Heart of Darkness* (1902): the communication to England of the denied undercurrents of reality and England's ambiguous reception of that intelligence. In *Frankenstein* as in *Heart of Darkness*, the suggestion is rather strong that England cannot or will not absorb this stunning new perception of reality. Just as Kurtz's fiancé almost a century later cannot imagine Kurtz's "horror," so Mrs. Saville's silence, the absence of her replies, suggests that Walton's stunning discovery has fallen on deaf ears.

The novel begins with Walton, isolated from his society at the North Pole, attempting to achieve glory. He prowls the frozen north "to accomplish some great purpose"; instead, he finds an almost dead Victor Frankenstein, who tells him a story that, in this setting, becomes a parable for Walton. Frankenstein, too, has isolated himself from society to fulfill his great expectations, and he has reaped the whirlwind.

Frankenstein tells Walton of his perfect early family life, one of complete kindness and solicitude. It is a scene across which never a shadow falls. Out of this perfection, Victor rises to find a way of conquering death and ridding himself and humankind of the ultimate shadow, the only shadow in his perfect middle-class life. Like a man possessed, Frankenstein forges ahead, fabricating a full, male, human body from the choicest corpse parts he can gather. He animates the creature and suddenly is overwhelmed by the wrongness of what he has done. In his success, he finds utter defeat. The reanimated corpse evokes only disgust in him. He abandons it in its vulnerable, newborn state and refuses to take any responsibility for it. From that day, his life is dogged by tragedy. One by one, all his loved ones are destroyed by the monster, who at last explains that he wanted only to love his creator but that his adoration turned to murderous hate in his creator's rejection of him. Ultimately, Frankenstein feels that he must destroy the monster or, at the very least, die trying. He succeeds at both. After Frankenstein's death in the presence of Walton—the only man other than Frankenstein to witness the monster and live—the monster mourns the greatness that could have been and leaves Walton with the intention of hurling himself onto Frankenstein's funeral pyre.

The critical task regarding this fascinating work has been to identify what it is that Frankenstein has done that has merited the punishment that followed. Is the monster a kind of retribution for people's arrogant attempt to possess the secrets of life and death, as in the expulsion from Eden? Is it the wrath of the gods visited on people for stealing the celestial fire, as in the Prometheus legend, a favorite fiction of Percy Shelley? Or is this a rather modern vision of the self-destructiveness involved in the idealistic denial of the dark side of human reality? Is this a criticism of Romantic optimism, of the denial of the reality of evil except as the utterly disposable dead hand of tradition? The mystery endures because critics have suggested all these possibilities; critics have even suggested a biographical reading of the work. Some have suggested that Victor Frankenstein is Shelley's shrewd insight into her husband's self-deceived, uncritical belief in the power of his own intelligence and in his destined greatness.

VALPERGA

Valperga, Shelley's second novel, has a fairy tale aura of witches, princes, maidens in distress, castles, and prophecies. The author uses all these fantasy apparatuses but actually deflates them as being part of the fantasy lives of the characters that they impose on a fully logical and pragmatic reality. The novel pits Castruccio, the Prince of Lucca, a worldly, Napoleonic conqueror, against the lost love of his youth, the beautiful and spiritual Euthanasia. Castruccio's one goal is to gain power and military dominion, and since he is enormously capable and charismatic, not to mention lucky, he is successful. Nevertheless, that he gains the world at the price of his soul is clearly the central point of the novel.

To gain worldly sway, he must destroy Valperga, the ancestral home of his love, Euthanasia. He must also turn Italy into an armed camp that teems with death and in which the soft virtues of love and family cannot endure. His lust for power raises to predominance the most deceitful and treacherous human beings because they are the ones who function best in the context of raw, morally unjustified power.

In the midst of all this, Castruccio, unwilling to recognize his limits, endeavors to control all. He wants to continue his aggrandizing ways and have the love of Euthanasia. Indeed, he wants to marry her. She reveals her undying love for him, but will only yield to it if he yields his worldly goals, which he will not do. As his actions become more threatening to her concept of a moral universe, Euthanasia finds that she must join the conspirators against him. She and her cohorts are betrayed, and all are put to death, with the exception of Euthanasia. Instead, Castruccio exiles her to Sicily. En route, her ship sinks, and she perishes with all aboard. Castruccio dies some years later, fighting one of his endless wars for power. The vision of the novel is that only pain and suffering can come from a world obsessed with power.

Surely the name Euthanasia is a remarkable choice for the novel's heroine. Its meaning in Shelley's time was "an easy death"; it did not refer to the policy of purposefully terminating suffering as it does today. Euthanasia's death is the best one in the story because she dies with a pure heart, never having soiled herself with hurtful actions for the purpose of self-gain. Possibly, the import of Shelley's choice is that all that one can hope for in the flawed, Hobbesian world of *Valperga* is the best death possible, as no good life can be imagined. It is probable that this bleak vision is at least obliquely connected with the comparatively recent trauma of Percy Shelley's death and Mary Shelley's grief and desolation.

THE LAST MAN

The degenerating spiral of human history is the central vision of *The Last Man*. Set in the radically distant future of the twenty-first century, this novel begins with a flourishing civilization and ends with the entire population of the world, save one man, decimated by the plague. Lionel Verney, the last man of the title, has nothing to anticipate except an endless journey from one desolate city to another. All the treasures of humankind are his and his alone; all the great libraries and coffers are open only to him. All that is denied to him—forever, it seems—is human companionship.

The novel begins before Lionel Verney's birth. It is a flashback narrated by Lionel himself, the only first-person narrator possible in this novel. Lionel describes his father as his father had been described to him, as a man of imagination and charm but lacking in judgment. He was a favorite of the king, but was forced out of the king's life by the king's new wife, a Marie Antoinette figure. The new queen, depicted as an arrogant snob, disapproves of Verney's father and effects his estrangement from the king by working on her husband's gullible nature.

Verney's father, in ostracized shame, seeks refuge in the country, where he marries a simple, innocent cottage girl and thus begets Lionel and his sister Perdita. Verney's father can never, however, reconcile himself to his loss of status and dies a broken man. His wife soon follows, and Lionel and Perdita live like wild creatures until chance brings the king's son, Adrian, into their path. Their friendship succeeds where the aborted friendship of their fathers failed, despite the continued disapproval of the queen.

What is remarkable to the modern reader is that Shelley, having set her story two hundred years in the future, does not project a technologically changed environment. She projects instead the same rural, agrarian, hand- and animal-driven society in which she lived. What does change, however, is the political system. The political system of *The Last Man* is a republican monarchy. Kings are elected, but not at regular intervals. The bulk of the novel concerns the power plays by which various factions intend to capture the throne by election rather than by war.

Adrian and Lionel are endlessly involved with a dashing, Byronic figure named Lord Raymond, who cannot decide whether he wants life in a cottage with Perdita, or life at the top. Ultimately, Raymond, like the protagonist of *Valperga*, wants to have both. He marries Perdita and gives up all pretensions to power, but then returns with her to rule the land. Power does not make him or his wife happy.

Despite the sublimation of the power process into an electoral system, the rage for power remains destructive, degenerating finally into war. The plague that appears and irrevocably destroys humankind is merely an extension of the plague of people's will to power. Not only Raymond and Perdita but also their innocent children, Lionel's wife, Iris, and Adrian's sister, who stayed home to eschew worldly aspirations, are destroyed. No one is immune.

Lionel's survival carries with it a suggestion of his responsibility in the tragedy of humankind. His final exile in a sea of books and pictures suggests that those who commit themselves solely to knowledge and art have failed to deal with the central issues of life. In simply abdicating the marketplace to such as Lord Raymond, the cultivators of the mind have abandoned humanity. Through Lionel, they reap a bitter reward, but perhaps the implication is that it is a just reward for their failure to connect with their fellow human beings.

A number of critics consider *The Last Man* to be Mary Shelley's best work after *Frankenstein*. Like *Frankenstein*, this novel rather grimly deals with the relationship between knowledge and evil. Its greatest drawback for modern audiences, however, is its unfortunate tendency to inflated dialogue. Every sentence uttered is a florid and theatrical speech. The bloated characterizations obscure the line of Shelley's inventive satire of people's lemminglike rush to the sea of power.

THE FORTUNES OF PERKIN WARBECK

The Fortunes of Perkin Warbeck attempts to chronicle the last, futile struggles of the House of York in the Wars of the Roses. Perkin Warbeck was a historical character who claimed to be Richard, the son of Edward IV of England. Most scholars believe that Richard died in the tower with his brother Edward; Perkin Warbeck claimed to be that child. Warbeck said that he had survived the tower, assumed another identity, and intended to reclaim the usurped throne held by Henry VII.

Shelley's novel assumes that Perkin was indeed Richard and documents his cheerless history from his childhood to his execution in manhood by Henry VII. The novel attempts to explore once more man's fruitless quest for power and glory. Richard is an intelligent, virtuous young man who finds true companionship even in his outcast state, and the love of a number of women, each different, utterly committed, and true. He is unable, however, to forsake the dream of conquest and live simply. As he presses onward to claim the throne, he suffers a series of crushing losses, not one of which will he yield to as a revelation of the wrongheadedness of his quest. His rush toward the throne achieves only the death of innocent persons. When he is executed at the end of the novel, his wife Katherine is given the last words. She needs to find a way of continuing to live without him. She is urged by his adherents to forsake the world, and for his sake to live a reclusive life. Although Katherine appears only briefly in the interminable scenes of war and the grandiose verbiage through which the reader must trudge, her appearance at the end of the novel and her refusal to forsake the world in her grief are the most impressive moments in the work.

In refusing to retreat from the world, Katherine commits herself to the only true value in the novel, love, a value that all the senseless suffering of Richard's quest could not destroy. Katherine, as the widow of the gentle but misguided warrior, becomes a metaphor for the endurance of love in a world that has its heart set on everything but love. Her final, gracious words are a relaxing change from the glory-seeking bombast of the action, "Permit this to be, unblamed—permit a heart whose sufferings have been and are, so many and so bitter, to reap what joy it can from the strong necessity it feels to be sympathized with—to love." Once again, Shelley's basic idea is an enthralling one, but her execution of her plan includes a grandiose superfluity of expression and incident.

LODORE

Lodore and Shelley's last novel, *Falkner*, form a kind of reconciliation couplet to end her exploration of loss and desolation. Reward for persistence in loving through the trials of death and social obliquity is her final vision. In *Lodore*, an extremely long parade of fatal misunderstandings, the central image is the recovery of a lost mother. The novel begins veiled in mystery. Lord Lodore has exiled himself and his fairylike, delicate daughter, Ethel, to the forests of Illinois in far-off America. Lord Lodore is without his wife, who has done something unnamed and perhaps unnameable to provoke this unusual separation. Reunion with her is the central action of the plot.

Lord Lodore is a perfect gentleman amid the cloddish but honest American settlers. His one goal is to produce the perfect maiden in his daughter, Ethel. Father and daughter are entirely devoted to each other. A series of flashback chapters reveal that Lady Lodore, very much the junior of Lord Lodore, had been overly influenced by her mother, who had insinuated herself between husband and wife and alienated her daughter's affections from Lord Lodore. Lord and Lady Lodore lived what life they had together always on the brink of rapprochement, but utterly confounded by the wiles of the mother-in-law, who managed to distort communicated sentiments to turn husband and wife away from each other, finally effecting a radical separation that neither Lord nor Lady Lodore wanted.

The American idyll ends for Ethel and her father when Ethel is about fifteen years old. The unwanted attentions of a suitor threaten Ethel's perfect life, and her father moves his household once more. Lodore thinks of reestablishing the bond with his estranged wife but is killed in a duel hours before departing for England. His last thoughts of reconciliation are buried with him, because the only extant will is one recorded years ago when he vindictively made Lady Lodore's inheritance dependent on her never seeing Ethel again. Ethel returns to England shaken and abandoned, but not to her mother. Instead, she lives with Lodore's maiden sister. Ethel is wooed and won by a gentleman, Edward Villiers, coincidentally one of the few witnesses to her father's death and many years older than herself. The marriage of this truly loving couple is threatened because Edward, reared in luxury, is in reduced financial circumstances owing to the irresponsibility of his father, one of the few truly despicable characters in the novel.

Much suffering ensues, during which Edward and Ethel endeavor to straighten out priorities: Which is more important, love or money? Should they part to give Ethel a chance at a more comfortable life, or should they endure poverty for love? They choose love, but Edward is taken to debtor's prison, Ethel standing by for the conjugal visits that the prison system permits.

Through a series of chance encounters, Lady Lodore, now a seemingly shallow woman of fashion, becomes aware of Ethel's needs and of her need to be a mother to the young woman. Telling no one but her lawyer what she intends, she impoverishes herself to release Edward from prison and to set the couple up appropriately. She then removes herself to a humble country existence, anticipating the blessings of martyrdom. She is, however, discovered, the mother and daughter are reunited, and Lady Lodore is even offered an advantageous marriage to a rich former suitor who originally was kept from her by the machinations of his sisters.

Lodore includes many particulars that are close to the biographical details of the author's life: the penury and social trials of her marriage to Shelley, the financial irresponsibility of her father, and the loss of her mother. Shelley's familiarity with her material appears to have dissolved the grandiose pretensions of the previous novels, which may have sprung from her distance from their exotic settings and situations. *Lodore* has the force of life despite its melodramatic plot. If it were more widely available, it would be a rich source of interest for historians and literary scholars. It contains an interesting image of America as envisioned by the early nineteenth century European. It also contains a wealth of interest for students of women's literature.

FALKNER

If *Lodore* offers a happy ending with the return of a long-lost mother, then *Falkner* finds contentment in the restoration of an estranged father. Here, the father is not the biological parent, but a father figure, Rupert Falkner. The plot is a characteristic tangle of gothic convolutions involving old secrets and sins, obdurate Catholic families, and the pure love of a young girl.

The delightful Elizabeth Raby is orphaned at the age of six under severe circumstances. Because her fragile, lovely parents were complete strangers to the little town in Cornwall to which they had come, their death left Elizabeth at the mercy of their landlady. The landlady is poor, and Elizabeth is a financial burden. The landlady keeps her only because she suspects that the now decimated, strange little family has noble connections. Thus begins a typical Shelley fiction—with abandonment, innocence, and loss of love.

The plot is set in motion by a mysterious stranger who identifies himself as "John Falkner." Falkner undertakes the guardianship of Elizabeth, not only because of her charm but also because of an unfinished letter found in the family cottage. This letter connects Elizabeth's mother to one "Alithea." The reader comes to learn that Falkner was Alithea's lover, that he carries the guilt of her ruin and death since Alithea was a married woman, and that her husband continues to bear his wife's seducer a vindictive grudge. Happily, for the moment, Alithea's husband believes that the seducer was surnamed Rupert. Alithea's husband was and is an unsuitable mate for a sensitive woman, and the marriage was one from which any woman would have wanted to flee. Alithea's infraction was only against the letter of the marriage bond, not its spirit.

The vindictive husband has conceived a hatred for Alithea's son, Gerard, on account of Alithea's connection with "Rupert." Elizabeth, Falkner's ward, coincidentally meets and forms an attachment to Gerard. Falkner repeatedly attempts to separate them because of his guilty feelings. Their attachment blooms into a love that cannot be denied, and Falkner is forced to confess all to Gerard after the boy saves Falkner's life. He is the infamous Rupert, Rupert Falkner.

With the revelation comes the separation of Elizabeth and Gerard, she to stand loyally with Falkner, he to defend his father's honor. For the first time in his life, Gerard finds himself on his father's side, but familiarity breeds contempt. Gerard wants to fight a manly duel for honor, while his father wants to crush Falkner for economic gain in the legal system. Gerard finds this an inexcusable pettiness on his father's part. He then joins Elizabeth to defend Falkner in court. To do this, they will need to go to America to bring back a crucial witness, but the witness arrives and saves them the voyage: Falkner is acquitted. The legal acquittal is also metaphorical: In comparison with the ugly sins of greed, the sins of passion are pardonable.

Elizabeth, the reader knows, is also the product of an elopement in defiance of family, a sin of passion. The proud Catholic family that once spurned her decides to acknowledge Elizabeth. Gerard and Elizabeth, both wealthy and in their proper social position, marry. Falkner will have a home with them in perpetuity.

Once again, Shelley's fictional involvement in the domestic sphere tones down her customary floridity and affords the reader fascinating insights into the thinking of the daughter of an early feminist, who was indeed an independent woman herself. It can only clarify history to know that such a woman as Mary Shelley can write in her final novel that her heroine's studies included not only the "masculine" pursuits of abstract knowledge but also needlework and "the careful inculcation of habits and order . . . without which every woman must be unhappy—and, to a certain degree, unsexed."

Martha Nochimson

OTHER MAJOR WORKS

SHORT FICTION: *Mary Shelley: Collected Tales and Stories*, 1976.

PLAYS: *Midas*, pb. 1922; *Proserpine*, pb. 1922.

NONFICTION: *History of a Six Weeks' Tour Through a Part of France, Switzerland, Germany, and Holland*, 1817 (with Percy Bysshe Shelley); *Lardner's Cabinet Cyclopaedia*, 1838 (numbers 63, 71, 96); *Rambles in Germany and Italy*, 1844; *The Letters of Mary Shelley*, 1980 (2 volumes; Betty T. Bennett, editor).

MISCELLANEOUS: *Mary Shelley's Literary Lives, and Other Writings*, 2002 (Nora Crook, editor).

BIBLIOGRAPHY

Baldick, Chris. *In Frankenstein's Shadow: Myth, Monstrosity, and Nineteenth-Century Writing*. Oxford, England: Clarendon Press, 1987. Analyzes the structure of modern myth as it adapted and misread Shelley's novel before the release of the 1931 film adaptation. Focuses on the novel *Frankenstein* as itself a monster that is assembled, speaks, and escapes like its protagonist. Includes footnotes, illustrations, an appendix summarizing the novel's plot, and an index.

Bennett, Betty T., and Stuart Curran, eds. *Mary Shelley in Her Times*. Baltimore: Johns Hopkins University Press, 2000. Collection of essays presents an examination of Shelley and her works in the full context of her life and times. Addresses all of Shelley's writings rather than concentrating only on her best-known novel.

Fisch, Audrey A., Anne K. Mellor, and Esther H. Schor, eds. *The Other Mary Shelley: Beyond "Frankenstein."* New York: Oxford University Press, 1993. Valuable collection of critical essays illuminates Shelley's major and less well-known works, including her novels *The Last Man* and *Valperga*. The essays by Mary Jean Corbett, Mary Favret, Morton D. Paley, and Esther H. Schor are particularly recommended.

Garrett, Martin. *Mary Shelley*. New York: Oxford University Press, 2003. Biography provides a general overview for readers new to Shelley's work. Discusses Shelley's early, formative years and includes a rich collection of illustrations and excerpts from diaries and letters.

Hoobler, Dorothy, and Thomas Hoobler. *The Monsters: Mary Shelley and the Curse of "Frankenstein."* New York: Little, Brown, 2006. Biography describes Shelley's creation of *Frankenstein* and demonstrates how the themes of this novel corresponded to the events of Shelley's life.

Mellor, Anne K. *Mary Shelley: Her Life, Her Fiction, Her Monsters*. London: Methuen, 1988. Argues against trends of analysis that subordinate Shelley to her husband, Percy Bysshe Shelley. Extends feminist and psychoanalytic criticism of *Frankenstein* to include all of Shelley's life and work, arguing that her stories are creations of the family she never enjoyed. Includes illustrations, chronology, ample notes, bibliography, and index.

Morrison, Lucy, and Staci Stone. *A Mary Shelley Encyclopedia*. Westport, Conn.: Greenwood Press, 2003. Reference volume contains alphabetically arranged and cross-referenced entries providing information about Shelley's family, friends, homes, works, characters, literary influences, and themes, among other topics.

Smith, Johanna M. *Mary Shelley*. New York: Twayne, 1996. Devotes a chapter to Shelley's biography, then divides Shelley's work into categories for closer discussion. More descriptive than analytical, this is an accessible introduction to Shelley's literary career. Includes selected bibliography.

Spark, Muriel. *Mary Shelley*. London: Constable, 1988. Revision of Spark's *Child of Light*, published in 1951, reassesses the view that Shelley craved respectability after her husband's death. Skillfully narrates Shelley's life and then analyzes her writings. Includes illustrations, selected bibliography, and index.

Sunstein, Emily. *Mary Shelley: Romance and Reality*. Boston: Little, Brown, 1989. One of the most complete biographies of Shelley available. Chapter notes explicitly identify key primary sources of information about Shelley's life and work, and an appendix provides detailed listings of works definitively identified as Shelley's as well as works that might be attributed to her.

JUN'ICHIRŌ TANIZAKI

Born: Tokyo, Japan; July 24, 1886
Died: Yugawara, Japan; July 30, 1965

OTHER LITERARY FORMS

The history of the novel in Japan is quite different from its history in the West, and the distinctions normally observed between the short story and the novel do not apply there. If, arbitrarily, one refers to Japanese works of fewer than one hundred pages of prose fiction as "short stories," Jun'ichirō Tanizaki (tah-nee-zahk-ee) is as famous for his short stories as for his longer works. Typical of his early period, "Shisei" (1910; "The Tattooer," 1963) indicates his early interest in sexual symbolism. "Akuma" (1912; Satan) deals with male masochism, and "Otsuya goroshi" (1913; a springtime case) deals with murder and amorality in Tokyo. Later, Tanizaki wrote such remarkable stories as "Ashikari" (1932; English translation, 1936), "Shunkinshō" (1933; "A Portrait of Shunkin," 1936), "Mōmoku monogatari" (1931; "A Blind Man's Tale," 1963), and the exquisite "Yume no ukihashi" (1959; "The Bridge of Dreams," 1963).

Tanizaki also wrote a number of plays, including *Aisureba koso* (pb. 1921; all because of love), *Okumi to Gohei* (pb. 1922), and *Shirogitsune no yu* (pb. 1923; *The White Fox*, 1930). In 1932, he began translating Murasaki Shikibu's *Genji monogatari* (c. 1004; *The Tale of Genji*, 1936-1941, 1951-1954) into modern Japanese; over the years, he produced several revisions of it. *Bunshō tokuhon* (1934; a manual of style), in which he outlined his craftsmanlike attitude toward composing fiction, is often called a minor masterpiece of criticism. Although he published several highly accomplished reviews and essays, he seldom was persuaded to undertake them, believing that he ought to concentrate on his fiction.

ACHIEVEMENTS

Jun'ichirō Tanizaki was recognized as a remarkable talent even in his twenties and continued to be so recognized throughout a long and prolific career, which outlasted several publications of his complete works. At first, he was considered shockingly Western by his contemporaries; during the 1920's, however, he gradually began to incorporate more conservative Japanese literary elements, implicitly warning his readers of the dangers of being overly Westernized. Late in his career, his characters are not endangered by Western culture, enjoying, for example, Western clothes and houses as everyday realities in modern Japan.

Tanizaki's mastery of a carefully composed style and his insight into the psychology of his characters place him among the great writers of twentieth century world literature. A slow, careful writer, Tanizaki argued that one of the most important elements of Japanese is its "vagueness" in comparison to other languages, a vagueness that allows the Japanese author to suggest motives, feelings, and details in delicate strokes rather than in precise exposition. Considering the imagination crucial, Tanizaki often dealt with sensational material and abnormal states of mind; by controlling his style, he did not allow his intensity to become hysterical. Despite their bizarre aberrations, his characters rarely become unbelievable as human beings, because of the objective manner in which he treats them. Like many great writers, Tanizaki was also able to assimilate opposing elements such as tradition and innovation, imagination and realism, and the influences of West and East.

BIOGRAPHY

Jun'ichirō Tanizaki was born in the heart of downtown Tokyo. For generations, his ancestors had lived there as members of the merchant class engaged in rice-brokering and printing and had little of the traditional samurai-class interest in affairs of state. Despite the traditional male-dominated culture of Japan, Tanizaki's grandfather and father were considered feminists, his father nearly worshiping Tanizaki's mother. The boy, as a result, was drawn to his mother very strongly, thus establishing the reverential attitude toward women seen in so many of his works. Tanizaki was also a handsome boy, but not a strong one, and, consequently, was often bullied by older classmates, perhaps encouraging a masochistic streak.

During Tanizaki's primary education, a young teacher noticed the boy's talents and gave him special instruction in Japanese and Chinese classics. It is often reported that Tanizaki became known as the brightest student ever to graduate from the First Municipal Secondary School of Tokyo. He entered Tokyo Imperial University in 1908, where he studied Japanese classical literature. He helped found the literary magazine of the university, *Shinshicho*, in which he published several short stories that received praise from older writers such as Mori Ogai and Nagai Kafu. After only a year, however, because he did not pay his fees, he left the university without finishing his degree.

Tanizaki's unfinished education did not hinder him unduly, because he was becoming known as a writer. A notorious frequenter of the "Bluff," or foreign sections of Yokohama, he wore checked suits and gaudy ties and was strongly under the influence of Decadent Western writers such as Edgar Allan Poe, Charles Baudelaire, and Oscar Wilde; Tanizaki translated Wilde's *Lady Windermere's Fan* (1892) in 1919. This lifestyle changed when he moved to Okamoto in 1923 after the Great Earthquake. In the Hakone mountains south of Yokohama, during the disaster, he first was delighted that all he despised of the old Japan had been destroyed. He predicted a new, modern Tokyo with wide boulevards, film theaters, and citizens wearing comfortable Western clothing. Yet, as time passed, he began to seek the traditional roots of Japanese literature and went, as is often asserted, from being merely a good author to being a great one.

By 1930, Tanizaki was so famous that his complete works were published. His personal life was almost as sensational as his fiction. After encouraging his wife, Chiyoko, to have an affair with his friend, Sato Haruo, they were divorced in 1930 after fifteen years of marriage. In 1931, he married Furukawa Tomiko, a literary student whom he divorced in 1934. In 1935, he married his last wife, Morita Matzuko, formerly married to an Ōsaka millionaire and patron of several artists and writers, including Tanizaki.

With the rise of militarism in Japan, Tanizaki's work—with its interest in aestheticism and sexuality—was considered improper, and he was forced to suppress the amorous passages of his translation of *The Tale of Genji*, which he had begun in 1935. His longest novel, *The Makioka Sisters*, was not published during the war because of the amorous content, but when it was finally released, it—along with his earlier works—established Tanizaki as possibly the most significant twentieth century Japanese author. In 1949, he received Japan's Imperial Prize for Literature.

During the 1950's and 1960's, Tanizaki returned to some of the themes of his earlier career. The publication of the first episode of *The Key* in the magazine *Chuo koron* in 1956 created a sensation in Japan as customers snatched up copies, partly because of its sexual content. It also became well known in the United States, as did "The Bridge of Dreams" and *Diary of a Mad Old Man*, as a result of a new Western interest in Japanese films (such as Akira Kurosawa's 1951 film of Ryūnosuke Akutagawa's "Rashomon") and literature (notably the works of Yasunari Kawabata and Yukio Mishima). In 1960, a film version of *The Key* was released in the United States as *Odd Obsession*. In 1964, Tanizaki was elected honorary member of the American Academy of Arts and Letters and the National Institute of Arts and Letters. He spent his last few years struggling with various illnesses and living in a Western-style house on the Izu Coast. At the time of his death, Tanizaki was one of the leading candidates for a Nobel Prize.

ANALYSIS

Jun'ichirō Tanizaki's early literary career was characterized by a deep interest in Western literature. Although as a student he studied Japanese literature and had a nostalgia for classical Japanese works, he once commented that about 1918, "I had come to detest Japan, even though I was obviously a Japanese." Assiduously reading Baudelaire, Wilde, and especially Poe, he asserted the supremacy of the imagination in literature, as opposed to the naturalism of many of his contemporaries, arguing that even Gustave Flaubert and Émile Zola could not have produced their naturalistic works without being highly imaginative.

Once using Wilde's aphorism "Nature imitates art" as an epigraph to a story, Tanizaki believed that the representation of reality was not the primary function of literature; it was rather the presentation of truth. "The artist," he wrote, "justifies his existence only when he can transform his imagination into truth." This truth, in Tanizaki's view, was primarily psychological. Imagination allowed the author to see the subconscious depths of humanity. The writer perceived what people were, not what they could be. There was no need for a writer to justify his (or her) works for social or moral reasons, and Tanizaki was seen as an exponent of aestheticism.

As might be expected, the early influence of the Decadent authors led to intense, macabre works. They are, by turn, gothic, grotesque, hedonistic, diabolic, and erotic. Tanizaki's first important work, "The Tattooer," is typical. Seikichi is a master tattooer who has become so great he only tattoos according to his vision of his client's character. Further, he delights in the suffering his needles cause his clients. His obsession becomes the creation of a masterwork on the skin of a woman who meets his requirements of character as well as beauty. After four years, he sees the foot of a woman disappear into a palanquin, knows instantly that she is the one he has been searching for, but loses the palanquin in the crowd. The next spring, she appears at his house, and after he reveals her true, vampirish nature, he creates an exquisite tattoo of a black widow spider on her back and finds himself the slave of his own creation.

There are several elements characteristic of Tanizaki's work in this story. In most of his works, a man delights in his utter servitude to the woman he adores. Seikichi goes from sadist to masochist as the result of finding his perfect woman, and although Tanizaki devotes this work to the psychological and artistic obsessions of the tattooer, he was generally more interested in his women characters, because they expressed an ideal before which his men groveled. This subservient role has been frequently associated with Tanizaki's attitude toward his mother, who died in 1917. One will also note the foot fetishism implicit in Seikichi's first noticing the young girl. Throughout Tanizaki's career, women's feet play a large role in the sexual relationships between his characters. This is obvious in such works as "Fumiko no ashi" in which an old man is infatuated with the feet of his mistress and dies in ecstasy as Fumiko presses his forehead under her foot, but it reveals itself in other ways as well: Frequently, Tanizaki devotes more detail to his description of a woman's feet than he does to his description of her face.

Despite Tanizaki's interest in Western writers, many elements of his early work were derived from traditional Japanese literature. Throughout his career, he felt no hesitation in setting his stories in the Japanese past. "The Tattooer," for example, occurs in the

Tokugawa period of the seventeenth century. In 1919, in the middle of his Decadent interests, the same year as "Fumiko no ashi" and his translation of *Lady Windermere's Fan*, he published a volume of erotic stories in the style of the Japanese 1830's and two novellas in the Chinese style. As they are depicted in works by Tanizaki, women are often portrayed as treacherous, cruel creatures in classical Japanese literature. The seventeenth century novelist Ihara Saikaku wrote many risqué stories, in some of which the heroine's insatiable sexual appetite exhausts the hero. Finally, grotesque and diabolic motifs are very common in classical Japanese literature, and it is perhaps too easy to overemphasize the influence of Poe's and Wilde's content on Tanizaki, when he was more interested in adapting their conception of art in his reaction against naturalism.

There is no doubt, however, that Tanizaki's work changed at the beginning of the 1920's, particularly after he moved from Tokyo to the more conservative Kansai (Kyōto, Ōsaka, and Kōbe) region after the Great Earthquake. Although in his later work he retained his masochistic heroes, characters for whom there are few precedents in traditional Japanese literature, he began to acknowledge more strongly the values and practices of his culture.

NAOMI

Naomi marks the division between Tanizaki's Westernized period and his more tradition-oriented works from the 1920's through the 1940's. Although, like so many of his works, *Naomi* tells of a man's quest for the ideal woman, there is much implied criticism of Japanese worship of the West, despite the fact that the novel seems to have been based on W. Somerset Maugham's *Of Human Bondage* (1915).

Joji, the narrator in *Naomi*, is attracted to a European-looking waitress named Naomi. Her features make him think of Mary Pickford, and he asks her if she would like to go to a film. Instead of the usual polite evasions, she says (like Mildred in *Of Human Bondage*), "I don't mind if I do." Eventually, he takes her home with the intention of remaking her into his ideal of beauty—a woman he will not be ashamed of in front of blond foreigners—and marrying her within a few years. Naomi is given Western clothes, practices playing the piano, speaking English, and dancing. All of this merely encourages her decadent tendencies. He learns she has been unfaithful and attempts to leave her. He discovers he cannot, however, and gives in completely to her. She can do as she wishes, have whatever lover she wishes, as long as she remains his wife.

Joji is a fool as much in his obsessive love of Western things as in his love of the girl. He is ashamed of his racial identity. His shortness, his protruding teeth, his dark complexion, and other typically Japanese features embarrass him, but he is proud of his European-style Yokohama house. He is degraded by his sense of both cultural and sexual inferiority. Often offended by Naomi's crudity, he excuses it because of his fascination with her; to be humiliated by her is an honor. Even when she dresses and behaves like a prostitute, he is filled with masochistic pride that she is his.

SOME PREFER NETTLES

Tanizaki's next major novel, *Some Prefer Nettles*, deals with similar themes. This work tells of a character, Kaname, whose superficial Western tastes are gradually replaced by an appreciation of traditional Japanese culture. Kaname is unhappily married to Misako. He has lost sexual interest in her but is tormented by uncertainty over what to do about it. He encourages her to have an affair while he finds sexual satisfaction with a Eurasian prostitute. There is a superficial resemblance between this plot and certain events in Tanizaki's own life. Bored with his first wife, Chiyoko, one night at dinner he calmly asked Sato Haruo, poet and friend, if he would like to marry her. In 1930, after encouraging the affair, Tanizaki divorced Chiyoko, and she married Sato. Obviously, this arrangement was on his mind during the writing of *Some Prefer Nettles*, and his ambivalence is perhaps reflected by the book itself.

Far more important, however, in assessing the book, is the struggle in Kaname between his appreciation of Western culture and his appreciation of the merchants' culture of old Japan surviving in Ōsaka, particularly represented in this novel by the Bunraku, or puppet theater. At the end of the novel, Kaname confuses a puppet with the Ōsaka beauty O-hisa, showing perhaps that the old way of life is a fantasy that cannot be recaptured. Edward G. Seidensticker, who translated the novel, argues that Kaname (and Tanizaki) is attempting to return to the peace of childhood, although the adult knows the new world is here to stay. In his essay "In'ei raisan" (1934; *In Praise of Shadows*, 1955), Tanizaki wrote "I know as well as anyone that I am dreaming, and that, having come this far, we cannot turn back."

It should also be noted that whatever ambivalence or vagueness readers might find in *Some Prefer Nettles* and other Tanizaki novels is as much a reflection of his aesthetic as of any personal feelings. He always insisted on exploiting the vagueness of Japanese and objected to writers who were too clear. One cannot, for example, know exactly what will happen to Kaname the day after the novel closes. Primary among Tanizaki's goals in writing was to achieve poetic suggestiveness, which the last scene certainly does.

THE MAKIOKA SISTERS

During the late 1930's, Tanizaki continued his rediscovery of traditional Japanese culture by beginning his translation of *The Tale of Genji*, a work that, in many ways, influenced the composition of *The Makioka Sisters*, his longest and, many argue, his greatest novel. Although Tanizaki was always a slow, very careful writer, wartime circumstances forced him to work even more slowly than usual. He spent many years on *The Makioka Sisters*, and censorship prevented complete publication of the work until 1948.

Before Tanizaki began writing the novel, he delineated a precise plan and followed it nearly to the conclusion. Despite this detailed planning, *The Makioka Sisters*—unlike his usual lean, straightforward novels—is a sprawling, indirect novel in the episodic form often favored by Japanese authors. Complex characterization and diverse social forces create many layers of action and emotion to give the book a texture quite different from that of Tanizaki's typical works, which focus on a single character.

In the novel, the four Makioka sisters represent various aspects of Japanese culture during the 1930's. Once a rich Ōsaka merchant family, the Makiokas have declined. Tsuruko, the eldest, is the most conservative, trying to hang on to a way of life they have outlived. Taeko, the youngest, seems the brightest, the most talented, and the most corrupted by the Tokyo-style intelligentsia with its Western fads. Sachiko, with her husband, Teinosuke, holds the family together by mediating between the impulses that tear at it. Yukiko, despite her traditional beauty, is too shy to deal effectively with her sisters or the world about her.

Most of the novel concerns the attempt to find the aging Yukiko a husband; the Japanese title *Sasameyuki* (thin snow) refers to the number of *miai* (marriage arrangements) that fail. Tsuruko generally insists on going through the slow traditional investigation of potential husbands, while Sachiko recognizes the diminishing value of Yukiko as a bride and tries to carry the arrangements out in a reasonable, though not hurried, time. Taeko, who intends to marry a Westernized playboy, must wait for her elder sister's marriage before marrying on her own. Yukiko is so introverted that she often seems indifferent to the whole struggle, except when she rejects another candidate.

This plot, however, is not Tanizaki's main concern. Using details from his wife Tomiko's family history, he re-creates Ōsaka as it was before the war, revealing foreign influences that would inevitably destroy that way of life—the clothing, the foreign films, the German neighbors, the visit to the White Russians, Taeko's desire to go to Paris to learn dressmaking—and the traditional Japanese customs as they were then practiced. Attention is devoted to the cherry blossom festival, Taeko's dollmaking, Kabuki, Japanese dance, and the old house of the Makiokas. The elegant Ōsaka dialect is spoken by the main characters and the Tokyo dialect is portrayed as being corrupted. Despite these contrasts, *The Makioka Sisters* is not a didactic work that preaches the superiority of the old ways over the new. It captures a particular way of life at a certain period in a certain place. Free of the grotesqueness that characterizes his early works and of the obsessive characters that populate most of his works, *The Makioka Sisters* is a panoramic view of diverse characters with complex motivations, a work unusual in Tanizaki's oeuvre but indisputably a masterpiece.

Unlike many writers, who, once they have achieved an integrated work such as *The Makioka Sisters*, run out of things to say, Tanizaki remained as creative in the final decades of his life as he had earlier. Entering the third phase of his career, he returned to many of the themes that had occupied him in his youth; with a more detached and sometimes ironic point of view, he dealt with the obsessions of sex in old age. Composed of the parallel diaries of a fifty-six-year-old professor and his forty-five-year-old wife, *The Key* progresses through the former's attempt to expand the sexual abilities of the latter, a woman whom he loves madly but who no longer satisfies him. Once again, one might note the autobiographical resonance of the professor's gradually directing his wife into the young Kimura's arms. One might also note the return of the devouring woman as the wife encourages the eating of beef and incites his jealousy, in spite of her knowledge of her husband's rising blood pressure, which eventually kills him.

THE KEY

The Key created a sensation on its publication, no doubt largely because of its frank treatment of sex; like other works of literature—Gustave Flaubert's *Madame Bovary* (1857) and D. H. Lawrence's *Lady Chatterley's Lover* (1928)—which achieved notoriety before their literary merits were admitted, *The Key*'s craftsmanship can now be assessed more objectively. Presenting one diary in the *katakana* script and the other in the *hiragana* script, Tanizaki exploits the differences between the two characters' perceptions of the situation. Further, he complicates the ostensibly sincere presentations of the diaries by having each character aware that the other may be reading what is written. This complex treatment of point of view turns an apparently simple, short work into a multilayered psychological study.

DIARY OF A MAD OLD MAN

Tanizaki's last novel, *Diary of a Mad Old Man*, also consists mainly of a diary, but by a man even older than the protagonist of *The Key*. Also suffering from high blood pressure, he is sexually impotent as well. Nevertheless, he is attracted to his daughter-in-law, Satsuko, estranged from her husband and having an affair with another man. As in many of Tanizaki's works, the narrator devotes much attention to Satsuko's feet as sexual objects, and he thinks often of his mother. He compares Satsuko's feet many times with those of his mother, and he delights in kissing Satsuko's feet and biting her toes when she comes from the shower. Her feet also become associated with the Buddhist goddess of mercy, and the old man plans for his daughter-in-law's footprints to be carved on his tombstone.

Objectively treated, *Diary of a Mad Old Man* is a great deal less sensational than it would appear from a plot summary. The artistic coolness that Tanizaki worked so hard to achieve saves the work from any pornographic content. Further, the novel is comic in its attitude toward the main character, satirizing the high intensity of Tanizaki's early works. Several of his works have comic elements—he was fond of cats and often wrote of them in a lighthearted vein—and Tanizaki seems to have ended his career looking back on his extraordinary achievements with a whimsical detachment.

J. Madison Davis

OTHER MAJOR WORKS

SHORT FICTION: "Kirin," 1910; "Shōnen," 1910; "Shisei," 1910 ("The Tattooer," 1963); "Hōkan," 1911; "Akuma," 1912; "Kyōfu," 1913 ("Terror," 1963); "Otsuya goroshi," 1913; "Haha o kouruki," 1919 ("Longing for Mother," 1980); "Watakushi," 1921

("The Thief," 1963); "Aoi Hano," 1922 ("Aguri," 1963); "Mōmoku monogatari," 1931 ("A Blind Man's Tale," 1963); "Ashikari," 1932 (English translation, 1936); "Shun-kinshō," 1933 ("A Portrait of Shunkin," 1936); *Hyofu*, 1950; "Yume no ukihashi," 1959 ("The Bridge of Dreams," 1963); *Yume no ukihashi*, 1960 (collection); *Kokumin no bungaku*, 1964; *Tanizaki Jun'ichirō shu*, 1970; *Seven Japanese Tales*, 1981; *The Gourmet Club: A Sextet*, 2001 (Anthony H. Chambers and Paul McCarthy, translators).

PLAYS: *Aisureba koso*, pb. 1921; *Okumi to Gohei*, pb. 1922; *Shirogitsune no yu*, pb. 1923 (*The White Fox*, 1930); *Mumyō to Aizen*, pb. 1924; *Shinzei*, pb. 1949.

NONFICTION: *Bunshō tokuhon*, 1934; "In'ei raisan," 1934 ("In Praise of Shadows," 1955); *Kyō no yume, Ōsaka no yume*, 1950; *Yōshō-jidai*, 1957 (*Childhood Years: A Memoir*, 1988).

TRANSLATION: *Genji monogatari*, 1936-1941, 1951-1954 (of Murasaki Shikibu's medieval novel).

MISCELLANEOUS: *Tanizaki Jun'ichirō zenshu*, 1930 (12 volumes); *Tanizaki Jun'ichirō zenshu*, 1966-1970 (28 volumes).

BIBLIOGRAPHY

Chambers, Anthony Hood. *The Secret Window: Ideal Worlds in Tanizaki's Fiction*. Cambridge, Mass.: Harvard University Press, 1994. Chambers analyzes seven of Tanizaki's novels and novellas, focusing on the characters' attempts to create "ideal worlds" and the elements of fantasy in these works. Includes notes and a bibliography.

Gessel, Van C. *Three Modern Novelists: Soseki, Tanizaki, Kawabata*. New York: Kodansha International, 1993. The sixty-five-page chapter on Tanizaki concentrates on his approach to modernism. Includes detailed notes but no bibliography.

Golley, Gregory L. "Tanizaki Junichiro: The Art of Subversion and the Subversion of Art." *Journal of Japanese Studies* 21 (Summer, 1995): 365-404. Examines the "return to Japan" inaugurated by Tanizaki's *Some Prefer Nettles*. Discusses themes and images in the work and suggests that Tanizaki's traditionalist fiction both championed and undermined the idea of an essential Japanese traditional culture.

Ito, Ken K. *Visions of Desire: Tanizaki's Fictional Worlds*. Stanford, Calif.: Stanford University Press, 1991. A critical biography, with chapters arranged in chronological order of Tanizaki's life and work. Ito primarily focuses his analysis on Tanizaki's best-known works that have been translated into English, and pays special attention to Tanizaki's language, narrative style, and his male characters' projection of their desires upon women. Includes notes, a bibliography, and a section on names and sources.

Keene, Donald. *Dawn to the West: Japanese Literature of the Modern Era—Fiction*. New York: Holt, Rinehart and Winston, 1984. A massive study of the fiction produced since the Japanese enlightenment of the nineteenth century. Chapter 20 is devoted exclusively to Tanizaki, and he is discussed in the introduction and in several other chapters in association with other writers and literary movements.

_____. *Five Modern Japanese Novelists*. New York: Columbia University Press, 2003. Keene devotes a chapter to Tanizaki in his tribute to five twentieth century Japanese novelists. Includes his personal recollections of Tanizaki, with whom he was acquainted, and discusses the writer's works.

_____. *Japanese Literature: An Introduction for Western Readers*. New York: Grove Press, 1955. Unlike the comprehensive treatment in *Dawn to the West*, this is a brief introduction to Japanese literature. Tanizaki is briefly mentioned in the introduction and chapter 4, "The Japanese Novel," but is discussed throughout chapter 5, "Japanese Literature Under Western Influence."

Lippit, Noriko Miuta. *Reality and Fiction in Modern Japanese Literature*. White Plains, N.Y.: M. E. Sharpe, 1980. Lippit considers the struggle of several Japanese writers to define the function of art and literature, both socially and personally. The sections on Tanizaki deal with his aesthetic preference for fantasy and complex structure, with a comparison to Edgar Allan Poe. Includes notes.

Suzuki, Tomi. *Narrating the Self: Fictions of Japanese Modernity*. Stanford, Calif.: Stanford University Press, 1996. Two of the chapters are devoted to Tanizaki: "Allegories of Modernity in Tanizaki Jun'ichirō's *Fool's Love*" (also known as *Naomi*) and the epilogue, "Tanizaki's Speaking Subject and the Creation of Tradition." Includes notes and a bibliography.

Ueda, Makoto. "Tanizaki Jun'ichirō." In *Modern Japanese Writers and the Nature of Literature*. Stanford, Calif.: Stanford University Press, 1976. Discusses Tanizaki as one of the eight major writers who make up the majority of modern Japanese fiction familiar to Western readers. Provides an introduction to major literary theories underlying Japanese novels and stories. Supplemented by source notes, a bibliography, and an index.

Yamanouchi, Hisaaki. *The Search for Authenticity in Modern Japanese Literature*. New York: Cambridge University Press, 1978. Discusses twelve modern Japanese writers, analyzing the ways each dealt with difficult personal, social, and intellectual questions in art. The sections on Tanizaki focus on the concept of eternal womanhood in his works. Includes notes, a bibliography, and an index.

BIBLIOGRAPHY

Every effort has been made to include studies published in 2000 and later. Most items in this bibliography contain a listing of secondary sources, making it easier to identify other critical commentary on novelists, movements, and themes.

THEORETICAL, THEMATIC, AND HISTORICAL STUDIES

Altman, Janet Gurkin. *Epistolarity: Approaches to a Form.* Columbus: Ohio State University Press, 1982. Examines the epistolary novel, explaining how novelists use the letter form to develop characterization, further their plots, and develop meaning.

Beaumont, Matthew, ed. *Adventures in Realism.* Malden, Mass.: Blackwell, 2007. Fifteen essays explore facets of realism, which was critical to the development of the novel. Provides a theoretical framework for understanding how novelists attempt to represent the real and the common in fiction.

Brink, André. *The Novel: Language and Narrative from Cervantes to Calvino.* New York: New York University Press, 1998. Uses contemporary theories of semiotics and narratology to establish a continuum between early novelists and those of the postmodern era in their conscious use of language to achieve certain effects. Ranges across national boundaries to illustrate the theory of the development of the novel since the seventeenth century.

Brownstein, Rachel. *Becoming a Heroine: Reading About Women in Novels.* New York: Viking Press, 1982. Feminist survey of novels from the eighteenth century through the latter half of the twentieth century. Examines how "becoming a heroine" defines for women a sense of value in their lives. Considers novels by both men and women, and discusses the importance of the traditional marriage plot.

Bruzelius, Margaret. *Romancing the Novel: Adventure from Scott to Sebald.* Lewisburg, Pa.: Bucknell University Press, 2007. Examines the development of the adventure novel, linking it with the medieval romance tradition and exploring readers' continuing fascination with the genre.

Doody, Margaret Anne. *The True Story of the Novel.* New Brunswick, N.J.: Rutgers University Press, 1996. Traces the roots of the novel, traditionally thought to have been developed in the seventeenth century, to classical Greek and Latin texts that exhibit characteristics of modern fiction.

Hale, Dorothy J., ed. *The Novel: An Anthology of Criticism and Theory, 1900-2000.* Malden, Mass.: Blackwell, 2006. Collection of essays by theorists and novelists. Includes commentary on the novel form from the perspective of formalism, structuralism, poststructuralism, Marxism, and reader response theory. Essays also address the novel through the lenses of sociology, gender studies, and feminist theory.

_____. *Social Formalism: The Novel in Theory from Henry James to the Present.* Stanford, Calif.: Stanford University Press, 1998. Emphasizes the novel's special ability to define a social world for readers. Relies heavily on the works of contemporary literary and cultural theorists. Provides a summary of twentieth century efforts to identify a theory of fiction that encompasses novels of many kinds.

Hart, Stephen M., and Wen-chin Ouyang, eds. *A Companion to Magical Realism*. London: Tamesis, 2005. Essays outlining the development of Magical Realism, tracing its roots from Europe through Latin America to other regions of the world. Explores the political dimensions of the genre.

Hoffman, Michael J., and Patrick D. Murphy, eds. *Essentials of the Theory of Fiction*. 2d ed. Durham, N.C.: Duke University Press, 1996. Collection of essays by influential critics from the late nineteenth century through the twentieth century. Focuses on the essential elements of fiction and the novel's relationship to the world it depicts.

Lodge, David. *The Art of Fiction: Illustrated from Classic and Modern Texts*. New York: Viking Press, 1993. Short commentaries on the technical aspects of fiction. Examples from important and minor novelists illustrate literary principles and techniques such as point of view, suspense, character introduction, irony, motivation, and ending.

Lynch, Deirdre, and William B. Walker, eds. *Cultural Institutions of the Novel*. Durham, N.C.: Duke University Press, 1996. Fifteen essays examine aspects of long fiction produced around the world. Encourages a redefinition of the genre and argues for inclusion of texts not historically considered novels.

Moretti, Franco, ed. *The Novel*. 2 vols. Princeton, N.J.: Princeton University Press, 2006. Compendium exploring the novel from multiple perspectives, including as an anthropological, historical, and sociological document; a function of the national tradition from which it emerges; and a work of art subject to examination using various critical approaches.

Priestman, Martin, ed. *The Cambridge Companion to Crime Fiction*. New York: Cambridge University Press, 2003. Essays examine the nature and development of the genre, explore works by writers (including women and ethnic minorities) from several countries, and establish links between crime fiction and other literary genres. Includes a chronology.

Scaggs, John. *Crime Fiction*. New York: Routledge, 2005. Provides a history of crime fiction, explores key subgenres, and identifies recurring themes that suggest the wider social and historical context in which these works are written. Suggests critical approaches that open crime fiction to serious study.

Shiach, Morag, ed. *The Cambridge Companion to the Modernist Novel*. New York: Cambridge University Press, 2007. Essays explaining the concept of modernism and its influence on the novel. Detailed examination of works by writers from various countries, all influenced by the modernist movement. Includes a detailed chronology.

Vice, Sue. *Holocaust Fiction*. New York: Routledge, 2000. Examines controversies generated by novels about the Holocaust. Focuses on eight important works, but also offers observations on the polemics surrounding publication of books on this topic.

Zunshine, Lisa. *Why We Read Fiction: Theory of Mind and the Novel.* Columbus: Ohio State University Press, 2006. Applies theories of cognitive psychology to novel reading, explaining how experience and human nature lead readers to constrain their interpretations of a given text. Provides numerous examples from well-known novels to illustrate how and why readers find pleasure in fiction.

THE GOTHIC NOVEL

Ahern, Stephen. *Affected Sensibilities: Romantic Excess and the Genealogy of the Novel, 1680-1810.* New York: AMS Press, 2007. Explores the rise and rapid demise of various forms of fiction that feature excessive sensibility. Considers amatory fiction, sentimental fiction, and gothic narratives produced during the eighteenth century.

Cavallaro, Dani. *The Gothic Vision: Three Centuries of Horror, Terror, and Fear.* New York: Continuum, 2005. Study of the gothic novel from its earliest manifestations in the eighteenth century to the early twenty-first century. Through the lenses of contemporary cultural theories, examines readers' fascination with novels that invoke horror, terror, and fright.

Norton, Rictor, ed. *Gothic Readings. The First Wave, 1764-1840.* London: Leicester University Press, 2000. Sketches the careers of important Gothic novelists, provides samples from their works, and discusses the development of the genre. Includes commentary on Gothic fiction from eighteenth and nineteenth century critics and readers.

Richetti, John, ed. *The Cambridge Companion to the Eighteenth Century Novel.* New York: Cambridge University Press, 1996. Focuses on the cultural and historical context in which the novel developed. Chapters explore the work of major figures, the role of women writers, and the rise of gothic fiction.

Laurence W. Mazzeno

GLOSSARY OF LITERARY TERMS

absurdism: A philosophical attitude, pervading much of modern drama and fiction, that underlines the isolation and alienation that humans experience, having been thrown into what absurdists see as a godless universe devoid of religious, spiritual, or metaphysical meaning. Conspicuous in its lack of logic, consistency, coherence, intelligibility, and realism, the literature of the absurd depicts the anguish, forlornness, and despair inherent in the human condition. Counter to the rationalist assumptions of traditional humanism, absurdism denies the existence of universal truth or value.

allegory: A literary mode in which a second level of meaning, wherein characters, events, and settings represent abstractions, is encoded within the surface narrative. The allegorical mode may dominate an entire work, in which case the encoded message is the work's primary reason for being, or it may be an element in a work otherwise interesting and meaningful for its surface story alone. Elements of allegory may be found in Jonathan Swift's *Gulliver's Travels* (1726) and Thomas Mann's *Der Zauberberg* (1924; *The Magic Mountain*, 1927).

anatomy: Literally the term means the "cutting up" or "dissection" of a subject into its constituent parts for closer examination. Northrop Frye, in his *Anatomy of Criticism* (1957), uses the term to refer to a narrative that deals with mental attitudes rather than people. As opposed to the novel, the anatomy features stylized figures who are mouthpieces for the ideas they represent.

antagonist: The character in fiction who stands as a rival or opponent to the *protagonist*.

antihero: Defined by Seán O'Faoláin as a fictional figure who, deprived of social sanctions and definitions, is always trying to define himself and to establish his own codes. Ahab may be seen as the antihero of Herman Melville's *Moby Dick* (1851).

archetype: The term "archetype" entered literary criticism from the psychology of Carl Jung, who defined archetypes as "primordial images" from the "collective unconscious" of humankind. Jung believed that works of art derive much of their power from the unconscious appeal of these images to ancestral memories. In his extremely influential *Anatomy of Criticism* (1957), Northrop Frye gave another sense of the term wide currency, defining the archetype as "a symbol, usually an image, which recurs often enough in literature to be recognizable as an element of one's literary experience as a whole."

atmosphere: The general mood or tone of a work; atmosphere is often associated with setting but can also be established by action or dialogue. A classic example of atmosphere is the primitive, fatalistic tone created in the opening description of Egdon Heath in Thomas Hardy's *The Return of the Native* (1878).

bildungsroman: Sometimes called the "novel of education," the bildungsroman focuses on the growth of a young *protagonist* who is learning about the world and finding his or her place in life; typical examples are James Joyce's *A Portrait of the Artist as a*

Young Man (1914-1915, serial; 1916, book) and Thomas Wolfe's *Look Homeward, Angel* (1929).

biographical criticism: Criticism that attempts to determine how the events and experiences of an author's life influence his or her work.

bourgeois novel: A novel in which the values, preoccupations, and accoutrements of middle-class or bourgeois life are given particular prominence. The heyday of the bourgeois novel was the nineteenth century, when novelists as varied as Jane Austen, Honoré de Balzac, and Anthony Trollope both criticized and unreflectingly transmitted the assumptions of the rising middle class.

canon: An authorized or accepted list of books. In modern parlance, the literary canon comprehends the privileged texts, classics, or great books that are thought to belong permanently on university reading lists. Recent theory—especially feminist, Marxist, and poststructuralist—critically examines the process of canon formation and questions the hegemony of white male writers. Such theory sees canon formation as the ideological act of a dominant institution and seeks to undermine the notion of canonicity itself, thereby preventing the exclusion of works by women, minorities, and oppressed peoples.

character: Characters in fiction can be presented as if they were real people or as stylized functions of the plot. Usually characters are a combination of both factors.

classicism. A literary stance or value system consciously based on the example of classical Greek and Roman literature. While the term is applied to an enormous diversity of artists in many different periods and in many different national literatures, "classicism" generally denotes a cluster of values including formal discipline, restrained expression, reverence for tradition, and an objective rather than a subjective orientation. As a literary tendency, classicism is often opposed to *Romanticism*, although many writers combine classical and romantic elements.

climax/crisis: The term "climax" refers to the moment of the reader's highest emotional response, whereas "crisis" refers to a structural element of plot, a turning point at which a resolution must take place.

complication: The point in a novel when the *conflict* is developed or when the already existing conflict is further intensified.

conflict: The struggle that develops as a result of the opposition between the *protagonist* and another person, the natural world, society, or some force within the self.

contextualist criticism: A further extension of *formalist criticism*, which assumes that the language of art is constitutive. Rather than referring to preexistent values, the artwork creates values only inchoately realized before. The most important advocates of this position are Eliseo Vivas (*The Artistic Transaction*, 1963) and Murray Krieger (*The Play and Place of Criticism*, 1967).

conventions: All those devices of stylization, compression, and selection that constitute the necessary differences between art and life. According to the Russian Formalists, these conventions constitute the "literariness" of literature and are the only proper concern of the literary critic.

deconstruction: An extremely influential contemporary school of criticism based on the works of the French philosopher Jacques Derrida. Deconstruction treats literary works as unconscious reflections of the reigning myths of Western culture. The primary myth is that there is a meaningful world that language signifies or represents. The deconstructionist critic is most often concerned with showing how a literary text tacitly subverts the very assumptions or myths on which it ostensibly rests.

defamiliarization: Coined by Viktor Shklovsky in 1917, this term denotes a basic principle of Russian Formalism. Poetic language (by which the Formalists meant artful language, in prose as well as in poetry) defamiliarizes or "makes strange" familiar experiences. The technique of art, says Shklovsky, is to "make objects unfamiliar, to make forms difficult, to increase the difficulty and length of perception. . . . Art is a way of experiencing the artfulness of an object; the object is not important."

detective story: The so-called classic detective story (or mystery) is a highly formalized and logically structured mode of fiction in which the focus is on a crime solved by a detective through interpretation of evidence and ratiocination; the most famous detective in this mode is Arthur Conan Doyle's Sherlock Holmes. Many modern practitioners of the genre, however, such as Dashiell Hammett, Raymond Chandler, and Ross Macdonald, have de-emphasized the puzzlelike qualities of the detective story, stressing instead characterization, theme, and other elements of mainstream fiction.

determinism: The belief that an individual's actions are essentially determined by biological and environmental factors, with free will playing a negligible role. (See *naturalism.*)

dialogue: The similitude of conversation in fiction, dialogue serves to characterize, to further the *plot*, to establish *conflict*, and to express thematic ideas.

displacement: Popularized in criticism by Northrop Frye, this term refers to the author's attempt to make his or her story psychologically motivated and realistic, even as the latent structure of the mythical motivation moves relentlessly forward.

dominant: A term coined by Roman Jakobson to refer to that which "rules, determines, and transforms the remaining components in the work of a single artist, in a poetic canon, or in the work of an epoch." The shifting of the dominant in a *genre* accounts for the creation of new generic forms and new poetic epochs. For example, the rise of *realism* in the mid-nineteenth century indicates realistic conventions becoming dominant and *romance* or fantasy conventions becoming secondary.

doppelgänger: A double or counterpart of a person, sometimes endowed with ghostly qualities. A fictional character's doppelgänger often reflects a suppressed side of his or her personality. One of the classic examples of the doppelgänger motif is found in

Fyodor Dostoevski's novella *Dvoynik* (1846; *The Double*, 1917); Isaac Bashevis Singer and Jorge Luis Borges, among others, offer striking modern treatments of the doppelgänger.

epic: Although this term usually refers to a long narrative poem that presents the exploits of a central figure of high position, the term is also used to designate a long novel that has the style or structure usually associated with an epic. In this sense, for example, Herman Melville's *Moby Dick* (1851) and James Joyce's *Ulysses* (1922) may be called epics.

episodic narrative: A work that is held together primarily by a loose connection of self-sufficient episodes. *Picaresque novels* often have episodic structure.

epistolary novel: A novel made up of letters by one or more fictional characters. Samuel Richardson's *Pamela: Or, Virtue Rewarded* (1740-1741) is a well-known eighteenth century example. In the nineteenth century, Bram Stoker's *Dracula* (1897) is largely epistolary. The technique allows for several different points of view to be presented.

euphuism: A style of writing characterized by ornate language that is highly contrived, al-literative, and repetitious. Euphuism was developed by John Lyly in his *Euphues, the Anatomy of Wit* (1578) and was emulated frequently by writers of the Elizabethan Age.

existentialism: A philosophical, religious, and literary term, emerging from World War II, for a group of attitudes surrounding the pivotal notion that existence precedes essence. According to Jean-Paul Sartre, "Man is nothing else but what he makes himself." For-lornness arises from the death of God and the concomitant death of universal values, of any source of ultimate or a priori standards. Despair arises from the fact that an individual can reckon only with what depends on his or her will, and the sphere of that will is severely limited; the number of things on which he or she can have an impact is pathetically small. Existentialist literature is antideterministic in the extreme and rejects the idea that heredity and environment shape and determine human motivation and behavior.

exposition: The part or parts of a fiction that provide necessary background information. Exposition not only provides the time and place of the action but also introduces readers to the fictive world of the story, acquainting them with the ground rules of the work.

fantastic: In his study *The Fantastic* (1970), Tzvetan Todorov defines the fantastic as a *genre* that lies between the "uncanny" and the "marvelous." All three genres embody the familiar world but present an event that cannot be explained by the laws of the familiar world. Todorov says that the fantastic occupies a twilight zone between the uncanny (when the reader knows that the peculiar event is merely the result of an illusion) and the marvelous (when the reader understands that the event is supposed to take place in a realm controlled by laws unknown to humankind). The fantastic is thus essentially unsettling, provocative, even subversive.

feminist criticism: A criticism advocating equal rights for women in political, economic, social, psychological, personal, and aesthetic senses. On the thematic level, the feminist reader should identify with female characters and their concerns. The object is to provide a critique of phallocentric assumptions and an analysis of patriarchal ideologies inscribed in a literature that is male-centered and male-dominated. On the ideological level, feminist critics see gender, as well as the stereotypes that go along with it, as a cultural construct. They strive to define a particularly feminine content and to extend the *canon* so that it might include works by lesbians, feminists, and women writers in general.

flashback: A scene in a fiction that depicts an earlier event; it may be presented as a reminiscence by a character in the story or may simply be inserted into the narrative.

foreshadowing: A device to create suspense or dramatic irony in fiction by indicating through suggestion what will take place in the future.

formalist criticism: Two particularly influential formalist schools of criticism arose in the twentieth century: the Russian Formalists and the American New Critics. The Russian Formalists were concerned with the conventional devices used in literature to defamiliarize that which habit has made familiar. The New Critics believed that literary criticism is a description and evaluation of its object and that the primary concern of the critic is with the work's unity. Both schools of criticism, at their most extreme, treated literary works as artifacts or constructs divorced from their biographical and social contexts.

genre: In its most general sense, this term refers to a group of literary works defined by a common form, style, or purpose. In practice, the term is used in a wide variety of overlapping and, to a degree, contradictory senses. Tragedy and comedy are thus described as distinct genres; the novel (a form that includes both tragic and comic works) is a genre; and various subspecies of the novel, such as the *gothic* and the *picaresque,* are themselves frequently treated as distinct genres. Finally, the term "genre fiction" refers to forms of popular fiction in which the writer is bound by more or less rigid conventions. Indeed, all these diverse usages have in common an emphasis on the manner in which individual literary works are shaped by particular expectations and conventions; this is the subject of genre criticism.

genre fiction: Categories of popular fiction in which the writers are bound by more or less rigid conventions, such as in the *detective story,* the *romance,* and the *Western.* Although the term can be used in a neutral sense, it is often used dismissively.

gothic novel: A form of fiction developed in the eighteenth century that focuses on horror and the supernatural. In his preface to *The Castle of Otranto* (1765), the first gothic novel in English, Horace Walpole claimed that he was trying to combine two kinds of fiction, with events and story typical of the medieval romance and character delineation typical of the realistic novel. Other examples of the form are Matthew Gregory

Lewis's *The Monk: A Romance* (1796; also known as *Ambrosio: Or, The Monk*) and Mary Wollstonecraft Shelley's *Frankenstein: Or, The Modern Prometheus* (1818).

grotesque: According to Wolfgang Kayser (*The Grotesque in Art and Literature*, 1963), the grotesque is an embodiment in literature of the estranged world. Characterized by a breakup of the everyday world by mysterious forces, the form differs from fantasy in that the reader is not sure whether to react with humor or with horror and in that the exaggeration manifested exists in the familiar world rather than in a purely imaginative world.

Hebraic/Homeric styles: Terms coined by Erich Auerbach in *Mimesis: The Representation of Reality in Western Literature* (1953) to designate two basic fictional styles. The Hebraic style focuses only on the decisive points of narrative and leaves all else obscure, mysterious, and "fraught with background"; the Homeric style places the narrative in a definite time and place and externalizes everything in a perpetual foreground.

historical criticism: In contrast to *formalist criticism*, which treats literary works to a great extent as self-contained artifacts, historical criticism emphasizes the historical context of literature; the two approaches, however, need not be mutually exclusive. Ernst Robert Curtius's *European Literature and the Latin Middle Ages* (1948) is a prominent example of historical criticism.

historical novel: A novel that depicts past historical events, usually public in nature, and features real as well as fictional people. Sir Walter Scott's Waverley novels established the basic type, but the relationship between fiction and history in the form varies greatly depending on the practitioner.

implied author: According to Wayne Booth (*The Rhetoric of Fiction*, 1961), the novel often creates a kind of second self who tells the story—a self who is wiser, more sensitive, and more perceptive than any real person could be.

interior monologue: Defined by Édouard Dujardin as the speech of a character designed to introduce the reader directly to the character's internal life, the form differs from other kinds of monologue in that it attempts to reproduce thought before any logical organization is imposed on it. See, for example, Molly Bloom's long interior monologue at the conclusion of James Joyce's *Ulysses* (1922).

irrealism: A term often used to refer to modern or postmodern fiction that is presented self-consciously as a fiction or a fabulation rather than a mimesis of external reality. The best-known practitioners of irrealism are John Barth, Robert Coover, and Donald Barthelme.

local colorists: A loose movement of late nineteenth century American writers whose fiction emphasizes the distinctive folkways, landscapes, and dialects of various regions. Important local colorists include Bret Harte, Mark Twain, George Washington Cable, Kate Chopin, and Sarah Orne Jewett. (See *regional novel*.)

Marxist criticism: Based on the nineteenth century writings of Karl Marx and Friedrich Engels, Marxist criticism views literature as a product of ideological forces determined by the dominant class. However, many Marxists believe that literature operates according to its own autonomous standards of production and reception: It is both a product of ideology and able to determine ideology. As such, literature may overcome the dominant paradigms of its age and play a revolutionary role in society.

metafiction: This term refers to fiction that manifests a reflexive tendency, such as Vladimir Nabokov's *Pale Fire* (1962) and John Fowles's *The French Lieutenant's Woman* (1969). The emphasis is on the loosening of the work's illusion of reality to expose the reality of its illusion. Other terms used to refer to this type of fiction include "irrealism," "postmodernist fiction," "antifiction," and "surfiction."

modernism: An international movement in the arts that began in the early years of the twentieth century. Although the term is used to describe artists of widely varying persuasions, modernism in general was characterized by its international idiom, by its interest in cultures distant in space or time, by its emphasis on formal experimentation, and by its sense of dislocation and radical change.

motif: A conventional incident or situation in a fiction that may serve as the basis for the structure of the narrative itself. The Russian Formalist critic Boris Tomashevsky uses the term to refer to the smallest particle of thematic material in a work.

motivation: Although this term is usually used in reference to the convention of justifying the action of a character from his or her psychological makeup, the Russian Formalists use the term to refer to the network of devices that justify the introduction of individual *motifs* or groups of motifs in a work. For example, "compositional motivation" refers to the principle that every single property in a work contributes to its overall effect; "realistic motivation" refers to the realistic devices used to make a work plausible and lifelike.

multiculturalism: The tendency to recognize the perspectives of those traditionally excluded from the canon of Western art and literature. In order to promote multiculturalism, publishers and educators have revised textbooks and school curricula to incorporate material by and about women, members of minority groups, persons from non-Western cultures, and homosexuals.

myth: Anonymous traditional stories dealing with basic human concepts and antinomies. According to Claude Lévi-Strauss, myth is that part of language where the "formula *tradutore, tradittore* reaches its lowest truth value. . . . Its substance does not lie in its style, its original music, or its syntax, but in the story which it tells."

myth criticism: Northrop Frye says that in myth "we see the structural principles of literature isolated." Myth criticism is concerned with these basic principles of literature; it is not to be confused with mythological criticism, which is primarily concerned with finding mythological parallels in the surface action of the *narrative*.

narrative: Robert Scholes and Robert Kellogg, in *The Nature of Narrative* (1966), say that by "narrative" they mean literary works that include both a story and a storyteller. The term "narrative" usually implies a contrast to "enacted" fiction such as drama.

narratology: The study of the form and functioning of *narratives*; it attempts to examine what all narratives have in common and what makes individual narratives different from one another.

narrator: The *character* who recounts the *narrative*, or story. Wayne Booth describes various dramatized narrators in *The Rhetoric of Fiction* (1961): unacknowledged centers of consciousness, observers, narrator-agents, and self-conscious narrators. Booth suggests that the important elements to consider in narration are the relationships among the narrator, the author, the characters, and the reader.

naturalism: As developed by Émile Zola in the late nineteenth century, naturalism is the application of the principles of scientific *determinism* to fiction. Although it usually refers more to the choice of subject matter than to technical conventions, those conventions associated with the movement center on the author's attempt to be precise and scientifically objective in description and detail, regardless of whether the events described are sordid or shocking.

New Criticism: See *formalist criticism.*

novel: Perhaps the most difficult of all fictional forms to define because of its multiplicity of modes. Edouard, in André Gide's *Les Faux-monnayeurs* (1925; *The Counterfeiters*, 1927), says the novel is the freest and most lawless of all *genres*; he wonders if fear of that liberty is the reason the novel has so timidly clung to reality. Most critics seem to agree that the novel's primary area of concern is the social world. Ian Watt (*The Rise of the Novel*, 2001) says that the novel can be distinguished from other fictional forms by the attention it pays to individual characterization and detailed presentation of the environment. Moreover, says Watt, the novel, more than any other fictional form, is interested in the "development of its characters in the course of time."

novel of manners: The classic examples of this form might be the novels of Jane Austen, wherein the customs and conventions of a social group of a particular time and place are realistically, and often satirically, portrayed

novella, novelle, nouvelle, novelette, novela: Although these terms often refer to the short European tale, especially the Renaissance form employed by Giovanni Boccaccio, the terms often refer to that form of fiction that is said to be longer than a short story and shorter than a novel. "Novelette" is the term usually preferred by the British, whereas "novella" is the term usually used to refer to American works in this *genre*. Henry James claimed that the main merit of the form is the "effort to do the complicated thing with a strong brevity and lucidity."

phenomenological criticism: Although best known as a European school of criticism practiced by Georges Poulet and others, this so-called criticism of consciousness is also propounded in the United States by such critics as J. Hillis Miller. The focus is less on individual works and *genres* than it is on literature as an act; the work is not seen as an object but rather as part of a strand of latent impulses in the work of a single author or an epoch.

picaresque novel: A form of fiction that centers on a central rogue figure, or picaro, who usually tells his or her own story. The plot structure is normally *episodic*, and the episodes usually focus on how the picaro lives by his or her wits. Classic examples of the mode are Henry Fielding's *The History of Tom Jones, a Foundling* (1749; commonly known as *Tom Jones*) and Mark Twain's *Adventures of Huckleberry Finn* (1884).

plot/story: "Story" refers to the full *narrative* of *character* and action, whereas "plot" generally refers to action with little reference to character. A more precise and helpful distinction is made by the Russian Formalists, who suggest that "plot" refers to the events of a narrative as they have been artfully arranged in the literary work, subject to chronological displacement, ellipses, and other devices, while "story" refers to the sum of the same events arranged in simple, causal-chronological order. Thus story is the raw material for plot. By comparing the two in a given work, the reader is encouraged to see the narrative as an artifact.

point of view: The means by which the story is presented to the reader, or, as Percy Lubbock says in *The Craft of Fiction* (1921), "the relation in which the narrator stands to the story"—a relation that Lubbock claims governs the craft of fiction. Some of the questions the critical reader should ask concerning point of view are the following: Who talks to the reader? From what position does the narrator tell the story? At what distance does he or she place the reader from the story? What kind of person is he or she? How fully is he or she characterized? How reliable is he or she? For further discussion, see Wayne Booth, *The Rhetoric of Fiction* (1961).

postcolonialism: Postcolonial literature emerged in the mid-twentieth century when colonies in Asia, Africa, and the Caribbean began gaining their independence from the European nations that had long controlled them. Postcolonial authors, such as Salman Rushdie and V. S. Naipaul, tend to focus on both the freedom and the conflict inherent in living in a postcolonial state.

postmodernism: A ubiquitous but elusive term in contemporary criticism, "postmodernism" is loosely applied to the various artistic movements that followed the era of so-called high modernism, represented by such giants as James Joyce and Pablo Picasso. In critical discussions of contemporary fiction, the term "postmodernism" is frequently applied to the works of writers such as Thomas Pynchon, John Barth, and Donald Barthelme, who exhibit a self-conscious awareness of their modernist predecessors as well as a reflexive treatment of fictional form.

protagonist: The central *character* in a fiction, the character whose fortunes most concern the reader.

psychological criticism: While much modern literary criticism reflects to some degree the impacts of Sigmund Freud, Carl Jung, Jacques Lacan, and other psychological theorists, the term "psychological criticism" suggests a strong emphasis on a causal relation between the writer's psychological state, variously interpreted, and his or her works. A notable example of psychological criticism is Norman Fruman's *Coleridge, the Damaged Archangel* (1971).

psychological novel: A form of fiction in which *character*, especially the inner lives of characters, is the primary focus. This form, which has been of primary importance at least since Henry James, characterizes much of the work of James Joyce, Virginia Woolf, and William Faulkner. For a detailed discussion, see *The Modern Psychological Novel* (1955) by Leon Edel.

realism: A literary technique in which the primary convention is to render an illusion of fidelity to external reality. Realism is often identified as the primary method of the novel form: It focuses on surface details, maintains a fidelity to the everyday experiences of middle-class society, and strives for a one to one relationship between the fiction and the action imitated. The realist movement in the late nineteenth century coincides with the full development of the novel form.

reception aesthetics: The best-known American practitioner of reception aesthetics is Stanley Fish. For the reception critic, meaning is an event or process; rather than being embedded in the work, it is created through particular acts of reading. The best-known European practitioner of this criticism, Wolfgang Iser, argues that indeterminacy is the basic characteristic of literary texts; the reader must "normalize" the text either by projecting his or her standards into it or by revising his or her standards to "fit" the text.

regional novel: Any novel in which the character of a given geographical region plays a decisive role. Although regional differences persist across the United States, a considerable leveling in speech and customs has taken place, so that the sharp regional distinctions evident in nineteenth century American fiction have all but disappeared. Only in the South has a strong regional tradition persisted to the present. (See *local colorists.*)

rhetorical criticism: The rhetorical critic is concerned with the literary work as a means of communicating ideas and the means by which the work affects or controls the reader. Such criticism seems best suited to didactic works such as satire.

roman à clef: A fiction wherein actual people, often celebrities of some sort, are thinly disguised.

romance: The romance usually differs from the novel form in that the focus is on symbolic events and representational characters rather than on "as-if-real" characters and events. Richard Chase says that in the romance, character is depicted as highly stylized, a function of the plot rather than as someone complexly related to society. The romancer is more likely to be concerned with dreamworlds than with the familiar world, believing that reality cannot be grasped by the traditional novel.

Romanticism: A widespread cultural movement in the late eighteenth and early nineteenth centuries, the influence of which is still felt. As a general literary tendency, Romanticism is frequently contrasted with *classicism.* Although many varieties of Romanticism are indigenous to various national literatures, the term generally suggests an assertion of the preeminence of the imagination. Other values associated with various schools of Romanticism include primitivism, an interest in folklore, a reverence for nature, and a fascination with the demoniac and the macabre.

scene: The central element of *narration*; specific actions are narrated or depicted that make the reader feel he or she is participating directly in the action.

science fiction: Fiction in which certain givens (physical laws, psychological principles, social conditions—any one or all of these) form the basis of an imaginative projection into the future or, less commonly, an extrapolation in the present or even into the past.

semiotics: The science of signs and sign systems in communication. According to Roman Jakobson, semiotics deals with the principles that underlie the structure of signs, their use in language of all kinds, and the specific nature of various sign systems.

sentimental novel: A form of fiction popular in the eighteenth century in which emotionalism and optimism are the primary characteristics. The best-known examples are Samuel Richardson's *Pamela: Or, Virtue Rewarded* (1740-1741) and Oliver Goldsmith's *The Vicar of Wakefield* (1766).

setting: The circumstances and environment, both temporal and spatial, of a *narrative.*

spatial form: An author's attempt to make the reader apprehend a work spatially in a moment of time rather than sequentially. To achieve this effect, the author breaks up the *narrative* into interspersed fragments. Beginning with James Joyce, Marcel Proust, and Djuna Barnes, the movement toward spatial form is concomitant with the *modernist* effort to supplant historical time in fiction with mythic time. For the seminal discussion of this technique, see Joseph Frank, *The Widening Gyre* (1963).

stream of consciousness: The depiction of the thought processes of a *character*, insofar as this is possible, without any mediating structures. The metaphor of consciousness as a "stream" suggests a rush of thoughts and images governed by free association rather than by strictly rational development. The term "stream of consciousness" is often used loosely as a synonym for *interior monologue.* The most celebrated example of stream of consciousness in fiction is the monologue of Molly Bloom in James Joyce's *Ulysses* (1922); other notable practitioners of the stream-of-consciousness technique include Dorothy Richardson, Virginia Woolf, and William Faulkner.

structuralism: As a movement of thought, structuralism is based on the idea of intrinsic, self-sufficient structures that do not require reference to external elements. A structure is a system of transformations that involves the interplay of laws inherent in the system itself. The study of language is the primary model for contemporary structuralism. The structuralist literary critic attempts to define structural principles that operate intertextually throughout the whole of literature as well as principles that operate in *genres* and in individual works. One of the most accessible surveys of structuralism and literature available is Jonathan Culler's *Structuralist Poetics* (1975).

summary: Those parts of a fiction that do not need to be detailed. In *Tom Jones* (1749), Henry Fielding says, "If whole years should pass without producing anything worthy of . . . notice . . . we shall hasten on to matters of consequence."

thematics: According to Northrop Frye, when a work of fiction is written or interpreted thematically, it becomes an illustrative fable. Murray Krieger defines thematics as "the study of the experiential tensions which, dramatically entangled in the literary work, become an existential reflection of that work's aesthetic complexity."

tone: The dominant mood of a work of fiction. (See *atmosphere.*)

unreliable narrator: A narrator whose account of the events of the story cannot be trusted, obliging readers to reconstruct—if possible—the true state of affairs themselves. Once an innovative technique, the use of the unreliable narrator has become commonplace among contemporary writers who wish to suggest the impossibility of a truly "reliable" account of any event. Notable examples of the unreliable narrator can be found in Ford Madox Ford's *The Good Soldier* (1915) and Vladimir Nabokov's *Lolita* (1955).

Victorian novel: Although the Victorian period extended from 1837 to 1901, the term "Victorian novel" does not include the later decades of Queen Victoria's reign. The term loosely refers to the sprawling works of novelists such as Charles Dickens and William Makepeace Thackeray—works that frequently appeared first in serial form and are characterized by a broad social canvas.

vraisemblance/verisimilitude: Tzvetan Todorov defines vraisemblance as "the mask which conceals the text's own laws, but which we are supposed to take for a relation to reality." Verisimilitude refers to a work's attempts to make the reader believe that it conforms to reality rather than to its own laws.

Western novel: Like all varieties of *genre fiction*, the Western novel—generally known simply as the Western—is defined by a relatively predictable combination of *conventions*, *motifs*, and recurring themes. These predictable elements, familiar from many Western films and television series, differentiate the Western from *historical novels* and idiosyncratic works such as Thomas Berger's *Little Big Man* (1964) that are also set in the Old West. Conversely, some novels set in the contemporary West are regarded as Westerns because they deal with modern cowboys and with the land itself in the manner characteristic of the *genre*.

Charles E. May

GUIDE TO ONLINE RESOURCES

WEB SITES
The following sites were visited by the editors of Salem Press in 2009. Because URLs frequently change, the accuracy of these addresses cannot be guaranteed; however, long-standing sites, such as those of colleges and universities, national organizations, and government agencies, generally maintain links when sites are moved or updated.

American Literature on the Web

http://www.nagasaki-gaigo.ac.jp/ishikawa/amlit

Among this site's features are several pages providing links to Web sites about specific genres and literary movements, southern and southwestern American literature, minority literature, literary theory, and women writers, as well as an extensive index of links to electronic text collections and archives. Users also can access information for five specific time periods: 1620-1820, 1820-1865, 1865-1914, 1914-1945, and since 1945. A range of information is available for each period, including alphabetical lists of authors that link to more specific information about each writer, time lines of historical and literary events, and links to related additional Web sites.

Books and Writers

http://www.kirjasto.sci.fi/indeksi.htm

This broad, comprehensive, and easy-to-use resource provides access to information about hundreds of authors throughout the world, extending from 70 B.C.E to the twenty-first century. Links take users from an alphabetical list of authors to pages featuring biographical material, lists of works, and recommendations for further reading about individual authors; each writer's page also includes links to related pages on the site. Although brief, the biographical essays provide solid overviews of the authors' careers, their contributions to literature, and their literary influences.

The Canadian Literature Archive

http://www.umanitoba.ca/canlit

Created and maintained by the English Department at the University of Manitoba, this site is a comprehensive collection of materials for and about Canadian writers. It includes an alphabetical listing of authors with links to additional Web-based information. Users also can retrieve electronic texts, announcements of literary events, and videocasts of author interviews and readings.

A Celebration of Women Writers

http://digital.library.upenn.edu/women

This site presents an extensive compendium of information about the contributions of women writers throughout history. The "Local Editions by Authors" and "Local Editions by Category" pages include access to electronic texts of the works of numerous writers, including Louisa May Alcott, Djuna Barnes, Grazia Deledda, Edith Wharton, and Virginia Woolf. Users can also access biographical and bibliographical information by browsing lists arranged by writers' names, countries of origin, ethnicities, and the centuries in which they lived.

Contemporary Writers

http://www.contemporarywriters.com/authors

Created by the British Council, this site offers "up-to-date profiles of some of the U.K. and Commonwealth's most important living writers (plus writers from the Republic of Ireland that we've worked with)." The available information includes biographies, bibliographies, critical reviews, news about literary prizes, and photographs. Users can search the site by author, genre, nationality, gender, publisher, book title, date of publication, and prize name and date.

Internet Public Library: Native American Authors

http://www.ipl.org/div/natam

Internet Public Library, a Web-based collection of materials, includes this index to resources about writers of Native American heritage. An alphabetical list of authors enables users to link to biographies, lists of works, electronic texts, tribal Web sites, and other online resources. The majority of the writers covered are contemporary Indian authors, but some historical authors also are featured. Users also can retrieve information by browsing lists of titles and tribes. In addition, the site contains a bibliography of print and online materials about Native American literature.

LiteraryHistory.com

http://www.literaryhistory.com

This site is an excellent source of academic, scholarly, and critical literature about eighteenth, nineteenth, and twentieth century American and English writers. It provides numerous pages about specific eras and genres, including individual pages for eighteenth, nineteenth, and twentieth century literature and for African American and postcolonial literature. These pages contain alphabetical lists of authors that link to articles, reviews, overviews, excerpts of works, teaching guides, podcast interviews, and other materials. The eighteenth century literature page also provides access to information about the eighteenth century novel.

Literary Resources on the Net

http://andromeda.rutgers.edu/~jlynch/Lit

Jack Lynch of Rutgers University maintains this extensive collection of links to Internet sites that are useful to academics, including numerous Web sites about American and English literature. This collection is a good place to begin online research about the novel, as it links to hundreds of other sites with broad ranges of literary topics. The site is organized chronically, with separate pages for information about the Middle Ages, the Renaissance, the eighteenth century, the Romantic and Victorian eras, and twentieth century British and Irish literature. It also has separate pages providing links to Web sites about American literature and to women's literature and feminism.

LitWeb

http://litweb.net

LitWeb provides biographies of more than five hundred world authors throughout history that can be accessed through an alphabetical listing. The pages about each writer contain a list of his or her works, suggestions for further reading, and illustrations. The site also offers information about past and present winners of major literary prizes.

The Modern Word: Authors of the Libyrinth

http://www.themodernword.com/authors.html

The Modern Word site, although somewhat haphazard in its organization, provides a great deal of critical information about writers. The "Authors of the Libyrinth" page is very useful, linking author names to essays about them and other resources. The section of the page headed "The Scriptorium" presents "an index of pages featuring writers who have pushed the edges of their medium, combining literary talent with a sense of experimentation to produce some remarkable works of modern literature." The site also includes sections devoted to Samuel Beckett, Umberto Eco, Gabriel García Márquez, James Joyce, Franz Kafka, and Thomas Pynchon.

Novels

http://www.nvcc.edu/home/ataormina/novels/default.htm

This overview of American and English novels was prepared by Agatha Taormina, a professor at Northern Virginia Community College. It contains three sections: "History" provides a definition of the novel genre, a discussion of its origins in eighteenth century England, and separate pages with information about genres and authors of nineteenth century, twentieth century, and postmodern novels. "Approaches" suggests how to read a novel critically for greater appreciation, and "Resources" provides a list of books about the novel.

Outline of American Literature

http://www.america.gov/publications/books/outline-of-american-literature.html

This page of the America.gov site provides access to an electronic version of the ten-chapter volume *Outline of American Literature*, a historical overview of prose and poetry from colonial times to the present published by the U.S. Department of State. The work's author is Kathryn VanSpanckeren, professor of English at the University of Tampa. The site offers links to abbreviated versions of each chapter as well as access to the entire publication in PDF format.

Voice of the Shuttle

http://vos.ucsb.edu

One of the most complete and authoritative places for online information about literature, Voice of the Shuttle is maintained by professors and students in the English Department at the University of California, Santa Barbara. The site provides thousands of links to electronic books, academic journals, association Web sites, sites created by university professors, and many, many other resources about the humanities. Its "Literature in English" page provides links to separate pages about the literature of the Anglo Saxon era, the Middle Ages, the Renaissance and seventeenth century, the Restoration and eighteenth century, the Romantic age, the Victorian age, and modern and contemporary periods in Britain and the United States, as well as a page focused on minority literature. Another page on the site, "Literatures Other than English," offers a gateway to information about the literature of numerous countries and world regions.

ELECTRONIC DATABASES

Electronic databases usually do not have their own URLs. Instead, public, college, and university libraries subscribe to these databases, provide links to them on their Web sites, and make them available to library card holders or other specified patrons. Readers can visit library Web sites or ask reference librarians to check on availability.

Canadian Literary Centre

Produced by EBSCO, the Canadian Literary Centre database contains full-text content from ECW Press, a Toronto-based publisher, including the titles in the publisher's Canadian fiction studies, Canadian biography, and Canadian writers and their works series, *ECW's Biographical Guide to Canadian Novelists*, and *George Woodcock's Introduction to Canadian Fiction*. Author biographies, essays and literary criticism, and book reviews are among the database's offerings.

Literary Reference Center

EBSCO's Literary Reference Center (LRC) is a comprehensive full-text database designed primarily to help high school and undergraduate students in English and the humanities with homework and research assignments about literature. The database contains massive amounts of information from reference works, books, literary journals, and other materials, including more than 31,000 plot summaries, synopses, and overviews of literary works; almost 100,000 essays and articles of literary criticism; about 140,000 author biographies; more than 605,000 book reviews; and more than 5,200 author interviews. It also contains the entire contents of Salem Press's MagillOnLiterature Plus. Users can retrieve information by browsing a list of authors' names or titles of literary works; they can also use an advanced search engine to access information by numerous categories, including author name, gender, cultural identity, national identity, and the years in which he or she lived, or by literary title, character, locale, genre, and publication date. The Literary Reference Center also features a literary-historical time line, an encyclopedia of literature, and a glossary of literary terms.

MagillOnLiterature Plus

MagillOnLiterature Plus is a comprehensive, integrated literature database produced by Salem Press and available on the EBSCO*host* platform. The database contains the full text of essays in Salem's many literature-related reference works, including *Masterplots*, *Cyclopedia of World Authors*, *Cyclopedia of Literary Characters*, *Cyclopedia of Literary Places*, *Critical Survey of Long Fiction*, *Critical Survey of Short Fiction*, *World Philosophers and Their Works*, *Magill's Literary Annual*, and *Magill's Book Reviews*. Among its contents are articles on more than 35,000 literary works and more than 8,500 writers, poets, dramatists, essays, and philosophers, more than 1,000 images, and a glossary of more than 1,300 literary terms. The biographical essays include lists of authors' works and secondary bibliographies, and almost four hundred overview essays offer information about literary genres, time periods, and national literatures.

NoveList

NoveList is a readers' advisory service produced by EBSCO. The database provides access to 155,000 titles of both adult and juvenile fiction as well information about literary awards, book discussion guides, feature articles about a range of literary genres, and "recommended reads." Users can search by author name, book title, or series title or can describe the plot to retrieve the name of a book, information about the author, and book reviews; another search engine enables users to find titles similar to books they have enjoyed reading.

Rebecca Kuzins

GEOGRAPHICAL INDEX

SUBJECT INDEX